The Canadian GED®
FOR
DUMMIES®

The Canadian GED® FOR DUMMIES®

by Murray Shukyn and
Dale E. Shuttleworth, PhD

John Wiley & Sons Canada, Ltd.

The Canadian GED® For Dummies®

Published by
John Wiley & Sons Canada, Ltd
6045 Freemont Boulevard
Mississauga, Ontario, L5R 4J3

www.wiley.com

For general information on John Wiley & Sons Canada, Ltd., including all books published by Wiley Publishing, Inc., please call our distribution centre at 1-800-567-4797. For reseller information, including discounts and premium sales, please call our sales department at 416-646-7992. For press review copies, author interviews, or other publicity information, please contact our publicity department, Tel. 416-646-4582, Fax 416-236-4448.

For technical support, please visit www.wiley.com/techsupport.

Wiley also publishes its books in a variety of electronic formats. Some content that appears in print may not be available in electronic books.

Library and Archives Canada Cataloguing in Publication Data

Shukyn, Murray, 1938-
    The Canadian GED for dummies / Murray Shukyn, Dale E. Shuttleworth.

Includes index.
ISBN 978-0-470-68091-9

    1. General educational development tests—Study guides. 2. High school equivalency examinations—Canada—Study guides. I. Shuttleworth, Dale E. (Dale Edwin), 1938– II. Title.

LB3060.33.G45S57 2010   373.126'2   C2010-902899-6

Printed in the United States

1 2 3 4 5 RRD 14 13 12 11 10

WILEY

About the Authors

Murray Shukyn, associate director of The Training Renewal Foundation, is a graduate of the University of Toronto with professional qualifications as a teacher at the elementary and secondary levels, including special education. During an extensive career spanning more than thirty years, he has taught at the elementary, secondary, and university levels. Murray has also taught professional development programs for teachers and training courses for adult learners. He is acknowledged as a Canadian leader in the field of alternative education through his work in the creation of such innovative programs for the Toronto Board of Education as SEED, Learnxs, Subway Academy, SOLE, and ACE. In 1995, he became associate director at The Training Renewal Foundation, which introduced the GED to the province of Ontario. Over the years, he has been a consultant to government, media, and public relations companies, as well as an author of textbooks and numerous articles in magazines and periodicals. He is a coauthor of the third and fourth Canadian editions of *How to Prepare for the GED,* published by Barron's Educational Series in the United States.

Dale E. Shuttleworth, PhD, is the executive director of The Training Renewal Foundation. Dale's career as a community educator has included experience as a teacher, school-community worker, consultant, principal, coordinator, superintendent, and university lecturer. In the fields of education and community economic development, he is a founder of the Learnxs Foundation, Inc., Youth Ventures Developments of Metropolitan Toronto, the Learning Enrichment Foundation, the York Business Opportunities Centre, the Centre for Community and Economic Renewal, and The Training Renewal Foundation. He is a coauthor of the third and fourth Canadian editions of *How to Prepare for the GED,* published by Barron's Educational Series in the United States, and the author of *School Management in Transition,* published by Routledge Falmer in 2003, *Enterprise Learning in Action,* published by Routledge in London and New York, and *Schooling for Life,* published by the University of Toronto Press in 2010. He has been the recipient of the prestigious Dag Hammarskjold Gold Medal for Excellence in Education.

In 1995, Dale created the GED Preparation Centre pilot project, which brought the High School Equivalency Certificate to the Province of Ontario. In 2000, he was named lead author/consultant for a study on "Innovations in School Management," conducted by the Organization for Economic Co-operation and Development (OECD) in Paris, France, resulting in the publishing of the book, *New School Management Approaches* in 2001.

Authors' Acknowledgements

We wish to express our appreciation to Marilyn Shuttleworth, who assisted us in the preparation of this manuscript; The Training Renewal Foundation for the opportunity to work in the world of the GED; and the late Peter Kilburn, former Canadian GED administrator, for his inspiration, friendship, and encouragement in introducing us to the potential of the GED to be a source of fulfillment and liberation in the lives and careers of so many adult learners who have dropped out of traditional schooling accreditation systems.

Publisher's Acknowledgements

We're proud of this book; please send us your comments at `http://dummies.custhelp.com`. For other comments, please contact our Customer Care Department within the U.S. at 877-762-2974, outside the U.S. at 317-572-3993 or fax 317-572-4002.

Some of the people who helped bring this book to market include the following:

Acquisitions and Editorial

Project Editor, U.S.: Chad Sievers

Editor, Canada: Robert Hickey

Copy Editor: Heather Ball

Production Editor: Lindsay Humphreys

Cover photo: ©iStock/Palto/New Opportunities

Cartoons: Rich Tennant (`www.the5thwave.com`)

Composition

Project Coordinator: Lynsey Stanford

Layout and Graphics: Carl Byers, Erin Zeltner

Proofreader: Lisa Young Stiers

Indexer: Christine Karpeles

John Wiley & Sons Canada, Ltd

    Bill Zerter, Chief Operating Officer

    Jennifer Smith, Publisher, Professional & Trade Division

    Alison MacLean, Managing Editor, Professional & Trade Division

    Karen Bryan, Vice-President, Publishing Services

Publishing and Editorial for Consumer Dummies

    Diane Graves Steele, Vice President and Publisher, Consumer Dummies

    Kristin Ferguson-Wagstaffe, Product Development Director, Consumer Dummies

    Ensley Eikenburg, Associate Publisher, Travel

    Kelly Regan, Editorial Director, Travel

Composition Services

    Debbie Stailey, Director of Composition Services

Contents at a Glance

Table of Contents

Introduction

*P*erhaps you've applied for a job and have been refused an interview because you don't have a high school diploma or a GED. Or maybe you were up for a promotion at work, but when your boss found out you didn't finish high school, he said you weren't eligible for the new job. Maybe you've always wanted to go to college or university but couldn't even apply because the post-secondary institution of your choice requires a high school diploma or equivalent (the GED) for admission. Or perhaps your kids are just about to graduate from high school, and you're motivated to finish, too.

Whatever your reasons are for wanting to earn a high school diploma — whether we've mentioned them here or not — this book is for you. It takes you through the process of preparing to take the GED tests — which, if you pass them, offer you the equivalent of a high school diploma or certificate without all the time-consuming bells and whistles of a traditional high school education.

About This Book

If you want a high school diploma, you can always go back and finish high school the old-fashioned way. Of course, it may take you a few years, and you may have to quit your job to do it. Plus, you'd have to sit in a class with teenagers for eight or so hours a day (and probably be treated like one, too).

For most people, this situation doesn't sound too appealing. This book presents a different solution: to earn a high school diploma in the shortest time possible. If you don't mind preparing yourself for a series of challenging tests that determine whether you've mastered key skills, you can get a *General Educational Development* (GED) diploma that's the equivalent of a high school education — and you can do so in much less than four years.

If taking the GED tests to earn your diploma sounds like a great idea to you, this book is a necessary study tool. It's a fun and friendly instruction manual for succeeding on the GED tests. It isn't a subject-matter preparation book — that is, it doesn't take you through the basics of math and then progress into algebra, geometry, and so on. It does, however, prepare you for the GED by giving you detailed information about each test, two sets of full-length practice tests that you can take to help you prepare for taking the real GED tests, and plenty of easy-to-understand answers and explanations for those tests. Use this book as your first stop. After taking the first set of practice tests and going through the answers and explanations, you can determine which subject areas you need to work on.

Conventions Used in This Book

To help you navigate your way around in this book, we use the following conventions:

- *Italics* to emphasize certain words and to point out new words or phrases that we define in the text

- **Boldface** to indicate key words in bulleted lists and action parts of numbered steps

- Monofont to set apart Web addresses from the rest of the text

Throughout the book, we refer to the diploma you receive upon passing the GED tests. Depending on where you live, however, you may receive either a diploma or a certificate. Whenever we mention diploma, we ask that you keep in mind that the piece of paper you receive when you pass might be called a certificate.

Assumptions

Here's who we think you are:

- ✔ You meet your province or territory's requirements regarding age, residency, and the length of time since leaving school that make you eligible to take the GED tests. (Check with your local GED administrator to find out your local requirements.)
- ✔ You're serious about getting a high school diploma as quickly as you can.
- ✔ You're willing to put in the time to prepare, keeping in mind that you have a lot of other responsibilities, too.
- ✔ You feel that getting a high school diploma is a priority in your life.
- ✔ You want a fun and friendly guide that helps you achieve your goal.
- ✔ You want to gain some insight from the experience of others.

If any of these descriptions sounds like you, welcome aboard. We've prepared an enjoyable tour of the GED.

What You Don't Have to Read

You probably have a very busy life with numerous responsibilities like children, a job or two, and social activities. You may not have the time to read every single word we write. The good news is you don't have to. If you want to read just the essential information that can help you prepare for the GED, you can skip the sidebars. The sidebars are the areas of text on a gray background. They add a little background information, but they're not essential to your understanding of the subject.

How This Book Is Organized

This book has seven parts, each of which prepares you for the GED. The first part gives you the ins and outs of the GED, each of the next five parts deals specifically with one of the five tests, and the last part includes some fun tips for maximizing your test scores and being successful on the GED tests. The following sections explain each part in a little more detail.

Part 1: Putting the GED into Perspective

If you've never heard of the GED tests, you can use Part I to find out everything you need to know about the GED as a whole, including what it covers and who can take it. If you have heard of the GED, turn to this part to find out some extra information and some handy tips for succeeding on all five of the GED tests. You also find out how to register for the tests and how to figure out your scores after you receive them.

Part II: Minding Your Ps and Qs: The Language Arts, Writing Test

This part tells you everything you ever wanted to know about the Language Arts, Writing Test and provides you with two practice tests (and the answers that go with them) to help you prepare for this test. Here, you test your ability to organize content, improve sentence structure, and correct grammatical mistakes. You also get to try writing an essay for Part II of this test. Don't panic! This essay isn't a full research essay — it's a short essay that uses your experiences and knowledge as research. And, to help you do your best, this part offers you a handful of pointers and strategies to keep in mind as you take the test.

Part III: Finding Your Way: The Social Studies Test

This part is all about the Social Studies Test. Here, you get a chance to take inventory of your skills in understanding principles and concepts in history, geography, economics, and civics. You get to practise answering multiple-choice questions based on both textual and visual materials (these visual materials include maps, cartoons, and graphs). You also find some pointers and strategies to help you do your best on the test. Like the other test-specific parts of this book, this part offers you two full practice tests and the answers that go with them. Go through these tests and read their corresponding answer explanations as you prepare for the Social Studies Test.

Part IV: Peering at Your Specimen: The Science Test

For the Science Test, you're expected to know some scientific vocabulary and have a very basic understanding of scientific principles. Don't panic! You don't have to understand Beilstein's categorization of organic chemicals, but you do need to know basic concepts like the fact that carbon is present in many forms on earth. With a little bit of practice (*Hint:* check out Part IV) and some outside reading, you can become much more comfortable with the Science Test and amaze yourself with how much you already know about the topics it covers.

This part provides all the details you need to know about the Science Test, including the skills it tests you on, the test's format, and a few strategies to help you do your best on the real test. It also offers you a tonne of practice answering questions about physics, chemistry, and earth sciences. And, then, to help you prepare for the real test, it provides all the answers and explanations so you'll know which questions you got right, which ones you missed, and why.

Part V: Checking Your Comprehension: The Language Arts, Reading Test

This part focuses on preparing you for the Language Arts, Reading Test, by showing you the test's format, the skills it tests you on, and some strategies to help you do well on test day. This test examines your ability to understand literary passages. The good news is that no matter where the passages on this test come from — works of fiction, non-fiction, or every-day workplace documents — everything you need to know to answer the questions is in the passages themselves.

To help you get ready to answer questions about the passages that appear on this test, take the two practice tests in this part. Then read the answers and explanations that go with them to find out what you may need to practise a little more before you take the real test.

Part VI: Counting All the Possible Solutions: The Mathematics Test

If you cringe at the words *mathematics, calculations,* and *problem solving* — or if you're one of the rare few who gets excited about them — this part is for you. Here, you discover all the details about the Mathematics Test you need to know, including the skills it tests you on, the different answer formats it uses (and instructions on how to use them), and some strategies that can help you do well on the test. Go through the practice tests in this part, and then read all the answers and explanations to find out what you did right and what you did wrong (and why). If you're not great at math, don't worry! We're here to help you get familiar with the Mathematics Test so that you can feel calm and confident as you sit down to take the real test.

Part VII: The Part of Tens

This part is a treat to read — and you can review it in no time at all. Here you discover some key ways to prepare for the tests and improve your scores, ten ways to be successful on the GED, and ten ways to use your GED diploma after you pass the tests.

Icons Used in This Book

Icons — little pictures that you see in the margins of this book — highlight bits of text that you want to pay special attention to. Here's what they mean:

Whenever we want to tell you a special trick or technique that can help you succeed on the GED tests, we mark it with this icon. Keep an eye out for it.

This icon points out information you want to burn into your brain. Think of the text with this icon as the sort of stuff you'd tear out and put on a bulletin board or your refrigerator.

Take this icon seriously! Although the world won't end if you don't heed the advice next to these icons, the warnings are important to your success in preparing to take the GED tests.

We use this icon sparingly to point out additional technical information that you don't need to lose sleep over. When you see this icon, feel free to skip the material next to it if you're short on time.

Where to Go from Here

Some people like to read books from beginning to end. Others prefer to read only the chapters or sections that interest them. Still others look in the index or table of contents for specific information they need to know now. However you want to approach this book is fine with us — just don't peek at the practice tests until the moment you're ready to take them (and be sure not to look at the answers until *after* you take the tests!).

Part I
Putting the GED into Perspective

The 5ᵗʰ Wave   By Rich Tennant

"I always get a good night's sleep the day before a test so I'm relaxed and alert the next morning. Then I grab my pen, eat a banana, and I'm on my way."

In this part . . .

*O*kay, you want to earn your high school diploma but don't have time to attend classes eight or so hours a day for four years, so you've turned to the GED for help. And now you need help preparing for the GED! Lucky for you, this part of the book is here to help you get started in your test planning and preparation. It introduces you to the GED and gives you a brief look at each of the five tests. It gives you a chance to see what the GED expects you to know to receive your high school equivalency diploma, as well as what you need to prepare for. It also offers some logistical help with how to schedule the test so you can make sure you're eligible to take it before you sign up. Plus, it gives you a peek inside how the tests are scored so you can be at the top of the heap when all the results come in.

Here you can also find plenty of tips for succeeding on the GED tests. You find out what to take with you and what to leave at home, what to do if you have special needs, and how to manage your time. Finally, it explains the importance of practice tests. The more practice you get, the better prepared you'll be for what the test throws at you, so don't hesitate — turn the page and get ready to meet the GED head on!

Chapter 1

Taking a Quick Glance at the GED

- -

In This Chapter

▶ Reviewing the different GED test sections and questions

▶ Registering for the exam

▶ Knowing that you can take the GED when English is your second language

▶ Understanding what your scores mean and how they're determined

- -

The General Educational Development (GED) tests measure whether you understand what Grade 12 and CEGEP students across the country are supposed to have learned before they graduate. When you pass these tests, you earn a high school equivalency certificate or diploma, which can open many doors for you — perhaps doors that you don't even know exist at this point.

Ready to get started? This chapter gives you the basics of the GED tests: what the tests look like, how to answer the questions on them, how to schedule the tests, and what to do after you get your scores back.

Reviewing the Test Sections

The GED tests include the following five tests, each of which you can take separately:

✔ Language Arts, Writing, Parts I and II

✔ Social Studies

✔ Science

✔ Language Arts, Reading

✔ Mathematics, Parts I and II

Although you can take each of the five tests separately, you must take both parts of the Language Arts, Writing or Mathematics tests at the same time.

The following sections offer a closer look into what these tests cover and how they're set up.

Language Arts, Writing Test

The Language Arts, Writing Test is split into two parts (which we explain further in the following sections):

✔ Part I asks you to rewrite and revise passages. This part focuses on your grammar, punctuation, and spelling skills.

✔ Part II asks you to write an essay on a given topic. This part examines your skills in organizing your thoughts and writing clearly.

You have to pass both parts to get a score in this test. If you pass one part of the test but not the other, you must retake both parts the next time.

Language Arts, Writing Test, Part 1

The Language Arts, Writing Test, Part I, has 50 multiple-choice questions and a time limit of 75 minutes. In this test, you're asked to edit and revise material that's given to you. This material comes from the following sources:

- ✔ **Workplace materials:** Work-related letters, memos, and instructions that you may see on the job

- ✔ **How-to books:** Samples of general reference books that are supposed to make you richer, stronger, and lighter, or a better cook, driver, investor, or student (or anything else you want to become better at)

- ✔ **Informational works:** Documents that present you with information (often dry and boring information), such as the instructional manual for your DVD player

You find three question types in this part of the Language Arts, Writing Test:

- ✔ **Correction:** You're asked to correct sentences presented to you.

- ✔ **Revision:** You're presented with a sentence that has a word or phrase underlined. If the sentence needs a correction, one of the answer choices will be better than the word or phrase underlined. If no correction is needed, either one of the answer choices will be the same as the underlined portion, or one of the choices will be something like "no correction needed."

- ✔ **Construction shift:** You have to correct a sentence by altering the sentence structure. The original sentence may not be completely wrong, but it can be improved with a little editing.

See Chapter 4 for the lowdown on this test, Chapters 5 and 7 for full-length practice Language Arts, Writing Tests, and Chapters 6 and 8 for answers and explanations to those tests.

To give you an idea of what the questions on this test look like, consider the following examples:

Questions 1 and 2 are based on the following business letter.

Dear Mr. Snyder:

(1) I have received your letter of February 3 and offer my apologi for the mistake in your account. (2) The charge for your cheques should have been $16.20, not $1,620.00. (3) I have credited the entire amount, making your cheques free. (4) I hope this settles the matter.

1. Sentence 1: **I have received your letter of February 3 and offer my apologi for the mistake in your account.**

   How can this sentence be improved?

   (1) insert a semicolon after <u>February 3</u>

   (2) change <u>February</u> to <u>Feb.</u>

   (3) insert a period after <u>February 3</u> and capitalize <u>and</u>

   (4) change <u>apologi</u> to <u>apology</u>

   (5) no correction needed

   The correct answer is Choice (4). The correct spelling is *apology*.

2. Sentence 3: **I have credited the entire amount, making your cheques free.**

   How can this sentence be improved?

   (1) change <u>credited</u> to <u>credit</u>

   (2) change the comma after <u>amount</u> to a semicolon

   (3) change <u>free</u> to <u>freely</u>

   (4) change the comma after <u>amount</u> to a colon

   (5) no correction needed

   The correct answer is Choice (5). The sentence is correct in its current form.

Language Arts, Writing Test, Part II

In this part of the Language Arts, Writing Test, you write an essay in 45 minutes. Because the two parts of the Writing Test are given together, however, you can share time between the two parts. If you finish Part I in less than 75 minutes, you can use the extra time on Part II.

The topic you're given to write on may sound like a question from a beauty pageant, like these examples:

> ✔ What aspects of Canadian culture do you feel are unique to Canada?

> ✔ How have computers allowed you to accomplish everyday tasks more efficiently?

 See Chapter 4 for more examples of essay topics, and try writing full-length essays in the practice tests in Chapters 5 and 7. Time yourself so that you're taking them under the same conditions as the real GED tests.

In your essay, you give your opinion or explain your viewpoint and then back it up with your own experiences and facts from your life. This essay isn't a research paper. The information for the essay topics on this test is in your head — not in a library.

When you write this essay, compose a series of interconnected paragraphs on a single topic. Not only should the entire essay begin with an introduction and end with a conclusion, but each paragraph needs an introductory sentence and a concluding sentence, as well.

 Write only on the assigned topic. To make sure you understand what the topic is about, read it several times. Off-topic essays don't receive scores (and if you don't receive a score on Part II of the Writing Test, you have to take both Parts I and II all over again).

Two different people grade your essay, and, as they do, they look for the following:

> ✔ Material that's clearly organized

> ✔ Main points that are well focused

> ✔ Ideas that are well developed

> ✔ Words that are used properly

> ✔ Sentences that are well structured

> ✔ Sentences that use proper grammar, punctuation, and spelling

Note: Neat writing or printing makes grading easier for your real-life graders, so take some time to practise writing neatly before the test.

 Read print or online newspapers and watch TV news for a few months before the tests. Doing so gives you some material with which to back up your opinions and viewpoints in your essay.

Social Studies Test

For the Social Studies Test, you have to answer 50 multiple-choice questions in 70 minutes. These questions deal with the following subject areas:

- ✔ Canadian history (25 percent)
- ✔ World history (15 percent)
- ✔ Civics and government (25 percent)
- ✔ Economics (20 percent)
- ✔ Geography (15 percent)

The questions in this test are based on written texts, pictures, charts, tables, graphs, photographs, political cartoons, diagrams, or maps. These textual and pictorial excerpts come from a variety of sources, such as government documents, academic texts, material from work-related documents, and atlases.

See Chapter 9 for more information about the Social Studies Test, and be sure to take the full-length practice tests in Chapters 10 and 12. (Then check out Chapters 11 and 13 for the answers and explanations.)

You may see the following types of problems on the Social Studies Test:

Question 1 is based on the following table.

Type of Religion	Date Started (Approximate)	Sacred Texts
Buddhism	500 BC	None
Christianity	33 AD	Bible (Old Testament and New Testament)
Hinduism	4000 BC	Vedas; Upanishads
Islam	600 AD	Qur'an; Hadith
Judaism	2000 BC	Hebrew Bible; Talmud

1. According to the table, Hinduism

   (1) started in 600 AD

   (2) uses the Qur'an as one of its sacred texts

   (3) is the oldest religion

   (4) has no known sacred texts

   (5) has one known sacred text

The correct answer is Choice (3). The table shows that Hinduism is the oldest of the five religions listed because it began in 4000 BC.

Question 2 is based on the following excerpt from the diary of Christopher Columbus.

Monday, 6 August. The rudder of the caravel Pinta became loose, being broken or unshipped. It was believed that this happened by the contrivance of Gomez Rascon and Christopher Quintero, who were on board the caravel, because they disliked the voyage. The Admiral says he had found them in an unfavourable disposition before setting out. He was in much anxiety at not being able to afford any assistance in this case, but says that it somewhat quieted his apprehensions to know that Martin Alonzo Pinzon, Captain of the Pinta, was a man of courage and capacity. Made progress, day and night, of twenty-nine leagues.

2. Why would Rascon and Quintero have loosened the rudder?

(1) They were trying to repair the rudder.

(2) The Admiral found them in an unfavourable disposition.

(3) The captain was very competent.

(4) They wanted to stop to fish.

(5) They did not want to be on the voyage.

The correct answer is Choice (5). This answer is the only one supported by the text. The others may be related to statements in the excerpt, but they don't answer the question.

Science Test

When you take the Science Test, you have to answer 50 multiple-choice science questions in 80 minutes. The questions deal with the following topics:

✔ Life science (45 percent)

✔ Physical science, including chemistry and physics (35 percent)

✔ Earth and space science (20 percent)

Some of the information the questions refer to appears in passages that you read before answering the questions. Other information is presented in charts, figures, graphs, maps, or tables. Chapter 14 discusses these different formats in detail. Turn to Chapters 15 and 17 to take two full-length sample Science Tests that are similar to the real ones. (Don't forget to go to Chapters 16 and 18 to find the answers and explanations to those tests — after you finish taking them, of course!)

Most of the information you need to answer the questions on the Science Test is in the passages and other excerpts, although to get a perfect score, you're expected to have picked up a bit of science information throughout your life. However, even if you answer correctly only the questions based entirely on information presented, you should get a score high enough to pass.

Here are some sample problems that may be on the Science Test:

Questions 1 and 2 are based on the following excerpt from a press release.

A key feature of the Delta 4's operation is the use of a common booster core, or CBC, a rocket stage that measures some 150 feet long and 16 feet wide. By combining one or more CBCs with various upper stages or strap-on solid rocket boosters, the Delta 4 can handle an extreme range of satellite applications for military, civilian, and commercial customers.

1. The CBC in this context is the

(1) Canadian Broadcasting Corporation

(2) common booster core

(3) cooperative boosters corps

(4) civilian barbers cooperative

(5) common ballistic cavalier

The correct answer is Choice (2), which is the only answer choice the passage mentions.

2. How can the Delta 4 handle a wide range of applications?

   (1) using the Delta 4 with different names

   (2) developing a Delta 5

   (3) continuing research

   (4) using the CBC as the base of a rocket ship

   (5) creating a common core booster

The correct answer is Choice (4). The passage says that "By combining one or more CBCs with various upper stages or strap-on solid rocket boosters . . . ," so Choice (4) comes closest to answering the question.

Language Arts, Reading Test

The Language Arts, Reading Test includes 40 multiple-choice questions that you must answer in 65 minutes. Seventy-five percent of the questions are based on passages from literature and include at least one work from each of the following:

- Drama
- Poetry
- Prose fiction (that is, novels and short stories) written before 1920
- Prose fiction written between 1920 and 1960
- Prose fiction written after 1960

Twenty-five percent of the questions are based on non-fiction texts. These passages come from any of the following sources:

- **Critical reviews of visual and performing arts:** Most people go to the theatre, movies, and concerts for entertainment, but if, after you leave, you tell other people your impression of what you saw, you're doing more than just watching for entertainment — you're critically reviewing the performance. In this test, some of the questions may be based on excerpts from critical reviews.
- **Non-fiction prose:** *Prose* is any written words not written as poetry. Prose is divided into two main categories: fiction and non-fiction. A made-up story is usually referred to as *prose fiction*. A work based on facts is considered *non-fiction prose*. A biography, an instruction manual, or a history text (even this book!) are all examples of non-fiction prose.
- **Workplace and community documents:** These documents are the types of materials you see on the job or in a community; they include workplace rules, employment contracts, wills, deeds, mortgage documents, instructions on how to use a voting machine, and income tax forms.

Chapter 19 gives you more information about the Language Arts, Reading Test, and Chapters 20 and 22 test your knowledge with full-length sample tests. (Don't forget to turn to Chapters 21 and 23 for the answers and explanations to those tests when you finish taking them.)

You may see questions like the following in the Language Arts, Reading Test:

Questions 1 and 2 are based on the following excerpt from a play.

Irvin and Mervin enter from stage left. Irvin is dressed sloppily in torn jeans, he wears a flannel shirt over a dirty T-shirt, and he has unkempt hair. Mervin is dressed more neatly in khakis, a blue button-down shirt open at the neck, and loafers.

Irvin: What you want to do, man?

Mervin: *(laughing)* With you or to you?

Irvin: *(looking up)* What do you mean by that?

Mervin: What are you wearing?

Irvin: What's wrong with it?

Mervin: What's not wrong with it?

Irvin: So what? You don't want to go to the mall now?

Mervin: Why would I want to go to the mall with you, looking like that?

Irvin: Aren't I your best friend?

Mervin: Can't you dress a little better?

Irvin: Would I be a better friend if I dressed more like you?

Irvin and Mervin look at each other and shuffle off toward the mall.

1. What form of sentence does the author use to create this conversation?
    (1) All of the dialogue is boring.
    (2) All of the dialogue is in questions.
    (3) Every sentence is in a different form.
    (4) This is the way I talk to my friends.
    (5) All of the dialogue is in exclamatory sentences.

    The correct answer is Choice (2). Each line of dialogue is a question.

2. According to the dialogue, why do Irvin and Mervin want to go to the mall?
    (1) The latest Harry Potter movie is playing there.
    (2) They are going to meet friends.
    (3) Irvin wants to shop for clothes.
    (4) Mervin works there.
    (5) They are looking for something to do.

    The correct answer is Choice (5). According to the first line of dialogue, they're looking for something to do. In another scene, you may find out that they're going to see a movie, meeting friends, shopping for clothes, or going to work, but GED questions are based only on the dialogue presented.

Mathematics Test, Parts 1 and 11

The Mathematics Test has two parts: Part I allows you to use a calculator; Part II doesn't. Each part has 25 questions, and you have 45 minutes to complete each part, for a total of 50 questions in 90 minutes.

The Mathematics Test covers four major areas:

- ✔ Algebra, equations, and patterns (20 to 30 percent)
- ✔ Data analysis, statistics, and probability (20 to 30 percent)
- ✔ Measurement and geometry (20 to 30 percent)
- ✔ Number operations (20 to 30 percent)

Eighty percent of the questions are multiple choice; the other 20 percent require you to answer the question yourself in what is called an *alternate-format grid*.

An alternate-format grid is either a standard grid or a coordinate-plane grid. Instead of getting a set of multiple-choice answers to choose from, you come up with an answer and enter it on whichever of these two grids you're given on the answer sheet. (You might need to practise using the coordinate-plane grid — if you need help and reading through Chapter 24 isn't enough, get a friend who understands math or a tutor to help you.)

Chapter 24 gives you a lot more information about the Mathematics Test, including how to answer the different types of questions and how to prepare for the subject areas tested. Check out Chapters 25 and 27 for two full-length practice Mathematics Tests, and don't forget to turn to Chapters 26 and 28 for the answers and explanations.

Consider the following questions (one traditional multiple-choice question and two questions that you have to answer using alternate-format grids) that are similar to what you may see on the Mathematics Test:

1. A right-angle triangle has a hypotenuse of 5 cm and one side that is 3 cm long. What is the length of the other side in cm?

   (1) 3

   (2) 48

   (3) 243

   (4) 6

   (5) 4

The correct answer is Choice (5). Using the Pythagorean Relationship (a formula that the Formula page of the test gives you), you know that $a^2 + b^2 = c^2$, where c is the hypotenuse and a and b are either of the other two sides. Because you know the hypotenuse and one side, turn the equation around so that it reads $a^2 = c^2 - b^2$.

To get c^2, you square the hypotenuse: $5 \times 5 = 25$.

To get b^2, square this side: $3 \times 3 = 9$.

Now solve the equation for a: $a^2 = 25 - 9$ or $a^2 = 16$. Take the square root of both sides, and you get: $a = 4$.

The Mathematics Test presents real-life situations in the questions. So if you find yourself answering 37 metres to a question about the height of a room or $3 for an annual salary, recheck your answer because you're probably wrong.

2. Barb is counting the number of boxes in a warehouse. In the first storage area, she finds 24 boxes. The second area contains 30 boxes. The third area contains 28 boxes. If the warehouse has 6 storage areas where it stores boxes, and the areas have an average of 28 boxes, what is the total number of boxes in the last three areas? Record your answer on the standard grid.

	⊘	⊘	⊘	
⊙	⊙	⊙	⊙	⊙
⓪	⓪	⓪	⓪	⓪
①	①	①	①	①
②	②	②	②	②
③	③	③	③	③
④	④	④	④	④
⑤	⑤	⑤	⑤	⑤
⑥	⑥	⑥	⑥	⑥
⑦	⑦	⑦	⑦	⑦
⑧	⑧	⑧	⑧	⑧
⑨	⑨	⑨	⑨	⑨

The correct answer is 86 (which you record on the standard grid provided). If the warehouse has 6 storage areas and they have an average of 28 boxes in each, they have $6 \times 28 = 168$ boxes in the warehouse. The first three areas have $24 + 30 + 28 = 82$ boxes in them. The last three areas must have $168 - 82 = 86$ boxes in them.

8	6			
	⊘	⊘	⊘	
⊙	⊙	⊙	⊙	⊙
⓪	⓪	⓪	⓪	⓪
①	①	①	①	①
②	②	②	②	②
③	③	③	③	③
④	④	④	④	④
⑤	⑤	⑤	⑤	⑤
⑥	●	⑥	⑥	⑥
⑦	⑦	⑦	⑦	⑦
●	⑧	⑧	⑧	⑧
⑨	⑨	⑨	⑨	⑨

3. A rectangle has one corner on the origin. The base goes from the origin to the point (3,0). The right side goes from (3,0) to (3,4). Draw the missing point on the coordinate-plane grid.

The correct answer is to shade the missing point at (0,4). If you shade the three points given on the coordinate-plane grid, you see that a fourth point at (0,4) creates the rectangle. Just be sure, however, that you don't draw on the GED test book as you're taking the test! Instead, draw the point as the following coordinate-plane grid shows:

It's a Date: Scheduling the Test

To take the GED, you can't just drop in to the testing site any time and take the test. You have to schedule it based on the available testing dates. Each local testing centre sets its own schedule for the five GED tests, which means that your province or territory decides how and when you take the five tests. Schedules for the tests vary by location. Tests may be offered once every week or just once every couple of months.

Your local GED administrator can give you all the information you need about scheduling the test. To find the administrator in your area, log on to www.acenet.edu/resources/ GED/center_locator.cfm. This Web site also gives the policies for taking the GED in each province and territory. Ask local school districts and community colleges if they have information about test centres, as well.

Taking all five of the GED tests together takes seven hours and five minutes, with breaks in between the tests. Depending on your local testing centre, you may have to take all the tests in one sitting (which is rare), or you may be able to break the tests up into two or more sittings. Some provinces and territories allow you to take one test each time you go to the testing centre, and some offer the tests in the evenings or on weekends.

The upcoming sections answer some questions you may have before you schedule your test date.

Discovering whether you're eligible

Before you schedule your GED tests, make sure you meet the requirements. These are the situations that mean you're eligible to apply to take the GED tests:

- ✔ **You're not currently enrolled in a high school.** If you're currently enrolled in a high school, you're expected to complete your diploma there. The purpose of the GED tests is to give people who aren't in high school a chance to get an equivalent high school diploma.

- ✔ **You're not a graduate of high school.** If you're a high school graduate, you should have a diploma, which means you don't need to take the GED.

- ✔ **You meet provincial or territorial requirements for age, residency, and the length of time since leaving high school.** Check with your local GED administrator to determine what the requirements are concerning these criteria. Or visit www2.acenet.edu/gedtest/policy/index.cfm?region=canada and click on your province or territory to see its policies.

Knowing when you can take the tests

When can you take the GED tests? If you're eligible and prepared, you can apply to take the GED tests as soon as you want. Just contact your local testing centre to get a test schedule, and then pick a day (or days) that works for you.

You can also apply to take the tests if you're not prepared, but if you do that, you don't stand a very good chance of passing. You can retake the tests only a limited number of times (check with your local testing centre to find out how many times you can retake the test), and in most jurisdictions taking the test costs money. To save time and money, prepare before you jump in to take the tests.

Signing up

To sign up for the test, follow these steps:

1. **Contact your local GED administrator to make sure you're eligible or check www2. acenet.edu/gedtest/policy/index.cfm?region=canada.**

2. **Ask the office for an application (if needed) or an appointment.**

3. **Complete the application (if needed).**

Are special accommodations available?

If you have unique circumstances such as chronic health problems, a mental health condition, or learning disability, don't let that stop you from getting your GED certificate or diploma. Test centres make every effort to give everyone fair access to the tests. The GED Testing Service in Washington, DC, which is GED Central, lists specific disabilities for which it may make special accommodations:

✔ Medical disabilities, such as cerebral palsy, epilepsy, or blindness

✔ Emotional disabilities, such as schizophrenia, major depression, attention deficit disorder, or Tourette Syndrome

✔ Specific learning disabilities, including perceptual handicaps, brain injury, minimal brain dysfunction, dyslexia, and developmental aphasia

If you need to make special arrangements, plan ahead so that everything is in order before test day. Regardless of your circumstances, you have to handle the mental demands of the test, and getting organized ahead of time can ease your stress so you can focus on studying.

Here's what you need to do:

✔ Contact the GED Testing Service or your local GED centre and explain your disability.

✔ Request any forms that you have to fill out for your special circumstances.

✔ Ensure that you have a recent diagnosis by a physician or other qualified professional.

✔ Complete all the proper forms and submit them with a medical or professional diagnosis.

For more information go to `www.acenet.edu/Content/NavigationMenu/ged/test/Take/Accommodations_Disab.htm`.

4. **Return the application to the proper office, with payment, if necessary.**

The fees vary by province and territory, so contact your local administrator or testing site to find out what you have to pay to take the tests. In some areas, if you fall into a low-income bracket, you may have the fees paid for you. Check for acceptable forms of payment (cheque, credit card, debit card) and follow the rules. You don't want to get stuck on a technicality.

Working with unusual circumstances

If you feel that you have a special circumstance that prevents you from taking the GED tests, contact the GED administrator in your area. If, for example, the tests are going to be held on your Sabbath, the testing centre may make special arrangements for you.

When applying for special circumstances, keep the following guidelines in mind:

✔ Document everything in your appeal for special consideration.

✔ Contact the GED administrator in your area as early as you can.

✔ Be patient. Special arrangements can't be made overnight. The administrator often has to wait for a group with similar issues to gather so he can make arrangements for the entire group.

Taking the GED When English Is Your Second Language

English doesn't have to be your first language for you to take the GED. The GED tests are offered in English, French, and Spanish. If you want to take the test in Spanish or French, contact your local GED administrator to apply.

If English, French, or Spanish isn't your first language, you must decide whether you read and write English as well as or better than 40 percent of high school graduates because you may be required to pass an English as a Second Language (ESL) Placement Test. If you write and read English well, prepare for and take the tests (either in English, French, or Spanish). If you don't read or write English well, take additional classes to prepare yourself in English until you think you're ready. Check out the "Your Language" section at www.acenet.edu/ Content/NavigationMenu/ged/test/Take/ESL_Test_GED.htm for more information about the language component.

In many ways, the GED tests are like the TOEFL (the Test of English as a Foreign Language) comprehension tests. If you've completed the TOEFL tests with good grades, you're likely ready to take the GED. If you haven't taken the TOEFL tests, enrol in a GED preparation course to see whether you have difficulty understanding the subjects and skills tested on the test. GED courses provide you not only with some insight into your comprehension ability, but also with a teacher to discuss your skills and struggles with.

Eyeing What You Have to Score to Pass the GED

To pass the tests, you have to score at least 410 on each one and have an average score of 450 on the five tests. If you pass, congratulate yourself: You've scored better than at least 40 percent of today's high school graduates, and you're now a graduate of the largest virtual school in the country!

The following sections address a few more points about how the GED tests are scored and what you can do if you score poorly on some or all of the tests.

Identifying how scores are determined

Except for the essay, each correct answer is worth one point. No matter how hard or easy the question is, if you get it right, you get one point. In each test, the points you get are totalled, and the total converts to a standard score, ranging from 200 to 800 on each test. The method of converting to standard scores is not a secret, but it is a complicated statistical process and not worth worrying about. Do as well as you can, and concentrate on preparing for the tests.

Because you don't lose points for incorrect answers, make sure you answer all the questions on each test. After all, a guessed answer can get you a point. Leaving an answer blank can't get you anything but a zero.

Web sites that can help you plan to take the GED

The Internet is a helpful and sometimes scary place. Some Web sites can help you in your GED preparation, while others just want to sell you something. You have to be on alert to separate the good from the bad. Here are a couple of essential ones:

✔ `www.acenet.edu/AM/Template.cfm? Section=GED_TS`: This Web site is the main site for the GED Testing Service. It contains all the essential information you need as you get ready for the GED.

✔ `www.acenet.edu/Content/Navigation Menu/ged/test/admin_canada.htm`: This site tells you the name of the GED administrator for your province or territory.

If you want to see what's out there, enter *GED* into any search engine and relax while you try to read about 22,000,000 entries ranging from the helpful to the useless. We suggest leaving this last activity until after you've passed the tests. As useful as the Internet can be, it can be a big time waster. And right now, you need to spend your time preparing for the tests — and leave the rest for after you get your certificate or diploma.

Knowing what to do if you score poorly on one or more tests

If you discover that your average score is less than 450 on any of the tests, start planning to retake the test(s) — and make sure you leave plenty of time for additional studying and preparing.

As soon as possible after seeing your results, contact your local GED administrator to find out the rules for retaking tests. Some provinces or territories may ask that you wait for a certain amount of time. Some may ask that you attend a preparation course and show that you've completed it before you can take the GED tests again. Some may charge you an additional fee.

No matter what score you receive on your first round of tests, don't be afraid to retake any of them that you didn't pass. Now that you've taken them once, you know what you need to work on, and you know exactly what to expect on test day. Just take a deep breath, and be prepared for the next round.

Chapter 2

Navigating the GED Testing System: The Who, When, and How

....

In This Chapter
▶ Figuring out who takes the GED
▶ Understanding why people take the tests
▶ Using pre-tests to help you prepare for the GED
▶ Managing your time before and during the tests

....

You may be wondering why you should consider taking the GED tests, or, if you've already decided to take them, you may be curious about why you should spend a lot of time preparing for them. The truth is that the GED is the best substitution for a high school diploma you can find in Canada today.

But why do you even need a high school diploma or its equivalent? To answer this question, take a serious look at the world today. Education level has become one of the main assets that employers look for when they're hiring. In Canada, the number of people who have completed high school has increased sharply in the last few years. More and more people have university degrees or college diplomas or certificates, which means that when you apply for a job, chances are good that other applicants will have more education than you. Also, today's industries are shifting from place to place, and your skills alone may no longer be valued where you live. So, you need to make yourself more competitive. And the GED certificate or diploma helps you do that.

Think of yourself as a product that people should want to buy. Your product needs interesting and enticing ingredients and superb marketing. A high school diploma is one of the necessary ingredients, and it needs to appear prominently on your resumé for all your potential employers to see.

This chapter gives you a clear idea of why you may want to take the GED and of who else is in a similar situation. This chapter also points out some general tidbits that can help you find your way through the GED test maze and come out ahead. Preparing for the GED will definitely cut into your TV time and social life — and require some sacrifices and a real commitment from you — but in the end, passing the tests will be worth all the effort and time.

Identifying Who Takes the GED

People who take the GED are people like you — they want a high school diploma but, for whatever reason, don't have one. Check out the following sections to get a better picture of who takes the GED.

People who didn't finish high school

Most people who take the GED tests dropped out of high school for some reason and didn't receive a high school diploma. Perhaps you dropped out of school to help your family with living expenses. Perhaps school just wasn't right for you. Perhaps you had a baby and couldn't take care of your newborn and go to school at the same time.

Whatever your situation, if you're looking to take the GED tests, all that matters is

✔ You're not currently enrolled in school (and haven't been for a specified period of time).

✔ You've reached a certain minimum age.

The amount of time you've been out of school and the age you need to be to take the GED depend on provincial or territorial requirements. You can find out whether you qualify by contacting your local GED administrator or reviewing your region's GED testing policies online (www2.acenet.edu/gedtest/policy/index.cfm?region=canada).

If you meet the qualifications, you're eligible to take the tests. If you decide to go for it, making sure you're prepared is the next step — and we can help. This book is chock-full of information and helpful hints to get you through the whole GED process.

Newcomers to Canada

If you've come to Canada from another country, you may have graduated from a school that's equivalent to Canadian high school but have difficulty proving it. Not all Canadian employers or schools will immediately accept documents from another country, especially if they're in another language, which leaves you with a huge problem. Fortunately, the GED comes to the rescue. The GED certificate or diploma is recognized all across the United States and Canada; it's as close to a universal diploma as you can get. Preparing for and passing the GED tests get you a certificate or diploma that says you're the equivalent of a high school graduate, which is helpful if you're having trouble proving your level of education.

In general, the GED tests are in English and require a level of English understanding that is equal to that of most Grade 12 students. If English isn't your first language and you have trouble reading it, consider beefing up your English-speaking and -reading skills before taking the GED. We suggest you take some English classes to improve your skills. Although the GED test is also available in French, not all test centres offer the test in all languages, so you have to check with your local test centre first. Some test centres also require that you prove you can read English and may require that you take an English as a second language (ESL) test in addition to the GED tests. Check all this out first with your local test administrator and avoid any last-minute surprises. To find out if your jurisdiction requires the ESL test, contact your local testing centre or the provincial administrator. (Just a note of reality — you may not be able to speak to the provincial or territorial administrator in person, but anyone in the office can give you the information you need.)

Opening Doors: Why People Take the GED

People take the GED tests because they want better opportunities in the workforce or in the world of education, and the GED can open many doors. If you're considering taking the GED, you may be in one of the following situations:

✔ **You want a better-paying job.** Most employers base their pay offer on your qualifications and experience. The GED certificate or diploma is a widely recognized credential and can help you get up the rungs on the pay scale.

✔ **You want to get in to a college, university, or other post-secondary institution.** Post-secondary institutions want to see that you can succeed in their courses. Some may accept you if you're older than a certain age and ask that you pass certain courses or take specific exams before admitting you. Most accept a high school diploma or equivalent. The GED is widely accepted as the equivalent of a high school diploma.

✔ **You want to enter a field that requires a high school diploma.** Many occupations and apprenticeships require a high school diploma or equivalent to enter. The GED certificate or diploma is the key to this lock.

✔ **You want to feel better about yourself.** Accomplishing a challenge makes you feel good about yourself. Passing the GED tests is a challenging task, and when you accomplish it, you can pat yourself on the back — just don't strain anything while doing it. It may be better to have friends and relatives pat you on the back. Then you can just enjoy all the attention.

No matter what your situation is, the GED tests offer you a way to reach your goals.

Eyeing the Importance of Pre-testing with the Practice Tests

If you knew everything that would be on a particular test, you could just walk in and ace it, right? And on the off chance that you didn't pass, you could simply take it again and again until you passed, couldn't you? Actually, you couldn't. The GED has strict rules about retaking it. You usually have to wait a period of time before retaking it, and you can only retake it a limited number of times. These limits are set by the local authorities, so check with your local administrator. That's why you should prepare *before* you take the tests, so you pass the first time.

The following sections discuss one of the best ways to prepare for the GED tests — pre-tests. A *pre-test,* or *practice test,* is an informal test that covers the same material that the real test covers to help you get a feel for that material and the test format. Read on to find out how you can use pre-tests to your advantage to help you get ready for the GED.

Using practice tests to prepare for the GED

How you use the practice tests is key to how well you do when you take the real GED. You can take practice tests individually or in a group (depending on your preference) to give you an idea of how you may do on the real test. Essentially, practice tests assist you to prepare for the real GED tests by showing you what you don't know and what you need to work on. Armed with this information, you can prepare for the real tests more efficiently.

Just because the practice test has the word *test* in it doesn't mean you have to panic. Repeat to yourself, "This practice test is my friend and only wants to help me." The practice tests in this book do just that — help you practise for the real tests. They help you discover your weaknesses and strengths, so you can concentrate on subject areas that you need to study more, which can definitely improve your chances of success on the real tests.

We supply several practice tests throughout this book to help you know what to expect on test day. Before each set of tests in each part, we provide you with a chapter that outlines what's unique about that particular test. *Note:* Not all tests on the GED are the same, and knowing as much as possible about each one will help you pass it. (For example, the Language Arts Test has a different format than the Math Test.) After you read the initial chapter in each part, you're ready to take the ensuing practice tests.

Working your way through a practice test

To get the most out of the practice tests in this book, you need to know what to do when taking them. Set yourself up as if you were going to take the real test. Time yourself and don't take a break to check the answers. The closer you come to real test conditions, the better the result will be when you take the real test.

When taking any practice tests in this book, keep the following steps in mind:

1. **Carefully read the instructions at the beginning of each test.**

   Normally, the person giving the real test makes sure that everyone understands the instructions before starting. If you have any questions about the directions, ask — don't wait until the clock is ticking. The instructions for the practice tests are as close as possible to the instructions for the real tests. If you're worried, ask your local administrator beforehand about the instructions. The administrator will answer any questions he or she can ahead of time.

2. **Know the time restrictions for the real test, and stick to them as you take the practice test.**

   Timing is very important in the GED tests. At the beginning of each test, the directions tell you how much time you have. Make sure you stick to the time. Use an alarm clock, have a friend keep an eye on the time, or do anything else you have to do to make sure you don't go over the time limit.

   During the real test, the person giving the test (*the proctor*) will remind you about the time allotment and what will happen at the end of the test. Usually, they tell you to put your writing instruments down and close your books. Whatever the proctor tells you to do, make sure you do it. This is not the time to show how much of an individual you are. Be part of the crowd and follow instructions.

3. **Prepare for the practice test the way you would prepare for the real test.**

   Have your writing instruments ready. Have enough scrap paper to make notes on. Make photocopies of the answer sheets or tear them out of this book so that you don't have to keep flipping back and forth. Find an uncomfortable chair to sit on — test centres aren't famous for their comfortable seats. Concentrate on the test — not the chair — and you'll be fine. The other way around can be a recipe for disaster.

4. **Make a mental plan beforehand so you know how to answer the questions in the allotted time.**

   Before you start taking the test, you know how many questions are on it and how much time you have to answer them. You also know about how many minutes you can safely spend on each question. Make a mental plan of how you're going to use this information. (See "Managing Your Time for the GED" later in this chapter.) Obviously, you can't time each question, but you may feel comfortable timing each set of five or ten questions to make sure you stay on track. You may want to set aside a few minutes at the beginning to scan over the questions and start with the easy ones. Or you may read all the questions and start with the even-numbered ones and finish with the odd-numbered ones. Whatever you choose, decide ahead of time and do it.

5. **Focus on each question and choose the best possible answer.**

   Be sure to record all your answers on your answer sheet. If possible, leave some time at the end of the test for review. Don't over-think the questions. You're looking for the *best answer* as stated or suggested by the question and any other material presented to you. If your previous knowledge tells you that the best answer according to the passage isn't the correct answer, play the multiple-choice game. Choose the best answer based on the material presented to you. In doing so, if your previous knowledge is flawed or if you forget something, you can still get the right answer and pass the test.

6. **After you finish all the questions or run out of time, make some notes on your scrap paper about the difficulty of the test.**

   Make notes about which questions you found difficult and which ones you found easy. Make notes about how you felt as you took the test. Did you have enough time? Did specific sections cause you trouble? Make notes on everything you remember about the test — these notes will come in handy later.

7. **Check the answers to see how you did.**

   You can find the answers and their explanations in the chapter immediately following the practice test chapter. For each question, compare your answer to the correct answer. If you got it wrong, read the explanation to try to figure out why. And if you're not sure why it's wrong, ask somebody who can help you. Even if you got the answer correct, read the explanation anyway. You may find out a bit more about doing a particular type of question.

8. **When you finish checking your answers, add up the number of questions you answered correctly.**

   On the real test, the scores are computed using a complex calculation that we don't do here. To be on the safe side, though, consider that getting 80 percent of the answers correct leaves you with a safe margin for error. If you got more than 20 percent of the questions wrong, you have work to do.

9. **Review the questions you missed, even if you only missed one, and read the notes you made right after you finished the test (in Step 6).**

   If your notes say that you knew you had problems with these questions when you answered them, compare your notes with the answers. For example, if you felt you had trouble with the questions about graphs and you got most of the graph-related questions wrong, you need more help with graphs. If you got them right, you may be worrying too much or you may just need a quick review of graphs. Now you can review or create your plan of action for passing the test based on experience.

   In the introductory chapter for each test, we tell you what that particular test is evaluating. Go to the sections in the introductory chapter with headings that focus on the areas you need the most help with (based on your analysis of your answers and post-test notes). If you made the most mistakes in one or more areas, spend most of your time working on that area as you prepare to take another practice test. And remember: Sometimes you have to take a slight detour to get to your goal. If you're having a lot of trouble with a particular test or section, consider looking into a course, asking a friend, or getting a tutor. Whatever you decide to do, don't just pass it over.

10. **Go on to the second practice test if you did well on the first one or if you've finished any extra preparation you wanted to do.**

    Follow Steps 1 through 9 to complete that test the same way you did the first. If your score improves, congratulate yourself. If it doesn't and you get a less-than-perfect score, you may want to do some additional practice or join a GED preparation class.

    You can also find some sample questions for the GED at www.acenet.edu/Content/ NavigationMenu/ged/test/prep/sample_questions.htm. The questions on this site are all from the American tests, but in many cases that doesn't matter. The differences between the American and Canadian tests are few (although this book stresses the Canadian tests).

Managing Your Time for the GED

Time management becomes important as soon as you decide you need a high school diploma equivalency. If you had all the time in the world, you could just meander through preparation and planning. But in real life, you probably have deadlines, which means you can't take forever to do something. Managing your time well can improve your chances of accomplishing your goals.

In this section, we give you some hints about how to manage your time. To start, this section consists of about 800 words. Think about how long it takes you to read and understand an 800-word passage. Keep track of the time it actually takes. You can use that information as you plan how to use your time preparing for and taking the tests.

Before the tests

Prior to taking the GED, you have plenty of tasks to tend to, and you have to find time for them all. Before you start studying or doing any other preparation work, you need to have a firm grasp of what you need to do and how much time you have to do it — which is where we can help you.

Before the test, make sure you do the following:

1. **Make a list of everything you need to do to prepare for the GED.**

   We suggest you first look over the information on the GED Web site (`www.acenet. edu/AM/Template.cfm?Section=GED_TS`), consult your local administrator, and review material like this book to help you prepare. Create your own list based on your skills and the test areas you need the most help in. You can create a table like the one we provide you here to keep organized.

Step	Task	Estimated Time	Date Completed
1	Make sure that I can prove I'm eligible to write the GED tests.		
	Get a copy of my birth certificate.		
	Get a copy of my high school transcript to prove when I left school.		
	Check with my local GED administrator to find out the actual requirements and if I presently meet them.		
2	Buy a copy of a good preparation book (like this one!).		
3	Contact my local GED administrator to get a schedule of tests.		
4	Figure out how much time I have to prepare for a test.		
5	Look at my high school transcript and make a list of the subject areas I had the most trouble with so I know where to spend most of my preparation time.		
6	Begin preparing for the practice tests by reading the appropriate sections of this book.		

Step	Task	Estimated Time	Date Completed
7	Take the first practice test, check my answers, and read the explanations.		
8	Make a list of the tests in order with my lowest scores at the top and my best scores at the bottom.		
9	Review the time I have before the test I want to write and make any modifications to my schedule I think would help.		
10	If my test scores are low, consider a preparation class, a GED preparation group, or other forms of additional help, and estimate the time.		
11	Begin to work on preparation, starting with my weakest area.		
12	Do regular reviews of all areas, spending the most time on my weakest areas.		
13	When I think I am better prepared, take the second practice test and repeat steps 7 through 12.		
14	Review, and modify if necessary, the time to prepare for the test I plan to take.		
15	Register for the test.		
16	Read the sections in this book about what to expect on the test.		
17	Set up a review schedule, spending the most time on my weakest areas.		
18	Practise getting to the test.		
19	Take the test.		
20	Wait for results while considering a realistic plan and schedule if any of the results are low.		

2. **After you have your list, approximate how much time you need to complete each task, indicating both when you'd like to have it done and leaving space to fill in the date you actually complete it.**

   Estimate how long you think it may take you to finish a task. Remember that some tasks will take longer than others. For example, getting a copy of your high school transcript may only take a couple hours, while preparing for your weakest subject area may take 30 or 40 hours depending on how much time you need. Make sure to consider any lag time, because you won't always get immediate answers to questions, and you'll have to wait to see people or wait for documents to arrive the mail. Use a calendar and figure out when you should have each task completed.

Your plan for managing your time is written on paper, not carved in stone. As you work through the preparation process, you may realize that you need more time for one task, such as taking more math pre-tests, and less time for another task. If so, that's okay. Simply revise your schedule to take your new needs into consideration. After you complete a task, write down the date you completed it.

After you pass the test: What you can do with your GED

After passing the GED and receiving that beautiful certificate or diploma, you're ready to think about your future. In addition to the obvious celebrations for your personal graduation, you have plenty more to do. (See Chapter 31 for some interesting ways your life can change with a GED.) Consider the following ways you can improve your life with your new GED in hand:

✔ **You can qualify for a better job.** If you took the GED to get a better, higher-paying job, go for it. Having a GED may increase your chances of passing the initial screening process and getting an interview. During the interview, you can shine your way past the other qualified applicants. Make sure you let your prospective employer know that you passed a test that about 40 percent of high school graduates would have trouble passing. Furthermore, you've proved that you're a diligent worker by preparing and passing the GED after leaving school. You're dedicated, you know how to prepare, and you learn well — if you didn't, you couldn't have passed the test. Basically, you're worthy of being hired. With this attitude, you should do well in interviews and be on your way to getting a better job.

Take some information about the GED tests and certificate or diploma with you to your interview. Don't assume that every human resources person knows all about the GED. Go to the GED home page and download some information to strengthen your case. You can enter *GED ace* into a search engine or go to www.acenet.edu/AM/Template.cfm?Section=GED_TS. The "Publications and Research" and "News and Events" are full of interesting material to convince any doubter that the GED is a valid and worthwhile credential.

✔ **You can go to college, university, or some other post-secondary schooling.** With a GED, you can apply to and improve your chances of getting accepted at many post-secondary schools. Check with the school you're interested in about its admission requirements, and review its deadlines for applying and the courses it offers. Consult with the financial aid office to find out how you can pay for school or if financial assistance is available.

During the tests

After the GED starts, you're on strict timelines. The best thing you can do during the tests to manage your time is simple: Relax. Many students get so psyched up right when they sit down that they have trouble focusing on the test and waste valuable time.

During the test, use the following time-management strategies to help keep yourself on track and to finish the test on time. We include specific time-management strategies for each test in the part of the book that deals with each particular test.

✔ **Take deep breaths, relax, and focus on the task at hand.** Some people visualize themselves doing well on the test, others may even close their eyes and say a little prayer. Whatever you do, take a few minutes to relax, but remember you don't get extra time on the test to do this.

✔ **Skim the questions to spot the easy ones, and do those questions first.** After doing so, look at the time and quickly calculate how many questions are left and how many minutes you have to do them. To determine how much time you can spend on each question, divide the time remaining by the number of questions you have left. Be sure to add in a little extra time at the end for review (see the next bullet point for details). *Note:* In each part, we offer a chapter that outlines how many questions and how much time you have for each type of test. Use these chapters to create a mental game plan so you're prepared to manage your time when you get to the real tests.

✔ **Leave a few minutes at the end to review your answers.** You need a few minutes to make sure you answered everything correctly. Quickly look over your answers, but don't panic and change them because at the last minute you think an answer is wrong. Chances are good that the answer you selected first is the right one.

Chapter 3

Succeeding on Test Day

*Y*ou may have never taken a standardized test before. Or if you have, you may wake up sweating in the middle of the night from nightmares about your past experience. Whether you have or haven't felt the joys or sorrows of standardized tests, to succeed in the GED, you have to know how to perform well on this type of test, which consists mostly of multiple-choice questions.

You've come to the right spot to find out more about this type of test. This chapter explains some important pointers for what you can do the night before and the morning of the test and what you need to do during the test to be successful. It also explains some important test-taking strategies that can help you feel confident.

Leading Up to Test Time

Doing well on the GED involves more than walking into the test site and answering the questions. You need to be prepared for the challenges in the tests. To ensure you're ready, do the following leading up to the test:

✔ **Get enough sleep.** We're sorry if we sound like your parents, but it's true — you shouldn't take tests when you're approaching exhaustion. Plan your time so that you can get a good night's sleep for several days before the test. If you prepare ahead of time, you'll be ready and sleep easier.

✔ **Eat a good breakfast.** A healthy breakfast fuels your mind and body. The tests take several hours, and you definitely don't want to falter during that time. Eat some oatmeal, yogourt, and fresh fruit the morning of the test. You don't want your empty stomach fighting with your full brain.

✔ **Take some deep breaths.** During your trip to the testing site, prepare yourself mentally. Clear your head of all distractions, practise deep breathing, and imagine yourself acing the test. Don't panic.

✔ **Start at the beginning, not the end.** Remember that the day of the test is the end of a long journey of preparation, and not the beginning. Building mental muscles takes time.

✔ **Be on time.** Make sure you know the exact date and time the test begins and the exact location of the test site. Most examination centres don't let you enter if you're late. Don't take a chance — arrive early. If necessary, take a practice run to make sure you have enough time to get from your home or workplace to the testing centre. You don't need the added pressure of worrying about being late, which can create industrial-strength panic in the calmest of people.

Traffic happens. No one can plan for it, but you can leave extra time to make sure it doesn't ruin your day. Plan your route and practise it. Then leave extra time in case a meteor crashes into the street and the crowd that gathers around it stalls your progress.

Finding Out What to Take to the GED Tests

The GED may be the most important exam you ever take. Treat it seriously and come prepared. Make sure you bring the following items with you on test day:

✔ **You:** The most important thing to bring to the GED tests is you. If you enrol to take the tests, you have to show up; otherwise, you'll receive a big fat zero. If something unfortunate happens after you enrol, contact the test centre right away and explain your situation to the test administrators.

✔ **Correct identification:** Before test officials let you into the room to take the test, they want to make sure you're you. Bring the approved photo ID (your local GED office can tell you what's approved). Have your ID in a place where you can reach it easily. And when asked to identify yourself, don't pull out a mirror and say, "Yep, that's me."

✔ **Fees you still owe:** To take the GED, you must pay a registration fee, which varies from region to region. (Check with your local administrator about when and how to pay the fee.) If you don't pay the fee, you can't take the exam. Bring your receipt in case of any misunderstanding at the door.

✔ **Registration confirmation:** The registration confirmation is your proof that you registered. If you're taking the tests in an area where everybody knows you and everything you do, you may not need the confirmation, but we suggest you take it anyway. It's light and doesn't take up much room in your pocket.

✔ **Other miscellaneous items:** In the instructions you receive after you register for the tests, you get a list of what you need to bring with you to the test. Besides yourself and the items listed previously, bring or wear the following:

  • Comfortable clothes

  • Comfortable shoes

  • Wristwatch with a second hand (If you haven't changed the battery lately, you may want to do so beforehand.)

  • Two HB pencils or mechanical pencils; a pen for the essay (all of which may be provided for you at the testing centre, but why take a chance?)

The rules about what enters the testing room are strict. Don't take any chances. If something isn't on the list of acceptable items and isn't normal clothing, leave it at home. Do not bring the following:

✔ Books

✔ Calculator (one is provided for you — see Chapter 24)

✔ Notes or scratch paper

✔ MP3 player

✔ Cellphone (leave it at home or in your car)

✔ Anything valuable, like a notebook computer or radio that you don't feel comfortable leaving outside the room while you take the exams

If you're wondering whether or not you can bring a certain item, ask the test centre in advance. Check out www.acenet.edu/resources/GED/center_locator.cfm to find testing sites near you by entering your postal code into the search box. You can also call 800-62-MYGED, the GED information line for the American Council on Education in Washington.

Knowing What to Expect When You Get There

Usually you take the GED tests in a large room with at least one official (sometimes called a *proctor* or *examiner*) who's in charge of the test. The proctor gives each test taker a test booklet and an answer sheet when the test is scheduled to begin and then reads instructions aloud. Listen carefully to these instructions so you know when and if you can take bathroom breaks, how much time you have to take the test, and even more interesting information.

As soon as the proctor gives you permission to open the test booklet, skim the questions. Don't spend a lot of time skimming — just enough to spot the questions you absolutely know and the ones you know you'll need more time to answer. Mark the easy ones in the test booklet. After you finish skimming, answer all the questions you know first; that way you leave yourself much more time for the questions you're less sure of.

For each question — except for a few on the Mathematics Test (see Chapter 24) and the essay in Part II of the Language Arts, Writing Test (see Chapter 4) — you have five answers to choose from. Read each question carefully, keeping in mind that only one answer is correct. Choose the answer that's closest to the correct answer from the material in the question. If what you know is different from what the question says, go with the information in the question. A machine usually grades the tests, and the machine doesn't know what's in your head. Sometimes you have to choose the *best* answer, not the absolutely correct one.

You don't have to answer questions in order. Nobody except you will ever know in which order you answered the questions, so do the questions you know best first.

Because taking standardized tests probably isn't a usual situation for you, you may feel nervous. This is perfectly normal. Just try to focus on answering one question at a time, and push away any other thoughts. Sometimes taking a few deep breaths can clear your mind; just don't spend a lot of time focusing on your breath. After all, your main job is to pass these tests.

Throughout the test, keep your eyes on your paper. If you glance around the room, the GED examiner may wonder what you're doing. Never become the object of an examiner's attention during a test. In the worst-case scenario, he or she may think you're cheating and disqualify your test. In the best-case scenario, he or she may think you're looking for someone to invite for coffee afterwards.

Throughout the test, the examiner will periodically tell you how much time has elapsed or how much time is left. Listen to these reminders. When time is up, immediately stop writing, put down your pencil, and breathe a sigh of relief. When the test is over, hand in your answer sheet and test booklet. Listen for instructions on what to do or where to go next.

Discovering Important Test-Taking Strategies

You can increase your score by practising — and mastering — a few smart test-taking strategies. To help you do so, we give you some tips in this section for planning your time, determining the question type, figuring out how to answer the different types of questions, guessing intelligently, and reviewing your work.

Watching the clock

You only have a certain amount of time for each test in the GED exam, so time management is an important part of succeeding. You need to plan ahead and use your time wisely.

When the test begins, check your watch and write down the time you start and the time you have to finish. (Write these times near the top of your answer sheet in very light pencil marks that you can erase before handing it in.) This way, you don't waste time figuring out how much time you have left partway through the test. Don't try to remember the time; instead, write it down.

During the test, your proctor will warn you — perhaps more than once — about how much time remains. Check the times you're told against the times you write down at the beginning of the test. Table 3-1 shows you how much time you have, on average, for each question in each test.

Table 3-1	Time per Question for Each GED Test		
Test	Number of Questions	Time Limit (Minutes)	Time per Question (Minutes)
Language Arts, Writing, Part I	50	75	1.5
Language Arts, Writing, Part II	1 essay	45	45
Social Studies	50	70	1.4
Science	50	80	1.6
Language Arts, Reading	40	65	1.6
Mathematics, Parts I and II	50	90	1.8

As you can see from this table, if you take two minutes for each question, you won't have time to answer all the questions on the test. The following general time-management tips can help you complete each exam on time:

- **Measure the time you have to answer each question without spending more time on timing than answering.** Group questions together. For example, plan to do five questions in seven minutes. Doing so helps you complete all the questions and leaves you several minutes for review.

- **Keep calm and don't panic.** Spend your time answering questions, not panicking.

- **Practise using the sample tests in this book.** The more you practise timed sample test questions, the easier managing timed tests becomes. Practising helps you get used to doing something under pressure and in a limited amount of time.

Identifying different question types

To answer the questions correctly, you don't have to know too much about how the test makers developed the questions. But you do need some understanding of how they were constructed. Knowing the type of question you're dealing with can make answering them easier and you will face fewer surprises.

For example, some questions in the Math Test require a special form for the answer. Knowing the question type can shape the way you think about the answer. Some questions ask you to analyze material from a passage, which means the information you need is in the passage. Others ask you to infer from the passage, which means that all the information may not be in the passage. Although none of the GED tests are labelled with the following titles, the questions test your skills in the following areas.

Analysis

Analysis questions require you to break down information and look at how the bits are related to one another. Analyzing information in this way is part of reasoning and requires you to

- Separate facts from opinions.

- Realize that when an assumption isn't stated it may not necessarily be true. Assumptions stated in the passage or question help you find the best answer.

- Identify a cause-and-effect relationship. For example, you have to eat an ice-cream cone quickly in hot weather. The cause is the hot weather and the effect is that the ice cream melts quickly.

- Infer. You may be asked to reach a conclusion based on evidence presented in the question. *Inferring* means that you'll reach a conclusion. In the preceding example, you can infer that you should stay in an air-conditioned space to eat your ice cream or eat it very quickly.

- Compare. If you consider the similarities between ideas or objects, you're *comparing* them. Saying that the world is like a basketball because both are round is an example of a comparison.

- Contrast. If you consider the differences between ideas or objects, you're *contrasting* them. Saying that the world isn't like a basketball because it is so much larger and has an irregular surface is an example of a contrast.

You develop most of these skills simply by interacting with people. For example, by talking about sports with your friends (or rivals), you quickly figure out how to separate fact from opinion and how to infer, compare, contrast, and identify cause-and-effect relationships. In other social situations, you come to realize when an assumption isn't stated. For example, you assume that your significant other is going to join you for a coffee the night before an important test, such as the GED, but, in reality, you get disappointed because he is planning on going to bed early. Unstated assumptions can get you into trouble in life and on the GED tests.

Application

Application questions require you to use the information presented to you in one situation to help you in a different situation. You've been applying information left and right for most of your life, but you probably didn't realize it. For example, when you use the information from the morning newspaper to make a point in an argument in the afternoon, you use your application skills.

Comprehension

A *comprehension* question asks whether you understand written material. The GED test makers expect you to be able to state the information presented on the test in your own words, develop a summary of the ideas presented, discuss the implications of those ideas, and draw conclusions from those implications. You need to develop these comprehension skills to understand what the multiple-choice questions are asking you and to answer the questions successfully.

The best way to increase your comprehension is to read extensively and to have another person ask you questions about what you read. You can also use books that specifically help you with your comprehension by presenting you with written material and asking you questions about it. (One of those books is in your hands!) All the other For Dummies test preparation books, as well as *AP English Literature & Composition For Dummies* by Geraldine Woods (Wiley), have reading comprehension as a major focus, too. Check out these books to improve your comprehension if you still have difficulty after using this book.

Synthesis

Synthesis questions require you to take apart blocks of information presented to you and put the pieces back together to form a hypothesis, theory, or story. Doing so gives you a new understanding or twist on the information that you didn't have before. Have you ever discussed something that happened, giving it your own twist and explanation to create a brand new story? If so, you've already used your synthesis skills.

Evaluation

Any time someone presents you with information or an opinion, you judge it to make sure it rings true in your mind. This *evaluation* helps you make decisions about the information presented before you decide to use it. If the clerk behind the ice-cream counter suggests you get a raspberry cone because everyone knows that raspberry melts slower than all the other flavours, you may be a bit suspicious of the information, especially if you notice that the clerk has four containers of raspberry ice cream and only one of each other flavour. You may evaluate what the clerk said as biased or even incorrect.

Cognitive skills

Mental skills that you use to get knowledge are called *cognitive skills* and include reasoning, perception, and intuition. They're particularly important in reading for understanding, which is what you do on the GED tests. You can increase your knowledge and comprehension by reading books, researching on the Web, or watching documentaries. After you read or watch something new, discuss it with others to make sure you understand and can use the information in conversation.

Addressing and answering questions

When you start the tests, you want to have a game plan on how to answer the questions. The following tips help you address each multiple-choice question:

- ✔ **Whenever you read a question, ask yourself, "What is this question really asking?"** Doing so helps you focus on what you need to find out to answer the question. You may even want to decide quickly what skills are required to answer the question (see the preceding section for more on these skills). Then try to answer it.

- ✔ **Try to eliminate some answers.** The questions are straightforward, so don't look for hidden or sneaky answers. The questions ask for an answer based on the information given. If you don't have enough information to answer the question, one of the answers will say so.

✔ **Find the best answer and quickly verify that it answers the question.** If it does, mark it in the answer book and go on. If it doesn't, mark the question in the question booklet and come back to it after you answer all the other questions, if you have time.

Guess for success: Using intelligent guessing

The multiple-choice questions provide you with five possible answers. You get one point for every correct answer, and nothing is subtracted for incorrect answers, which means you can guess on the questions you don't know for sure without fearing that you'll lose points. However, you don't want to guess willy-nilly on all the questions; instead, guess logically by eliminating as many wrong choices as possible and then choosing from just two or three possibly correct ones.

When the question gives you five possible answers and you randomly choose one, you have a 20 percent chance of guessing the correct answer without even reading the question. Of course, we don't recommend using this method during the test.

If you know that one of the answers is definitely wrong, you now have just four answers to chose from and have a 25 percent chance (1 in 4) of choosing the correct answer. If you know that two of the answers are wrong, you leave yourself only three possible answers to choose from, giving you a 33 percent (1 in 3) chance of guessing right — much better than 20 percent. And, finally, if you know that three of the answers are wrong, your chances of choosing the correct answer move up to 50 percent, which is as good as a random choice gets!

If you don't know the answer to a question, try to spot the wrong choices using the following tips:

✔ **Make sure you're really answering the question.** Wrong choices usually don't answer the question; that is, they may sound good, but they answer a different question than the one the test asks.

✔ **When two answers seem very close, consider both answers carefully, because they both can't be right — but they both *can* be wrong.** Answers that are very close are sometimes given to see whether you really know the answer.

✔ **Look for opposite answers in the hopes that you can eliminate one.** If two answers contradict each other, both can't be right, but both can be wrong.

✔ **Trust your instincts.** Some choices may just strike you as wrong when you first read them. If you prepare for these exams, you probably know more than you think.

Leaving time for review

Having a few minutes at the end of a test to check your work is a great way to ease your mind. These few minutes give you a chance to look at any questions you may have had trouble with. If you've chosen an answer for every question, relax for the last few minutes before time is called. Remember the following tips as you review your answers:

✔ Although you technically have a minute and a half for each question, on average, try to do each question in a minute or so. The extra seconds you don't use the first time through the test add up for time at the end of the test to review. Some questions require more thought and decision making than others. Use your extra seconds to answer those questions.

✔ Do *not* try to change a lot of answers at the last minute. Second-guessing yourself can lead to trouble. If you have prepared well and done lots of sample questions, you probably have a good chance of getting the correct answers the first time. Ignoring all your preparation and knowledge to play a hunch isn't a good idea at the race track or on a test.

✔ Check that your answers are displayed properly. Make sure that the circles are filled and that you don't have any stray marks on the answer sheet. A machine may read your doodles as answers or miss a partially completed circle.

Keeping Your Head in the Game

To succeed on the GED, you need to be prepared. In addition to studying the content and skills needed for the five different tests, you also want to be mentally prepared. You may be nervous, but you can't let your nerves get the best of you. Stay calm and take a deep breath. Remember the following pointers to help you stay focused:

✔ **Take time to relax.** Passing the GED tests is an important milestone in life. Make sure you leave a bit of time to relax, both while you prepare for the tests and just before you take them. Relaxing has a place in preparing, as long as it doesn't become your main activity.

✔ **Make sure you know the rules of the room before you begin.** If you have questions about using the bathroom during the test or what to do if you finish early, ask the proctor before you begin. If you don't want to ask these questions in public, call the GED office before the test day and ask your questions. If you are a member of Facebook, send your questions to www.facebook.com/group.php?gid=46193757671, which is an easy way to go if you get caught in a jungle of unanswered voice mails. For general GED questions, call 800-62-MYGED during regular office hours (remember that the office is in Washington, DC) or check out www.acenet.edu.

✔ **Keep your eyes on your paper.** Everybody knows not to look at other people's papers during the test, but, to be on the safe side, don't stretch, roll your eyes, or do anything else that may be mistaken for looking at another person's test.

✔ **Stay calm.** Your nerves use up a lot of energy. Concentrate on the test. You can be nervous or panicky some other time.

Part II
Minding Your Ps and Qs: The Language Arts, Writing Test

The 5th Wave   By Rich Tennant

YOUNG STEPHEN KING SUBMITS HIS GED WRITING SAMPLE.

©RICHTENNANT

"I finished my essay early, so I wrote essays on all the other questions, and then I had some time, so I wrote a few more essays on some spooky stuff I've been thinking about."

In this part . . .

This part takes you inside the Language Arts, Writing Test, giving you the lowdown on both Parts I and II. On this test, you get a chance to answer multiple-choice questions and write a short essay. Lucky you!

To keep yourself from panicking, all you have to do is prepare for these tasks — which is where this part comes in handy. Here you find out how the Language Arts, Writing Test, is put together and on which skills it tests you. With that information in hand, you can become familiar with what you're expected to know before taking the tests — and this familiarity will prove incredibly beneficial on test day. As an added bonus, we also offer you some strategies that can help you do your best on this test.

After cramming your head with test details, we give you a chance to test your skills and preparation on two full-length practice tests. Each of the tests has an answer chapter with explanations to help you understand why the answers are what they are, as well as suggestions for how to write a well-thought-out essay.

Chapter 4

The Write Stuff: Preparing for the Language Arts, Writing Test, Parts I and II

....

In This Chapter

▶ Taking a look at the format of the Language Arts, Writing Test, Parts I and II

▶ Knowing what kinds of questions appear on Part I and knowing how to prepare for them

▶ Preparing to write an essay for Part II and practising with some sample prompts

....

The Language Arts, Writing Test evaluates your skills in comprehending and applying concepts in grammar and writing. In case you don't already know, *grammar* is the basic structure of language (you know — subjects, verbs, sentences, fragments, periods, commas, and all that). Most of what you're tested on (both in writing and grammar) is stuff you've picked up over the years, either in school or just by living and speaking and reading, but, to help you better prepare for this test, we give you some more skill-building tips in this chapter.

As you may have gathered from this chapter's title, the Language Arts, Writing Test comes in two parts. Much of Part I determines how well you know grammar by asking you 50 multiple-choice questions about it.

Part II of this test is different from all the other GED tests because you have to write an essay. In spite of its name, however, Part II doesn't consist of a real essay so much as a series of related paragraphs. You aren't expected to produce a book-length opus complete with documented research. Rather, you have 45 minutes to write a coherent series of inter-related paragraphs on a given topic and use the rules of grammar and correct spelling in writing it. Examiners look for a five-paragraph essay that is well-organized and sticks to the topic given.

This chapter gives you the lowdown on the Language Arts, Writing Test and offers you some helpful tips to assist you in succeeding on it.

Understanding the Test Format

As we mention earlier, the Language Arts, Writing Test breaks down into two parts, each of which has its own question type. Having a basic understanding of the two question types used in these two parts can help you avoid any surprises when you sit down to take the test. The following sections explain what types of questions you encounter on Part I and Part II and offer you some advice on how to prepare for them so that you can answer them with ease.

Grasping what's on Part 1

Part I of the Language Arts, Writing Test consists of 50 multiple-choice questions, which you have 75 minutes to complete. The questions ask you to read and then revise and edit documents that may include how-to information, informational texts, and workplace material. Don't worry — just because you haven't studied grammar for years doesn't mean you don't know it. You probably know more than you think. And, lucky for you, all the questions in this part are multiple choice, which means you don't have to come up with the answers all on your own.

To answer a question or set of questions in this part, you need to carefully read the passage that goes with it. Always read the entire document before answering the corresponding questions, because the questions make more sense when you have an idea of what the whole passage is about. As you read each document, think to yourself, "Can I correct this passage? If so, how?"

Grasping what's on Part 11

This 45-minute test has only one question on it, and it's a topic on which you have to write a short essay. You can add any time you have left after completing Part I of the Language Arts, Writing Test to your time for Part II.

For this part of the test, you're given one topic and a few instructions. Your task is to write approximately two pages (one front and one back) on that topic. Remember that you can't write about another topic or a similar topic — if you do, you'll receive zero points for your essay, and you'll have to retake the entire Language Arts, Writing Test.

The instructions that accompany your essay topic require that you use your personal observations, knowledge, and experience as you write about your given topic.

Passing Part 1

The Language Arts, Writing Test, Part I requires you to draw on all your previous knowledge of grammar. To help you succeed on this test, we provide insightful information in the following sections that deals with what skills this part of the test covers, what types of questions you'll encounter, what you can do to prepare, how you can manage your time, and what actual problems look like. With this information in hand, you can stare this test straight in the eyes on test day.

Looking at the skills Part 1 covers

Part I of the Language Arts, Writing Test evaluates you on the following types of skills related to grammar. Note that unlike the other GED tests, Part I of this test expects that you *know* or at least *are familiar with* the rules of grammar; looking at the passages provided won't do you much good if you don't understand the basics of these rules already.

✔ **Mechanics (25 percent; 12 or 13 questions):** You don't have to become a professional grammarian to pass this test, but you should know or review basic grammar. Check out *English Grammar For Dummies,* 2nd Edition, by Geraldine Woods (Wiley) to review what you should know or may have forgotten. The mechanics of writing include the following:

- **Capitalization:** You have to recognize which words start with a capital letter and which words don't. All sentences start with a capital letter, but so do titles, like "Miss," "Prime Minister," and "Senator," when they're followed by a person's last name. Names of cities, provinces, territories, and countries are also capitalized.

- **Punctuation:** This area of writing mechanics includes everyone's personal favourite — commas. (Actually, most people hate commas because they aren't sure how to use them, but the basic rules are simple to apply after you know them.) The more you read, the better you get at punctuation. If you're reading and don't understand why punctuation is or isn't used, check with your grammar guidebook or the Internet.

- **Spelling:** You don't have to spot a lot of misspelled words, but you do have to know how to spell contractions and possessives and understand the different spellings of homonyms.

- **Contractions:** This area of writing mechanics has nothing to do with those painful moments before childbirth! Instead, *contractions* are formed when the English language shortens a word by leaving out a letter or a sound. For example, when you say or write *can't*, you're using a shortened form of *cannot*. In this example, *can't* is the contraction.

  The important thing to remember about contractions is that the *apostrophe* (that's a single quotation mark) takes the place of the letter or letters that are left out.

- **Possessives:** Do you know people who are possessive? They're all about ownership, right? So is the grammar form of possessives. *Possessives* are words that show ownership or possession, usually by adding an apostrophe to a person or object's name. If Marcia owns a car, that car is *Marcia's* car. The word *Marcia's* is a possessive.

✔ **Organization (15 percent; 7 or 8 questions):** On the test, you're asked to correct passages by changing the order of sentences or leaving out certain sentences when they don't fit. You have to work with passages to turn them into logical, organized paragraphs. You may be asked to work with paragraphs to form a better composition by changing them around or editing them by improving or adding topic sentences or making sure that all the sentences are about the same topic. The important thing to remember is that the questions are all multiple choice, which means you have only a limited number of options for making the passages better. Read the questions carefully and you should have no problems.

✔ **Sentence structure (30 percent; 15 questions):** Every language has rules about the order in which words should appear in a sentence. You get a chance to improve sentences through your understanding of what makes a good sentence. Extensive reading before the test can give you a good idea of how good sentences are structured and put together. The advice here, as always, is read, read, and read some more.

✔ **Usage (30 percent; 15 questions):** Usage questions make up one of the largest portions of the test. Grammar has a wide variety of rules, and these questions test your knowledge and understanding of many of them. Subjects and verbs must agree. Verbs have tenses that must be consistent. Pronouns must refer back to nouns properly. If the last three sentences sound like Greek to you, make sure you review grammatical usage rules.

Having a firm grasp of these writing mechanics can help you get a more accurate picture of the types of questions you'll encounter on Part I of this test. The next section focuses more on the specific passage materials you'll face.

Identifying the types of passages in Part I

The passages that the questions in Part I are based on come in the following three forms:

- **How-to texts:** Each of these articles or excerpts consists of 200 to 300 words and deals with topics of interest to the reader, such as how to pass the GED tests, how to write a great resumé, how to build a fence, or how to do anything else that the general public may want to know about.

- **Informational texts:** These articles or excerpts provide information or analysis on a topic. They may be position papers, support papers, or critical evaluations of a subject. Each of these documents consists of about 200 to 300 words and tries to convey information to the reader.

- **Workplace material:** These articles or excerpts are all around you; they include letters, meeting notes, executive summaries, and applications. Each of these documents consists of about 200 to 300 words and normally discusses the everyday topics that you're probably already familiar with.

Regardless of what type of passage the questions in Part I are based on, your job is to correct the grammar. Grammar doesn't change with the type of passage, so, although you should be familiar with the various types of passages, you need to be most familiar with the rules of grammar so you can use them to improve the passages.

Preparing for Part I: Tactics that work

To succeed on Part I of the Language Arts, Writing Test, you can prepare in advance by reviewing rules of grammar, punctuation, and spelling and by familiarizing yourself with the format and subject matter of the Part I test. Here are some of the best ways you can prepare:

- **Read as often as you can.** This strategy is the best one for passing this test, and it's by far the simplest because reading exposes you to correct grammar.

  Keep in mind that what you read makes a difference. Reading catalogues may increase your product knowledge and improve your research skills, but reading literature is preferable because it introduces you to so many rules of grammar. Reading fiction exposes you to interesting words and sentences. It shows you how paragraphs tie into one another and how each paragraph has a topic and generally sticks to it. Reading historical fiction can give you some insight into what led up to today and can also help you with the Social Studies Test (see Chapter 9 for more on the Social Studies Test). Just because we didn't mention something here doesn't mean you shouldn't read it. Read everything you can get your hands on, including newspapers, textbooks, and much more. If you choose to read material online, be aware that not all spelling will be correct nor will all "facts" be accurate. Blogs and e-mails aren't always written by professionals. Other material is written by credible sources and will help you understand concepts. Just learn to differentiate between the two.

- **Master the rules of basic grammar.** On this test, you don't have to define a gerund and give an example of one, but you do have to know about verb tenses, subject/verb agreement, pronoun/antecedent agreement, possessives, and the like. As your knowledge of grammar and punctuation improves, have a bit of fun by correcting what you read in small-town newspapers and low-budget novels — both sometimes have poor editing.

- **Practise grammar in everyday speaking.** As you review the rules of grammar, practise them every day as you talk to your friends, family, and co-workers. Although correct grammar usually "sounds" right to your ears, sometimes it doesn't because you and the people you talk to have become used to using incorrect grammar. If you see a rule that seems different from the way you talk, put it on a flashcard and practise it as you go through your day. Before long, you'll train your ears so that correct grammar sounds right.

Correcting other people's grammar out loud doesn't make you popular, but correcting it in your head can help you succeed on this test.

✔ **Understand punctuation.** Know how to use commas, semicolons, colons, and other forms of punctuation. To find out more about punctuation and when and why to use its different forms, check out a grammatical reference book like *English Grammar For Dummies,* 2nd Edition, by Geraldine Woods (Wiley).

✔ **Practise writing and reading.** Write as much and as often as you can, and then review it for errors. Look for and correct mistakes in punctuation, grammar, and spelling. If you're not able to find any, ask someone who knows grammar and punctuation for help.

✔ **Keep a journal or blog.** Journals and blogs are just notebooks (physical or virtual) in which you write a bit about your life every day. They both provide good practice for personal writing. Blogging or responding to blogs gives you practice in public writing because others see what you write. Whether you use a personal journal or a public blog, keep in mind that the writing is the important part. If public writing encourages you to write more and more often, do it. If not, consider writing a private journal or diary.

✔ **Improve your spelling.** As you practise writing, keep a good dictionary handy. If you're not sure of the spelling of any word, look it up. Add it to a spelling list that you keep and practise from. In addition, get a list of common *homonyms* (words that sound the same but are spelled differently and have different definitions), and review them every day. (You need to know, for example, the difference between *their, there,* and *they're.*) Many dictionaries contain a list of homonyms.

✔ **Keep in mind that these questions are multiple choice.** Multiple-choice questions always give you the correct answer. Of course, they also tell you four other answers that are incorrect, but all you have to do is find the correct one! As you practise speaking and writing correctly, you tune your ears so that the correct answer sounds right, which, believe it or not, makes finding it easier on the test.

✔ **Take practice tests.** Take as many practice tests as you can. Be strict about time limitations, and check your answers when you're finished. Don't move on until you know and understand the correct answer. (Check out Chapters 5 and 7 for two sample tests and Chapters 6 and 8 for their answers.) The time you spend taking and reviewing these practice tests is well worth it.

Managing your time for Part 1

To complete Part I of the Language Arts, Writing Test, you have to answer 50 questions in 75 minutes, which breaks down to one and a half minutes per question. However, because the questions on this test are based on passages (of between 200 and 300 words), you have to give yourself enough time to read the passages, too. The upside is that you don't have to read a different passage for each question (because each passage is followed by a set of questions). The downside is that you have to remember the material you read about in each passage long enough to answer all the questions based on it.

You basically have two options for reading passages and answering questions in this part of the test. Before we explain these two options, imagine that you're faced with a passage of about 300 words followed by ten questions. You have 15 minutes to complete these ten questions (one and a half minutes times ten). Here are your two options for moving through this passage and its corresponding questions:

- ✔ **Option No. 1:** For this option, you spend half a minute reading and understanding each question and the answer choices that follow, which takes about five minutes total. Then you spend about three minutes reading the passage, knowing what to look for, and you take the remaining seven minutes to answer the questions and review your answers. As you may recognize, we suggest using this option for managing your time on most of the GED tests (see Chapter 1).

- ✔ **Option No. 2:** Answering questions using Option No. 2 means taking a slightly different angle to managing your time than we discuss for most other tests on the GED. With this option, you begin by reading the passage as quickly as you can without sacrificing understanding. This option calls on your speed-reading skills, which allow you to spend less time reading the passage (and have more time left to choose and review your answers).

Remember that speed reading allows you to increase your reading speed *without* hurting your comprehension. If you want to try out speed-reading by yourself, pick up any reading material and try to train your eyes to read down a line in the middle of each page, allowing your peripheral vision to catch the words at each edge. You can use your finger to increase the speed at which you read by moving it along the same line you read along. You can also practise your speed-reading skills by setting a timer and decreasing the time you have to read a page each time you start reading a new page of a book. Try anything that helps you read faster. Developing your speed-reading skills improves your scores in all the GED tests, but especially this one because it uses longer passages. Check out *Speed Reading For Dummies* by Richard Sutz (Wiley) for more info.

Practising for Part 1 with some sample problems

Before you take Part I of the Language Arts, Writing Test, make sure you take plenty of practice tests so you're well versed with the types of problems you'll face. Take the following sample problems to help you get started. When you finish these, move on to Chapters 5 and 7 to take the full-length practice tests.

Questions 1 through 4 refer to the following passage.

Project WKE
(1) **Referral:** Workers will refer dependant of WOW recipients to WKE.

(2) **Intake:** Intake process will involve a series of interviews and the use of transferable skills inventories combined with the evaluation of credentials.

(3) **Assessment:** A holistic asesment will be prepared and discussed with clients as preparation for additional experiences and training.

(4) **Pre-Employment Training:** Pre-employment training will include confidence building, interpersonal skills, goal setting, career path planning, problem-solving, resumé preparation, basic computer literacy, educational upgrading and child development and parenting skills as required.

(5) **Job Readiness Training:** Experiences, such as job-shadowing and mentoring, will be provided as needed for clients ready to enter the work farce in a supportive environment. Other clients will be provided with additional skills in sectoral analysis, cold calling, budgeting,

time management, development of job search strategies, preparation and presentation of Prior Learning Assessment and Recognition Portfolios, development and evaluation of transferable skills inventories, interview techniques, and follow-up.

(6) **Referral:** Clients will be referred to appropriate community agencies, if required. If desired by the client, alternate career pathways will be investigated and career paths planned for these alternate careers.

(7) **Skill Enhancement:** Clients will have the opportunity to enhance the following skills: computer literacy, prior learning assessment and recognition, assistance in gaining additional certification, use of computers and Internet in job search and career research, and academic skills.

(8) **Supportive Job Search Activities (if unemployed):** Unemployed clients will be introduced to Supportive Job Search activities where they may volunteer for periods of time in positions congruent with their career plans to gain real world experience.

(9) **Employment Retention (if employed):** Employed clients will be able to call in to WKE to assist in the retention of clients in workplaces. Employers will be able to contact WKE if problems arise on the job and WKE will provide support, advice and mediation to try to maintain employment.

1. Section 1: **Workers will refer dependent of WOW recipients to WKE.**

   Which change should be made to Section 1?

   (1) omit <u>will</u>

   (2) change <u>dependant</u> to <u>dependant(s)</u>

   (3) place a comma after <u>Workers</u>

   (4) change <u>WOW</u> to <u>wow</u>

   (5) no changes necessary

   The correct answer is Choice (2). Because the sentence refers to the plural "recipients," you can't logically assume that there'd be more than one dependant, but you need a word that allows for the possibility.

2. Section 3: **A holistic asesment will be prepared and discussed with clients as preparation for additional experiences and training.**

   Which change should be made to Section 3?

   (1) change <u>holistic</u> to <u>wholistic</u>

   (2) change <u>will be prepared</u> to <u>was prepared</u>

   (3) change <u>clients</u> to <u>patience</u>

   (4) change <u>asesment</u> to <u>assessment</u>

   (5) no changes necessary

   The correct answer is Choice (4). This question requires you to correct a spelling mistake. Always be careful of double letters. Many English words have double letters that are pronounced like single letters.

3. Section 5: **Experiences, such as job-shadowing and mentoring, will be provided as needed for clients ready to enter the work farce in a supportive environment. Other clients will be provided with additional skills in sectoral analysis, cold calling, budgeting, time management, development of job search strategies, preparation and presentation of Prior Learning Assessment and Recognition Portfolios, development and evaluation of transferable skills inventories, interview techniques, and follow-up.**

Which change should be made to Section 5?

(1) change <u>job-shadowing</u> to <u>jobshadowing</u>

(2) change <u>supportive</u> to <u>support</u>

(3) change <u>additional</u> to <u>a whole lot of</u>

(4) change <u>skills</u> to <u>skill</u>

(5) change <u>farce</u> to <u>force</u>

The correct answer is Choice (5). The word *farce* refers to a comic drama or film; this section is referring to a retraining program, which is definitely more serious.

4. Section 9: **Employed clients will be able to call in to WKE to assist in the retention of clients in workplaces. Employers will be able to contact WKE if problems arise on the job and WKE will provide support, advice and mediation to try to maintain employment.**

Which change should be made to Section 9?

(1) change <u>retention</u> to <u>resistence</u>

(2) rewrite the first sentence like this: <u>Employed clients will be able to call in to WKE if problems arise on the job.</u>

(3) omit <u>if problems arise</u>

(4) change <u>support, advice and mediation</u> to <u>supportive advice, and mediation</u>

(5) change <u>assist in the retention of clients</u> to <u>assist in the release of clients</u>

The correct answer is Choice (2). Of all the suggestions made, this one makes the most sense in the context of the passage. If you read the passage carefully, clients call in to WKE if they have problems on the job. The original wording suggests otherwise.

 As you practise doing these types of questions (here and in Chapters 5 and 7), remember to read the questions first; doing so gives you an idea of what you need to look for in the passage as you read it. Also, be sure to read the questions carefully — they aren't trick questions, but they do expect you to be a good reader.

Revealing some helpful pointers for Part 1

Remember the following tips as you move through Part I:

✔ **Read the questions quickly before you read the entire passage.** This way, you'll know what to look for in the passage.

✔ **Read carefully.** As you read the passages, look for errors and hard-to-read sentences. The more carefully you read the passages, the better chance you have of getting the right answers when you move on to the questions.

Passing Part II

Part II of the Language Arts, Writing Test asks you to write an essay on an assigned topic that two essay graders will then read (find out more about these graders and what they're looking for in the "Revealing some helpful pointers for Part II" section). You have 45 minutes to read the given topic and write your corresponding essay. This part of the test checks your literacy and understanding. If you can understand the essay topic you're given and are literate, you can successfully complete this part with no problem.

Keep in mind that writing this essay isn't that different from writing a letter or a blog — except that here you must explain or clarify the subject for the reader without rambling on until you run out of space.

If you don't pass this part of the Language Arts, Writing Test, you have to take both parts over again. That fact alone should be all the incentive you need to practise writing.

Looking at the writing skills Part II covers

Two trained essay readers grade your essay by focusing on five major criteria or skills. By having a clear understanding of the main skills covered in this part of the test, you can ensure that you address all of them when writing your essay — which helps you get a better score. The GED Testing Service defines the five essay criteria you need to address as follows:

- ✔ **Response to the prompt:** This criterion refers to how well you answer the topic, including whether or not the focus of the response shifts as you write.

- ✔ **Organization:** This criterion refers to whether or not you show the reader through your essay that you have a clear idea about what you're writing and that you're able to establish a definable plan for writing the essay.

- ✔ **Development and details:** This criterion refers to your ability to expand on initial concepts or statements with examples and specific details instead of using generic lists or reiterating the same information.

- ✔ **Conventions of edited Canadian English:** This criterion refers to your ability to appropriately use edited written English, including applying the basic rules of grammar that you're tested on in Part I, such as sentence structure, mechanics, usage, and so forth.

- ✔ **Word choice:** This criterion refers to your ability to use appropriate words to express your ideas.

The evaluators grade your essay as inadequate, marginal, adequate, or effective, depending on your success in each of these five categories. Go to www.acenet.edu/Content/NavigationMenu/ged/etp/writing_2_test_descr.htm for a more in-depth breakdown of these five criteria and what the evaluators look for in an essay that receives a passing score. Read the sections on what constitutes a passing score very carefully. If you don't pass, you have to rewrite the entire test.

Preparing for Part II: Tactics that work

As you prepare for the Language Arts, Writing Test, Part II, do the following:

- ✔ **Read and read some more.** Just like for Part I (and most other tests on the GED), reading is important. Reading exposes you to well-crafted sentences, which can help you improve your own writing. Reading also expands your horizons and provides you with little bits of information you can work into your essay.

As you read, make an outline of the paragraphs or chapters you read to see how the material ties together. Try rewriting some of the paragraphs from your outline, and compare what you write to the original. Yours may not be ready for prime time, but this little exercise gives you practice in writing organized, cohesive sentences and paragraphs, which can go a long way in this part of the test.

✔ **Practise writing neatly.** You can't take a computer and printer into the test for Part II, so you have to express your thoughts the old-fashioned way — with a pen and paper. Remember way back in grade school when you learned how to write neatly? Well, call on all your good-handwriting skills (no matter how buried they may be). Graders have to read your essay to score it, so make reading your writing as easy as possible.

Really neat, beautiful penmanship is easy to read, but it takes a long time to write. You need something in between chicken scratch and calligraphy — legible writing that you can write quickly. Neat and quick are the important words here (after all, this is a timed test like all the others!).

✔ **Practise editing your own work.** After the test starts, the only person able to edit your essay is you. If that thought scares you, practise editing your own work now. Take a writing workshop, or get help from someone who knows how to edit. Practise writing a lot of essays, and don't forget to review and edit them as soon as you're done writing.

✔ **Review how to plan an essay.** Few people can sit down, write a final draft of an essay the first time around, and receive a satisfactory grade on it. Instead, you have to plan what you're going to write. The best way to start is to jot down everything you know about a topic without worrying about the order. From there, you can organize your thoughts into groups. Check out the "Managing your time for Part II" section for more help on planning your essay.

✔ **Practise writing on a topic (and not going off topic!).** Your essay must relate to the given topic as closely as possible. If the test asks you to write about your personal goals, and you write about a hockey game you once played in, you can kiss your good score goodbye.

To help you practise staying on topic, read the newspaper and write a letter to the editor or a response to a columnist. Because you're responding to a very narrow topic that appeared in a particular newspaper article, you have to do so clearly and concisely — if you ever want to see it in print. (You can also practise staying on topic by picking a newspaper article's title and writing a short essay about it. Then read the actual story and see how yours compares.)

✔ **Think about and use related examples.** If you're writing about how machines make life harder, the difficult experience you had trying to get your toaster fixed under warranty makes for a great example. In contrast, a story about painting your bike fluorescent pink doesn't make such a hot example. Remember that examples can provide great support to your essay's main points, but, to do so, they have to relate to the topic.

✔ **Practise general writing.** If writing connected paragraphs isn't one of your fortes, practise doing so! Write long e-mails. Write long letters. Write to your Member of Parliament. Write to your friends. Write articles for community newspapers. Write short stories. Write anything you want — whatever you do, just keep writing.

✔ **Write practice essays.** Check out the "Practising with some sample essays" section later in this chapter to read a sample essay. Then see Chapters 5 and 7 for some more practice essay prompts (in actual test format). Write essays based on the topics given, and then ask a knowledgeable friend or former teacher to grade them for you. You can also turn to Chapters 6 and 8 to read a couple of sample essays based on the same topics you're given in Chapters 5 and 7 to write about. You may want to take a preparation class in which you're assigned practice topics to write about, too. When you're finished practising, practise some more.

Managing your time for Part II

You have 45 minutes to finish your essay for Part II of the Language Arts, Writing Test, and, in that time, you have four main tasks:

- ✔ Plan
- ✔ Draft
- ✔ Edit and revise
- ✔ Rewrite

The following sections take a closer look at these tasks and explain how you can successfully complete each one in the time you have.

 Taking ten minutes to plan, twenty minutes to draft, five minutes to edit and revise, and ten minutes to rewrite is a good plan for action. Keep in mind that this is a tight schedule, though, so if it makes your writing too sloppy to read, consider allowing more time for rewriting. No one but you will see anything but the final version.

Planning

Before you begin writing your essay, read the topic carefully several times, and ask yourself what the topic means to you. Then, on scratch paper, write down everything you can think of that relates to the topic, no matter how silly it seems (this act of writing is called *brainstorming,* which is like dumping out the contents of a portion of your brain). Don't worry about the order of your ideas or the ideas you think of. Just let everything flow onto the paper. You can sort through all the information in the next phase.

For example, if the essay question asks you to discuss a major milestone in your life, you may choose to centre your essay around the following topic: "Passing the GED will be a major milestone in my life." In your essay, you need to explain why passing the test is the major milestone for you at this moment and how you plan to use the GED to better your life. The planning stage of your essay writing is when you jot down everything you can think of about the GED and its effect on your life. The points you jot down here should include your personal observations, experience, and knowledge.

After you write down these points, sit back for a moment to reflect. (Don't reflect too long, though, because you still have an essay to write. Just take a few minutes.) Look over your points and find an introduction, such as, "I have accomplished many things in my life, but my major milestone will be passing the GED tests." Write this sentence down beneath your brainstorming notes. Beneath this sentence, write down the points you came up with earlier that strongly back up your introduction.

Now write down a concluding sentence, such as, "Of all my accomplishments, passing the GED tests will be the most important because it will open doors that are closed to me now." Glancing at your introduction and the essay topic, select points that strengthen your conclusion. Some of these points may be the same ones you used in your introduction.

Next, plan a path from your introduction to your conclusion. The path may be several points long. Here's an example of an essay plan from introduction to conclusion:

- ✔ **Introduction:** "I have accomplished many things in my life, but my major milestone will be passing the GED tests."
  - • List my accomplishments.
  - • Discuss my goals.
  - • Discuss what's stopping me from reaching my goals.

- • Tie in which of these things I may be able to eliminate by having a GED diploma.

- • Discuss which goals are attainable with the GED diploma.

- • Envision how my life will change as I accomplish those goals.

✔ **Conclusion:** "Of all my accomplishments, passing the GED tests will be the most important because it will open doors that are closed to me now."

Now reflect again. Can you add any more points to improve the essay? Don't just add points to have more points, though. This isn't a contest in which the one with the most points wins. This is an essay in which the one with the best points, logically written, gets the passing grade.

Look over your planning path and your points. Can you combine any parts of the path to make it tighter? For example:

✔ **Introduction:** "I have accomplished many things in my life, but my major milestone will be passing the GED tests."

- • List my accomplishments.

- • Discuss my goals and what's stopping me from reaching them.

- • Tie in which of these things I may be able to eliminate by having a GED diploma, and discuss which goals are attainable with the GED diploma.

- • Envision how my life will change as I accomplish those goals.

✔ **Conclusion:** "Of all my accomplishments, passing the GED tests will be the most important because it will open doors that are closed to me now."

Now that you have the outline, you're ready to go on to the next step — drafting your essay.

Drafting

During the drafting stage of writing your essay, you think in more detail about the main points you came up with in the planning stage. As you add new details (called *subpoints*) under each main point, your essay begins to take shape.

Here's an example of what the drafting process may look like for the "major milestone in life" topic:

Introduction: "I have accomplished many things in my life, but my major milestone will be passing the GED tests."

✔ List my accomplishments:

- • I coach youth hockey.

- • I have kept a job for four years.

- • I got a small promotion.

- • I got married.

✔ Discuss my goals and what's stopping me from reaching them:

- • People expect more education from hockey coaches in the minor leagues.

- • Many promotions are blocked to me because of my education.

- • My children may be embarrassed to have an uneducated parent.

- • My boss likes people with diplomas and certificates.

✔ Tie in which of these things I may be able to eliminate by having a GED diploma, and discuss which goals are attainable with the GED diploma:

- I may be able to coach in the minors.

- I can apply for more promotions.

- My boss may like me more.

- My children will be impressed by my accomplishment.

- I will have graduated from high school.

✔ Envision how my life will change as I accomplish those goals:

- As a minor-league coach, my picture will be in the papers.

- I could become a manager at my company.

- I may be invited to lunch by my boss to discuss ideas.

- I could be invited to my children's classes to talk about the importance of education.

- I will have a diploma to hang on the wall.

Conclusion: "Of all my accomplishments, passing the GED tests will be the most important because it will open doors that are closed to me now. The doors are open — promotion, dreams, recognition — and that creates so many more possibilities."

Notice how each main point becomes a paragraph. The subpoints you come up with during the drafting process form the sentences in each paragraph.

Each paragraph starts with an *introductory sentence,* which hints at what is to come, and ends with a *transition sentence* that leads from the paragraph you're on to the next one. Your subpoints are your sentences within the paragraphs. If you put your sentences in a logical order from introduction to transition, you start to see paragraphs — as well as your essay — emerging.

Editing and revising

Now comes the hard part. You have to be your own editor. Turn off your ego and remember that every word is written on scratch paper, not carved in stone. Make your work better by editing and revising it. Make this the best piece of writing you've ever done — in a 45-minute time block, of course.

Rewriting

Your essay has to be well written, but it also has to be readable. Neatly rewrite your edited work — in pen — in the proper place in the answer booklet. Two graders have to read this essay, so write neatly and clearly. Write large enough to be read. Leave some room between lines. If you make a mistake, neatly cross it out and move on. Scratch-outs don't count against you.

Practising with some sample essays

To help you get a feel for how the essay grader evaluates your essay, look at the sample essay that follows. The sample essay is based on this topic:

The Worst Traffic Control Idea — Ever

Write an essay explaining the positive and/or negative aspects of this idea. Use examples to support your point of view and be as specific as possible.

Use the five criteria we explain in the "Looking at the writing skills Part II covers" section to mark up the essay, pointing out its strengths and weaknesses. Also keep in mind the characteristics of a good essay that evaluators look for, which we list in the "Revealing some helpful pointers for Part II" section.

Speed Bumps

We have all driven down a quiet residential street and without warning hit a bump in the road, so severe, that our teeth rattled. Well, we may have been going ever so slightly over the speed limit but needing dental work is not the usual punishment for speeding.

Living in a society where unenforced laws get ignored has presented a problem in many areas. Just look at all the Ponzi schemes being uncovered all around the world. Wherever there has been no enforcement, there has been an increase in crime but a little bit of speeding is not that serious a crime.

In Jamaica they call speed bumps, "Sleeping Policemen" because they do the job of speed control without the police being present. In St. Maarten, they have installed them on highways to keep the speed down in dangerous areas. But here, in Canada, do we need these ugly bumps in the road? We all know that these are just a political solution to calm down voters who do not want speeding traffic through their neighbourhood. No one seems to care about the negative aspects of these devices.

Cars are most efficient at constant speed but speed bumps cause the driver to slow down and speed up all through the area, increasing pollution and wasting gas. Even bicyclists, the darlings of many city politicians, have trouble with speed bumps. If you go too fast over one of these bumps on a bicycle, you may become airborne and fly off your bicycle. That will do damage to your body.

Speed bumps are hard to see and force drivers to take their eyes off the road. This causes a dangerous situation. Who knows what could pass in front of a car while the driver is looking carefully for the next bump which will shatter teeth and probably destroy the car's suspension. Is there no justice for the driver on the roads?

Now that you have a sample essay to look at, try writing your essay that addresses the traffic control topic. When you're done, evaluate it using the same criteria you used to mark up the sample essay. Then write an essay on one of the following topics and mark it up in the same way (don't forget to use your personal experience and knowledge for support):

- ✔ Should the Government Bail Out Industries?
- ✔ Video Games Teach People Many Skills
- ✔ One Job the Guidance Department Forgot to Tell Me About
- ✔ Reality Television is the Most Unreal Programming Available

Revealing some helpful pointers for Part II

In addition to evaluating the main criteria or skills we list in the "Looking at the writing skills Part II covers" section, essay graders look for the following characteristics in your essay (if you have all these characteristics, your chances of receiving a high score are pretty good):

✔ Main points that focus on the topic

✔ Clear and organized main points and subpoints — both in the paragraphs and throughout the entire essay

✔ Logically and clearly developed ideas

✔ Transitions throughout the essay for a smooth flow between ideas

✔ Good vocabulary

✔ Proper punctuation

✔ Correct spelling

Knowing what essay graders are looking for in your essay can help you meet all their expectations. Here are a few other tips and ground rules to remember as you prepare for Part II of the Language Arts, Writing Test:

✔ **You have only 45 minutes to write an essay of about 250 words based on a single topic.** An essay usually consists of a number of paragraphs, each of which contains a topic sentence stating a main idea or thought. Be sure each paragraph relates to the overall topic of the essay. And, for the most part, make sure to place a topic sentence at the beginning of each paragraph to help readers focus on the main point you want them to understand.

✔ **You can prepare your essay by using the scratch paper provided.** You're given scratch paper at the test site. Use it to make notes and write down your rough work so that your final essay is well organized and neat. The graders don't look at it, so what you write on the scratch paper is just for you.

✔ **You must write about the topic and only about the topic.** You're graded for writing an essay on the topic, so make sure you really do write on the topic you're given. One of the easiest ways to fail this test is to write about something that isn't on topic.

Keep in mind that the topic is always a brief one about an issue or situation that's familiar to you.

✔ **The essay tests your ability to write about an issue that has positive and/or negative implications but about which you have some general knowledge.** The essay doesn't test how much you know about a topic; instead, it tests your ability to express yourself in writing.

✔ **You need to use stuff from your life to make your points stronger.** You're writing an essay about you, your life, and your experiences, so don't forget to use real examples to strengthen your main points. Specific examples and details support your point of view, so use them liberally.

✔ **Effective paragraphs use a variety of sentence types: statements, questions, commands, exclamations, and even quotations.** Vary your sentence structure and word choice to spark the readers' interest. Some sentences may be short, and others may be long to catch the readers' attention.

✔ **Paragraphs create interest in several ways: by developing details, by using illustrations and examples, by presenting events in a time or space sequence, by providing definitions, by classifying persons or objects, by comparing and contrasting, and by demonstrating reasons and proof.** Organize your paragraphs and sentences in a way that both expresses your ideas and creates interest.

✔ **The readers want to see that you can express your ideas clearly and logically.** They're also reading to make sure that you stick to the topic given.

Chapter 5

Practice Test — Language Arts, Writing Test: Parts I and II

. . . .

The Language Arts, Writing Test measures your ability to use clear and effective English. It is a test of English as it should be written, not as it may be spoken. This test includes both multiple-choice questions and an essay. The following directions apply only to the multiple-choice section; a separate set of directions is given for the essay.

The multiple-choice section consists of documents with lettered paragraphs and numbered sentences. Some of the sentences contain an error in sentence structure, usage, or mechanics (punctuation and capitalization). After reading the numbered sentences, answer the multiple-choice questions that follow. Some questions refer to sentences that are correct as written. The best answer for these questions is the one that leaves the sentence as originally written. The best answer for some questions is the one that produces a document that is consistent with the verb tense and point of view used throughout the text.

You have 120 minutes (two hours) to complete both parts of the test. You can spend up to 75 minutes on the 50 multiple-choice questions, leaving the remaining time for the essay. Work carefully, but do not spend too much time on any one question. Answer every question. You will not be penalized for incorrect answers. You may begin working on the essay section of this test as soon as you complete the multiple-choice section.

Answer Sheet for Language Arts, Writing Test: Part 1

1	① ② ③ ④ ⑤		26	① ② ③ ④ ⑤
2	① ② ③ ④ ⑤		27	① ② ③ ④ ⑤
3	① ② ③ ④ ⑤		28	① ② ③ ④ ⑤
4	① ② ③ ④ ⑤		29	① ② ③ ④ ⑤
5	① ② ③ ④ ⑤		30	① ② ③ ④ ⑤
6	① ② ③ ④ ⑤		31	① ② ③ ④ ⑤
7	① ② ③ ④ ⑤		32	① ② ③ ④ ⑤
8	① ② ③ ④ ⑤		33	① ② ③ ④ ⑤
9	① ② ③ ④ ⑤		34	① ② ③ ④ ⑤
10	① ② ③ ④ ⑤		35	① ② ③ ④ ⑤
11	① ② ③ ④ ⑤		36	① ② ③ ④ ⑤
12	① ② ③ ④ ⑤		37	① ② ③ ④ ⑤
13	① ② ③ ④ ⑤		38	① ② ③ ④ ⑤
14	① ② ③ ④ ⑤		39	① ② ③ ④ ⑤
15	① ② ③ ④ ⑤		40	① ② ③ ④ ⑤
16	① ② ③ ④ ⑤		41	① ② ③ ④ ⑤
17	① ② ③ ④ ⑤		42	① ② ③ ④ ⑤
18	① ② ③ ④ ⑤		43	① ② ③ ④ ⑤
19	① ② ③ ④ ⑤		44	① ② ③ ④ ⑤
20	① ② ③ ④ ⑤		45	① ② ③ ④ ⑤
21	① ② ③ ④ ⑤		46	① ② ③ ④ ⑤
22	① ② ③ ④ ⑤		47	① ② ③ ④ ⑤
23	① ② ③ ④ ⑤		48	① ② ③ ④ ⑤
24	① ② ③ ④ ⑤		49	① ② ③ ④ ⑤
25	① ② ③ ④ ⑤		50	① ② ③ ④ ⑤

Language Arts, Writing Test: Part 1

Do not mark in this test booklet. Record your answers on the separate answer sheet provided. To record your answers, fill in the numbered circle on the answer sheet that corresponds to the answer you select for each question in the test booklet.

EXAMPLE:

Sentence 1: **We were all honoured to meet governor Phillips and his staff.**

Which correction should be made to sentence 1?

(1) change <u>were</u> to <u>was</u>

(2) insert a comma after <u>honoured</u>

(3) change <u>governor</u> to <u>Governor</u>

(4) insert a comma after <u>Phillips</u>

(5) no correction is necessary

(On Answer Sheet)
① ② ● ④ ⑤

In this example, the word "governor" should be capitalized; therefore, answer space 3 would be marked on the answer sheet.

Do not rest the point of your pencil on the answer sheet while you are considering your answer. Make no stray or unnecessary marks. If you change an answer, erase your first mark completely. Mark only one answer space for each question; multiple answers will be scored as incorrect. Do not fold or crease your answer sheet. All test materials must be returned to the test administrator.

Note: Refer to Chapter 6 for the answers for Parts I and II of this practice test.

DO NOT BEGIN TAKING THIS TEST UNTIL TOLD TO DO SO

Directions: Choose the <u>one best answer</u> to each question.

Questions 1 through 10 refer to the following business letter.

BETA Café Equipment, Inc.
Unit 6, 700 Millway Ave.
Concord, ON L4K 3W7

John Charles
Executive Director
Canadian Specialty Coffee Association
Suite 301, 425 Pacific Drive
Vancouver, BC V6B 4Z3

Dear Mr. Charles:

(A)

(1) Thank you for you're interest in our new company, which serves the rapidly expanding specialty coffee industry. (2) BETA Café Equipment, Inc. were formed in 2009 to provide an affordable source of reconditioned Italian espresso/cappuccino machines for new businesses entering the industry.

(B)

(3) During our first year of operation BETA plans to repair and recondition 500 machines for use in restaurants and cafés. (4) This will generate revenue of more then $1,000,000. (5) Almost half a million dollars will be created for returning thirteen jobs to the local economy.

(C)

(6) BETA will purchase used equipement, which will be shipped to our centralized repair and reconditioning depot. (7) After total rebuilding, equipment will be forwarded to regional sales offices to be sold to local restaurants and cafés at a much lower price than comparable new equipment. (8) Entrepreneurs wishing to start new specialty coffee businesses particularly should be interested in our products.

(D)

(9) To learn more about BETA please consult our Web site at www.betace.com or give us a call at our toll-free number, 1-555-TRY-BETA. (10) Any assistence you can provide in sharing this information with your membership will be very much appreciated.

Yours truly,

Edwin Dale, President

Go on to next page

1. Sentence 1: **Thank you for you're interest in our new company, which serves the rapidly expanding specialty coffee industry.**

   Which correction should be made to sentence 1?

   (1) change <u>you're</u> to <u>your</u>

   (2) place a comma after <u>serves</u>

   (3) change <u>interest</u> to <u>concern</u>

   (4) insert <u>but</u> after <u>rapidly</u>

   (5) place <u>expanding</u> before <u>rapidly</u>

2. Sentence 2: **BETA Café Equipment, Inc. <u>were formed</u> in 2009 to provide an affordable source of reconditioned Italian espresso/cappuccino machines for new businesses entering the industry.**

   What is the best way to write the underlined portion of this sentence?

   (1) was being formed

   (2) had formed

   (3) was formed

   (4) is formed

   (5) have been formed

3. Sentence 3: **During our first year of operation BETA plans to repair and recondition 500 machines for use in restaurants and cafés.**

   What correction should be made to sentence 3?

   (1) insert a colon after <u>operation</u>

   (2) insert a comma after <u>operation</u>

   (3) insert a comma after <u>recondition</u>

   (4) insert a semicolon after <u>machines</u>

   (5) place a question mark after <u>cafés</u>

4. Sentence 4: **This will generate revenue of more then $1,000,000.**

   What correction should be made to sentence 4?

   (1) change <u>$1,000,000</u> to <u>$100,000</u>

   (2) change <u>generate</u> to <u>genarate</u>

   (3) insert <u>about</u> after <u>will</u>

   (4) replace <u>will</u> with <u>may</u>

   (5) change <u>then</u> to <u>than</u>

5. Sentence 5: **Almost half a million dollars will be created returning thirteen new jobs to the local economy.**

   The most effective revision of sentence 5 would begin with which group of words?

   (1) Thirteen new jobs will be created, returning

   (2) Half a million dollars will be created almost

   (3) Created will be thirteen new jobs almost

   (4) Almost half a million jobs will be created

   (5) no correction required

6. Sentence 6: **BETA will purchase used equipement, which will be shipped to our centralized repair and reconditioning depot.**

   What correction should be made to sentence 6?

   (1) change <u>repair</u> to <u>repare</u>

   (2) insert a colon after <u>purchase</u>

   (3) change <u>equipement</u> to <u>equipment</u>

   (4) replace <u>depot</u> with <u>depote</u>

   (5) insert a comma after <u>repair</u>

7. Sentence 7: **After total rebuilding, equipment <u>will be forwarded</u> to regional sales offices to be sold to local restaurants and cafés at a much lower price than comparable new equipment.**

   Which is the best way to rewrite the underlined portion of this sentence?

   (1) will forward

   (2) be forwarded

   (3) forwarded

   (4) will be

   (5) no correction required

Go on to next page ➡

8. Sentence 8: **Entrepreneurs wishing to start new specialty coffee <u>businesses particularly should be interested</u> in our products.**

   What correction should be made to the underlined portion?

   (1) businesses should particularly be interested

   (2) businesses should be particularly interested

   (3) businesses particularly should be interested

   (4) businesses should be interested particularly

   (5) particularly businesses should be interested

9. Sentence 9: **To learn more about BETA please consult our Web site at www.betace.com or give us a call at our toll-free number, 1-555-TRY-BETA.**

   Which addition should be made to sentence 9?

   (1) no addition required

   (2) insert a colon after <u>Web site</u>

   (3) insert a comma after <u>please</u>

   (4) insert a comma after <u>BETA</u>

   (5) insert a period after <u>www.betace.com</u>

10. Sentence 10: **Any assistence you can provide in sharing this information with your membership will be very much appreciated.**

    Which correction should be made to sentence 10?

    (1) change <u>membership</u> to <u>member</u>

    (2) insert a comma after <u>provide</u>

    (3) change <u>appreciated</u> to <u>appreciate</u>

    (4) change <u>assistence</u> to <u>assistance</u>

    (5) change <u>you</u> to <u>I</u>

Go on to next page

> *Questions 11 through 20 refer to the following prospectus.*

Marketing

(A)

(1) BETAs product is reconditioned Italian café equipment.

(2) The initial's priority will be espresso/cappuccino machines.

(3) There are four ways of marketing the reconditioned machines (a) direct sales (b) sales through a network of distributors (c) leasing directly (d) leasing through a network of distributors.

(4) Direct sales and leasing will take time, because establishing a network of distributors will be the priority in year one.

(5) In order for BETA to be successful, a trained workforce are essential.

(6) A secondary business will be reconditioning machines too order.

Sales

(B)

(7) All estimates for potential units reconditioned and soled or leased are conservative.

(8) The initial mix of leasing and sales is estimated to be 20 percent leasing and 80 percent sales for the first year.

Raw Material

(C)

(9) The average trade-in for an espresso machine will be $75, while the average price paid for used machines will be $250.

(10) Twenty percent of the machines acquired will be trade-ins, the balance will be purchased.

Go on to next page

11. Sentence 1: **BETAs product is recondi- tioned Italian café equipment.**

    Which correction should be made to sen- tence 1?

    (1) insert an apostrophe before the *s* in BETAs

    (2) change <u>Italian</u> to <u>italian</u>

    (3) replace <u>is</u> with <u>are</u>

    (4) insert a comma after <u>reconditioned</u>

    (5) change <u>reconditioned</u> to <u>recondition</u>

12. Sentence 2: **The initial's priority will be espresso/cappuccino machines.**

    Which change should be made to sen- tence 2?

    (1) insert <u>to</u> after <u>will</u>

    (2) replace <u>will</u> with <u>may</u>

    (3) change <u>priority</u> to <u>prior</u>

    (4) change <u>initial's</u> to <u>initial</u>

    (5) no correction required

13. Sentence 3: **There are four ways of market- ing the reconditioned machines (a) direct sales (b) sales through a network of dis- tributors (c) leasing directly (d) leasing through a network of distributors.**

    Which punctuation should be added to sen- tence 3?

    (1) add a colon after <u>machines</u>

    (2) add a semicolon after <u>ways</u>

    (3) add a comma after <u>directly</u>

    (4) add a comma after <u>ways</u>

    (5) add a colon after <u>marketing</u>

14. Sentence 4: **Direct sales and marketing will take time, because establishing a net- work of distributors will be the priority in year one.**

    Which is the most effective revision to begin sentence 4?

    (1) Because establishing a network of dis- tributors will be the priority in year one,

    (2) Direct sales and marketing since estab- lishing a network,

    (3) The priority in year one will take time,

    (4) A network of distributors will take time,

    (5) Because direct sales and marketing will take time,

15. Sentence 5: **In order for BETA to be suc- cessful, a trained workforce are essential.**

    Which correction should be made to sen- tence 5?

    (1) replace <u>to be</u> with <u>being</u>

    (2) remove the comma after <u>successful</u>

    (3) change <u>are</u> to <u>is</u>

    (4) change <u>for</u> to <u>four</u>

    (5) replace <u>trained</u> with <u>train</u>

16. Sentence 6: **A secondary business will be reconditioning machines too order.**

    Which change should be made to sen- tence 6?

    (1) change <u>will be</u> to <u>would be</u>

    (2) change <u>reconditioning</u> to <u>recondition</u>

    (3) change <u>machines</u> to <u>machine</u>

    (4) replace <u>too</u> with <u>to</u>

    (5) change <u>secondary</u> to <u>second</u>

17. Sentence 7: **All estimates for potential units reconditioned and soled or leased are conservative.**

    Which correction should be made to sentence 7?

    (1) change <u>for</u> to <u>four</u>

    (2) change <u>soled</u> to <u>sold</u>

    (3) replace <u>are</u> with <u>is</u>

    (4) change <u>estimates</u> to <u>estimate</u>

    (5) place a comma after <u>reconditioned</u>

18. Sentence 8: **The initial mix of leasing and sales is estimated to be 20 percent leasing and 80 percent sales for the first year.**

    Which revision should be made to sen- tence 8?

    (1) move <u>for the first year</u> between <u>sales</u> and <u>is</u>

    (2) change <u>is</u> to <u>are</u>

    (3) change <u>sales</u> to <u>sails</u>

    (4) move <u>is estimated to</u> between <u>mix</u> and <u>of</u>

    (5) change <u>first</u> to <u>1st</u>

Go on to next page ⟶

19. Sentence 9: **The average trade-in for an espresso machine will be $75, while the average price paid for used machines will be $250.**

Which revision should be made to sentence 9?

    (1) remove the comma after <u>$75</u>

    (2) change <u>an</u> to <u>a</u>

    (3) change <u>will be</u> to <u>should be</u>

    (4) change <u>paid</u> to <u>payed</u>

    (5) insert <u>price</u> after <u>trade-in</u>

20. Sentence 10: **Twenty percent of the machines acquired will be** <u>trade-ins, the balance</u> **will be purchased.**

Which is the best way to improve the underlined portion of sentence 10?

    (1) remove the comma after <u>trade-ins</u>

    (2) change to <u>trade-ins, while the balance</u>

    (3) change to <u>traded, the balance</u>

    (4) change to <u>trade-ins the balance</u>

    (5) no correction required

Go on to next page

Questions 21 through 30 refer to the following executive summary.

Marketing

Drycleaning and Laundering Industry Adjustment Committee
Report on the Local Labour Market Partnership Project
April 2007 – August 2009

Executive Summary

(A)

(1) Over the past two years, the Drycleaning and Laundering Industry Adjustment Committee has worked hard to become a cohesive group focused on assessing and addressing the human resource implications associated with changes in the fabricare industry. (2) As of August 2009, the Committee has an active membership of over 15 individuals involved in all aspects of the project. (3) The Committee, which has great difficulty speaking with one voice, has taken responsibility for undertaking actions that will benefit this large, highly fragmented industry.

(B)

(4) During the initial period that the Committee was in existence, its work focused on out-reaching to and building a relationship with key individuals within the industry. (5) One of its first steps was to undertake a Needs Assessment Survey within the industry.

(C)

(6) During the first year, the Committee explored ways of meeting the needs identified in the Needs Assessment Survey, including raising the profile of the industry and offering on-site training programs, particularly in the areas of spotting and pressing. (7) A great deal of feasibility work was undertaken during this phase yet each possible training solution proved to be extremely difficult and costly to implement.

(D)

(8) As the Committee moved into its second year, it officially established a joint project with the National Fabricare Association to achieve goals in two priority areas: mentorship, train-ing, and profile building.

(E)

(9) During this passed year, much effort and vision has gone into achieving the goals estab-lished by the Industry Adjustment Committee and the Association. (10) The new priority areas have provided an opportunity for the industry to do the following

- Introduce technology
- Build capacity and knowledge
- Enhance skills
- Build partnerships and networks

Go on to next page

21. Sentence 1: **Over the past two years, the Drycleaning and Laundering Industry Adjustment Committee has worked hard to become a cohesive group focused on assessing and addressing the human resource implications in the fabricare industry.**

    Which is the best way to improve sentence 1?

    (1) remove the comma after <u>years</u>
    (2) place a period after <u>group</u> and start a new sentence beginning with <u>It has focused on</u>
    (3) place a comma after <u>group</u>
    (4) change <u>focused</u> to <u>focussed</u>
    (5) place a period after <u>group</u> and start a new sentence beginning with <u>To become focused</u>

22. Sentence 2: **As of August 2009, the Committee has an active membership of over 15 individuals involved in all aspects of the project.**

    Which revision should be made to sentence 2?

    (1) change <u>has</u> to <u>have</u>
    (2) remove the comma after <u>2009</u>
    (3) change <u>individuals</u> to <u>individual's</u>
    (4) change <u>aspects</u> to <u>aspect</u>
    (5) remove <u>over</u>

23. Sentence 3: **The Committee, which has great difficulty speaking with one voice, has taken responsibility for undertaking actions that will benefit this large, highly fragmented industry.**

    Which revision is required to improve sentence 3?

    (1) remove the comma after <u>large</u>
    (2) change <u>Committee</u> to <u>committee</u>
    (3) move <u>,which has great difficulty speaking with one voice,</u> to the end of the sentence after <u>industry</u>
    (4) change <u>has taken</u> to <u>have taken</u>
    (5) no correction required

24. Sentence 4: **During the initial period that the Committee was in existence, its work focused on outreaching to and building a relationship with key individuals within the industry.**

    Which correction should be made to sentence 4?

    (1) change <u>its</u> to <u>it's</u>
    (2) change <u>outreaching to</u> to <u>reaching out to</u>
    (3) place a comma after <u>period</u>
    (4) change <u>outreaching</u> to <u>out-reaching</u>
    (5) change <u>within</u> to <u>between</u>

25. Sentence 5: **One of its first steps was to undertake a Needs Assessment Survey within the industry.**

    Which change should be made to sentence 5?

    (1) change <u>its</u> to <u>it's</u>
    (2) change <u>first</u> to <u>1st</u>
    (3) change <u>within</u> to <u>with</u>
    (4) change <u>was</u> to <u>were</u>
    (5) no correction required

26. Sentence 6: **During the first year, the Committee explored ways of meeting the needs identified in the Needs Assessment Survey including raising the profile of the industry and offering on-site training programs, particularly in the areas of spotting and pressing.**

    Which is the best way to improve sentence 6?

    (1) insert a comma after <u>including</u>
    (2) place a period after <u>Survey</u> and start a new sentence with <u>These included</u>
    (3) place a period after <u>industry</u> and start a new sentence with <u>Offering on-site</u>
    (4) remove the comma after <u>programs</u>
    (5) no correction required

Go on to next page

27. Sentence 7: **A great deal of feasibility work was undertaken during this phase yet each possible training solution proved to be extremely difficult and costly to implement.**

    Which correction should be made to sentence 7?

    (1) change <u>was</u> to <u>were</u>

    (2) change <u>proved</u> to <u>prove</u>

    (3) insert a comma after <u>undertaken</u>

    (4) insert a comma after <u>phase</u>

    (5) change <u>difficult</u> to <u>difficulty</u>

28. Sentence 8: **As the Committee moved into its second year, it officially established a joint project with the National Fabricare Association to achieve goals in two priority areas: mentorship, training, and profile building.**

    What correction should be made to sentence 8?

    (1) change <u>its</u> to <u>it's</u>

    (2) change <u>Association</u> to <u>association</u>

    (3) change <u>with</u> to <u>between</u>

    (4) change <u>two</u> to <u>three</u>

    (5) no correction required

29. Sentence 9: **During this passed year, much effort and vision has gone into achieving the goals established by the Industry Adjustment Committee and the Association.**

    What correction should be made to sentence 9?

    (1) insert a comma after <u>Committee</u>

    (2) change <u>passed</u> to <u>past</u>

    (3) change <u>into</u> to <u>in</u>

    (4) change <u>goals</u> to <u>goal</u>

    (5) remove the comma after <u>year</u>

30. Sentence 10: **The new priority areas have provided an opportunity for the industry to do the following**

    • **Introduce technology**

    • **Build capacity and knowledge**

    • **Enhance skills**

    • **Build partnerships and networks**

    What punctuation should be added to sentence 10?

    (1) place a semicolon after <u>technology</u>

    (2) place a semicolon after <u>knowledge</u>

    (3) place a semicolon after <u>skills</u>

    (4) place a semicolon after <u>following</u>

    (5) place a colon after <u>following</u>

Go on to next page

> *Questions 31 through 40 refer to the following information piece.*

Prior Learning Assessment and Recognition

Introduction

(A)

(1) This course is based on a Prior Learning Assessment and Recognition (PLAR) model, as a component of the PLAR, which utilizes preparation for a standardized challenge examination. (2) In addition candidates are guided through the creation of a portfolio, which can be evaluated by a college for admission or advanced standing. (3) This is an opportunity for adults, who have learned in non-formal as well as formal venues, to document and assess their prior learning. (4) The course is intents and concentrated and is not meant for every applicant.

(B)

(5) Candidates, who score low in the pre-test, should be directed to remedial programs before beginning such a rigorous course. (6) Those who extremely score well in a pre-test may be advised to arrange immediately to take a challenging test, such as one of the GED tests. (7) This course is meant for candidates who will gain from review and re-mediation but do not require extensive teaching.

Rationale

(C)

(8) This course is designed to help adult learners gain acknowledgement and accreditation of their prior learning in preparation for post secondary study. (9) Students will learn methods for documenting prior knowledge and will develop skills while becoming reacquainted with educational environments and developing the skills needed to succeed in such environments. (10) Through the use of assessment tools and councilling, students will gain a realistic understanding of their levels of competence, personal strengths, weaknesses, and learning styles.

Go on to next page

31. Sentence 1: **This course is based on a Prior Learning Assessment and Recognition (PLAR) model, as a component of the PLAR, which utilizes preparation for a standardized challenge examination.**

    Which is the best way to improve sentence 1?

    (1) no improvement required

    (2) delete as a component of the PLAR,

    (3) change is to has

    (4) change utilizes to utilized

    (5) place a comma after Assessment

32. Sentence 2: **In addition candidates are guided through the creation of a portfolio, which can be evaluated by a college for admission or advanced standing.**

    Which correction should be made to sentence 2?

    (1) insert a comma after candidates

    (2) change are guided to is guided

    (3) change by to through

    (4) insert a comma after addition

    (5) change portfolio to port-folio

33. Sentence 3: **This is an opportunity for adults, who have learned in non-formal as well as formal venues, to document and assess there prior learning.**

    Which correction should be made in sentence 3?

    (1) change there to their

    (2) remove the comma after adults

    (3) change an to a

    (4) change venues to venue

    (5) no correction required

34. Sentence 4: **The course is intents and concentrated and is not meant for every applicant.**

    Which correction should be made to sentence 4?

    (1) change is not to are not

    (2) change not to only

    (3) change meant to mend

    (4) place a comma after concentrated

    (5) change intents to intense

35. Sentence 5: **Candidates, who score low in the pre-test, should be directed to remedial programs before beginning such a rigorous course.**

    Which improvement should be made to sentence 5?

    (1) remove the comma after candidates

    (2) remove the comma after pre-test

    (3) remove both the comma after candidates and the comma after pre-test

    (4) change before to after

    (5) change pre-test to post-test

36. Sentence 6: Those who extremely score well **in a pre-test may be advised to arrange immediately to take a challenging test, such as one of the GED tests.**

    Which is the best way to write the underlined portion of this sentence?

    (1) Extremely those who score well

    (2) Those who score well extremely

    (3) Those who score extremely well

    (4) Those extremely who score well

    (5) no correction required

37. Sentence 7: **The course is meant for candidates who will gain from review and re-mediation but do not require extensive teaching.**

    Which correction should be made to sentence 7?

    (1) change review to revue

    (2) place a comma after candidates

    (3) place a comma after re-mediation

    (4) change re-mediation to remediation

    (5) no correction required

Go on to next page

38. Sentence 8: **This course is designed to help adult learners gain acknowledgement and accreditation of their prior learning in preparation for post secondary study.**

    Which change should be made to sentence 8?

    (1) change <u>post secondary</u> to <u>post-secondary</u>

    (2) change <u>acknowledgement</u> to <u>acknowledge</u>

    (3) change <u>prior learning</u> to <u>prior-learning</u>

    (4) change <u>their</u> to <u>there</u>

    (5) no correction required

39. Sentence 9: **Students will learn methods for documenting prior knowledge and will develop skills while becoming reacquainted with educational environments and developing skills needed to succeed in such environments.**

    Which is the best way to improve sentence 9?

    (1) remove <u>for documenting</u>

    (2) remove <u>and developing skills needed to succeed in such environments</u>

    (3) remove <u>prior knowledge</u>

    (4) remove <u>with educational environments</u>

    (5) no correction required

40. Sentence 10: **Through the use of assessment tools and councilling, students will gain a realistic understanding of their levels of competence, personal strengths, weaknesses, and learning styles.**

    Which correction should be made to sentence 10?

    (1) change <u>realistic</u> to <u>real</u>

    (2) change <u>levels</u> to <u>level</u>

    (3) change <u>weaknesses</u> to <u>weeknesses</u>

    (4) change <u>students</u> to <u>students'</u>

    (5) change <u>councilling</u> to <u>counselling</u>

Go on to next page

> *Questions 41 through 50 refer to the following business letter.*

CanLearn Study Tours, Inc.
2500 Big Beaver Rd.
Halifax, NS B3J 2B1

Dr. Dale Worth, Ph.D.
Registrar
BEST Institute of Technology
75 Ingram Drive
Toronto ON M5H 2N2

Dear Dr. Worth:

(A)

(1) Our rapidly changing economic climate has meant both challenges never before known. (2) It has been said that only those organizations who can maintain loyalty and commitment among their employees, members, and customers will continue to survive and prosper in this age of continuous learning and globalization.

(B)

(3) Since 1974, CanLearn Study Tours, Inc. have been working with universities, colleges, school districts, voluntary organizations, and businesses to address the unique learning needs of their staff and clientele. (4) These have included educational travel programs that explore the following, artistic and cultural interests, historic and archeological themes, environmental and wellness experiences, and new service patterns. (5) Professional development strategies have been organized to enhance international understanding and boost creativity. (6) Some organizations have used study tours to build and maintain their membership or consumer base. (7) Other organizations discover a new soarce of revenue in these difficult economic times.

(C)

(8) The formats has varied from a series of local seminars to incentive conferences or sales promotion meetings. (9) Our professional services, including the best possible transportation and accommodation at the most reasonable rates, have insured the success of these programs.

(D)

(10) We would appreciate the opportunity to share our experiences in educational travel and discuss the ways we may be of service to your organization.

Yours sincerely,

Todd Croft, M.A., President
CanLearn Study Tours, Inc.

Go on to next page

41.   Sentence 1: **Our rapidly changing economic climate has meant both challenges never before known.**

      Which improvement should be made to sentence 1?

      (1) insert <u>and opportunities</u> between <u>challenges</u> and <u>never</u>
      (2) change <u>has meant</u> to <u>have meant</u>
      (3) change <u>known</u> to <u>none</u>
      (4) change <u>challenges</u> to <u>challenge</u>
      (5) no correction required

42.   Sentence 2: **It has been said that only those organizations who can maintain loyalty and commitment among their employees, members, and customers will continue to survive and prosper in this age of continuous learning and globalization.**

      Which change should be made to sentence 2?

      (1) insert a comma after <u>commitment</u>
      (2) change <u>has been</u> to <u>had been</u>
      (3) change <u>who</u> to <u>that</u>
      (4) change <u>those</u> to <u>these</u>
      (5) no correction required

43.   Sentence 3: **Since 1974, CanLearn Study Tours, Inc.** <u>have been working</u> **with universities, colleges, school districts, voluntary organizations, and businesses to address the unique learning needs of their staff and clientele.**

      Which is the best way to write the underlined portion of sentence 3?

      (1) had been working
      (2) has been working
      (3) will be working
      (4) shall be working
      (5) no correction required

44.   Sentence 4: **These have included educational travel programs that explore the following, artistic and cultural interests, historic and archeological themes, environmental and wellness experiences, and new service patterns.**

      Which correction should be made to sentence 4?

      (1) insert a comma after <u>have included</u>
      (2) change the comma after <u>following</u> to a colon
      (3) change the comma after <u>interests</u> to a colon
      (4) change the comma after <u>themes</u> to a colon
      (5) change the comma after <u>experiences</u> to a colon

45.   Sentence 5: **Professional development strategies have been organized to enhance international understanding and boost creativity.**

      Which change should be made to sentence 5?

      (1) change <u>strategies</u> to <u>strategy</u>
      (2) change <u>boost</u> to <u>boast</u>
      (3) change <u>have been organized</u> to <u>has been organized</u>
      (4) change <u>enhance</u> to <u>enhancing</u>
      (5) no correction required

46.   Sentence 6: **Some organizations' have used study tours to build and maintain their membership and consumer base.**

      Which correction should be made to sentence 6?

      (1) change <u>Some</u> to <u>All</u>
      (2) change <u>their</u> to <u>there</u>
      (3) change <u>have used</u> to <u>has used</u>
      (4) change <u>organizations'</u> to <u>organizations</u>
      (5) change <u>base</u> to <u>bays</u>

Go on to next page

47. Sentence 7: **Other organizations discover a new soarce of revenue in these difficult economic times.**

    Which change should be made to sentence 7?

    (1) change <u>organizations</u> to <u>organization's</u>

    (2) change <u>soarce</u> to <u>source</u>

    (3) change <u>these</u> to <u>this</u>

    (4) change <u>discover</u> to <u>discovering</u>

    (5) no correction required

48. Sentence 8: **The formats has varied from a series of local seminars to incentive conferences or sales promotion meetings.**

    Which revision should be made to sentence 8?

    (1) add a comma after <u>seminars</u>

    (2) add an apostrophe after <u>sales</u>

    (3) change <u>formats</u> to <u>format</u>

    (4) add a period after <u>seminars</u>

    (5) no correction required

49. Sentence 9: **Our professional services, including the best possible transportation and accommodation at the most reasonable rates, have insured the success of these programs.**

    Which correction should be made to sentence 9?

    (1) change <u>services</u> to <u>service</u>

    (2) replace <u>insured</u> with <u>ensured</u>

    (3) remove the comma after <u>services</u>

    (4) remove the comma after <u>rates</u>

    (5) no correction required

50. Sentence 10: **We would appreciate the opportunity to share our experiences in educational travel and discuss the ways we may be of service to your organization.**

    Which revision should be made to sentence 10?

    (1) change <u>would appreciate</u> to <u>appreciate</u>

    (2) insert a comma after <u>share</u>

    (3) insert a comma after <u>ways</u>

    (4) change <u>may</u> to <u>will</u>

    (5) no correction required

Go on to next page ⟶

Language Arts, Writing Test: Part II

Look at the box on the following page. In the box, you find your assigned topic and the letter of that topic.

You must write on the assigned topic **ONLY.**

Mark the letter of your assigned topic in the appropriate space on your answer sheet booklet.

You have 45 minutes to write on your assigned essay topic. If you have time remaining in this test period after you complete your essay, you may return to the multiple-choice section. Do not return the Language Arts, Writing Test booklet until you finish both Parts I and II of the Language Arts, Writing Test.

Two evaluators will score your essay according to its overall effectiveness. Their evaluation will be based on the following features:

✔ Well-focused main points

✔ Clear organization

✔ Specific development of your ideas

✔ Control of sentence structure, punctuation, grammar, word choice, and spelling

REMEMBER, YOU MUST COMPLETE BOTH THE MULTIPLE-CHOICE QUESTIONS (PART I) AND THE ESSAY (PART II) TO RECEIVE A SCORE ON THE LANGUAGE ARTS, WRITING TEST.

To avoid having to repeat both parts of the test, be sure to observe the following rules:

✔ Before you begin writing, jot notes or outline your essay on the sheets provided.

✔ For your final copy, write legibly in ink so that the evaluators can read your writing.

✔ Write on the assigned topic. If you write on a topic other than the one assigned, you will not receive a score for the Language Arts, Writing Test.

✔ Write your essay on the lined pages of the separate answer sheet booklet. Only the writing on these pages will be scored.

Note that if you do not pass one portion of the test, you must take both parts over again.

DO NOT BEGIN TAKING THIS TEST UNTIL TOLD TO DO SO

Topic C

Many people enjoy a hobby or special interest in their spare time.

Write an essay that encourages someone else to enjoy a hobby or special interest. Use your personal experiences, knowledge gained, relationships formed, and so on to develop your ideas.

Part II is a test to determine how well you can use written language to explain your ideas.

In preparing for your essay, you should take the following steps:

✔ Read the DIRECTIONS and the TOPIC carefully.

✔ Plan your essay before you write. Use the scratch paper provided to make any notes. These notes will be collected but not scored.

✔ Before you turn in your essay, reread what you have written and make any changes that will improve your essay.

Your essay should be long enough to develop the topic adequately.

Note: Refer to Chapter 6 for the answers for Parts I and II of this practice test.

END OF TEST

Answer Sheet for Language Arts, Writing Test: Part II

Use a No. 2 pencil to write the letter of your essay topic in the box, then fill in the corresponding circle.

TOPIC | (A)(B)(C)(D)(E)(F)(G)(H)(I)(J)(K)(L)(M)(N)(O)(P)(Q)(R)(S)(T)(U)(V)(W)(X)(Y)(Z)

Chapter 6

Answers and Explanations for the Language Arts, Writing Test

Answer Key for Part 1

After taking the Language Arts, Writing Test, Part I, in Chapter 5, use this section to check your answers.

1. **1**	18. **1**	35. **3**
2. **3**	19. **5**	36. **3**
3. **2**	20. **2**	37. **4**
4. **5**	21. **2**	38. **1**
5. **1**	22. **5**	39. **2**
6. **3**	23. **3**	40. **5**
7. **5**	24. **2**	41. **1**
8. **2**	25. **5**	42. **3**
9. **4**	26. **2**	43. **2**
10. **4**	27. **4**	44. **2**
11. **1**	28. **4**	45. **5**
12. **4**	29. **2**	46. **4**
13. **1**	30. **5**	47. **2**
14. **1**	31. **2**	48. **3**
15. **3**	32. **4**	49. **2**
16. **4**	33. **1**	50. **5**
17. **2**	34. **5**	

Analysis of the Answers for Part 1

If you aren't sure why an answer was incorrect, use this section to get quick explanations of the answers. If you correctly answered a question, you may still want to read the explanations to get a better understanding of the thought process that helped you choose the correct answer.

1. **1.** Change *you're* (which means "you are") to *your*. *Your* indicates ownership of the new company, which is the meaning you want. The other choices are either grammatically incorrect or do nothing to make the sentence clearer.

2. **3.** The verb tense must be the singular *was,* not the plural *were.* Singular subjects always take singular verbs.

3. **2.** The sentence needs a comma after *operation* to separate the introductory adverb clause.

4. **5.** *Homonyms* are words that sound alike but are spelled differently and have different meanings, such as *then* and *than.* The correct word to use in this sentence is *than. Than* is used for comparisons, while *then* refers to time sequences. Because this sentence needs a word that indicates a comparison, *than* is the correct answer.

5. **1.** Although you can revise this sentence in many ways, the answer that makes the most sense is "Thirteen new jobs will be created, returning half a million dollars to the local economy." This change improves the organization of the sentence.

6. **3.** *Equipment* is the correct spelling.

To improve your spelling skills, read as much as you can before you take the GED Language Arts, Writing Test, Part I. Seeing words spelled correctly (as you do when you read published works) is a great way to help you recognize when words are misspelled on this test.

7. **5.** The sentence is correct. No changes are needed, so the answer is *no correction required.*

Some sentences on the test are correct. Don't correct grammar and punctuation if the sentence looks right to you.

8. **2.** To improve the sentence structure, insert *particularly* (an adverb modifying *interested*) before *interested.* This change makes the sentence easier to read and understand.

9. **4.** You need a comma after *BETA* to separate the introductory adverb phrase from the rest of the sentence.

10. **4.** Correct the spelling error: Change *assistence* to *assistance.*

11. **1.** Apostrophes have two uses: to take the place of a missing letter or to indicate possession. You need to add an apostrophe before the *s* in *BETA* because it's a singular possessive. The text indicates that the product belonging to BETA is reconditioned Italian café equipment, which means you need the apostrophe to show this relationship.

12. **4.** You need to eliminate the extra apostrophe in this sentence. The correct form of the word is *initial.*

13. **1.** You need a colon after *machines* to indicate to readers that a list is coming.

14. **1.** The sentence "Direct sales and marketing will take time, because establishing a network of distributors will be the priority in year one" isn't easy to understand, and it doesn't flow easily. Phrases starting with *because* usually make more sense at the beginning of the sentence. You can then write, "Because establishing a network of distributors will be the priority in year one, direct sales and marketing will take time." Because the meaning of the second section flows from the meaning of the first section, this sentence is an improvement from the original.

15. **3.** The singular noun *workforce* doesn't belong with the plural verb *are.* The subject and verb in a sentence must always agree, so you need to use the singular verb *is* rather than the plural *are.*

16. **4.** *Too* means "also," which isn't what you need in this sentence. Replace *too* with *to.*

Before taking the GED Language Arts, Writing Test, Part I, study a list of *homonyms* — words that sound the same but are spelled differently and have different meanings. The test includes several incorrect homonyms to test your ability to differentiate between them.

17. **2.** Correct the homonym spelling error from *soled* to *sold. Sold,* the word you want to use, is the past tense of *sell.*

18. **1.** The sentence "The initial mix of leasing and sales is estimated to be 20 percent leasing and 80 percent sales for the first year" could be misunderstood. The best way to correct this sentence is to change it around to read, "The initial mix of leasing and sales for the first year is estimated to be 20 percent leasing and 80 percent sales." When you read a sentence and words are out of order or make reading awkward, go back and correct them.

19. **5.** Because the sentence is talking about price, add the word *price* to clarify the meaning.

20. **2.** Changing the sentence to read *trade-ins, while the balance* improves the sentence structure. Another way to correct the original sentence is to replace the comma with a semicolon; however, because that's not an answer given, you must pick Choice (2).

21. **2.** Avoid the overly long and complex sentence, "Over the past two years, the Drycleaning and Laundering Industry Adjustment Committee has worked hard to become a cohesive group focused on assessing and addressing the human resource implications in the fabricare industry." To improve it, create two new sentences, such as the following: "Over the past two years, the Drycleaning and Laundering Industry Adjustment Committee has worked hard to become a cohesive group. It has focused on assessing and addressing the human resource implications in the fabricare industry."

22. **5.** Remove *over* to clarify the meaning of the sentence. If you know that the group has 29 members (or however many it has over 15), say so.

23. **3.** The sentence in question says that the *committee* has great difficulty speaking in one voice, which may be true. However, a more accurate statement is that the *industry* has great difficulty speaking in one voice. You know this statement is true because the sentence given describes the industry as *fragmented.* A better organization for the sentence is, "The Committee has taken responsibility for undertaking actions that will benefit this large, highly fragmented industry, which has great difficulty speaking with one voice."

24. **2.** *Outreaching* isn't a verb; *reaching out* is.

25. **5.** No correction is required because none of the other options improves the sentence.

Are you thinking that we made a mistake in the sentence just above? Well, we didn't; it's correct. The noun *none* goes with the verb *improves.* The prepositional phrase *of the other options* doesn't determine how the noun and verb agree. *None* is a singular noun and, therefore, goes with *improves,* not *improve.* If this situation comes up on your test, replace *none* with *not one* (in your head), ignore any prepositional phrases between *none* and the verb, and see whether *not one* agrees with the verb given.

26. **2.** The sentence "During the first year, the Committee explored ways of meeting the needs identified in the Needs Assessment Survey including raising the profile of the industry and offering on-site training programs, particularly in the areas of spotting and pressing" is simply too long to be understood. Find a logical place to break it into two sentences. The first part of the sentence discusses the uses of the Needs Assessment Survey; the second discusses the type of training. You can split the sentence into two smaller, more easily understood, sentences, as follows: "During the first year, the Committee explored ways of meeting the needs identified in the Needs Assessment Survey. These included raising the profile of the industry and offering on-site training programs, particularly in the areas of spotting and pressing."

27. **4.** Insert a comma after *phase* to improve the sentence structure. Because this compound sentence is joined by the conjunction *yet*, it needs the comma to ensure that the two thoughts remain separate.

    A *compound sentence* contains two independent clauses or thoughts. The clauses have to be separated by a conjunction like *but* or *yet,* and the conjunction needs a comma before it.

28. **4.** This answer is a given: Three priority areas are listed, not two.

29. **2.** Correct the homonym spelling error from *passed* to *past.*

30. **5.** The introductory clause needs a colon at the end.

    If you thought the items in the list needed semicolons, they can have them or not, depending on *house style* (the style used and followed religiously by the company or publishing house writing or editing the text). However, if you use semicolons, you need to use them at the end of each component in the list, which isn't an answer choice.

31. **2.** The phrase *as a component of the PLAR* is unnecessary.

32. **4.** You need a comma after *in addition.*

    Not sure about commas? Check out *English Grammar For Dummies,* 2nd Edition, by Geraldine Woods (Wiley) for the lowdown on this tricky form of punctuation.

33. **1.** *Their* is possessive (showing belonging) and is the correct choice in this sentence. Correct the spelling error from *there* to *their.*

    The homonyms, *there, their,* and *they're* probably trip up more high school and college students than any other homonyms. Before heading into the GED Language Arts, Writing Test, Part I, know the differences between these three words!

34. **5.** *Intense* and *concentrated* are synonyms used in this sentence for emphasis, but *intense* is misspelled as *intents. Intents* is where you sleep on a camping trip.

35. **3.** The clause *who score low in the pre-test* is a *restrictive clause,* which means it refers to a specific noun — *candidates* in this case — and specifies something about the noun that the sentence needs to make sense to readers. Restrictive clauses aren't separated by commas because they're an integral part of the sentence.

    Contrast the restrictive clause with the *nonrestrictive clause,* which adds information about the noun that isn't essential to the meaning of the sentence. If you remove a nonrestrictive clause from the sentence, you can still fully understand the meaning of the sentence. Nonrestrictive clauses require commas to separate them from the sentence.

36. **3.** *Those who score extremely well* is the best order of the words. *Extremely,* an adverb, is best placed next to the word it modifies, which is *well.*

37. **4.** Correct the error in the spelling of *re-mediation.*

    Although exceptions exist, when a prefix that ends in a vowel (as *re-* does) precedes a consonant, no hyphen is used. In many (but not all) cases, when a prefix that ends in a vowel precedes another vowel, a hyphen is used.

38. **1.** When two adjectives (like *post* and *secondary* in the example) combine to modify one noun, they're almost always hyphenated. Keep in mind, however, that when an adverb and adjective (such as *newly formed*) combine to modify a noun, they're usually not hyphenated.

    If you have trouble remembering this rule, keep in mind that words ending in *–ly* and forming two-word adjectives are almost never hyphenated. English usage can be strange and irrational. It has many exceptions to rules and probably just as many rules about exceptions. Style manuals can help you write correctly in particular areas of writing.

39. **2.** The sentence "Students will learn methods for documenting prior knowledge and will develop skills while becoming reacquainted with educational environments and developing skills needed to succeed in such environments" is complex and redundant. Delete the entire phrase *and developing skills needed to succeed in such environments.*

Unless you're being paid by the word, always try to say what you mean in as few words as possible.

40. **5.** This sentence contains a spelling error. Correct the spelling error by changing *councilling* to *counselling*.

41. **1.** Although the word *both* refers to two options, here, you're given only one option — *challenges*. If you insert *and opportunities* between *challenges* and *never,* you include a second option and correct the sentence.

42. **3.** An organization is never a *who;* only people can be referred to as *who*. An organization is a collective noun made up of people, but the collective noun itself is an impersonal entity and doesn't qualify as a *who.*

Although the sentence may appear long and, therefore, may benefit from rewriting, the sentence is technically correct. Although commas do serve to make sentences clearer, you don't want to insert them unless punctuation rules make them correct.

43. **2.** CanLearn Study Tours is a single entity because it's one company. Therefore, it's a singular noun and needs the singular verb *has* instead of the plural *have*.

People like to refer to companies as *them* when, in fact, a company is always an *it.* Even though a company is made up of a lot of people, it's still a singular entity.

44. **2.** You need to insert a colon before the list to introduce it.

45. **5.** The options presented either make the sentence difficult to understand or introduce errors, so the correct answer is *no correction required.*

46. **4.** A stray apostrophe has landed on this sentence. The one after *organizations'* is unnecessary because you're not trying to show possession.

Get comfortable with using apostrophes — especially for possession — before taking the GED Language Arts, Writing Test, Part I.

47. **2.** Correct the spelling error by changing *soarce* to *source*.

48. **3.** *Formats* is plural, but *has* is a singular verb. Verbs and their subjects must agree.

Study both subject-verb agreement and pronoun-antecedent agreement before taking the Language Arts, Writing Test.

49. **2.** Correct the spelling error by changing *insured* to *ensured*.

Using *insure* is a common error. Use *insure* only when you mean the thing you buy to protect your car, house, health, life, and so on. This example has nothing to do with insurance, so use *ensure,* instead.

50. **5.** No correction is required. The other choices don't improve or correct the sentence.

Sample Essay for Part II

The topic for the practice test in Chapter 5 is as follows:

Many people enjoy a hobby or special interest in their spare time.

Write an essay that encourages someone else to enjoy a hobby or special interest. Use personal experiences, knowledge gained, relationships formed, and so on to develop your ideas.

As the test graders read and evaluate your essay, they look for the following:

✔ Well-focused main points

✔ Evidence of clear organization

✔ Specific development of your ideas

✔ Proper sentence structure

✔ Correct grammar

✔ Necessary punctuation

✔ Appropriate word choice

✔ Correct spelling

Although every essay will be unique, we provide a sample to give you a better idea of what the test graders expect to see in your essay. Compare the structure of this essay to yours.

> Hiking is a hobby I can recommend to anyone. Being outdoors, getting exercise, and spending quiet time alone are all facets of hiking that make it unique in today's mostly indoor, sedentary — and yet overly busy — life. Many areas — even large cities — offer parks with dirt or grass paths that are perfect for a daily hike.
>
> Hiking gets me outdoors, away from potentially harmful indoor air. Too much time indoors cuts humans off from the sun, which is vital to mental health, and can also lead to allergies or other illnesses from too much exposure to chemicals and other products that are trapped indoors. Just an hour per day of hiking can counteract many of the effects of spending too much time indoors.
>
> Hiking is also great exercise, because it works the heart, lungs, and leg muscles without adding stress to the knees and other joints. You can hike in your street clothes (although a good pair of hiking boots is a good idea), so hiking does not require the investment in gear that many forms of exercise do.
>
> Perhaps the best — and most unique — feature of hiking, however, is that it provides solace from our loud, fast-paced, materialistic world. When hiking — even in or near a large, metropolitan area — I see deer, listen to birdsongs, and watch squirrels busy with their work. Without the constant sound of a TV or radio in the background, I can focus on my own thoughts instead of on what is expected by society and promoted by advertisers. While on the trail, I can focus on the natural beauty around me instead of worrying about bills or comparing myself to others. This quiet disconnection from society helps me remember what is important in life.
>
> In short, hiking helps me break free of the work-a-day world by getting me outside to appreciate nature, encouraging me to exercise, and giving me long periods of restful silence. I recommend hiking to anyone.

After reading through the sample essay once, reread it and answer the following questions about it:

- ✔ Does this essay contain a series of main points that clearly relate to the topic? (Underline the main points to check.)

- ✔ Does each paragraph have an introductory sentence or thought?

- ✔ Does each paragraph have a concluding sentence or thought?

- ✔ Are the sentences within each paragraph well organized?

- ✔ Are the paragraphs organized in a natural flow from beginning to end? In other words, does each paragraph build on the previous one and lead to the next one?

- ✔ Have the ideas in the given topic and the first paragraph been developed throughout the essay?

- ✔ Are all the sentences grammatically correct?

- ✔ Are all the sentences properly structured?

- ✔ Are all the sentences correctly punctuated?

- ✔ Are all the words used correctly?

- ✔ Are all the words spelled correctly?

A test evaluator would probably have given this sample essay a high score, because it has all the attributes of a good essay that we list earlier in this section. It isn't perfect, but no one's asking you to write a perfect essay. Look over the list of characteristics the readers are looking for, and try to determine whether your practice essay satisfies those requirements. Ask a friend to answer the questions we list here about your essay. If you or your friend answers no to any questions, rewrite your essay until you and your friend can answer yes.

Make your essay more than a collection of grammatically correct sentences that flow from beginning to end. Make it interesting and even entertaining to read. After all, no one — not even professional test graders — wants to read a boring essay!

Note: Check out Chapter 4 for tips and ideas on mastering the Language Arts, Writing Test, Part II.

Chapter 7

Another Practice Test — Language Arts, Writing Test: Parts I and II

• •

*T*he Language Arts, Writing Test measures your ability to use clear and effective English. It is a test of English as it should be written, not as it may be spoken. This test includes both multiple-choice questions and an essay. The following directions apply only to the multiple-choice section; a separate set of directions is given for the essay.

The multiple-choice section consists of documents with lettered paragraphs and numbered sentences. Some of the sentences contain an error in sentence structure, usage, or mechanics (punctuation and capitalization). After reading the numbered sentences, answer the multiple-choice questions that follow. Some questions refer to sentences that are correct as written. The best answer for these questions is the one that leaves the sentence as originally written. The best answer for some questions is the one that produces a document that is consistent with the verb tense and point of view used throughout the text.

You have 120 minutes (two hours) to complete both parts of the test. You can spend up to 75 minutes on the 50 multiple-choice questions, leaving the remaining time for the essay. Work carefully, but do not spend too much time on any one question. Answer every question. You will not be penalized for incorrect answers. You may begin working on the essay section of this test as soon as you complete the multiple-choice section.

Answer Sheet for Language Arts, Writing Test: Part 1

1. ① ② ③ ④ ⑤ 26. ① ② ③ ④ ⑤
2. ① ② ③ ④ ⑤ 27. ① ② ③ ④ ⑤
3. ① ② ③ ④ ⑤ 28. ① ② ③ ④ ⑤
4. ① ② ③ ④ ⑤ 29. ① ② ③ ④ ⑤
5. ① ② ③ ④ ⑤ 30. ① ② ③ ④ ⑤
6. ① ② ③ ④ ⑤ 31. ① ② ③ ④ ⑤
7. ① ② ③ ④ ⑤ 32. ① ② ③ ④ ⑤
8. ① ② ③ ④ ⑤ 33. ① ② ③ ④ ⑤
9. ① ② ③ ④ ⑤ 34. ① ② ③ ④ ⑤
10. ① ② ③ ④ ⑤ 35. ① ② ③ ④ ⑤
11. ① ② ③ ④ ⑤ 36. ① ② ③ ④ ⑤
12. ① ② ③ ④ ⑤ 37. ① ② ③ ④ ⑤
13. ① ② ③ ④ ⑤ 38. ① ② ③ ④ ⑤
14. ① ② ③ ④ ⑤ 39. ① ② ③ ④ ⑤
15. ① ② ③ ④ ⑤ 40. ① ② ③ ④ ⑤
16. ① ② ③ ④ ⑤ 41. ① ② ③ ④ ⑤
17. ① ② ③ ④ ⑤ 42. ① ② ③ ④ ⑤
18. ① ② ③ ④ ⑤ 43. ① ② ③ ④ ⑤
19. ① ② ③ ④ ⑤ 44. ① ② ③ ④ ⑤
20. ① ② ③ ④ ⑤ 45. ① ② ③ ④ ⑤
21. ① ② ③ ④ ⑤ 46. ① ② ③ ④ ⑤
22. ① ② ③ ④ ⑤ 47. ① ② ③ ④ ⑤
23. ① ② ③ ④ ⑤ 48. ① ② ③ ④ ⑤
24. ① ② ③ ④ ⑤ 49. ① ② ③ ④ ⑤
25. ① ② ③ ④ ⑤ 50. ① ② ③ ④ ⑤

Language Arts, Writing Test: Part 1

Do not mark in this test booklet. Record your answers on the separate answer sheet provided. To record your answers, fill in the numbered circle on the answer sheet that corresponds to the answer you select for each question in the test booklet.

EXAMPLE:

Sentence 1: **We were all honoured to meet governor Phillips and his staff.**

Which correction should be made to sentence 1?

(1) change <u>were</u> to <u>was</u>

(2) insert a comma after <u>honoured</u>

(3) change <u>governor</u> to <u>Governor</u>

(4) insert a comma after <u>Phillips</u>

(5) no correction is necessary

(On Answer Sheet)

① ② ● ④ ⑤

In this example, the word "governor" should be capitalized; therefore, answer space 3 would be marked on the answer sheet.

Do not rest the point of your pencil on the answer sheet while you are considering your answer. Make no stray or unnecessary marks. If you change an answer, erase your first mark completely. Mark only one answer space for each question; multiple answers will be scored as incorrect. Do not fold or crease your answer sheet. All test materials must be returned to the test administrator.

Note: Refer to Chapter 8 for the answers for Parts I and II of this practice test.

DO NOT BEGIN TAKING THIS TEST UNTIL TOLD TO DO SO

> **Directions:** Choose the <u>one best answer</u> to each question.

> *Questions 1 through 10 refer to the following excerpt, which is adapted from* Customer Service
> For Dummies *by Karen Leland and Keith Bailey (Wiley).*

Fix the Problem

(1) This step requires you to listen to each customers assessment of the problem. (2) Your job when she explains the situation from her perspective is to fully absorb what she is saying about her unique set of circumstances. (3) After you identify the customer's problem, the next step, obviously, is to fix it. (4) Sometimes, you can easily remedy the situation by changing an invoice, redoing an order, waving or refunding charges, or replacing a defective product. (5) At other times, fixing the problem is more complex because the damage or mistake cannot be repaired simply. (6) In these instances, mutually exceptable compromises need to be reached.

(7) Whatever the problem, this step begins to remedy the situation and gives the customer what she needs to resolve the source of the conflict. (8) Don't waste time and effort by putting the horse before the cart and trying to fix the wrong problem. (9) Its easy to jump the gun and think that you know what the customer is about to say because you've heard it all a hundred times before. (10) Doing so loses you ground on the recovery front and farther annoys the customer. (11) More often than not, what you think the problem is at first glance, is different from what it becomes upon closer examination.

---

1. Sentence 1: **This step requires you to listen to each customers assessment of the problem.**

    Which correction should be made to sentence 1?

    (1) change <u>requires</u> to <u>required</u>

    (2) change <u>customers</u> to <u>customers'</u>

    (3) change <u>assessment</u> to <u>assessing</u>

    (4) change <u>customers</u> to <u>customer's</u>

    (5) no correction required

2. Sentence 2: **Your job when she explains the situation from her perspective is to fully absorb what she is saying about her unique set of circumstances.**

    The most effective revision of sentence 2 would begin with which group of words?

    (1) When she explains the situation from her perspective,

    (2) Your job when she explains,

    (3) What she is saying about,

    (4) Her unique set of circumstances,

    (5) no correction required

3. Sentence 4: **Sometimes, you can easily remedy the situation by changing an invoice, redoing an order, waving or refunding charges, or replacing a defective product.**

    Which correction should be made to sentence 4?

    (1) change <u>redoing</u> to <u>re-doing</u>

    (2) change <u>invoice</u> to <u>invoise</u>

    (3) change <u>waving</u> to <u>waiving</u>

    (4) change <u>defective</u> to <u>defected</u>

    (5) no correction required

4. Sentence 5: **At other times fixing the problem is more complex because the damage or mistake cannot be repaired simply.**

    Which is the best way to improve this sentence?

    (1) add a comma after <u>because</u>

    (2) add a semicolon after <u>times</u>

    (3) add a comma after <u>times</u>

    (4) add a comma after <u>mistake</u>

    (5) add a semicolon after <u>mistake</u>

Go on to next page

5. Sentence 6: **In these instances, mutually exceptable compromises need to be reached.**

   Which correction should be made to sentence 6?

   (1) remove the comma after <u>instances</u>

   (2) change <u>these</u> to <u>those</u>

   (3) change <u>need</u> to <u>needed</u>

   (4) change <u>exceptable</u> to <u>acceptable</u>

   (5) no correction required

6. Sentence 7: **Whatever the problem, this step begins to remedy the situation and gives the customer what she needs to resolve the source of the conflict.**

   Which is the best way to begin sentence 7? If the original is the best way, choose option (1).

   (1) Whatever the problem,

   (2) This step begins to remedy,

   (3) What she needs to resolve,

   (4) To resolve the source of the conflict,

   (5) To remedy the situation,

7. Sentence 8: **Don't waste time and effort by putting the horse before the cart and trying to fix the wrong problem.**

   Which change should be made to sentence 8?

   (1) change <u>waste</u> to <u>waist</u>

   (2) revise to read <u>the cart before the horse</u>

   (3) change <u>trying</u> to <u>try</u>

   (4) change <u>Don't</u> to <u>Doesn't</u>

   (5) no correction required

8. Sentence 9: **Its easy to jump the gun and think you know what the customer is about to say because you've heard it all a hundred times before.**

   What correction should be made to sentence 9?

   (1) replace <u>is</u> with <u>was</u>

   (2) change <u>heard</u> to <u>herd</u>

   (3) replace <u>you've</u> with <u>you had</u>

   (4) change <u>Its</u> to <u>It's</u>

   (5) no correction required

9. Sentence 10: **Doing so loses you ground on the recovery front and farther annoys the customer.**

   Which change should be made to sentence 10?

   (1) replace <u>loses</u> with <u>looses</u>

   (2) change <u>recovery</u> to <u>recover</u>

   (3) replace <u>farther</u> with <u>further</u>

   (4) change <u>you</u> to <u>your</u>

   (5) no correction required

10. Sentence 11: **More often than not, what you think the problem is at first glance, is different from what it becomes upon closer examination.**

    Which correction should be made to sentence 11?

    (1) remove the comma after <u>not</u>

    (2) remove the comma after <u>glance</u>

    (3) insert a comma after <u>different</u>

    (4) insert a comma after <u>from</u>

    (5) no correction required

Go on to next page

Questions 11 through 17 refer to the following business letter.

BEST Institute of Technology
75 Ingram Dr.
Toronto, ON M5H 2N2

To Whom It May Concern:

(1) I am pleased to comment on the relationship of our organization to Peta Jackson of the York Square Employment resource Centre. (2) The BEST Institute of Technology has partnered with the York Square ERC in recruiting candidates for our Café Technician and Operator training programs since April 2002.

(3) In support of the partnership, Peta provided the following services to our programs

- Set up information presentations as part of her job-readiness seminars
- Distributed print materials
- Counselled applicants
- Expedited meetings with potential candidates
- Arranged five graduating ceremonies held at York Square ERC

(4) Peta has always been a strong advocate for our program, which has trained more than 50 technicians and operators during the past 18 months. (5) The fact that York Square was our primary source of referrals are a tribute to Peta's efforts. (6) She has, with a high degree of professional competence, pursued her responsibilities. (7) On a personal level, it has been a joy to work with Peta and I wish her the very best in her future endeavours.

Dale Worth, Ph.D., Registrar

11. Sentence 1: **I am pleased to comment on the relationship of our organization to Peta Jackson of the York Square Employment resource Centre.**

Which revision should be made to sentence 1?

(1) change <u>to Peta Jackson</u> to <u>of Peta Jackson</u>
(2) change <u>pleased</u> to <u>please</u>
(3) change <u>resource</u> to <u>Resource</u>
(4) change <u>Centre</u> to <u>Center</u>
(5) no correction required

12. Sentence 2: **The BEST Institute of Technology has partnered with the York Square ERC in recruiting candidates for our Café Technician and Operator training programs since April 2002.**

Which is the best way to improve sentence 2?

(1) move <u>since April 2002</u> to the start of the sentence
(2) change <u>has partnered</u> to <u>have partnered</u>
(3) change <u>with</u> to <u>between</u>
(4) change <u>in recruiting</u> to <u>while recruiting</u>
(5) no correction required

Go on to next page

13. Sentence 3: **In support of the partnership, Peta provided the following services to our programs**

    - **Set up information presentations as part of her job-readiness seminars**
    - **Distributed print materials**
    - **Counselled applicants**
    - **Expedited meetings with potential candidates**
    - **Arranged five graduating ceremonies held at York Square ERC**

    Which correction should be made to sentence 3?

    (1) remove the comma after <u>partnership</u>

    (2) add a semicolon after <u>seminars</u>

    (3) add a semicolon after <u>materials</u>

    (4) insert a colon after <u>programs</u>

    (5) insert a comma after <u>services</u>

14. Sentence 4: **Peta <u>has always been</u> a strong advocate for our program, which has trained more than 50 technicians and operators during the past 18 months.**

    Which is the best way to write the underlined portion of this sentence? If the original is the best way, choose option (1).

    (1) has always been

    (2) always has been

    (3) has been always

    (4) have always been

    (5) always have been

15. Sentence 5: **The fact that York Square was our primary source of referrals are a tribute to Peta's efforts.**

    Which correction should be made to sentence 5?

    (1) change <u>Peta's</u> to <u>Petas'</u>

    (2) change <u>are</u> to <u>is</u>

    (3) change <u>was</u> to <u>were</u>

    (4) change <u>our</u> to <u>her</u>

    (5) no correction required

16. Sentence 6: **She has, with a high degree of professional competence and efficiency, pursued her responsibilities.**

    Which revision should be made to sentence 6?

    (1) move <u>, with a high degree of professional competence and efficiency,</u> after <u>She</u>

    (2) move <u>, with a high degree of professional competence and efficiency,</u> after <u>pursued</u>

    (3) move <u>, with a high degree of professional competence and efficiency</u> to the end of sentence after <u>responsibilities</u> and eliminate the comma

    (4) place <u>With a high degree of professional competence and efficiency,</u> at the front of the sentence before <u>She</u>

    (5) no correction required

17. Sentence 7: **On a personal level, it has been a joy to work with Peta and I wish her the very best in her future endeavours.**

    Which improvement should be made to sentence 7?

    (1) add a comma after <u>Peta</u>

    (2) change <u>endeavours</u> to <u>endeavors</u>

    (3) change <u>has been</u> to <u>have been</u>

    (4) move <u>on a personal level</u> to come after <u>Peta</u>

    (5) no correction required

Go on to next page

Questions 18 through 28 refer to the following example, which is adapted from Customer Service For Dummies *by Karen Leland and Keith Bailey (Wiley).*

The Care Token Coupon

(1) A new copy shoppe recently opened near our office. (2) Modern and full of new, streamlined, state-of-the-art copiers. (3) The store was just what I needed. (4) The first time I went over I waited 45 minutes to get served because of a shortage of trained staff. (5) They bounced back by apologizing, explaining the situation, and gave me a care token coupon that was worth 100 free copies. (6) Okay, I thought, fair enough, they're new and getting their act together, no big deal. (7) A week later, I went back and waited 30 minutes for service. (8) They apologised, explained the situation, and gave me a coupon for 100 free copies. (9) This time I was a little less understanding. (10) Two weeks later, I went back and the same thing happened again. (11) I didn't want another free coupon — they had bounced back just once too often. (12) My opinion of their services were so soured that I began looking for another copy shop.

18. Sentence 1: **A new copy shoppe recently opened near our office.**

    Which correction should be made to sentence 1?

    (1) change <u>copy</u> to <u>copie</u>

    (2) change <u>shoppe</u> to <u>shop</u>

    (3) change <u>opened</u> to <u>is opening</u>

    (4) change <u>a</u> to <u>an</u>

    (5) no correction required

19. Sentences 2 and 3: **Modern and full of new, streamlined, state-of-the-art copiers. The store was just what I needed.**

    Which improvement should be made to sentences 2 and 3?

    (1) combine the two sentences by changing <u>The</u> to <u>the</u> and replacing the period after <u>copiers</u> with <u>, and</u>

    (2) remove the hyphens from <u>state-of-the-art</u>

    (3) change <u>streamlined</u> to <u>streamlining</u>

    (4) change <u>store was</u> to <u>the copiers were</u>

    (5) no correction required

20. Sentence 4: **The first time I went over I waited 45 minutes to get served because of a shortage of trained staff.**

    Which is the best way to begin sentence 4?

    (1) Because to get served

    (2) I waited 45 minutes

    (3) To get served because

    (4) Because of a shortage

    (5) no correction required

21. Sentence 5: **They bounced back by apologizing, explaining the situation, and gave me a care token coupon that was worth 100 free copies.**

    Which correction should be made to sentence 5?

    (1) change <u>apologizing</u> to <u>apologized</u>

    (2) replace <u>explaining</u> with <u>explained</u>

    (3) change <u>gave</u> to <u>giving</u>

    (4) replace <u>was</u> with <u>were</u>

    (5) no correction required

Go on to next page

22. Sentence 6: **Okay, I thought, fair enough, they're new and getting their act together, no big deal.**

    Which revision should be made to sentence 6?

    (1) change thought to am thinking

    (2) change the one sentence into three sentences

    (3) change no to know

    (4) change getting to got

    (5) change the first they're to their

23. Sentence 7: **A week later I went back and waited 30 minutes for service.**

    Which addition should be made to sentence 7?

    (1) add a comma after later

    (2) add a comma after back

    (3) add a colon after back

    (4) add more after minutes

    (5) no correction required

24. Sentence 8: **They apologised, explained the situation, and gave me a coupon for 100 free copies.**

    Which correction is required for sentence 8?

    (1) change apologised to apologising

    (2) change explained to explaining

    (3) change apologised to apologized

    (4) change copies to copys

    (5) no correction required

25. Sentence 9: **This time I was a little less understanding.**

    Which correction should be made to sentence 9?

    (1) insert a comma after time

    (2) change was to am

    (3) change less to least

    (4) change understanding to understood

    (5) no correction required

26. Sentence 10: **Two weeks later, I went back and the same thing happened again.**

    Which is the best way to write the underlined portion of the sentence?

    (1) later, back I went,

    (2) back, later I went

    (3) later, I went back,

    (4) I, later, went back,

    (5) I went back later

27. Sentence 11: **I didn't want another free coupon — they had bounced back just once too often.**

    Which is the best way to revise sentence 11?

    (1) remove once

    (2) insert a period after coupon

    (3) change had to have

    (4) change another to no

    (5) no correction required

28. Sentence 12: **My opinion of their services were so soured that I began looking for another copy shop.**

    Which correction should be made to sentence 12?

    (1) change began to begun

    (2) insert a comma after soured

    (3) replace my with our

    (4) change were to was

    (5) no correction required

Go on to next page

> *Questions 29 through 41 refer to the following executive summary.*

Executive Summary
KWIK Stop Auto Centre

The correct approach for the 21st century

(1) Back in 1978, Morris James, President and Founder of KWIK Stop Auto Centre, foresaw changes necessary for the automotive-service industry. (2) The market was becoming much more sophisticated. (3) Combined with 5 years' experience as a licensed mechanic and owner/operator of a repair facility, this knowledge, led to the opening of KWIK Stop Auto Centre's first location.

(4) Morris James analyzed the "fast food" concept of providing high quality merchandize at affordable prices. (5) This concept combined with speedy service helped the industry grow every year. (6) Morris decided that the same principals should be applied to the automotive industry, and he started KWIK Stop as the first logical step.

(7) In 1987, Morris was relocated to Woodbridge and began searching for a new shop site to begin franchising. (8) The opening of a concord franchise became very profitable and proved Morris's theory to be correct. (9) He then opened the corporate store having established the validity of the concept in Etobicoke, in 1991.

(10) Now the challenge is to develop the corporate store in a way that it can not only function in its capacity as a profit centre but also be used as a hands-on training centre for future franchise owners.

(11) The start up costs will require some initial investment, but will be gained within the first three years. (12) We will look at this situation more in-depth within the plan. (13) The addition of a wide selection of accessories, for the customer, will broaden the impact of this new concept.

29. Sentence 1: **Back in 1978, Morris James, President and Founder of KWIK Stop Auto Centre, foresaw changes necessary for the automotive-service industry.**

    Which change should be made to sentence 1?

    (1) change <u>foresaw</u> to <u>forseen</u>

    (2) remove the comma after <u>1978</u>

    (3) remove the comma after <u>Centre</u> and add one after <u>changes</u>

    (4) move <u>necessary</u> to between <u>foresaw</u> and <u>changes</u>

    (5) no correction required

30. Sentence 2: **The market <u>was becoming</u> much more sophisticated.**

    Which is the best way to write the underlined portion of this sentence? If the original is the best way, choose option (1).

    (1) was becoming

    (2) will becoming

    (3) were becoming

    (4) is becoming

    (5) would becoming

Go on to next page ⟹

31. Sentence 3: **Combined with 5 years' experience as a licensed mechanic and owner/ operator of a repair facility, this knowledge, led to the opening of KWIK Stop Auto Centre's first location.**

    Which improvement should be made to sentence 3?

    (1) change years' to year's

    (2) remove the comma after knowledge

    (3) change licensed to licenced

    (4) move This knowledge, to the beginning of the sentence

    (5) change Centre's to Centres

32. Sentence 4: **Morris James analyzed the "fast food" concept of providing high quality merchandize at affordable prices.**

    What correction should be made to sentence 4?

    (1) change analyzed to analysed

    (2) change merchandize to merchandise

    (3) change concept to consept

    (4) delete of

    (5) no correction required

33. Sentence 5: **This concept combined with speedy service helped the industry grow every year.**

    Which change should be made to sentence 5?

    (1) add commas after concept and service

    (2) change helped to has helped

    (3) change grow to growing

    (4) change service to servicing

    (5) no correction required

34. Sentence 6: **Morris decided that the same principals should be applied to the automotive industry, and he started KWIK Stop as the first logical step.**

    Which correction should be made to sentence 6?

    (1) change principals to principles

    (2) change decided to had decided

    (3) change should be to shouldn't be

    (4) change industry to industries

    (5) no correction required

35. Sentence 7: **In 1987, Morris was relocated to Woodbridge and began searching for a new shop site to begin franchising.**

    Which is the best way to write the underlined portion of this sentence? If the original is the best way, choose option (1).

    (1) was relocated

    (2) is located

    (3) has located

    (4) relocated

    (5) will locate

36. Sentence 8: **The opening of a concord franchise became very profitable and proved Morris's theory to be correct.**

    Which revision should be made to sentence 8?

    (1) change concord to Concord

    (2) change franchise to franchize

    (3) change Morris's to Morris'

    (4) change profitable to profiting

    (5) no correction required

37. Sentence 9: **He then opened the corporate store having established the validity of the concept in Etobicoke, in 1991.**

    Which is the best way to begin this sentence? If the original is the best way, choose option (1).

    (1) He then opened the corporate store

    (2) Having established the validity of the concept

    (3) In Etobicoke, in 1991, he then opened

    (4) In 1991, he then opened

    (5) The validity of the concept having established

Go on to next page

38. Sentence 10: **Now the challenge is to develop the corporate store in a way that it can not only function in its capacity as a profit centre, but can also be used as a hands-on training centre for future franchise owners.**

    Which is the best way to improve sentence 10?

    (1) insert <u>, as a profit centre,</u> between <u>store</u> and <u>in</u>

    (2) change <u>can not only</u> to <u>only can not</u>

    (3) place a comma after <u>capacity</u>

    (4) change <u>challenge is</u> to <u>challenges are</u>

    (5) no correction required

39. Sentence 11: **The start up costs will require some initial investment but will be regained within the first three years.**

    Which correction should be made to sentence 11?

    (1) change <u>some</u> to <u>any</u>

    (2) change <u>start up</u> to <u>start-up</u>

    (3) add a comma after <u>investment</u>

    (4) change <u>within</u> to <u>between</u>

    (5) no correction required

40. Sentence 12: **We will look at this <u>situation more in-depth</u> within the plan.**

    Which is the best way to improve the underlined portion of this sentence? If the original is the best way, choose option (1).

    (1) situation more in-depth

    (2) more situation in-depth

    (3) situation in more depth

    (4) more in-depth situation

    (5) in-depth more situation

41. Sentence 13: **The addition of a wide selection of accessories, for the customer, will broaden the impact of this new concept.**

    Which revision should be made to sentence 13?

    (1) move <u>for the customer</u> to the end of the sentence and eliminate the commas

    (2) change <u>will broaden</u> to <u>broaden</u>

    (3) begin the sentence with <u>The impact of this new concept</u>

    (4) begin the sentence with <u>The customer will broaden</u>

    (5) change the commas after <u>accessories</u> and <u>customer</u> to semicolons

Go on to next page ⟶

> Questions 42 through 50 refer to the following passage, which is adapted from Customer Service For Dummies *by Karen Leland and Keith Bailey (Wiley).*

The Customer Chain

(1) The relationship among internal customers and external customers is what forms the customer chain. (2) If you have a backroom kind of job where you see the light of day, rarely, you can easily begin to feel that your work has little or no impact on external customers. (3) But if you look at the bigger picture, you can see that everyone in a company plays some part in fulfilling the customers needs. (4) Barely an hour goes by during the day when you are not, in some form or another, providing somebody for something. (5) Each interaction with an internal customer is an important link in a chain of events that always end up at the external customers' feet.

(6) About two years ago, the *Financial Post* ran an article entitled, Poorly treated employees treat the customer just as poorly. (7) We had dealt with a frightening percentage of managers who do not realize that their staffs are their internal customers. (8) That the quality of service that a company provides to its customers — we are convinced — is a direct reflection of how the staff of the company are treated by their managers. (9) View your staff members as some of your most important customers and treat them accordingly.

42. Sentence 1: **The relationship among internal customers and external customers is what forms the customer chain.**

Which correction should be made to sentence 1?

(1) replace <u>among</u> with <u>between</u>

(2) change <u>relationship</u> to <u>relations</u>

(3) replace <u>is what</u> with <u>was what</u>

(4) change <u>customer</u> to <u>customers'</u>

(5) no correction required

43. Sentence 2: **If you have a backroom kind of job,** <u>where you see the light of day, rarely,</u> **you can easily begin to feel that your work has little or no impact on external customers.**

Which is the best way to write the underlined portion of this sentence? If the original is the best way, choose option (1).

(1) where you see the light of day, rarely

(2) where the light of day you see rarely

(3) where you rarely see the light of day

(4) where you see rarely the light of day

(5) where rarely you see the light of day

44. Sentence 3: **But if you look at the bigger picture, you can see that everyone in a company plays some part in fulfilling the customers needs.**

Which correction should be made to sentence 3?

(1) replace <u>customers</u> with <u>customers'</u>

(2) change <u>bigger</u> to <u>biggest</u>

(3) replace <u>everyone</u> with <u>everybody</u>

(4) change <u>fulfilling</u> to <u>fulfiling</u>

(5) no correction required

45. Sentence 4: **Barely an hour goes by during the day when you are not, in some form or another, providing somebody for something.**

Which revision should be made to sentence 4?

(1) replace <u>barely</u> with <u>about</u>

(2) change <u>somebody for something</u> to <u>something for somebody</u>

(3) replace <u>during</u> with <u>over</u>

(4) change <u>providing</u> to <u>provided</u>

(5) no correction required

Go on to next page

46. Sentence 5: **Each interaction with an internal customer is an important link in a chain of events that always end up at the external customer's feet.**

    Which correction should be made to sentence 5?

    (1) replace <u>customer's</u> with <u>customers</u>

    (2) change <u>is</u> to <u>are</u>

    (3) change <u>with</u> to <u>between</u>

    (4) change <u>end</u> to <u>ends</u>

    (5) no correction required

47. Sentence 6: **About two years ago, the *Financial Post* ran an article entitled, Poorly treated employees treat the customer just as poorly.**

    Which addition should be made to sentence 6?

    (1) place quotation marks before <u>Poorly</u> and after <u>poorly</u>

    (2) remove the comma after <u>ago</u>

    (3) remove the comma after <u>entitled</u>

    (4) remove italics from <u>Financial Post</u>

    (5) no correction required

48. Sentence 7: **We had dealt with a frightening percentage of managers who do not realize that their staffs are their internal customers.**

    Which correction should be made to sentence 7?

    (1) replace <u>frightening</u> with <u>frightened</u>

    (2) change <u>staffs</u> to <u>staff</u>

    (3) change <u>had dealt</u> to <u>have dealt</u>

    (4) place an apostrophe after <u>managers</u>

    (5) no correction required

49. Sentence 8: **That the quality of service that a company provides to its customers — we are convinced — is a direct reflection of how the staff of the company are treated by their managers.**

    Which is the best way to begin sentence 8? If the original is best, choose option (1).

    (1) That the quality of service

    (2) We are convinced

    (3) How the staff of the company

    (4) That a company provides

    (5) A direct reflection of how

50. Sentence 9: **View your staff members as some of your most important customers and <u>treat them accordingly</u>.**

    Which is the best way to revise the underlined portion of the sentence?

    (1) accordingly treat them

    (2) treat accordingly them

    (3) them treat accordingly

    (4) remove <u>them</u>

    (5) no correction required

Go on to next page

Language Arts, Writing Test: Part II

Look at the box on the following page. In the box, you find your assigned topic and the letter of that topic.

You must write on the assigned topic **ONLY.**

Mark the letter of your assigned topic in the appropriate space on your answer sheet booklet.

You have 45 minutes to write on your assigned essay topic. If you have time remaining in this test period after you complete your essay, you may return to the multiple-choice section. Do not return the Language Arts, Writing Test booklet until you finish both Parts I and II of the Language Arts, Writing Test.

Two evaluators will score your essay according to its overall effectiveness. Their evaluation will be based on the following features:

✔ Well-focused main points

✔ Clear organization

✔ Specific development of your ideas

✔ Control of sentence structure, punctuation, grammar, word choice, and spelling

REMEMBER, YOU MUST COMPLETE BOTH THE MULTIPLE-CHOICE QUESTIONS (PART I) AND THE ESSAY (PART II) TO RECEIVE A SCORE ON THE LANGUAGE ARTS, WRITING TEST.

To avoid having to repeat both parts of the test, be sure to observe the following rules:

✔ Before you begin writing, jot notes or outline your essay on the sheets provided.

✔ For your final copy, write legibly in ink so that the evaluators can read your writing.

✔ Write on the assigned topic. If you write on a topic other than the one assigned, you will not receive a score for the Language Arts, Writing Test.

✔ Write your essay on the lined pages of the separate answer sheet booklet. Only the writing on these pages will be scored.

Note that if you do not pass one portion of the test, you must take both parts over again.

DO NOT BEGIN TAKING THIS TEST UNTIL TOLD TO DO SO

Topic B

Cellphones have certainly made a difference in our lives. You may own and use one or have put up with other people who use them while driving or at the movies. Cellphones have made our lives better, more difficult, or both.

Write an essay explaining the positive or negative effects — or both — of this innovation in communication. Use examples to support your point of view and be as specific as possible.

Part II is a test to determine how well you can use written language to explain your ideas.

In preparing for your essay, you should take the following steps:

- ✔ Read the DIRECTIONS and the TOPIC carefully.
- ✔ Plan your essay before you write. Use the scratch paper provided to make any notes. These notes will be collected but not scored.
- ✔ Before you turn in your essay, reread what you have written and make any changes that will improve your essay.

Your essay should be long enough to develop the topic adequately.

Note: Refer to Chapter 8 for the answers for Parts I and II of this practice test.

END OF TEST

Answer Sheet for Language Arts, Writing Test: Part II

Use a No. 2 pencil to write the letter of your essay topic in the box, then fill in the corresponding circle.

TOPIC ☐ ⒶⒷⒸⒹⒺⒻⒼⒽⒾⒿⓀⓁⓂⓃⓄⓅⓆⓇⓈⓉⓊⓋⓌⓍⓎⓏ

Chapter 8

Answers and Explanations for the Language Arts, Writing Test

. . . .

Answer Key for Part 1

After taking the Language Arts, Writing Test, Part I, in Chapter 7, use this section to check your answers.

1. **4**	18. **2**	35. **4**
2. **1**	19. **1**	36. **1**
3. **3**	20. **5**	37. **2**
4. **3**	21. **3**	38. **5**
5. **4**	22. **2**	39. **2**
6. **1**	23. **1**	40. **3**
7. **2**	24. **3**	41. **1**
8. **4**	25. **1**	42. **1**
9. **3**	26. **3**	43. **3**
10. **2**	27. **5**	44. **1**
11. **3**	28. **4**	45. **2**
12. **1**	29. **4**	46. **4**
13. **4**	30. **1**	47. **1**
14. **1**	31. **4**	48. **3**
15. **2**	32. **2**	49. **2**
16. **3**	33. **1**	50. **5**
17. **1**	34. **1**	

Analysis of the Answers for Part 1

If you aren't sure why an answer was incorrect, use this section to get quick explanations of the answers. If you correctly answered a question, you may still want to read the explanations to get a better understanding of the thought process that helped you choose the correct answer.

1. **4.** The *assessment* belongs to each customer and requires a possessive form of customer: *customer's*. The other answers neither correct nor improve the sentence.

2. **1.** The meaning of this sentence is that the clerk should listen to the customer, so put the most important information first. The best way to start this sentence is with the *When she explains the situation from her perspective* phrase.

3. **3.** *Waving* means to motion with the hand, while *waive* means to dismiss. It may be interesting to wave at a charge, but the proper meaning of the sentence is to dismiss (or not collect) the charge. These two words are *homonyms* (words that sound the same but have different spellings and meanings). You are expected to understand most homonyms for this test.

4. **3.** The only place you can use a comma in this sentence is after the introductory phrase *At other times*.

5. **4.** *Exceptable* may sound like a word, but it's not. The correct word to use is *acceptable*.

The more reading you do as you prepare for the test, the better your chances are for recognizing misspellings.

6. **1.** A gift for you: No correction is required.

If you chose Choice (5), keep in mind that this sentence has one subject and two verbs. These types of sentences don't require a comma between the two verbs. Not sure about subjects and verbs? Here, the subject is *step* and the two verbs are *begins* and *gives*. If the sentence had a second subject before the second verb, it would need a comma.

7. **2.** If you've ever seen an old Western movie, you know that the horse comes before the cart. Or you may have heard the expression, "Don't put the cart before the horse." In either case, the proper correction is to reverse the order of *horse* and *cart*.

8. **4.** *Its* is possessive (meaning that it shows that something belongs to *it*), while *it's* stands for "it is." Here, the sentence clearly means "it is."

Confusing these two words is a common error that's usually tested in some way. Master the difference between *its* and *it's*. *It's* means "it is" and is often confused with the possessive form of other words that use the apostrophe.

9. **3.** *Farther* always refers to distance. *Further* is a matter of degree. Here, you want degree, not distance.

If you didn't know the answer, this question is a good example of one that you can answer by intelligent guessing. Choice (1) isn't correct because *looses* isn't a word. Choice (2) doesn't make sense in the context of the sentence. Choice (4) isn't right because the person losing ground is you, and because you don't own the ground, you don't want to use a possessive. Now you just have to guess between Choices (3) and (5).

10. **2.** Commas used in moderation help sentences. Extra commas hurt sentences. A comma is never used to separate a subject from a verb.

11. **3.** In the letter, the *York Square Employment Resource Centre* is a title; as such, all words (except prepositions and articles) are capitalized.

12. **1.** Moving *since April 2002* is the only good answer here. The current sentence sounds as though the training programs have been in existence since April 2002 when, in fact, the partnership has been in existence since that time.

13. **4.** Most (although not all) lists begin with a colon. You don't need semicolons after the items in the list (the bullets serve as separators). You need a comma after the introductory phrase, which eliminates Choice (1), and you don't separate a direct object from an indirect object with a comma, which eliminates Choice (5).

14. **1.** No correction is required.

15. **2.** The subject of the sentence is *fact,* which is singular, but the verb is *are,* which is plural. Verbs must agree with their subjects.

16. **3.** In its current form, this sentence forces the reader to pause too long and remember too much. Rewriting it as "She has pursued her responsibilities with a high degree of professional competence and efficiency" is far more straightforward.

17. **1.** As is, this is a run-on sentence. To make it a compound sentence, just add a comma after <u>Peta</u>.

18. **2.** The word *shoppe* is quaint, but it isn't common usage. If you were living in Upper Canada 200 years ago, the answer would be different. Today, people use the shorter and more common *shop.*

19. **1.** Before the change, the first sentence is missing a verb, making it an incomplete sentence. Choice (2) is incorrect because *state-of-the-art* is acting as a single adjective to *copiers,* and multiword adjectives are nearly always hyphenated. Choice (4) is incorrect because the first sentence is clearly describing the store, not the copiers.

20. **5.** No change is required in this sentence. The copy shop may want to consider changing the way it hires and trains its staff, but that's another matter altogether.

21. **3.** Lists have to be parallel. In this case, you have *apologizing, explaining,* and *gave,* which aren't parallel (all three are verbs, but the first two are gerunds, while the second is an infinitive). Changing *gave* to *giving* makes the list parallel.

22. **2.** This is a classic run-on sentence, so you need to break it apart into separate sentences (in this case, three). A good change is as follows: "Okay, I thought, fair enough. They're new and getting their act together. No big deal." (Note that the third sentence doesn't appear to have a verb, but the implied subject and verb are *it is,* as in "It is no big deal.")

23. **1.** The correct answer is to add a comma after *later.* Most of the time, you want to set off an introductory clause with a comma; however, be aware that when the introductory clause is very short, the convention isn't always clear: Some people use the comma and others don't. On this test, however, you're always better off putting a comma after any introductory clause.

24. **3.** Change *apologised* to *apologized,* which is the correct spelling. The other answer choices do nothing to improve the sentence.

25. **1.** Add a comma after the introductory phrase. See the answer explanation to Question 23 for further details.

26. **3.** Whenever a sentence has two clauses, each with a subject and a verb, a comma has to separate them. In this sentence, *I went back* is a clause that has both a subject *(I)* and a verb *(went).* The clause *and the same thing happened again* also has a subject *(thing)* and a verb *(happened). Two weeks later* is an introductory phrase that requires a comma after *later.*

27. **5.** This answer is a gift. The sentence is correct as is.

A point of interest with this sentence is that it uses one of the dreaded *two/to/too* words. These words are all *homonyms:* words that sound the same but have different spellings and meanings. Here, the use of *too* is correct, but be sure you put these three words on your list of homonyms to study.

28. **4.** *My opinion* is a singular subject that needs a singular verb. *Were* is a plural verb and must be changed to the singular form *was.* Don't let that prepositional phrase *of their services* throw you off track. Just act as if that part of the sentence weren't there.

If you have trouble with singular and plural verbs and subject-verb agreement, try changing the subject into a pronoun. This sentence would become *It were* which sounds wrong. Changing it to *It was* sounds right. Trust your ears.

One exception to the "it sounds right" rule is the *subjunctive form* of verbs. Whenever something is contrary to fact, you use *were* with singular subjects. For example, "If I were taller" is correct. Look for terms and phrases like *if, I wish,* and *if only:* These words are usually followed by the subjunctive form of the verb.

29. **4.** This question is a good example of when using elimination can help you get the right answer. Choice (1) introduces the wrong verb tense. Choice (2) introduces a punctuation error because the comma is needed. Choice (3) introduces another punctuation error: This comma is also needed. When you plug in Choice (4), the sentence reads more smoothly, so you know you have a winner.

30. **1.** Choice (1) is the only option of all the ones presented that uses correct verb form and meaning. Choices (2), (3), and (5) all introduce errors in verb form; Choice (4) changes the sentence to present tense, which then changes its meaning.

31. **4.** The words *this knowledge* are out of place, but they're necessary to the sentence because they add to its meaning. You can improve the sentence by moving *This knowledge* to the front of the sentence and changing *Combined* to *combined*. Another way to change the sentence is to simply remove the comma after *knowledge* (because subjects and their verbs are never separated by commas), but that option isn't an answer choice.

32. **2.** This sentence contains a spelling mistake. Change *merchandize* to *merchandise*.

33. **1.** This sentence is badly in need of a comma transfusion. It should read, "This concept, combined with speedy service, helped the industry grow every year." These two little commas help the sentence by separating the phrase *combined with speedy service* from the rest of the sentence.

34. **1.** This sentence is fairly long and seems to ramble, but none of the options offers a way to split it into two. However, the sentence does have an error: Schools have *principals;* people and businesses (you hope!) have *principles*. These two words are *homonyms,* meaning that they sound alike but have different meanings and spellings.

35. **4.** You should change the underlined phrase to *relocated*. The other answer choices introduce new errors.

36. **1.** From the context of the passage, you can assume Concord is a town or city and deserves a capital letter at the beginning of the word.

37. **2.** The sentence is supposed to say that he (Morris James) had established the validity of the concept before (in 1991) and then (later) he wanted to establish a corporate store. Rewriting the sentence like this is clearer: "Having established the validity of the concept in Etobicoke in 1991, he then opened the corporate store." The other answer choices don't maintain this meaning.

Choice (4) may look good, but it changes the meaning of the sentence. He didn't open the corporate store in 1991; he established the validity of the concept in 1991.

38. **5.** Okay, this sentence is really long, but, technically, nothing is wrong with it. If you had the option of splitting it into two sentences, you'd want to do so. But because you're not given that option and all the other options are incorrect, leave it as is.

39. **2.** Here, *start up* is acting as an adjective for *costs*. Most multiword adjectives are hyphenated.

If you chose Choice (3), you must've thought that the second half of the sentence had a second subject in it. If so, reread that part of the sentence to try to find the subject. It's not there. This is a sentence with one subject *(cost)* and two verbs *(will require* and *will be regained)*. A sentence like this one, with only one subject and two verbs, doesn't require a comma. If it had a second subject before the second verb, it would need a comma.

40. **3.** Changing the phrase to *in more depth* improves the sentence structure. The other options don't make much sense when you plug them into the sentence.

41. **1.** Moving *on the customer* to the end of the sentence improves the sentence organization by placing the direct object *(the impact)* closer to the second indirect object *(the customer)*. (What's the first indirect object? *This new concept.*)

    If you chose Choice (5), you essentially said that the customer would have a wide selection of accessories added to him or her.

42. **1.** *Among* is used when comparing three or more entities; *between* is used to compare only two things. Here, you have two types of customers, so *between* is correct.

43. **3.** *Where you rarely see the light of day* is an improved word order because you want the adverb (in this case, *rarely*) to be as close as possible to the verb it modifies (in this case, *see*).

44. **1.** The needs belong to the customers, so you must make *customers* possessive by making it *customers'*.

45. **2.** *Providing somebody for something* doesn't make sense. You don't provide people for things; rather, you provide things for people.

46. **4.** Examine the phrase *that always end up*. What's the phrase referring to? *Important link*, right? Yes, but *link* is singular, so you don't say, *link . . . end*. Instead, you say *link . . . ends*.

47. **1.** "Poorly treated employees treat the customer just as poorly" is the title of a newspaper article and must be in quotation marks. Names of newspapers are in italics, while the stories that are in them are placed in quotes.

    The idea of the entire work (the newspaper) being in italics, while the inner works (the articles) are in quotes extends to other situations, as well. For example, a book title is in italics, while the name of each chapter is in quotes. A TV series is in italics, while the name of each episode is in quotes.

48. **3.** This sentence has two related problems. First, the past tense of *deal* is *dealt*, not *dealed*. Second, according to the context, you know that this action began in the past and continues in the present. You can indicate that timeline by using *have*. On the other hand, using *had* means that the action began in the past and also stopped in the past — in other words, that it isn't continuing today.

49. **2.** Putting *we are convinced* in the middle of the sentence interrupts the main point — to show a specific cause-and-effect relationship.

50. **5.** A final gift for you — no correction is needed, and all the other choices make the sentence worse.

Sample Essay for Part II

The topic for the practice test in Chapter 7 is as follows:

> Cellphones have certainly made a difference in our lives. You may own and use one or have put up with other people who use them while driving or at the movies. Cellphones have made our lives better, more difficult, or both.

> Write an essay explaining the positive or negative effects — or both — of this innovation in communication. Use examples to support your point of view and be as specific as possible.

As the test graders read and evaluate your essay, they look for the following:

- ✔ Well-focused main points
- ✔ Evidence of clear organization
- ✔ Specific development of your ideas
- ✔ Proper sentence structure
- ✔ Correct grammar
- ✔ Necessary punctuation
- ✔ Appropriate word choice
- ✔ Correct spelling

Although every essay will be unique, we provide a sample here to give you a better idea of what the test graders expect to see in your essay. Compare the structure of this essay to yours.

Cellphones make life easier

My children and I recently signed up for a family-rate calling plan——complete with four separate phones and phone numbers——so that we could communicate more easily. Although I put off the purchase for several years, thinking that having a cellphone would make me so accessible to others that I would never get any time to myself, the truth is, the phones have made all of our lives easier.

My three children attend three different schools. The youngest, Doug, is in the 4th grade and takes a free acting class year-round at the local playhouse. His lessons run from 4:00 to 5:00 three days per week, but he can sometimes catch rides home with other children in the class. Because I work until 5:30, my oldest daughter, Sydney, who is a junior in high school, waits for him to call to tell her whether he needs a ride. Before we had cellphones, Doug always had to find a working pay phone, and Sydney had to wait by the phone at home.

The middle child, Maggie, is in eighth grade and plays three sports: soccer, basketball, and track. I can usually pick her up from practice on my way home from work, but her practices end at different times every day. While she, too, used to have to hunt down a pay phone and call me at work, now she just calls and lets me know where she'll be waiting. I can run errands while I wait for her call instead of waiting at work or by the curb at her school.

The best part of the phones, though, is that whenever people want to reach any of the four of us, they call the number for the individual, not the entire family. I no longer answer the phone for all of Doug's, Maggie's, and Sydney's friends, and people trying to reach me no longer get a busy signal.

For us, cellphones are the ultimate convenience. In fact, we like our cellphones so much that we no longer have regular phone service in our home.

Note: To evaluate this sample essay, as well as your own, turn to Chapter 6 for a list of questions to ask yourself about both essays. For tips and ideas on mastering the Language Arts, Writing Test, Part II, check out Chapter 4.

Part III
Finding Your Way: The Social Studies Test

The 5th Wave   By Rich Tennant

In this part . . .

*I*n this part, you find questions, questions, and more questions about social studies in the form of sample test questions — but, lucky for you, you also get the answers and explanations that go along with them. In addition, this part explains what skills the Social Studies Test tests you on, what subject areas the test covers, and how the test is laid out so you get a better idea of what you need to do to get good marks on the test. It also offers you some helpful strategies you can use to do your best on the test.

Before taking the actual Social Studies Test, take the two practice tests in this part to determine how well you've mastered the required skills in social studies. Pretend they're real tests by timing yourself, following the instructions, and asking someone to act as the test administrator to keep you honest (if you can find someone willing to help). The closer you come to mimicking the real test conditions, the more you get out of practicing here and in all the other tests.

Chapter 9

A Graph, a Map, and You: The Social Studies Test

- -

In This Chapter

▶ Figuring out what the Social Studies Test covers and how it's formatted

▶ Surveying the types of questions on this test and knowing how to prepare for them

▶ Using the strategies that achieve the best results

▶ Managing your time and looking at sample problems

- -

Do you enjoy knowing about how events in the past may help you foretell the future? Do the lives of people in faraway places interest you? Do you care about politics? If you answered yes to any of these questions, you're going to like social studies! After all, social studies helps you discover how humans relate to their environment and to other people.

The GED Social Studies Test assesses your skills in understanding and interpreting concepts and principles in history, geography, economics, and civics. Consider this test as a crash course in where you've been, where you are, and how you can continue living there. You can apply the skills covered in the Social Studies Test to your experience in visual, academic, and workplace situations as a citizen, a consumer, or an employee. This test includes questions drawn from a variety of written and visual passages taken from academic and workplace materials, as well as from primary and secondary sources. The passages in this test are like the ones you read in daily newspapers and news magazines. Reading these news sources regularly can help you become familiar with the style and vocabulary of the passages you find here.

This chapter helps you prepare for the Social Studies Test.

Looking at the Skills the Social Studies Test Covers

The GED Social Studies Test requires you to draw on your previous knowledge of events, ideas, terms, and situations that may be related to social studies. From a big-picture perspective, the Social Studies Test and the skills it covers break down like this:

✔ **20 percent:** Relates to your ability to identify information and ideas and interpret their meaning.

✔ **20 percent:** Assesses your ability to use information and ideas in different ways to explore their meanings or solve a problem.

✔ **40 percent:** Measures your ability to use information or ideas to do the following:

- Determine the difference between facts and opinions.

- Arrive at conclusions using material.

- Influence other people's attitudes.

- Find other meanings or mistakes in logic.

- Identify causes and their effects.

- Recognize a writer's historical point of view.

- Compare and contrast differing views and opinions.

- Determine what impact these views and opinions may have both now and in the future.

✔ **20 percent:** Measures your ability to make judgments about the material's appropriateness, accuracy, and differences of opinion, as well as the role information and ideas play in influencing current and future decision making. These questions ask you to think about issues and events that affect you every day, making you a more informed citizen of the modern world. What a bonus for a test!

Being aware of what skills the Social Studies Test covers can help you get a more accurate picture of the types of questions you'll encounter. The next section focuses more on the specific subject materials in this test.

Understanding the Test Format

The Social Studies Test contains 50 multiple-choice questions that you must answer in 70 minutes, which means you have less than one and a half minutes per question. These 50 questions check your knowledge in the following subject areas:

✔ **Canadian history (25 percent; 12 or 13 questions):** You may read passages about Canada's First Nations, New France, the Seven Years' War, United Empire Loyalists, the War of 1812, the British North America Act, settlement, industrial development, or the Canadian Charter of Rights and Freedoms — and answer questions about them, of course. If you didn't have to answer questions, reading these passages would be a dream assignment, because Canadian history can be a lot of fun.

To practise for this section of the test, read articles and books about historical events and trends. Remember that 60 percent of these questions are based on visual passages, including illustrations, maps, and charts, so look at those, too. With practice, you can learn to read visual elements as well as you read text.

✔ **World history (15 percent; 7 or 8 questions):** The types of questions and sources of information in the world history questions are identical to those in the Canadian history section, except that they deal with history from around the world and go back much further than Canadian history does.

✔ **Civics and government (25 percent; 12 or 13 questions):** These passages are all about civic life, government, politics (especially the Canadian political system), Canada's relationships with other countries, and Canada's role in the world. Your job is to read and understand the passages and questions about those passages. You can find a lot of material about civics and government in newspapers and news magazines. If you don't have these publications at home, visit your public library (or go to your doctor's waiting room). Try to get a sense of what's going on by pretending you want to explain the issue to a friend. (Don't explain *all* the current issues to your friends, though, because you'll probably run out of friends before you run out of issues.)

- ✔ **Economics (20 percent; 10 questions):** Economics is the study of how the earth's resources are used to create wealth, which is then distributed and used to satisfy the needs of humankind. It involves banking and finance in both small businesses and large corporations. It includes workers and owners who import and export manufactured goods, natural resources, and services. You can find articles about economics on the Internet and in newspapers, magazines, textbooks, and software programs.

- ✔ **Geography (15 percent; 7 or 8 questions):** Geography passages usually read like a list of places you want to go. Geography deals with the world and what's going on in it, including the impact of weather and environmental conditions and the political divisions of land and its use by living creatures. For geography questions, you often have to read maps and answer questions about them. Although reading maps is a different kind of reading, with a little practice, it can be a fun and wonderful excuse for daydreaming about where you'd like to go on your next vacation.

  To help you prepare for the geography questions, you can read several good geographic magazines with fascinating articles and beautiful photographs. Plus, you can find Web sites and library books about every place on earth. The important thing is to read, read, and read some more to become comfortable with the language of geography.

The passages in the Social Studies Test are taken from the following two types of sources:

- ✔ **Academic material:** You find this material in a school — textbooks, maps, newspapers, magazines, software, and online material.

- ✔ **Workplace material:** You find this material on the job — manuals, documents, business plans, advertising and marketing materials, correspondence, and so on.

The material may be from primary or secondary sources, which means the following:

- ✔ **Primary sources:** The original documents, such as the British North American Act

- ✔ **Secondary sources:** Material written about an event or person, sometimes long after the event takes place or the person dies

Identifying the Types of Questions and Knowing How to Prepare for Them

The Social Studies Test contains two main types of questions. Having a basic understanding of these two types can help you prepare and avoid any surprises when you take the test.

As you read the passages in this test and get ready to answer the questions about them, you're expected to use the following skills:

- ✔ Comprehension

- ✔ Application

- ✔ Analysis

- ✔ Evaluation

Most adults regularly use these higher-level thinking skills. To better understand these skills, consider the following three examples:

- ✔ When you buy something new, you likely have to read the users' manual that came with it to figure out how to use what you bought. As you read the manual and follow its instructions, you use *comprehension* and *application skills*. You first have to understand what the manual says and then use that information to make the thing you bought work. Without comprehension and application skills, the clock on your DVD player might blink *12:00* forever.

✔ If you were in the checkout line of your favourite grocery store and saw a magazine that said the prime minister was born on Mars, you probably wouldn't run to your friends screaming about this amazing development. Instead, you'd likely first want to decide whether this new "fact" could possibly be true by doing some further research and clarifying your thinking. When you read or hear something and you take time to think about it before using the information in a discussion, you use *evaluation* and *application* skills.

✔ If someone said to you, "Canada is a dictatorship with the occasional outbreaks of democracy," you'd need to use the skill of *analysis* to either agree or disagree with that statement. Do the "occasional outbreaks of democracy" refer to the elections? In this case, what happens between elections? Can the prime minister make decisions without consulting the public or the elected representatives? Can an elected representative vote however he or she wants without considering the needs of his or her constituents? You get answers to these questions when you analyze the initial statement.

The following sections explain the two types of questions you encounter on this test and offer you advice on how to prepare so that you can solve them with ease on test day.

Questions about text passages

The first type of question you have to answer on the Social Studies Test is based on text passages. You read a textual excerpt or passage and then answer questions about it.

The best way to prepare for these types of questions is to read, read, read. In particular, these questions require you to read excerpts from documents such as the following:

✔ British North America Act

✔ Constitution Act

✔ War Measures Act

✔ Landmark Supreme Court cases

✔ Consumer information guides

✔ Voters' guides

✔ Atlases

✔ Tax forms

✔ Budget graphs

✔ Political speeches

✔ Almanacs

✔ Statistical abstracts

The more you read these types of documents, the more you think about what you read; and the more you think about what you read, the better prepared you are for the text-based questions on this test. You can find examples of each of these possible sources in libraries and on the Internet.

When you're preparing for the test and when you're reading these passages on the actual test, read between the lines and look at the implications and assumptions in the passages. An *implication* is something you can understand from what's written even though it isn't directly stated. An *assumption* is something you can accept as the truth even though proof isn't presented in the text.

When you take the test, read each question carefully so you know exactly what it's asking. If you're being asked for facts, they're presented to you in the passage. If you're asked for opinions, they may be either stated or implied in the passage (and they may disagree with your own opinions — but you still have to answer with the best choice based on the material presented). Keep in mind that you usually find opinions in textual passages, political cartoons, and works of art.

If a question doesn't specifically tell you to use additional information that isn't presented in the passage, use _only_ the information presented. An answer may be incorrect in your opinion, but according to the information presented, it's correct (or vice versa). Go with the information presented unless a question tells you to do otherwise.

Questions about visual materials

To make sure you don't get bored taking this test, only 40 percent of the questions are based on textual material. Another 40 percent are based on maps, graphs, tables, political cartoons, diagrams, photographs, and artistic works. The remaining 20 percent of the questions are based on a combination of visual material and text.

While the fact that at least 40 percent of the questions deal with visual material may seem overwhelming, consider the following:

✔ **You're probably already familiar with maps.** Travel maps (see Figure 9-1) help you get from place to place. Weather maps help you see what the weather has in store for your area. To help you prepare for the map-based questions on the test, study the maps you see on TV or in newspapers or magazines; try to figure out what they're showing you.

Figure 9-1: Peruse different maps like this one.

✔ **Every time you turn around, someone in the media is using a graph to make a point.** People use graphs to explain themselves so often because a graph can clearly show trends and relationships between different sets of information. The next time you see a graph, such as the ones in Figure 9-2, study it carefully to see whether you understand what the graph is telling you. (Keep in mind that graphs are also called *charts*.)

✔ **Tables are everywhere.** If you've ever looked at the nutrition label on a food product, you've read a table. Study any table you can find, whether in a newspaper or on a can of tuna. See Figure 9-3 for an example of a table that could appear on the Social Studies Test. (Note that tables are also sometimes called *charts*, which can be a little confusing. Remember that it doesn't matter whether a visual passage is a table, a cartoon, a drawing, or a graph — as long as you know how to read it.)

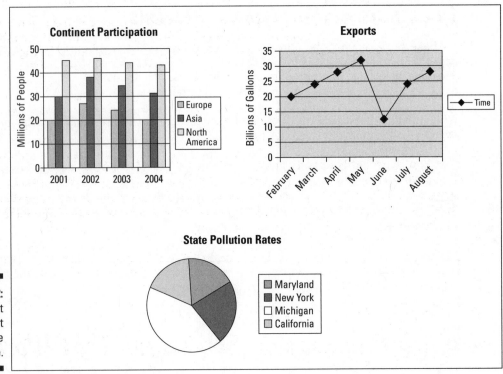

Figure 9-2:
Check out different graphs like these.

Impact on the Environment

Figure 9-3:
See if you can understand the basic information in tables like this one.

Type of Vehicle	MPG	Cost of Resources
SUV	12.8	$3,900
Sedan	19.6	$2,400
2-door	19.5	$2,700
All-wheel drive	17.2	$3,100
Sports car	18.6	$3,300

✔ **Political cartoons appear in newspapers every day.** If you don't read political cartoons in the daily newspaper (usually located on the Editorial or Op-Ed pages), give them a try. Some days, they're the best entertainment in the paper. Political cartoons in the newspaper are usually based on a recent event. If you want to get the most out of political cartoons, look for small details, facial expressions, and background clues. The cartoons on the test are obviously older than the ones in daily newspapers, so you may not get the context unless you've been reading newspapers or watching the news for the past several weeks or months.

✔ **You've no doubt seen countless photographs.** Photos are all around you. All you need to do to prepare for the photograph-based questions on the test is to begin getting information from the photographs you see. Start with newspapers or magazines, where photos provide information that connects directly to a story. See if you can determine what message the photograph carries with it, and how it relates to the story it supports.

✔ **You probably like to look at works of art.** On the Social Studies Test, you have a chance to "read" works of art. You look at a work of art and gather information you can use to answer the question. To get ready for the test, visit an art gallery, go online, and peruse library books. Lucky for you, some books even give some background or explanations for these works.

If you're unsure of how to read a map, go to any search engine and search for *map reading help* to find sites that explain how to read a map. If any of the other types of visual materials cause you concern, do the same thing — with the exception of political cartoons. If you try to follow the same procedure for political cartoons, you'll get a lot of actual cartoons but not a lot of explanations of them. Instead, look at some examples of political cartoons (either in the newspaper or online) to try to understand what the cartoonist is saying. Then look up the topic of the cartoon and the date to read some of the news stories they refer to. Talk about them with your friends. If you can explain a cartoon or carry on a logical discussion about the topic, you probably understand it.

All the visual items you have to review on this test are familiar. Now all you have to do is practise until your skills in reading and understanding them increase. Then you, too, can discuss the latest political cartoon or pontificate about a work of art.

Examining Preparation Strategies That Work

To improve your skills and get better results, try the following strategies when taking the Social Studies Test:

✔ **Take as many practice tests as you can.** The best way to prepare is to answer all the sample social studies questions you can find. Do practice tests (see Chapters 10 and 12), practice questions (see the "Practising with Sample Problems" section later in this chapter), and examples, such as those on the GED site (www.acenet.edu/Content/NavigationMenu/ged/test/prep/sample_questions.htm).

Consider taking a preparation class to get your hands on even more sample Social Studies Test questions. But remember that your task is to pass the test — not to collect every question ever written.

✔ **Practise reading a variety of documents.** As we mention in the previous section, read, read, and read some more. The documents you need to focus on include historic passages from original sources (such as the British North America Act, the Canadian Charter of Rights and Freedoms, and so on), as well as practical information for consumers (such as voters' guides, atlases, budget graphs, political speeches, almanacs, and tax forms).

✔ **Prepare summaries of the passages you read in your own words.** After you read these passages, summarize what you've read. Doing so can help you identify the main points of the passages, which is an important part of succeeding on the Social Studies Test. Ask yourself the following two questions when you read a passage or something visual like a graph:

- **What's the passage about?** When reading passages of text, ask yourself what the passage is about. The answer is usually in the first or last sentence. If you don't see the answer there, you may have to look carefully through the rest of the passage.

- **What's the visual material about?** When looking at maps, charts, graphs, political cartoons, diagrams, photographs, and artistic works, ask yourself what the visual material is about. Look for the answer in the title, labels, captions, and any other information that's included.

After you get an initial grasp of the main idea, determine what to do with it. Some questions ask you to use information you gain from one situation in another similar situation. If you know the main idea of the passage, you can apply it more easily to another situation.

✔ **Draft your own test questions that draw on the information from the passages you read.** Doing so can help you become familiar with social-studies-based questions. Look in newspapers and magazines for articles that fit into the general passage types tested on the Social Studies Test. Find a good summary paragraph, and develop a question that gets to the point of the summary.

✔ **Compose answers for each of your test questions.** Write out five answers to each of your test questions, only one of which is correct based on the passage. Creating your own questions and answers helps reduce your stress by showing you how answers are related to questions. It also encourages you to read and think about material that could be on the test. Finally, it gives you some idea of where to look for answers in a passage.

✔ **Discuss questions and answers with friends and family to make sure you understand and can properly use the material.** If your friends and family understand the question, you know it's a good question. Discussing your questions and answers with others gives you a chance to explain social studies topics and concepts, which is an important skill to have for this test.

Managing Your Time for the Social Studies Test

Remember that you have to answer 50 questions in 70 minutes to complete this test, which means you have less than one and a half minutes to spend on each question. Because you don't have a lot of time, you want to plan accordingly so you can answer every question and quickly review your answers.

As we mention earlier in this chapter, the questions on the Social Studies Test are based on both regular textual passages and visual materials like maps and charts, so, when you plan your time for answering the questions, consider the amount of time it takes to read both types of passages. (See the "Questions about visual materials" section of this chapter for advice on how you can get more comfortable with questions based on graphs, charts, and the like.)

When you come to a prose passage, read the questions first and then skim the passage looking for sections that answer the questions. If that doesn't work, read the passage carefully, looking for the answers. This way, you take more time only when needed.

Because you have such little time to gather all the information you can from a piece of visual material and answer a question about it, you can't study the map, chart, or cartoon all afternoon. You have to skim it the way you skim a paragraph. Reading the questions that relate to a particular visual passage first helps you figure out what to look for as you skim the material. The practice tests in Chapters 10 and 12 contain examples of questions based on visual materials, and so do the sample problems in the "Practising with Sample Problems" section in this chapter.

If you're unsure of how quickly you can answer questions based on visual materials, time yourself on a few and see. If your time comes out to be more than one and a half minutes, you need more practice.

Realistically, you have about 20 seconds to read the question and the possible answers, 40 seconds to look for the answer in the cartoon, and 10 seconds to fill in the circle for the answer. Dividing your time in this way leaves you less than 20 seconds for review or for time at the end of the test to spend on difficult questions. To finish the Social Studies Test completely, you really have to be organized and watch the clock. Check out Chapter 2 for more general time-management tips.

Practising with Sample Problems

The sample problems in this section give you a taste of what to expect in the practice tests in Chapters 10 and 12 of this book.

Remember that the Social Studies Test doesn't measure your ability to recall information, such as dates, facts, or events. It requires you to read a passage, analyze the information, evaluate its accuracy, and draw conclusions according to the printed text or visual materials in the passage. You then choose the one best answer to each question.

Questions 1 through 5 are based on the following passage.

Bridging both temperate and tropical regions, Mexico's terrain includes mountains, plains, valleys, and plateaus. Snow-capped volcanoes slope down to pine forests, deserts, and balmy tropical beaches. This diverse topography supports a variety of industries, including manufacturing, mining, petroleum, and agricultural production. As a member of the North American Free Trade Agreement (NAFTA), Mexico has the United States and Canada as main trading partners. In economic terms, Mexico boasts a GDP (gross domestic product) of $370 billion ($8,100 per person), which ranks it thirteenth in the world. Mexico currently enjoys an annual growth rate of over 6 percent. Beginning in 1985, Mexico began a process of trade liberalization and privatization. From 1982 to 1992, government-controlled enterprises were reduced from 1,155 to 217.

1. Which of the following are not part of Mexico's terrain?

    (1) plateaus

    (2) polar ice caps

    (3) mountains

    (4) valleys

    (5) plains

The correct answer is Choice (2) because the country doesn't lie either at the North or South Pole, where you find polar ice caps. The passage mentions the other answer choices — plateaus, mountains, valleys, and plains — but this question asks for what isn't mentioned.

2. Which adjectives demonstrate that the Mexican climate represents extremes in temperature?

    (1) sunny and rainy

    (2) dark and misty

    (3) plains and valleys

    (4) snow-capped and balmy

    (5) forests and deserts

    The correct answer is Choice (4). Snow-capped volcanoes represent an extremely low temperature, while balmy beaches refer to the higher temperatures found in a tropical climate. Other adjectives — such as sunny and rainy or dark and misty — don't refer to changes in temperature. Plains and valleys and forests and deserts are nouns that refer to terrain, not temperature.

3. What does diverse topography refer to?

    (1) differences in terrain

    (2) uniqueness in manufacturing

    (3) differences in agriculture

    (4) diversity of tropical beaches

    (5) abundance of petroleum production

    The correct answer is Choice (1). *Topography* is another word for terrain. *Diverse* means different. Manufacturing, agriculture, and petroleum production are types of industries. Tropical beaches are just one type of terrain.

4. Which countries are Mexico's trading partners in NAFTA?

    (1) the United States and the United Kingdom

    (2) France and Germany

    (3) North America

    (4) Canada and the United Kingdom

    (5) the United States and Canada

    The correct answer is Choice (5). The text states that the United States and Canada joined with Mexico to form the North American Free Trade Agreement. The United Kingdom, France, and Germany aren't partners in NAFTA.

5. What happened in Mexico between 1982 and 1992?

    (1) Government control of enterprises increased.

    (2) The government controlled fewer enterprises.

    (3) Mexico achieved the highest GDP in the world.

    (4) Mexico's growth rate was less than 6 percent.

    (5) Mexico won the World Cup.

    The correct answer is Choice (2). According to the passage, from 1982 to 1992, Mexico's government reduced its control of enterprises from 1,155 to 217. It didn't increase enterprise control, nor did Mexico achieve the highest GDP in the world — 12 countries were higher. The country's growth rate was more than 6 percent. And although Mexico would love to win the World Cup in soccer, the passage doesn't say it did so during the mentioned decade.

Questions 6 through 7 are based on the following graph:

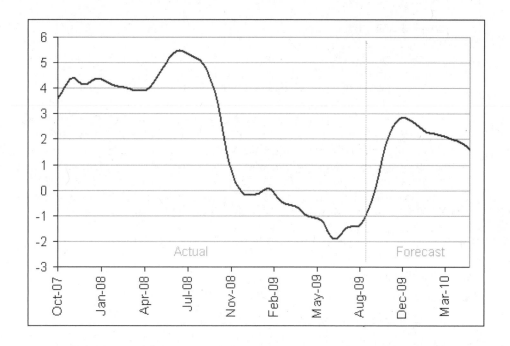

6. In what period was the inflation rate the highest?

    (1) January to April 2008

    (2) April to August 2008

    (3) August to November 2008

    (4) November 2008 to February 2009

    (5) February to May 2009

    The correct answer is Choice (2). The highest point on the graph occurs in the period represented by April to August 2008. If the *x*-axis (horizontal axis) of the graph had finer divisions, you could be more accurate in the timing, but, as it is, the graph indicates this level of accuracy.

7. In what period did the inflation rate first dip below zero?

    (1) January to April 2008

    (2) April to August 2008

    (3) August to November 2008

    (4) November 2008 to February 2009

    (5) February to May 2009

    The correct answer is Choice (4). The first time that the line on this graph passes through the horizontal line labeled *0* on the vertical axis (the *y*-axis) is during the period November 2008 to February 2009. The numbers below this horizontal line are negative.

Revealing Some Helpful Pointers

The following additional tips can serve you well in this test:

✔ **Don't assume.** Be extra careful with visual material and read it thoroughly. You want to be able to read visual material as accurately as you read text material, and doing so takes practice. Don't assume something is true just because it looks that way in a diagram, chart, or map. Visual materials can be precise drawings, with legends and scales, or they can be drawn in such a way that, at first glance, the information appears to be different than it really is. Verify what you think you see by making sure the information looks correct and realistic.

✔ **Be familiar with general graphical conventions.** Maps and graphs have conventions. The top of a map is almost always north. The horizontal axis is always the *x*-axis, and the vertical axis (the *y*-axis) is dependent on the *x*-axis. Looking at the horizontal axis first usually makes the information clearer and easier to understand.

See Chapter 1 for general rules that apply to all the GED tests.

Chapter 10

Practice Test — Social Studies Test

*T*he Social Studies Test consists of multiple-choice questions that measure general social studies concepts. The questions are based on short readings that often include a map, graph, chart, cartoon, or figure. Study the information given and then answer the question(s) following it. Refer to the information as often as necessary in answering the questions.

You have 70 minutes to answer the 50 questions in this booklet. Work carefully, but do not spend too much time on any one question. Be sure you answer every question.

Answer Sheet for Social Studies Test

1	① ② ③ ④ ⑤					26	① ② ③ ④ ⑤
2	① ② ③ ④ ⑤					27	① ② ③ ④ ⑤
3	① ② ③ ④ ⑤					28	① ② ③ ④ ⑤
4	① ② ③ ④ ⑤					29	① ② ③ ④ ⑤
5	① ② ③ ④ ⑤					30	① ② ③ ④ ⑤
6	① ② ③ ④ ⑤					31	① ② ③ ④ ⑤
7	① ② ③ ④ ⑤					32	① ② ③ ④ ⑤
8	① ② ③ ④ ⑤					33	① ② ③ ④ ⑤
9	① ② ③ ④ ⑤					34	① ② ③ ④ ⑤
10	① ② ③ ④ ⑤					35	① ② ③ ④ ⑤
11	① ② ③ ④ ⑤					36	① ② ③ ④ ⑤
12	① ② ③ ④ ⑤					37	① ② ③ ④ ⑤
13	① ② ③ ④ ⑤					38	① ② ③ ④ ⑤
14	① ② ③ ④ ⑤					39	① ② ③ ④ ⑤
15	① ② ③ ④ ⑤					40	① ② ③ ④ ⑤
16	① ② ③ ④ ⑤					41	① ② ③ ④ ⑤
17	① ② ③ ④ ⑤					42	① ② ③ ④ ⑤
18	① ② ③ ④ ⑤					43	① ② ③ ④ ⑤
19	① ② ③ ④ ⑤					44	① ② ③ ④ ⑤
20	① ② ③ ④ ⑤					45	① ② ③ ④ ⑤
21	① ② ③ ④ ⑤					46	① ② ③ ④ ⑤
22	① ② ③ ④ ⑤					47	① ② ③ ④ ⑤
23	① ② ③ ④ ⑤					48	① ② ③ ④ ⑤
24	① ② ③ ④ ⑤					49	① ② ③ ④ ⑤
25	① ② ③ ④ ⑤					50	① ② ③ ④ ⑤

Social Studies Test

Do not mark in this test booklet. Record your answers on the separate answer sheet provided. Be sure that all requested information is properly recorded on the answer sheet.

To record your answers, fill in the numbered circle on the answer sheet that corresponds to the answer you select for each question in the test booklet.

EXAMPLE:

Early colonists of North America looked for settlement sites with adequate water supplies and access by ship. For this reason, many early towns were built near

(1) mountains

(2) prairies

(3) rivers

(4) glaciers

(5) plateaus

(On Answer Sheet)
① ② ● ④ ⑤

The correct answer is "rivers"; therefore, answer space 3 would be marked on the answer sheet.

Do not rest the point of your pencil on the answer sheet while you are considering your answer. Make no stray or unnecessary marks. If you change an answer, erase your first mark completely. Mark only one answer space for each question; multiple answers will be scored as incorrect. Do not fold or crease your answer sheet. All test materials must be returned to the test administrator.

Note: See to Chapter 11 for the answers for this practice test.

DO NOT BEGIN TAKING THIS TEST UNTIL TOLD TO DO SO

Directions: Choose the <u>one best answer</u> to each question.

Questions 1 through 4 refer to the following passage, which is excerpted from Canadian History For Dummies, *2nd Edition, by Will Ferguson (Wiley).*

When Worlds Collide

This part deals with Canada's First Nations and their initial contact with Europeans, beginning with the Vikings and ending with the first tentative colonies in Newfoundland, the Maritimes, and along the St. Lawrence. The societies of Canada prior to first contact were incredibly complex and varied: ranging from the military and political alliances of the Iroquois to the northern trade empire of the Ojibwa; from the small-band subsistence hunters of the northern forests to the austere lifestyle of the plains; from the intricate arts and social caste system of the Pacific Coast to the survival techniques and adaptive genius of the Arctic Inuit. This wasn't an empty continent that the European explorers first stumbled upon. Far from it.

1. What does the excerpt's title, "When Worlds Collide," mean?

   (1) another Star Wars sequel

   (2) European explorers encounter First Nations societies

   (3) the Iroquois battle the Vikings

   (4) military and political alliances

   (5) colonies in Newfoundland and the Maritimes

2. Who were the first Europeans to reach Canada?

   (1) the British

   (2) the French

   (3) the Ojibwa

   (4) the Vikings

   (5) the Spanish

3. What were the Iroquois known for?

   (1) northern trading

   (2) military and political alliances

   (3) First Nations societies

   (4) social caste system

   (5) survival techniques

4. In general, what terms best describe the First Nations societies?

   (1) complex and varied

   (2) intricate arts

   (3) social caste system

   (4) subsistent hunters

   (5) adaptive genius

Go on to next page

> *Questions 5 through 9 refer to the following passage, which is excerpted from* CliffsQuickReview U.S. History I *by P. Soifer and A. Hoffman (Wiley).*

The Voyages of Christopher Columbus

Christopher Columbus, a Genoese sailor, believed that sailing west across the Atlantic Ocean was the shortest sea route to Asia. Ignorant of the fact that the Western Hemisphere lay between Europe and Asia and assuming the earth's circumference to be a third less than it actually is, he was convinced that Japan would appear on the horizon just three thousand miles to the west. Like other seafarers of his day, Columbus was untroubled by political allegiances; he was ready to sail for whatever country would pay for his voyage. Either because of his arrogance (he wanted ships and crews to be provided at no expense to himself) or ambition (he insisted on governing the lands he discovered), he found it difficult to find a patron. The Portuguese rejected his plan twice, and the rulers of England and France were not interested. With influential supporters at court, Columbus convinced King Ferdinand and Queen Isabella of Spain to partially underwrite his expedition. In 1492, Granada, the last Muslim stronghold on the Iberian Peninsula, had fallen to the forces of the Spanish monarchs. With the Reconquista complete and Spain a unified country, Ferdinand and Isabella could turn their attention to overseas exploration.

5. Which direction did Columbus sail to reach Asia?

   (1) east

   (2) south

   (3) north

   (4) west

   (5) northwest

6. What did he assume the earth's circumference to be?

   (1) three thousand miles

   (2) between Europe and Asia

   (3) a third less than it is

   (4) shortest sea route to Asia

   (5) across the Atlantic Ocean

7. How did Columbus feel about politics?

   (1) He was not troubled.

   (2) He was troubled.

   (3) He was ready to sail.

   (4) He was arrogant.

   (5) He was ambitious.

8. Which country finally agreed to provide funds for his plan?

   (1) Portugal

   (2) England

   (3) France

   (4) Japan

   (5) Spain

9. How were Ferdinand and Isabella convinced by Columbus?

   (1) They now had a unified country.

   (2) The Muslims were defeated.

   (3) The English and French were not interested.

   (4) They were convinced by influential supporters at court.

   (5) They were ready for overseas exploration.

Go on to next page ⟶

Questions 10 through 15 refer to the following passage, which is excerpted from Canadian History For Dummies, 2nd Edition, by Will Ferguson (Wiley).

Cartier's First Voyage

On April 20, 1534, Jacques Cartier sailed out of the French seaport of St. Malo with two ships and a crew of 61 men. His mission? "To discover certain isles and countries where it is said there must be great quantities of gold and other riches." Unlike Cabot, Cartier knew exactly where he was going. He had probably accompanied Verrazano on an earlier failed quest for a passage to the Orient, and he certainly had been to the cod-rich fisheries of Newfoundland at some point.

Cartier made one important discovery right at the start: By sailing through the narrow northern strait, he proved that Newfoundland was in fact an island. He also had a flair for description. Earlier, when he landed on the rugged coast of Labrador; he dubbed the region "the Land God Gave Cain." Then, sailing west, he discovered an isle he dubbed "the fairest land 'tis possible to see." It would later be known as Prince Edward Island, and Cartier's ringing endorsement is still proudly recalled in tourist brochures even today.

Cartier next sailed up the coast of what is now New Brunswick, where he was met enthusiastically by a band of Mi'kmaq, who were well-versed in trade and eager to acquire European goods. Cartier followed the coastline north to the Gaspé peninsula, where he made contact with a group of Iroquoian people who were on a seasonal fishing expedition. In the presence of their chief, Donnacona, the French explorer erected a large wooden cross emblazoned with the words *Vive le Roi de France* and claimed the land in the name of King François I.

10. What was Cartier's mission in his first voyage?

    (1) a passage to the Orient

    (2) cod-rich fisheries

    (3) Newfoundland

    (4) the narrow northern strait

    (5) isles and countries with gold and other riches

11. What did Cartier discover about Newfoundland?

    (1) It was an island.

    (2) It had a rugged coast.

    (3) It had cod-rich fisheries.

    (4) It was the fairest land.

    (5) It was a good place for tourists.

12. What were the Mi'kmaq known for?

    (1) their ability as fishermen

    (2) their interest in exploration

    (3) being Iroquoian people

    (4) their interest in trade

    (5) their agricultural skills

13. Who was Donnacona?

    (1) a French explorer

    (2) an Iroquoian chief

    (3) a Gaspé native

    (4) a native of Labrador

    (5) one of Cartier's crew

14. What symbol did Cartier use to claim the land?

    (1) European goods

    (2) a tourist brochure

    (3) the Gaspé peninsula

    (4) King François I

    (5) a large wooden cross

15. How do we know so much about Cartier's discoveries?

    (1) He accompanied Verrazano.

    (2) He sailed from St. Malo.

    (3) He had a flair for description.

    (4) He was a French explorer.

    (5) He befriended the First Nations people.

Go on to next page →

Questions 16 through 20 refer to the following passage, which is excerpted from Canadian History For Dummies, *2nd Edition, by Will Ferguson (Wiley).*

The Rise of New France

To encourage trade and to suss out the neighbourhood, [Samuel] Champlain began sending out men to live among their Native allies, to learn their language and customs, and to become familiar with the lay of land. Champlain, ever the mapmaker, wanted to chart the geography of the fur trade, and the adventurers he sent out, later dubbed *coureurs de bois,* "runners of the woods," played an important role in this. They also helped bridge the culture gap between Native and Canadien societies.

The coureurs de bois were the forerunners of the French *voyageurs,* or "travellers," who would paddle deep into the continent each year in flotillas of canoes to collect furs. The "original coureur de bois" was Étienne Brûlé, who spent 20 years among the Huron and whose life reads like an adventure novel. When Champlain arrived in Huronia, Brûlé had already spent five years there and was on hand to greet him. Brûlé acted as an interpreter, cartographer, diplomat, and spy. He even died in a suitably dramatic fashion, in an incident shrouded by mystery, apparently assassinated by the Huron when he attempted to negotiate a trade deal that would have bypassed them.

In the early years, New France was little more than a trading post perched on the edge of a vast frontier. Until settlers took up the plow and made a commitment to stay, the colony would never take root. And so, in 1617, Samuel Champlain asked Louis Hébert, a former Acadian colonist, to settle in New France. Not that Champlain had to twist his arm. Hébert was working as a pharmacist/herbalist back in Paris at the time, and he missed the freedom and adventure of the New World. So off he went, dragging his wife Marie and three children with him. Known as "the original habitants," Louis and Marie cleared the land and planted crops, making them both the first farmers and the first true settlers of New France. The slow transformation of New France had begun, from fur trading outpost to a colony of farming communities.

16. Who was chiefly responsible for the rise of New France?
    (1) Étienne Brûlé
    (2) Louis Hébert
    (3) Jacques Cartier
    (4) Marie Hébert
    (5) Samuel Champlain

17. How did Champlain gain the trust of the Huron?
    (1) He sent adventurers to live with them.
    (2) He charted their geography.
    (3) He acted as a spy.
    (4) He encouraged trade.
    (5) He made maps.

18. What became of Étienne Brûlé?
    (1) He bridged the cultural gap.
    (2) He wrote an adventure novel.
    (3) He was killed by the Huron.
    (4) He became a farmer.
    (5) He charted the fur trade.

19. Who were the "runners of the woods"?
    (1) travellers
    (2) coureurs de bois
    (3) voyageurs
    (4) habitants
    (5) original settlers

Go on to next page

20. Why were the Héberts important to the future of New France?

    (1) They were fur traders.

    (2) They were coureurs de bois.

    (3) They were its first farmers.

    (4) They were voyageurs.

    (5) They were from Acadia.

Questions 21 through 23 refer to the following political cartoon.

21. How does the cartoon depict the use of cellphones?

    (1) wonderful invention

    (2) aid to communication

    (3) medical breakthrough

    (4) useful appliance

    (5) injurious to health

22. How would you best describe the cellphone user in the cartoon?

    (1) foolhardy

    (2) talkative

    (3) considerate

    (4) courageous

    (5) cowardly

23. What source tells us that cellphones may represent a risk to health?

    (1) movies

    (2) scientific research

    (3) urban legends

    (4) popular opinion

    (5) crime reports

Go on to next page

Questions 24 through 26 refer to the following passage, which is excerpted from Canadian History for Dummies, *2nd Edition, by Will Ferguson (Wiley).*

On the Plains of Abraham

As the boats glided down the St. Lawrence, a French sentry spotted them and called out from the shore, but the British managed to bluff their way past and, just before dawn, they landed at the cove. An advance guard climbed the narrow trail and overpowered the French post at the top as the rest of the troops followed, pulling themselves up along handholds of roots and vines, up onto the Plains of Abraham. It was September 13, 1759.

Although the name has a nice Biblical ring to it, suggesting sacrifice and redemption, the plains were actually named after a settler who had farmed in the area. It was here that the future of Canada would be decided. By daybreak, [General] Wolfe had positioned more than 4,500 troops on the Plains of Abraham. The surprise was complete. General Montcalm had been convinced that the final attack, if it came, would be on the other side of the city at the Beauport shore. When an aide suggested the British might try to climb the cliffs, Montcalm had snorted with derision. "We do not need to imagine that the enemy has wings," he wrote in his journal, "so that in one night they can cross the river, disembark, and climb the obstructed cliffs." But now, they had done just that. As he hurried to assemble his troops, Montcalm looked out at the red coats that were lining up behind the city, and complained, "They have no right to be there."

Wolfe had managed to drag up only two light cannons. Montcalm decided that time was of the essence and that the British had to be attacked immediately, before they could dig in and strengthen their position. For the first time since the British arrived. Montcalm acted impulsively. He had 3,000 reinforcements somewhere behind the British lines — a message had been sent and they were on their way — but he didn't wait for them to arrive. Instead, Montcalm gathered the troops he had on hand and threw open the city gates . . .

The battle lasted only 15 minutes. The British had formed a "thin red line," two men deep, and the French advanced in a ragged charge, the regulars and the Canadiens stumbling over each other. Native snipers were picking off British soldiers from nearby woods, but Wolfe stood his ground.

---

24. How were the Plains of Abraham named?

  (1) from the Bible

  (2) by General Montcalm

  (3) by the British

  (4) after a settler

  (5) by General Wolfe

25. Why did the British climb the cliffs?

  (1) to surprise the enemy

  (2) to find a shortcut

  (3) to wait for daybreak

  (4) to cross the river

  (5) to reach the Beauport shore

26. What was the "thin red line"?

  (1) the French defenders

  (2) the Native snipers

  (3) the British troops

  (4) the Canadiens

  (5) the reinforcements

Go on to next page

Questions 27 through 30 refer to the following excerpt from Canadian History For Dummies, 2nd Edition, by Will Ferguson (Wiley).

The BNA Act Is Passed

The terms of Confederation were worked out at three separate conferences:

- **Charlottetown (September 1-9, 1864):** Delegates agree to the broad principles of a possible union.

- **Québec City (October 10-27, 1864):** The structure of the union, the division of power between national and provincial governments, and other details are hammered out.

- **London, England (over the winter of 1866-67):** Delegates meet one last time and make some minor, but important, changes to the Québec Resolutions (they improve the financial terms for the Maritimes and add a requirement for an "intercolonial railway" to be built).

On March 29, 1867, Queen Victoria signed the British North America Act (BNA Act), and on July 1, it came into effect. A new nation was born: *Canada*, consisting of 3.5 million people and four provinces. The original four, the "charter members of Confederation," so to speak, were as follows:

- Nova Scotia

- New Brunswick

- Québec (formerly the Canada East region)

- Ontario (formerly the Canada West region)

It is important to note that the BNA Act did *not* grant Canada full independence. Far from it. Canada was still a part of the British Empire. Canadians were still British citizens. The Queen was still the head of state, and in matters of diplomacy and international defence, Britain still called the shots. Even then, the BNA Act was a giant step forward nonetheless.

27. How were the terms of Confederation developed?

    (1) by Queen Victoria

    (2) by a series of three conferences

    (3) by the provinces

    (4) by the British Empire

    (5) by the head of state

28. Where was the division of power decided?

    (1) London

    (2) Charlottetown

    (3) Nova Scotia

    (4) Québec City

    (5) Ontario

29. What was the major outcome of the British North America Act?

    (1) an intercontinental railway

    (2) a division of power

    (3) a possible union

    (4) Confederation

    (5) full independence

30. According to the BNA Act, who was to be the head of state?

    (1) the prime minister

    (2) the Queen

    (3) the British Empire

    (4) the charter members

    (5) a premier

Go on to next page

Questions 31 through 35 refer to the following passage, which is excerpted from CliffsQuickReview U.S. History II *by P. Soifer and A. Hoffman (Wiley).*

The End of the Cold War

In July 1989, Gorbachev repudiated the Brezhnev Doctrine, which had justified the intervention of the Soviet Union in the affairs of communist countries. Within a few months of his statement, the Communist regimes in Eastern Europe collapsed — Poland, Hungary, and Czechoslovakia, followed by Bulgaria and Romania. The Berlin Wall came down in November 1989, and East and West Germany were reunited within the year. Czechoslovakia eventually split into the Czech Republic and Slovakia with little trouble, but the end of the Yugoslav Federation in 1991 led to years of violence and ethnic cleansing (the expulsion of an ethnic population from a geographic area), particularly in Bosnia-Herzegovina. The Soviet Union also broke up, not long after an attempted coup against Gorbachev in August 1991, and the Baltic states of Latvia, Estonia, and Lithuania were the first to gain their independence. That December, Gorbachev stepped down, and the old Soviet Union became the Commonwealth of Independent States (CIS). The CIS quickly disappeared, and the republics that had once made up the Soviet Union were recognized as sovereign nations. The end of the Cold War led directly to major nuclear weapons reduction agreements between President Bush and the Russian leaders, as well as significant cutbacks in the number of troops the United States committed to the defense of NATO.

31. Who or what caused the end of the Cold War?

   (1) the Soviet Union

   (2) Communist regimes

   (3) Gorbachev

   (4) Brezhnev

   (5) Eastern Europe

32. How were East and West Germany reunited?

   (1) the fall of the Berlin Wall

   (2) intervention of the Soviet Union

   (3) the Brezhnev Doctrine

   (4) the collapse of regimes

   (5) intervention of the United States

33. What is ethnic cleansing?

   (1) years of violence

   (2) the end of the Yugoslav Federation

   (3) expelling populations

   (4) the split of Czechoslovakia

   (5) the breakup of the Soviet Union

34. What happened to the republics of the Soviet Union?

   (1) They quickly disappeared.

   (2) They joined NATO.

   (3) They became the CIS.

   (4) They joined the Baltic states.

   (5) They became sovereign nations.

35. What was one of the results of the end of the Cold War?

   (1) more nuclear weapons

   (2) more tension between the United States and the former Soviet Union

   (3) no agreements between leaders

   (4) an increase in U.S. troops

   (5) cutbacks in U.S. troops

Go on to next page

> *Questions 36 through 40 refer to the following passage, which is excerpted from* Canadian History For Dummies, *2nd Edition, by Will Ferguson (Wiley).*

The Mounties

If you had to choose one all-Canadian symbol, it would probably be a red-coated Mountie, "rider of the plains." The image of the Mountie — a potent blend of myth and history — is as Canadian as the gunslinger is American, or the loyal samurai is Japanese. Created by an Act of Parliament in 1873, the North-West Mounted Police (NWMP) were one of John A.'s schemes, aimed at bringing law and order to the Canadian frontier. American whisky peddlers had crossed into Canadian territory and were selling rotgut to the Indians at illegal trading posts with names like Fort Whoop-Up and Robber's Roost.

In 1873, the violence to the south spilled north into Canada when a band of American-led wolf hunters ambushed and killed 36 Assiniboine at Cypress Hills, in what is now southwestern Saskatchewan. The Cypress Hills massacre gave an added sense of urgency to John A. Macdonald's plan for creating a paramilitary police force to patrol the western frontier. The red jackets the officers wore were chosen with care to distinguish them from the blue coats of the U.S. Cavalry to the south, where a long and bloody war against the Plains Indians was being waged.

The following year, 300 Mounted Police recruits made a gruelling two-month overland trek from Manitoba, led by the legendary Métis scout Jerry Potts. By the time the Mounties reached Fort Whoop-Up, the Americans had fled, tails between their legs. The Mounties, "stalwarts in scarlet jackets," established and asserted Canadian autonomy over the Northwest. The official motto was *Maintiens le Droit* ("Uphold the Right"), but the Americans added a new one: "They always get their man." In 1920, the force was reorganized as the Royal Canadian Mounted Police, or RCMP.

36. What created the North-West Mounted Police?

    (1) an Act of Parliament

    (2) one of John A.'s schemes

    (3) American whisky peddlers

    (4) Japanese samurai

    (5) the Cypress Hills massacre

37. Why did the officers wear red jackets?

    (1) to work with the Indians

    (2) to chase the wolf hunters

    (3) to distinguish them from the Cavalry

    (4) to patrol the western frontier

    (5) to establish law and order

38. What were the duties of the Mounties?

    (1) to stop the whisky peddlers

    (2) to be a paramilitary force

    (3) to protect the Plains Indians

    (4) to bring law and order to the frontier

    (5) all of the above

39. Who was Jerry Potts?

    (1) a Métis scout

    (2) a scarlet jacket

    (3) a wolf hunter

    (4) a Plains Indian

    (5) a U.S. Cavalry soldier

40. How did the Americans feel about the Mounties?

    (1) They hated them.

    (2) They feared them.

    (3) They respected their ability.

    (4) They resented them.

    (5) They joined them.

Go on to next page

Questions 41 through 45 refer to the following tables.

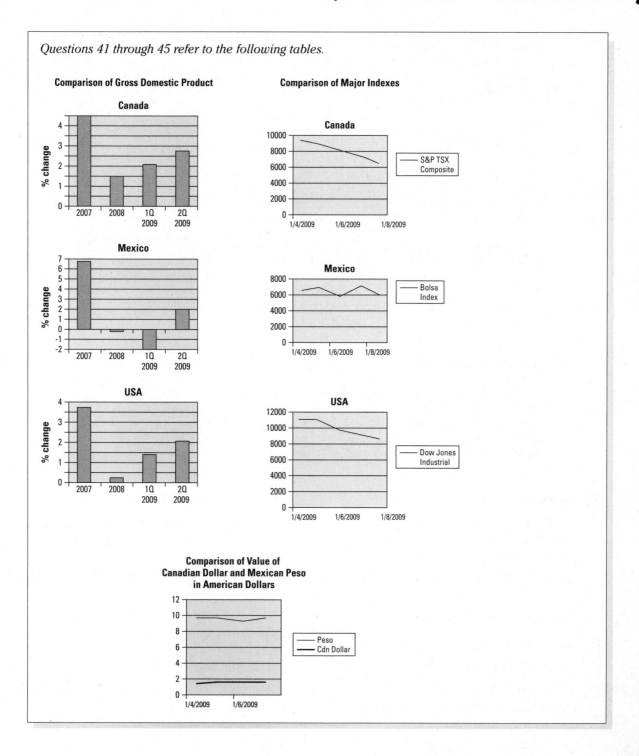

Comparison of Gross Domestic Product

Canada

Mexico

USA

Comparison of Major Indexes

Canada

Mexico

USA

Comparison of Value of
Canadian Dollar and Mexican Peso
in American Dollars

Go on to next page

41. By how much did the Mexican gross domestic product (GDP) outperform the U.S. GDP in the year 2007?

    (1) 8.4 percentage points

    (2) 2.8 percentage points

    (3) 0.7 percentage points

    (4) 5.9 percentage points

    (5) 1.3 percentage points

42. Why does Canada's GDP appear healthy as compared to that of the United States and Mexico?

    (1) Canada has consistently performed well.

    (2) Canada performed better than it did in 2Q.

    (3) Canada performed better in 1Q.

    (4) Canada performed better in 2008.

    (5) Canada performed better in 2007.

43. How did the Canadian dollar perform against the U.S. dollar, according to the graph?

    (1) moved higher

    (2) stayed the same

    (3) lost ground

    (4) finished even

    (5) did not change

44. How did the S&P TSX Composite Index compare on 1/4/2009 and 1/8/2009?

    (1) down almost 2,000

    (2) up about 1,000

    (3) about the same

    (4) up less than 300

    (5) down more than 3,000

45. According to the graph, how did the Dow Jones compare on 1/4/2009 and 1/8/2009?

    (1) down more than 5,000

    (2) up more than 1,000

    (3) about the same

    (4) up more than 300

    (5) down more than 2,000

Go on to next page

Questions 46 through 50 refer to the following political cartoon.

46. What is the setting for the cartoon?

    (1) living room

    (2) laboratory

    (3) playroom

    (4) library

    (5) kitchen

47. What problem has the researcher been studying?

    (1) the common cold

    (2) a rare blood disease

    (3) vision

    (4) hair loss

    (5) limited patents for medicines

48. How does the cartoonist depict drug companies?

    (1) caring

    (2) religious

    (3) greedy

    (4) generous

    (5) curious

49. Why is this solution important for the drug companies?

    (1) to share with all people

    (2) to make their employees famous

    (3) for good public relations

    (4) to make them look good to their customers

    (5) to increase their profits

50. What is the theme of the cartoon?

    (1) greed

    (2) inventing

    (3) curiosity

    (4) diligence

    (5) patience

END OF TEST

Chapter 11

Answers and Explanations for the Social Studies Test

. . . .

Answer Key

After taking the Social Studies Test in Chapter 10, use this section to check your answers.

1. **2**	18. **3**	35. **5**
2. **4**	19. **2**	36. **1**
3. **2**	20. **3**	37. **3**
4. **1**	21. **5**	38. **5**
5. **4**	22. **1**	39. **1**
6. **3**	23. **2**	40. **3**
7. **1**	24. **4**	41. **2**
8. **5**	25. **1**	42. **1**
9. **4**	26. **3**	43. **2**
10. **5**	27. **2**	44. **5**
11. **1**	28. **4**	45. **5**
12. **4**	29. **4**	46. **2**
13. **2**	30. **2**	47. **5**
14. **5**	31. **3**	48. **3**
15. **3**	32. **1**	49. **5**
16. **5**	33. **3**	50. **1**
17. **1**	34. **5**	

Analysis of the Answers

If you aren't sure why an answer is incorrect, use this section to get quick explanations of the answers. If you correctly answered a question, you may still want to read the explanations to get a better understanding of the thought process that helped you choose the correct answer.

1. **2.** The collision referred to in the passage's title is the clash of cultures between the European and First Nations societies. The other choices: Iroquois and Vikings, military and political, and Newfoundland and the Maritimes are not as relevant to the question. Movies had not been invented yet.

2. **4.** The *Vikings* reached Canada centuries before the British or French. The Spanish were not mentioned in the passage. The Ojibwa are among Canada's First Nations.

3. **2.** The passage states that the Iroquois formed *military and political alliances*. The other choices — northern trading, First Nations societies, social castes, and survival techniques — were not as relevant to the Iroquois.

4. **1.** The passage describes the First Nations societies, in general, as *complex and varied*. The other choices are characteristics of specific nations.

5. **4.** According to the passage, Columbus sailed *west to cross the Atlantic Ocean* in search of Asia.

6. **3.** Columbus thought the circumference was *a third less than it really is*. The other answers are incorrect, according to the passage.

7. **1.** Columbus was not troubled about political allegiances. He would sail for any country that was willing to pay for the trip. The other choices — that he was troubled, arrogant, ready to sail, or ambitious — don't refer to political allegiances.

8. **5.** Columbus finally got partial funding from the king and queen of Spain. Portugal, England, France, and Japan didn't provide any funding.

9. **4.** Columbus convinced Ferdinand and Isabella to fund the voyage by using *influential supporters at court*. The other answers — that they had a unified country, the Muslims were defeated, the English and French weren't interested, and they were ready for exploration — aren't the best answers.

10. **5.** According to the passage, Cartier's mission was to discover *gold and other riches*. The other choices — route to the Orient, fisheries, Newfoundland, and a northern straight — were secondary objectives, but not the prime mission.

11. **1.** Cartier found that Newfoundland was an *island*. Rugged coast and rich fisheries, while relevant, were not as important. Fairest land refers to Prince Edward Island, which tourists would not be visiting any time soon.

12. **4.** The Mi'kmaq people were traders — interested in European goods. They were not as well known as fishermen, explorers, or farmers. The Iroquois were a different nation.

13. **2.** Donnacona was an Iroquoian chief — not a native of the Gaspé or Labrador. He certainly was not a French explorer or member of Cartier's crew.

14. **5.** The symbol that Cartier used to claim ownership of the land was the *large wooden cross*. The King, goods, a brochure, or the Gaspé peninsula are not appropriate as symbols.

15. **3.** We know so much about Cartier's discoveries because *he had a flair for description*. The fact that he travelled with Verrazano, sailed from St. Malo, was an explorer, or was friendly with the First Nations people are not relevant choices.

16. **5.** *Samuel Champlain* was the builder of New France. Marie and Louis Hébert were original farmers, Étienne Brûlé was a coureur de bois, and Cartier was the discoverer, not the builder, of the settlement.

17. **1.** According to the passage, Champlain sent *adventurers* to live with the Huron to gain their trust. Other choices — charting, spying, trading, and mapping — are not as relevant.

18. **3.** *Étienne Brûlé was killed by the Huron.* While he may have bridged the cultural gap and charted the fur trade, these factors did not save him from an untimely death. He certainly did not become a farmer or an adventure novelist.

19. **2.** *Coureurs de bois,* which can be translated as "runners of the woods," is the best choice. Travellers and voyageurs are other characteristics. Habitants and original settlers do not apply.

20. **3.** The Héberts were the original *farmers* who settled New France. They were not fur traders, coureurs de bois, or voyageurs. The fact that they came from Acadia, while true, is not relevant to the question.

21. **5.** Some researchers believe cellphones are *injurious to your health*, particularly if they damage the brain or cause accidents while driving. The other answers — wonderful invention, aid to communication, medical breakthrough, and useful appliance — are all factors, but they aren't the ones the cartoon depicts.

22. **1.** The cellphone user is *foolhardy* in that he's driving dangerously by not paying enough attention to the road. Other choices, such as considerate and courageous, are incorrect. Talkative and cowardly aren't the best answers, according to the cartoon.

23. **2.** Some *scientific research* indicates that cellphones may represent a risk to health (radiation and brain tumours, for example). Movies, legends, opinion, and reports aren't correct choices, according to the cartoon.

24. **4.** The Plains of Abraham were named *after a settler who had farmed the area*. The choices of from the Bible or by Montcalm are not correct according to the passage. The British and by Wolfe are also incorrect.

25. **1.** The British troops scaled the cliffs at night to *surprise the French* who thought they'd cross the river and take a more direct, easier to defend shortcut. By daybreak the British were already assembled on the plains and ready for battle.

26. **3.** The *British troops* wore red coats and formed a line as they advanced toward the enemy. The French defenders, snipers, Canadiens, and reinforcements were dressed in different colours.

27. **2.** A *series of three conferences* developed the terms of Confederation. The other choices — Queen Victoria, the provinces, the British Empire, or the head of state — were involved but not the source of the terms.

28. **4.** According to the passage, the division of power was decided at the conference in *Québec City*. The other choices — London and Charlottetown — are not correct. No conferences were held in Nova Scotia or Ontario.

29. **4.** The major outcome of the BNA Act was *Confederation*. Other choices — a railway, division of power, or possible union — were not the major outcomes. Full independence was never achieved.

30. **2.** The head of state was to be *Queen Victoria*. The other choices are either incorrect or not mentioned in the passage.

31. **3.** *Gorbachev* ended the Cold War when he repudiated the Brezhnev Doctrine. Communist regimes, Brezhnev, Eastern Europe, and the Soviet Union are incorrect answers.

32. **1.** When *the Berlin Wall fell*, East and West Germany were once again united. Soviet intervention, the Brezhnev Doctrine, regimes collapsing, and U.S. intervention may have existed, but they aren't the best answers according to the passage.

33. **3.** According to the passage, *ethnic cleansing* refers to the expulsion of minority ethnic populations. The other answers are incorrect because they don't refer specifically to how people were expelled.

34. **5.** The former Soviet republics *became sovereign nations*. According to the passage, the Soviet republics didn't disappear, weren't invited to join NATO, and didn't become the Baltic states. The passage doesn't mention anything called CNS.

35. **5.** All the factors except Choice (5) are the opposite of what the last sentence of the passage states, so Choice (5) is the only correct answer.

36. **1.** The North-West Mounted Police, according to the passage, were created by an *Act of Parliament* — not just one of John A.'s schemes. Whisky peddlers, samurai, or a massacre do not make sense.

37. **3.** The officers wore red jackets to gain their own sense of identity and to *distinguish themselves* from the U.S. Cavalry, who dressed in blue. This helped them in their work with the Indians, chasing wolf hunters, patrolling the frontier, and establishing law and order.

38. **5.** All of the duties listed in Choices (1) to (4) were part of the Mounties' work.

39. **1.** Jerry Potts was a *Métis scout.* He did not wear a red jacket, nor was he a wolf hunter, Plains Indian, or U.S. soldier.

40. **3.** The Americans must have *respected the Mounties' ability* when they said, "They always get their man." They may also have hated them, feared them, or resented them, but they certainly did not join them.

41. **2.** The Mexican GDP was *2.8 percentage points higher* than the U.S. GDP. The other answers are simply incorrect, according to the graphs.

42. **1.** According to the GDP graphs, Canada's economy has *consistently performed well* when compared to the economies of the United States and Mexico.

43. **2.** The value of the Canadian dollar is a straight line, which means its value *stayed the same*.

44. **5.** On 1/4/2009, the index was just under 10,000, and on 1/8/2009, it was above 6,000. Thus, Choice (5) is the most correct.

45. **5.** The Dow Jones was *down by more than 2,000 points*, from around 11,000 to around 9,000, which makes Choice (5) the correct answer.

46. **2.** The setting for the cartoon is a *laboratory*, not a living room, playroom, library, or kitchen.

47. **5.** The researcher has been studying *limited patents for medicines*. You can tell this from the phrase *perpetual patents*.

48. **3.** The cartoonist depicts drug companies as *greedy*. Drug companies may also be caring or generous, but the cartoon doesn't suggest this. Drug companies certainly aren't religious, and the term *curious* just doesn't make sense in this context.

49. **5.** The solution is important for the drug companies because it will *increase their profits*. Other potential effects — sharing with people, making employees famous, improving public relations, and looking good — may all be important to people, but they aren't the primary reason for wanting the solution.

50. **1.** The overall theme of the cartoon is the *greed* of the drug companies.

Chapter 12

Another Practice Test — Social Studies Test

· ·

The Social Studies Test consists of multiple-choice questions that measure general social studies concepts. The questions are based on short readings that often include a map, graph, chart, political cartoon, or figure. Study the information given and then answer the question(s) following it. Refer to the information as often as necessary in answering the questions.

You have 70 minutes to answer the 50 questions in this test. Work carefully, but do not spend too much time on any one question. Be sure you answer every question.

Answer Sheet for Social Studies Test

1	① ② ③ ④ ⑤					26	① ② ③ ④ ⑤
2	① ② ③ ④ ⑤					27	① ② ③ ④ ⑤
3	① ② ③ ④ ⑤					28	① ② ③ ④ ⑤
4	① ② ③ ④ ⑤					29	① ② ③ ④ ⑤
5	① ② ③ ④ ⑤					30	① ② ③ ④ ⑤
6	① ② ③ ④ ⑤					31	① ② ③ ④ ⑤
7	① ② ③ ④ ⑤					32	① ② ③ ④ ⑤
8	① ② ③ ④ ⑤					33	① ② ③ ④ ⑤
9	① ② ③ ④ ⑤					34	① ② ③ ④ ⑤
10	① ② ③ ④ ⑤					35	① ② ③ ④ ⑤
11	① ② ③ ④ ⑤					36	① ② ③ ④ ⑤
12	① ② ③ ④ ⑤					37	① ② ③ ④ ⑤
13	① ② ③ ④ ⑤					38	① ② ③ ④ ⑤
14	① ② ③ ④ ⑤					39	① ② ③ ④ ⑤
15	① ② ③ ④ ⑤					40	① ② ③ ④ ⑤
16	① ② ③ ④ ⑤					41	① ② ③ ④ ⑤
17	① ② ③ ④ ⑤					42	① ② ③ ④ ⑤
18	① ② ③ ④ ⑤					43	① ② ③ ④ ⑤
19	① ② ③ ④ ⑤					44	① ② ③ ④ ⑤
20	① ② ③ ④ ⑤					45	① ② ③ ④ ⑤
21	① ② ③ ④ ⑤					46	① ② ③ ④ ⑤
22	① ② ③ ④ ⑤					47	① ② ③ ④ ⑤
23	① ② ③ ④ ⑤					48	① ② ③ ④ ⑤
24	① ② ③ ④ ⑤					49	① ② ③ ④ ⑤
25	① ② ③ ④ ⑤					50	① ② ③ ④ ⑤

Social Studies Test

Do not mark in this test booklet. Record your answers on the separate answer sheet provided. Be sure that all requested information is properly recorded on the answer sheet.

To record your answers, fill in the numbered circle on the answer sheet that corresponds to the answer you select for each question in the test booklet.

EXAMPLE:

Early colonists of North America looked for settlement sites with adequate water supplies and access by ship. For this reason, many early towns were built near

(1) mountains

(2) prairies

(3) rivers

(4) glaciers

(On Answer Sheet)

① ② ● ④ ⑤

(5) plateaus

The correct answer is "rivers"; therefore, answer space 3 would be marked on the answer sheet.

Do not rest the point of your pencil on the answer sheet while you are considering your answer. Make no stray or unnecessary marks. If you change an answer, erase your first mark completely. Mark only one answer space for each question; multiple answers will be scored as incorrect. Do not fold or crease your answer sheet. All test materials must be returned to the test administrator.

Note: See Chapter 13 for the answers for this practice test.

DO NOT BEGIN TAKING THIS TEST UNTIL TOLD TO DO SO

Directions: Choose the <u>one best answer</u> to each question.

Questions 1 through 5 refer to the following passage, which is excerpted from Canadian History For Dummies, *2nd Edition, by Will Ferguson (Wiley).*

The Winnipeg General Strike

By 1911, Winnipeg was the third largest city in Canada. It was also one of the most union-ized. Historian David Bercuson traces the showdown of 1919 all the way back to labour disputes in 1906, but it was the war and its aftermath that finally pushed things over the edge. The Great War, with its spiralling inflation and frantic employment, made workers aware of both their increasing power — and their increasing vulnerability. As early as 1917, there was talk of calling a city-wide general strike over conscription — an issue that union organizers opposed — and in 1918, when the Winnipeg City Council outlawed the right to strike for civic employees, municipal workers walked off the job in protest and were joined in sympathy strikes by other unions. Their actions shook the City Council to the core, and the city quickly backed down in defeat. The 1918 lesson was well learned: *Strength in numbers, victory through militancy.* It was, in a way, merely a warm-up for what was to come.

Returning veterans played a key role on both sides. They were, to a man, sick of war and longing for a permanent peace. They drifted into two opposing camps: one pro-reform and pro-union, the other *anti*-reform and *anti*-union. Ironically, both were inspired by the same wish: to see something good come out of World War I. Some were determined to change the social structure that they felt had led to war; others were just as determined to never see that structure again challenged. In 1919, the pot finally boiled over. More working hours were lost to strikes in 1919 than any other year in the nation's history, before or since.

Go on to next page

1. What notable characteristic made Winnipeg stand out among Canadian cities?

   (1) spiralling inflation

   (2) frantic employment

   (3) increasing power

   (4) increasing vulnerability

   (5) most unionized

2. What was the year of the first great showdown?

   (1) 1906

   (2) 1911

   (3) 1918

   (4) 1917

   (5) 1919

3. What was the primary cause of the city-wide general strike?

   (1) conscription

   (2) inflation

   (3) unemployment

   (4) labour disputes

   (5) the Great War

4. What factor most influenced the conflict?

   (1) permanent peace

   (2) opposing camps

   (3) the social structure

   (4) returning veterans

   (5) right to strike

5. What was the major impact of the general strike?

   (1) World War I

   (2) strength in numbers

   (3) lost hours

   (4) sick of war

   (5) more prosperity

Go on to next page

> *Questions 6 through 11 refer to the following passage, which is excerpted from* Canadian History For Dummies, *2nd Edition, by Will Ferguson (Wiley).*

The War Measures Act of 1970

On October 15, Québec Premier Robert Bourassa sent word to Ottawa, asking for federal intervention. Trudeau responded by invoking the War Measures Act, which gave the government sweeping, dictatorial powers. Far from being a unilateral imposition by Trudeau, the Act was passed with overwhelming support in the House of Commons: 190 to 16. Only the NDP stood opposed. Canada was now under martial law. Civil liberties were suspended, the FLQ was banned, and the police were allowed to arrest and detain citizens without trial — or even explanation. In a series of pre-dawn raids, police officers rounded up more than 450 people and held them without bail. (All but 25 of them would later be released.)

It was the first time in Canadian history that the War Measures Act had been used during peacetime — and the public wholeheartedly agreed. In fact, the 1970 imposition of the War Measures Act was probably one of the single most popular pieces of legislation ever passed in Canada. Almost 90 percent of the population supported it, and this support was just as strong among French Canadians as it was among English Canadians

6. Why did Premier Bourassa send word to Ottawa?

   (1) He wanted dictatorial powers.

   (2) He was asking for federal intervention.

   (3) He was seeking overwhelming support.

   (4) He wished to arrest citizens.

   (5) He wanted to round up people.

7. Who invoked the War Measures Act?

   (1) Bourassa

   (2) the NDP

   (3) civil liberties

   (4) Trudeau

   (5) the House of Commons

8. How did the House of Commons deal with the War Measures Act?

   (1) gave it overwhelming support

   (2) suspended it

   (3) banned it

   (4) placed it under martial law

   (5) gave it dictatorial powers

9. What were the results of the use of the War Measures Act?

   (1) martial law

   (2) suspended liberties

   (3) FLQ banned

   (4) citizens detained

   (5) all of the above

10. What was unique about the imposition of the War Measures Act?

    (1) The NDP opposed it.

    (2) It caused more than 450 people to be rounded up.

    (3) It was used during peacetime.

    (4) It was popular legislation.

    (5) It received population support.

11. How did members of the public feel about the War Measures Act?

    (1) They were violently opposed.

    (2) They strongly supported it.

    (3) They didn't pay attention.

    (4) They demanded an explanation.

    (5) They feared a loss of liberties.

Go on to next page

Questions 12 through 17 refer to the following passage, which is excerpted from
CliffsQuickReview U.S. History I by P. Soifer and A. Hoffman (Wiley).

The War of 1812

For the United States, the most obvious British target was Canada. Its population was small, many Canadians were actually Americans by birth, and a quick victory there would stop British plans to ruin American trade. The military facts painted a different picture, however. Thousands of Native Americans in the northwestern territories sided with the British when the war began, bolstering their strength, while the small U.S. army was composed of poorly trained state militiamen led by elderly and incompetent generals.

In July 1812, an American army led by General William Hull moved from Detroit into Canada. Almost immediately the Shawnee cut his supply lines, forcing him back to Detroit. Although Hull commanded two thousand men, he surrendered to a considerably smaller British and Native American force. Other embarrassments followed as the United States suffered defeat at Queenston Heights in western New York and the militia under General Henry Dearborn refused to march to Montreal from northeastern New York.

The United States fared better on Lake Erie in 1813. The Royal Navy could not reach the lake from the St. Lawrence River, so both the British and Americans raced to build ships on opposite sides of the lake. On September 10, 1813, the small American fleet under Oliver Hazard Perry defeated the British in the Battle of Lake Erie. "We have met the enemy, and they are ours," he reported, a victory statement that became legendary.

Less than three weeks later, on October 5, William Henry Harrison (a general by then) defeated a combined British and Native American force at the Battle of the Thames. Tecumseh was killed in this battle, ending Native Americans' hopes for a coalition that could stand against the advance of U.S. settlement. Despite these victories, U.S. efforts to capture Canada ended in a stalemate.

Go on to next page

12. Why was Canada a target for the United States?

    (1) Its citizens were American by birth.

    (2) It had a large population.

    (3) It was a British possession.

    (4) Americans had visited Canada many times.

    (5) It would protect American trade.

13. Whom did Native Americans support in the conflict?

    (1) the British

    (2) the Canadians

    (3) the Americans

    (4) the U.S. army

    (5) the French

14. Why did General Hull surrender?

    (1) He was forced back to Detroit.

    (2) He commanded only two thousand men.

    (3) He couldn't cross the Thames.

    (4) The British force was too strong.

    (5) His supply lines were cut.

15. What did Queenston Heights represent for the United States?

    (1) a victory

    (2) a proposal

    (3) an embarrassment

    (4) a refusal to march

    (5) a lot of suffering

16. What kept the Royal Navy fleet from Lake Erie?

    (1) the St. Lawrence River

    (2) the Detroit River

    (3) Lake Ontario

    (4) Lake St. Clair

    (5) not enough information given

17. What was the result of the War of 1812?

    (1) The Americans won.

    (2) The British won.

    (3) It ended in a stalemate.

    (4) The Native Americans won.

    (5) Tecumseh was killed.

Go on to next page

Questions 18 through 23 refer to the following passage, which is excerpted from Canadian History For Dummies, *2nd Edition, by Will Ferguson (Wiley).*

Patrioting Canada's Constitution

Hard to believe, but Canada was still not a fully independent nation. The country was governed under the terms of the British North America Act, first drafted by John A. Macdonald and the others back in 1867. The BNA Act was an act of *British* Parliament, and any changes to it had to be approved by Britain. This had become a mere formality, of course. But it still took time and energy, and — more importantly — it was a mouldy relic of colonial times. Britain would have gladly turned its remaining authority over to Canada, and Canada would have been more than happy to accept. There was just one snag: With Britain removed from the equation, how would future constitutional changes be made? If the Constitution were to come home, an "amending formula" had to be worked out first.

Attempts to *patriate* (bring home) Canada's Constitution had been made before, most notably during the 1920s and later in 1964, when Pearson had presented a blueprint for future constitutional changes. Dubbed "the Fulton-Favreau Formula" after its two key architects, it was approved by every premier in Canada, including Québec's Jean Lesage. But before the deal could be ratified, Daniel Johnson and the Union Nationale were elected and all bets were off. Canada's Constitution remained in the hands of Britain.

18. Who or what governed Canada after 1867?

    (1) the British Parliament

    (2) John A. Macdonald

    (3) the British North America Act

    (4) the Fulton-Favreau Formula

    (5) the Union Nationale

19. Who drafted the original BNA Act?

    (1) Lester Pearson

    (2) Pierre Trudeau

    (3) Jean Lesage

    (4) John A. Macdonald

    (5) Daniel Johnson

20. How does the passage describe the BNA Act?

    (1) amending formula

    (2) act of Parliament

    (3) mere formality

    (4) future blueprint

    (5) mouldy relic

21. What body was originally responsible for Canada's Constitution?

    (1) the British Parliament

    (2) the House of Commons

    (3) the House of Lords

    (4) the House of Representatives

    (5) the Senate

22. Through which method could the Constitution be brought home?

    (1) the Fulton-Favreau Formula

    (2) a blueprint for changes

    (3) a judicial decree

    (4) the premiers

    (5) an amending formula

23. How could Canada's Constitution be patriated and ratified?

    (1) If it remained in British hands.

    (2) If the people approved.

    (3) If every premier approved.

    (4) If the Queen consented.

    (5) If Québec agreed.

Go on to next page

> *Questions 24 through 29 refer to the following passage, which is excerpted from*
> CliffsQuickReview U.S. History II *by P. Soifer and A. Hoffman (Wiley).*

Causes of World War I

On June 28, 1914, a Serbian nationalist assassinated the Archduke Franz Ferdinand, the heir to the throne of Austria-Hungary. Austria demanded indemnities from Serbia for the assassination. The Serbian government denied any involvement with the murder and, when Austria issued an ultimatum, turned to its ally, Russia, for help. When Russia began to mobilize its army, Europe's alliance system, ironically intended to maintain the balance of power on the continent, drew one country after another into war. Austria's ally, Germany, declared war on Russia on August 1 and on France (which was allied with Russia) two days later. Great Britain entered the war on August 4, following Germany's invasion of neutral Belgium. By the end of August 1914, most of Europe had chosen sides: the Central Powers — Germany, Austria-Hungary, Bulgaria, and the Ottoman Empire (Turkey) — were up against the Allied Powers — principally Great Britain, France, Russia, and Serbia. Japan joined the Allied cause in August 1914, in hopes of seizing German possessions in the Pacific and expanding Japanese influence in China. This action threatened the Open Door Policy and led to increased tensions with the United States. Originally an ally of Germany and Austria-Hungary, Italy entered the war in 1915 on the side of Britain and France because they had agreed to Italian territorial demands in a secret treaty (the Treaty of London).

24. Where did the assassin of Archduke Ferdinand originate?

    (1) Great Britain

    (2) France

    (3) Russia

    (4) Serbia

    (5) Germany

25. How did Austria initially react to the assassination?

    (1) denied any involvement

    (2) demanded indemnities

    (3) turned to its ally

    (4) declared war

    (5) mobilized its army

26. Which countries were not allies?

    (1) Serbia and Russia

    (2) Austria and Hungary

    (3) Germany and France

    (4) France and Great Britain

    (5) Germany and Austria

27. What caused Great Britain to enter the war?

    (1) Germany invaded Belgium

    (2) Russia attacked Serbia

    (3) France invaded Russia

    (4) Austria invaded Hungary

    (5) Germany attacked Russia

28. Which country was not an Allied Power?

    (1) Great Britain

    (2) France

    (3) Germany

    (4) Russia

    (5) Serbia

29. Why did Italy join the Allies?

    (1) the Open Door Policy

    (2) increased tensions

    (3) business demands

    (4) the expanding Japanese influence

    (5) the Treaty of London

Go on to next page ⟹

Questions 30 through 33 refer to the following passage.

U.S. "Invades" Canada

Hilary Clinton, U.S. secretary of state, arrived in Canada for the G8 Summit yesterday with her verbal guns blazing. She does not agree with Prime Minister Harper on several issues and used her style of gunboat diplomacy to tell him publicly.

Canada has advised NATO that it will withdraw troops from Afghanistan. This goes against American policy and Clinton told Harper so in public. Most disagreements of this type are sorted out behind closed doors. Clinton chose the public arena to try to whip Canada into American shape. The war has been unpopular in both countries but that did not stop the U.S. from advocating more troops.

Although the Americans are embroiled in their own healthcare problems, Clinton gave Harper her views on abortion and maternal health and tried arm-twisting to solve their differences.

Harper is also in trouble with Clinton's America for convening a meeting on the Arctic Oceans. It seems our sovereignty has its limits with our neighbours.

Canadians are now wondering if this was the opening salvo in an invasion by coercion or just a misstep in what has been peaceful co-existence. Only time will tell.

30. How did Hilary Clinton arrive at the G8 Summit?

    (1) by Airforce One

    (2) with verbal guns blazing

    (3) with gunboat diplomacy

    (4) by special limousine

    (5) from Afghanistan

31. According to the passage, in what way is this type of political disagreement usually settled?

    (1) at NATO

    (2) in public

    (3) through peaceful co-existence

    (4) by going to war

    (5) behind closed doors

32. What is Harper's policy on Afghanistan?

    (1) withdraw troops

    (2) advocate more troops

    (3) offer healthcare assistance

    (4) discuss abortion and maternal health

    (5) give Arctic sovereignty

33. What was the topic of the disagreement between Clinton and Harper?

    (1) troop withdrawal

    (2) views on abortion

    (3) maternal health

    (4) Arctic sovereignty

    (5) all of the above

Go on to next page

> Questions 34 through 37 refer to the following passage, which is excerpted from Canadian History for Dummies, *2nd Edition, by Will Ferguson (Wiley).*

The Trudeau Legacy

On a snowy evening at the end of a leap year February in 1984, Pierre Elliott Trudeau went for a long walk and looked for signs of destiny in the sky. "But there were no signs," he said wistfully. "There were only snowflakes." The next day he announced his retirement.

Trudeau should have left two years earlier, after the triumph of the Constitution Act and the Charter of Rights and Freedoms. Instead, he lingered like an actor who stays on stage after the applause has petered out. In 1984, unemployment was high, the value of the Canadian dollar was in free fall, and the public was growing weary of Trudeau's aloof arrogance. It is highly unlikely he could have won another term.

With only a brief interruption, Pierre Trudeau was the prime minister of Canada for 15 tumultuous years — third-longest after Mackenzie King and John A. Macdonald. Economically, the Trudeau Era (1968–84) was an erratic time. According to Keynesian theory, economies should alternate between times of high unemployment and high inflation — but not both. Yet across Canada and much of the Western world a new phenomenon was born: "stagflation," a bewildering combination of inflation *and* high unemployment.

34. What did Trudeau look for during his long walk?

    (1) snowflakes

    (2) signs of destiny

    (3) the end of a leap year

    (4) a snowy evening

    (5) some peace and quiet

35. What was the result of Trudeau's long walk?

    (1) Constitution Act

    (2) Charter of Rights and Freedoms

    (3) high unemployment

    (4) his retirement announcement

    (5) a low Canadian dollar

36. What about Trudeau caused the public to grow weary?

    (1) his aloof arrogance

    (2) his lack of applause

    (3) his tumultuous years

    (4) his economics

    (5) his sense of humour

37. What does "stagflation" mean?

    (1) Keynesian theory

    (2) an erratic time

    (3) a new phenomenon

    (4) a brief interruption

    (5) inflation and high unemployment combined

Go on to next page

Questions 38 through 42 refer to the following timeline from Canadian History For Dummies, 2nd Edition, by Will Ferguson (Wiley).

A Timeline of World War I

Year	Date	Event
1914	June 28	Archduke Ferdinand of Austria assassinated — setting off a chain of events leading to World War.
	August 4	Britain declares war on Germany — as part of the Empire, Canada is automatically at war as well.
	October 3	Canada's first contingent sets sail for Europe.
1915	April 22 – 24	Ypres — Germans unleash the first gas attack.
	December	In his year-end address, Borden commits Canada to 500,000 more troops.
1916	July 1 – November 18	Battle of the Somme — more than 600,000 Allied troops are lost.
1917	April 6	United States declares war on Germany.
	April 9 – 12	Battle of Vimy Ridge — major Canadian victory.
	August 29	Military Service Act — conscription becomes law.
	October 12	Borden announces the creation of a Union government.
	October 26 – November 10	Battle of Passchendaele takes place.
	October – November	Communist forces under Lenin seize control of Russia and sue for peace with Germany.
	December 17	Borden's pro-conscriptionist Unionists defeat Laurier's.
1918	March 21	With troops no longer tied down on the Russian front, Germans launch a major offensive.
	March 29 – April 1	Easter Weekend riots occur in Québec City.
	April 12	All exemptions are cancelled; conscription begins in full force.
	August 8 – November 11	"Canada's 100 Days" — the Allies counterattack with the Canadians as the spearhead to victory.
	August 8 – 11	Battle of Amiens — Canadians lead the attack.
	August 26 – September 2	Canadians break through the Hindenburg Line.
	November 11	Germany surrenders.
1919	June 28	Treaty of Versailles formally ends the war.
1920	January 10	Canada becomes a founding member of the League of Nations.

Go on to next page

38. Why did Canada join World War I?

    (1) Archduke Ferdinand was assassinated.

    (2) Canada was part of the British Empire.

    (3) The United States declared war.

    (4) Conscription was introduced.

    (5) Many troops were killed.

39. Where did the Germans first attack with gas?

    (1) Vimy Ridge

    (2) Somme

    (3) Ypres

    (4) Passchendaele

    (5) Amiens

40. When did the United States enter the War?

    (1) 1916

    (2) 1918

    (3) 1914

    (4) 1915

    (5) 1917

41. Who was chiefly responsible for conscription?

    (1) Laurier

    (2) Lenin

    (3) Ferdinand

    (4) Borden

    (5) Hindenberg

42. How was Canada's contribution to the war effort recognized?

    (1) Easter Weekend riots occurred in Québec City.

    (2) The 100 days saw counterattacks.

    (3) Canada became a founding member of the League of Nations.

    (4) There was a spearhead to victory.

    (5) The Treaty of Versailles was enacted.

Go on to next page

> *Questions 43 through 46 refer to the following newscast.*

World Environmental News

Good evening and welcome to World Environmental News.

Our stories this evening: cyclones in Korea, flooding in Europe and India, volcanic eruptions in New Guinea, drought in Australia, tornadoes in the United States, hailstorms in Italy, earthquakes in Iran, and locusts in Denmark.

Now, let's look at our top stories.

Drought in Australia: The wheat fields west of Canberra, New South Wales, are in great danger today because of the ongoing drought. In the next week, farmers may have to write off this year's crop, and this will likely lead to financial ruin for many of them. To add to the misery, hundreds of thousands of sheep had to be sold because there was not enough water for them to drink.

Locusts in Denmark: The unseasonably warm weather in Denmark is proving to be inviting to the lowly locust. Normally found along the Mediterranean coast, the locust has been found far from its normal habitat. These discoveries in southwest Denmark are causing concern because locusts have not been seen in Denmark for over 50 years.

Hurricane near Mexico: Hurricane Herman is losing force off the Pacific coast of Mexico. The country is giving a sigh of relief as the hurricane winds down.

For wine drinkers: And a last note for you wine drinkers. The recent violent hailstorms in Italy are expected to cause a poor grape harvest. This means lower wine production and, consequently, higher prices.

There's more as nature lashes out. Tune in again for World Environmental News.

43. In which ocean is the tropical storm called Hurricane Herman located?

    (1) Pacific

    (2) Arctic

    (3) Atlantic

    (4) Indian

    (5) Antarctic

44. According to the newscast, where is the extreme drought causing major loss of wheat crops?

    (1) India

    (2) China

    (3) Saudi Arabia

    (4) Death Valley

    (5) Australia

45. Why have locusts been found in Denmark?

    (1) unseasonably warm weather

    (2) prevailing winds

    (3) foreign ships

    (4) wild birds

    (5) Mediterranean climate

46. What will be the impact of hailstorms in Italy?

    (1) lower olive oil prices

    (2) devastating floods

    (3) damaged cars

    (4) higher wine prices

    (5) more insurance coverage

Go on to next page

Questions 47 through 50 refer to the following political cartoon.

47. What happens if oil prices rise?

    (1) SUV sales decrease.

    (2) People stop travelling.

    (3) Oil companies make less profit.

    (4) Gas stations close.

    (5) Gasoline prices rise.

48. How does a rise in oil prices affect the cost of living?

    (1) has no impact

    (2) raises the cost of living

    (3) doesn't really matter

    (4) forces rich nations to pay more

    (5) protects the oil companies

49. What adjective best describes the characters in the cartoon?

    (1) smug

    (2) arrogant

    (3) wasteful

    (4) thoughtful

    (5) angry

50. What phrase does not describe the SUV or its occupants?

    (1) pollution creator

    (2) road warrior

    (3) energy saver

    (4) gas guzzler

    (5) monster truck

END OF TEST

Chapter 13

Answers and Explanations for the Social Studies Test

Answer Key

After taking the Social Studies Test in Chapter 12, use this section to check your answers.

1. **5**	18. **3**	35. **4**
2. **3**	19. **4**	36. **1**
3. **1**	20. **5**	37. **5**
4. **4**	21. **1**	38. **2**
5. **3**	22. **5**	39. **3**
6. **2**	23. **3**	40. **5**
7. **4**	24. **4**	41. **4**
8. **1**	25. **2**	42. **3**
9. **5**	26. **3**	43. **1**
10. **3**	27. **1**	44. **5**
11. **2**	28. **3**	45. **1**
12. **3**	29. **5**	46. **4**
13. **1**	30. **2**	47. **5**
14. **5**	31. **5**	48. **2**
15. **3**	32. **1**	49. **3**
16. **5**	33. **5**	50. **3**
17. **3**	34. **2**	

Analysis of the Answers

If you aren't sure why an answer is incorrect, use this section to get quick explanations of the answers. If you correctly answered a question, you may still want to read the explanations to get a better understanding of the thought process that helped you choose the correct answer.

1. **5.** By 1911, The notable characteristic that made Winnipeg stand out among Canadian cities was that it was known as one of the *most unionized* cities in Canada. The Great War caused spiralling inflation and frantic employment. The workers gained increasing power and vulnerability.

2. **3.** The first great showdown happened in *1918* when City Council outlawed the right to strike. As a result, more hours were lost to strikes in 1919. The other choices — 1906, 1911, and 1917 — are incorrect.

3. **1.** The imposition of *conscription* in 1917 led to a call for a city-wide general strike. Other factors, such as inflation and labour disputes, might also have been influential, but they were not the primary cause. Unemployment is not mentioned in the passage.

4. **4.** The *returning veterans* were the factor that most influenced the conflict. It was the veterans who were sick of war, wanted permanent peace, and established opposing camps. The social structure and the right to strike are not relevant to the question.

5. **3.** The major impact of the general strike was the *many hours of work that were lost* in 1919. World War I, strength in numbers, and sick of war were not major impacts. More prosperity is not mentioned in the passage.

6. **2.** Premier Bourassa approached Ottawa for the *intervention of the federal government* because of the crisis in Québec. Legally, he did not have dictatorial powers to arrest citizens and round up people, so he was seeking federal support.

7. **4.** According to the passage, it was *Prime Minister Trudeau* who invoked the War Measures Act. Of course, it also had to be approved by the House of Commons where the NDP opposed its passage. Bourassa and civil liberties are incorrect choices.

8. **1.** When the War Measures Act was presented to the House of Commons, it received *overwhelming support*. The Act, when passed, however, would result in suspensions, bans, martial law, and dictatorial powers.

9. **5.** The War Measures Act resulted in all of Choices (1) to (4) being imposed particularly in the province of Québec.

10. **3.** The unique thing about the War Measures Act was that it was *used during peacetime*. While the NDP opposed it, 450 people were rounded up, and it proved to be popular with the public, those are not the best answers.

11. **2.** The passage says that the public *strongly supported* the War Measures Act, which means the other choices — violently opposed, lack of attention, demanding an explanation, and loss of liberties — are incorrect answers because they're not specifically mentioned in the passage. You can only answer questions from the information in the passage.

12. **3.** Canada was a target for the United States because it was a British possession with a small population (refer to the first sentence of the passage).

13. **1.** The first paragraph states that Native Americans were *loyal to the British* in the war.

14. **5.** Hull surrendered because the Shawnee *cut his supply lines* (refer to the second paragraph of the passage).

15. **3.** The battle of Queenston Heights was a defeat for the United States — so it represented an *embarrassment*, not a victory. Refusal to march and suffering are also incorrect answers. A battle isn't ever likely to be considered a proposal, so that answer choice is wrong, too.

16. **5.** Although you may know that Niagara Falls kept the Royal Navy from sailing from the St. Lawrence River into Lake Erie, the passage doesn't tell you so. For this reason, *not enough information given* is the best answer here.

17. **3.** The last sentence of the passage states that the War of 1812 ended in a *stalemate*, with neither side claiming victory. The death of Tecumseh was also an outcome, but it wasn't the *overall* result of the war, which is why stalemate is the best answer.

18. **3.** After 1867, Canada was governed by the *British North America Act*. Although it was passed by the British Parliament, the BNA Act itself provided government for Canada. John A. Macdonald helped to draft the BNA Act. The Fulton-Favreau Formula and Union Nationale are incorrect answers.

19. **4.** *John A. Macdonald* drafted the BNA Act in 1867. The others — Pearson, Trudeau, Lesage, and Johnson — were leaders in the twentieth century.

20. **5.** The BNA Act is described in the passage as a *mouldy relic* of the time when Canada was a colony of Britain. Although it was also an act of Parliament, this is not the best description. Amending formula, mere formality, and future blueprint are not correct choices.

21. **1.** The *British Parliament*, which passed the BNA Act, was the body originally responsible for Canada's Constitution. Both the House of Commons and the House of Lords make up the Parliament. The House of Representatives and the Senate are part of the American government. Parliament and the Senate form the Canadian government.

22. **5.** For the Constitution to be brought home, an *amending formula* had to be approved by all provinces. Québec did not approve the Fulton-Favreau. Blueprint for changes, judicial decree, and through the premiers are not the best answers.

23. **3.** To be patriated and ratified, the Constitution must be *approved by all the premiers*. It would not be patriated if left in British hands. Approval by the people, consent by the Queen, and Québec's agreement are not the best answers.

24. **4.** Archduke Ferdinand was assassinated by a Serbian nationalist, so the correct answer is *Serbia*. Great Britain, France, Russia, and Germany are incorrect.

25. **2.** Austria *demanded indemnities* in response to the assassination. This answer comes directly from the passage.

26. **3.** *Germany and France* weren't allies in the war. Although the list of allies is rather confusing, the passage does sum up who was on which side.

27. **1.** You know that Great Britain entered the war *when Germany invaded Belgium* from the sentence that states, "Great Britain entered the war on August 4, following Germany's invasion of neutral Belgium."

28. **3.** *Germany* was not an Allied power. About halfway through the passage is a list of the Central powers (on one side of the war) and the Allied powers (on the other side).

29. **5.** Italy joined the Allies because of the *Treaty of London*. The Open Door Policy, increased tensions, territorial demands, and the expanding Japanese influence may have played a part, but, according to the passage, they aren't the best answers.

30. **2.** In the passage, the author describes Hilary Clinton as arriving at the G8 Summit "with her verbal guns blazing." This behaviour might be referred to as gunboat diplomacy, but that is not the best answer. The other choices — Airforce One, special limousine, and from Afghanistan — relate to transportation and are not supported by the passage.

31. **5.** Disagreements between friendly neighbours, such as the U.S. and Canada, are usually resolved *behind closed doors* as opposed to at NATO, in public, or going to war. Peaceful co-existence, while an outcome of settling disputes, is not the best answer.

32. **1.** The Canadian government's stated policy has been to *withdraw its troops from Afghanistan* by 2011. The U.S., on the other hand, has been advocating for more troops. Health issues and Arctic sovereignty are not relevant to Afghanistan.

33. **5.** *All of the above* is the only correct choice according to the issues of disagreement between Clinton and Harper described in the passage.

34. **2.** Trudeau took his long walk seeking *signs of his future destiny.* Although it happened to be a snowy evening at the end of a leap year, these are not relevant choices. The idea of peace and quiet does not appear in the passage.

35. **4.** The result of Trudeau's long walk was his decision to *announce his retirement.* The Constitution Act and the Charter of Rights and Freedoms were accomplishments during his tenure. High unemployment and a low dollar may have been factors in his decision to retire.

36. **1.** The public was growing weary of Trudeau because of the *aloof arrogance* he displayed. Lack of applause, tumultuous years, and his economics were not the best answers. His sense of humour was not mentioned in the passage.

37. **5.** According to the passage, stagflation is a combination of *high inflation and high unemployment.* Keynesian theory, erratic time, new phenomenon, and brief interruption are not part of the definition of stagflation.

38. **2.** Canada joined the fighting in World War I because it was *part of the British Empire.* While the Archduke's assassination was a cause of war breaking out, it was not the reason Canada became involved. The other answers — the United States' involvement, conscription, and the death toll of troops — while factors, were also not reasons for joining.

39. **3.** The Germans first used gas in their attack at *Ypres.* Other battles — Vimy Ridge, Somme, Passchendaele, and Amiens — were not the first time gas was used.

40. **5.** The United States did not enter the War until 1917. The other dates are incorrect answers according to the timeline.

41. **4.** When Borden's Unionist party came to power in 1917, he introduced conscription through the Military Service Act. Laurier's Liberals did not support conscription. The other answers — Lenin, Ferdinand, and Hindenberg — had nothing to do with conscription in Canada.

42. **3.** Canada's contribution to the War effort was recognized in 1920, when Canada became a *founding member of the League of Nations.* The other events, while part of the War, are not the correct answers.

43. **1.** According to the newscast, Hurricane Herman is located off Mexico's *Pacific* coast.

44. **5.** Extreme drought conditions exist in *Australia* because of a lack of rainfall.

45. **1.** Because of *unseasonably warm weather*, locusts were found in Denmark. Locusts are drawn to warm weather, so they're leaving the warm Mediterranean for usually chilly Denmark.

46. **4.** The hailstorms will ruin many of the grapes that are on the vines when the storm hits, which will result in a reduced grape harvest and *higher wine prices* in Italy. One principle of economics is the law of supply and demand: The less supply of something you have, the greater the demand is for that something, so the more you can charge for it. When something is in low supply, the price usually goes up.

47. **5.** If oil prices rise, *gasoline prices will rise* — this answer is best given the cartoon. Although you can guess that SUV sales may decrease and people may travel less as a result of higher oil prices, you don't have evidence of either of these results in the cartoon.

48. **2.** Because oil is used to fuel cars and some homes, if oil prices rise, the cost of living (which includes paying for gas and home heating) *will also rise.*

49. **3.** The characters in the cartoon are willing to *waste* gasoline to drive their car. When you waste gasoline, not only do you waste money, but you also waste all the natural resources and energy that went into getting the oil out of the ground and turning it into gasoline.

50. **3.** The SUV *isn't an energy saver.* That's the point of the cartoon.

Part IV
Peering at Your Specimen: The Science Test

In this part . . .

How is the Science Test different from the other GED tests, and what do you have to know to pass it? The secrets lie within this part, which tells you all about what you need to know for the Science Test and how to prepare for it. Here we also show you how the Science Test is set up and give you some strategies to follow to do your best.

Like in the other parts about the specific tests, we provide you with two practice tests to get your feet wet. You can see how you did on those tests by perusing the answers and explanations — take the time to congratulate yourself when you're right and figure out what went wrong when you aren't. We recommend that you take these practice tests after you've studied and brushed up your skills and science vocabulary. Mastering this set of practice tests tells you that you're ready to take the real GED tests. If you don't do as well as you'd hoped on these tests, you know you have a bit more preparation to do before you're ready for the real deal.

Chapter 14

From Aardvarks to Atoms: The Science Test

The Science Test is both the same as the other tests and different from them. Although the questions are multiple choice (like the other tests), they're based on scientific text passages or visual images, including diagrams, graphs, maps, and tables. To do well on the Science Test, you're expected to have a passing knowledge of scientific vocabulary, and one of the best ways to improve your scientific vocabulary is to read scientific material and look up any words you don't know. Rest easy that you aren't expected to know the difference between terms like fission and fusion — just being slightly familiar with them can help you on the test.

The Science Test covers material from life science, physical science (chemistry and physics), and earth and space science. Don't panic — you don't need to memorize material from those subjects. You just need to be able to read and understand the material and correctly answer questions about it. The hardest part of this test is understanding science vocabulary; to help you, we offer you more than one chance to improve your science vocabulary as you work through this chapter. We also help you get a feel for the Science Test's format. We show you the different types of questions that may appear on your test. Finally, we try to help you stay awake for what may be some of the driest material on any of the GED tests. After you understand the words on this test, along with its basic format and subject areas, try out the practice tests in Chapters 15 and 17.

Looking at the Skills the Science Test Covers

The Science Test doesn't test you on your knowledge of science, and you're not expected to memorize any scientific information to do well on this test. Instead, this test checks your ability to ferret out information presented to you in passages or visual materials.

If you're totally unfamiliar with science and its vocabulary, you'll likely have trouble with the questions on this test. You're expected to have some basic knowledge about how the physical world works, how plants and animals live, and how the universe operates. This test is about ideas that you observe and develop throughout your life, both in and out of school.

You probably know a little about traction, for example, from driving and walking in slippery weather. On the other hand, you may not know a lot about equilibrium other than what you read in school.

As you take the Science Test, you're expected to understand that science is all about inquiry. In fact, inquiry forms the basis of the *scientific method* — which is the process every good scientist follows when faced with an unknown. The steps of the scientific method are

1. **Ask questions.**

2. **Gather information.**

3. **Do experiments.**

4. **Think objectively about what you find.**

5. **Look at other possible explanations.**

6. **Draw one or more possible conclusions.**

7. **Test the conclusion(s).**

8. **Tell others what you found.**

Look at your studying for the Science Test as a scientific problem. The question you're trying to answer is "How can I increase my scientific knowledge?" Follow the scientific method to come up with a procedure to fix the problem. Hopefully, your solution includes reading, reading, and more reading! A high school science book is a great tool to use, as is a preparation book or course that teaches the basics of high school science. (Go to your local library to get your hands on a copy of one of these books, and check with your local school board or continuing education centre to find basic science courses in your area.)

Understanding the Test Format

The Science Test contains 50 multiple-choice questions, which you have 80 minutes to answer. As with the other tests, the information and questions on the Science Test are straightforward — no one is trying to trick you. To answer the questions, you have to read and interpret the passages or other visual materials provided with the questions (and to do so, you likely need a basic understanding of science and the words scientists use).

In terms of format, the 50 questions are grouped as sets. All the questions in a particular set refer to a given passage, chart, diagram, graph, map, or table. Your job is to read or review the material and decide on the best answer for each question based on the given material.

In terms of subject matter, the questions on the Science Test check your knowledge in the following areas:

✔ **Physical science (35 percent; 17 or 18 questions):** *Physical science* is the study of atoms, chemical reactions, forces, and what happens when energy and matter get together. As a basic review, keep the following in mind:

 • Everything is composed of atoms. (The paper this book is printed on is composed of atoms.)

 • When chemicals get together, they have a reaction — unless they're *inert* (which means they don't react with other chemicals; inert chemicals are sort of like anti-social chemicals).

 • You're surrounded by forces and their effects. (If the floor didn't exert a force up on you when you stepped down, you would go through the floor.)

For more information about physical science (which includes basic chemistry and basic physics), read and review a basic science textbook, which you can borrow from your local library (or from your local high school, if you call the office in advance and ask whether the school has any extras). You can also find information on the Internet by entering "basic" and the name of the subject into a search engine. For example, if you want to know more about physics, enter "basic physics" into a search engine. When reading this material, you may need definitions for some of the words or terms to make understanding the concepts easier. Use a good dictionary or the Internet to find these definitions. (If you use the Internet, enter any of the topics into a search engine and add "definition" after it. Become amazed at the number of hits, but don't read them all. After all, you want to write the test while you're still young enough to enjoy the results of your labours.)

✔ **Life science (45 percent; 22 or 23 questions):** *Life science* is the study of cells, heredity, evolution, and other processes that occur in living systems. All life is composed of *cells,* which you can see under a microscope. If you don't have access to a microscope and a set of slides with cells on them, look at life-science-related books or go online to see photographs of cells. When someone tells you that you look like your parents or that you remind them of another relative, they're talking about *heredity.* Reading a bit about heredity in biology-related books can help you practise answering some of the questions on the Science Test.

Use a biology textbook to help you review for this portion of the test. Get your hands on one at your local library or high school, or read up about biology on the Internet. (Remember that not all Internet sites are credible. Always verify your information at more than one source. If two or more sources say the same thing, it is probably more credible than a site that contradicts everything else you have ever read.)

✔ **Earth and space science (20 percent; 10 questions):** This area of science looks at the earth and the universe, specifically weather, astronomy, geology, rocks, erosion, and water.

When you look down at the ground as you walk, you're interacting with earth sciences. When you look up at the stars on a clear night and wonder what's really up there, you're thinking about space sciences. When you complain about the weather, you're complaining about earth sciences. In a nutshell, you're surrounded by earth sciences, so you shouldn't have a problem finding materials to read on this subject.

You don't have to memorize everything you read about science before you take the test. All the answers to the test questions are based on information provided in the passages or on the basic scientific knowledge you've acquired over the years. Any science reading you do prior to the test not only increases your basic knowledge but also improves your vocabulary. An improved science vocabulary increases your chances of reading the passages and answering the questions on the test quickly.

Identifying the Types of Questions and Knowing How to Tackle Them

Like the Social Studies Test, the Science Test has two main types of questions — questions about text passages and questions about visual materials (see Chapter 9 for details on the Social Studies Test). Having a basic understanding of these two question types can help you avoid any surprises when you take the test. In general, you can prepare for these questions similarly to how you prepare for the Social Studies Test. The following sections break down the two types of questions you encounter and offer you advice on how to solve them.

Like with all the other GED tests, make sure you read every word and symbol that appears on the Science Test, including every chart, diagram, graph, map, table, passage, and question. Information — both relevant and irrelevant — is all over the test, and you never know where you'll find what you need to answer the questions quickly and correctly. Don't skip something because it doesn't immediately look important. (Check out the "Examining Preparation Strategies That Work" section for more tips on how you can handle problems that may arise on this test.)

Questions about passages

The first question type on the Science Test is based on passages you have to read and understand. The written passages on this test — and the questions that accompany them — are very similar to a reading-comprehension test: You have to answer questions about textual material. The passages present everything you need to answer the questions — but you usually have to understand all the words in those passages to figure out what they're telling you (which is why we recommend that you read as much science information as you can prior to the test).

The difference between this test and other reading-comprehension tests is that the terminology and examples are all about science. The more you read about science, the more science words you'll know, understand, and feel comfortable seeing on the test — which can greatly improve your chances of success.

Keep the following tips and tricks in mind when answering questions about passages:

✔ **Read each passage and question carefully.** Some of the questions on the Science Test assume that you know a little bit from past experience. For example, you may be expected to know that a rocket is propelled forward by an engine firing backward. (On the other hand, you won't have to know the definition of nuclear fission — thank goodness!)

Regardless of whether a question assumes some basic science knowledge or asks for an answer that appears directly in the passage, you need to read each passage and corresponding question carefully. As you read, do the following:

- Try to understand the passage, and think about what you already know about the subject.

- If a passage has only one question, read that question extra carefully.

- If the passage or question contains words you don't understand, try to figure out what those words mean from the rest of the sentence or the entire passage.

✔ **Read each answer choice carefully.** Doing so helps you get a clearer picture of your options. If you select an answer without reading all the answers, you may end up picking the wrong one because, although that answer may seem right at first, another answer may be more correct.

- If one answer is right from your reading and experience, mark it.

- If you aren't sure which answer is right, exclude the answers you know are wrong and then exclude answers that may be wrong.

- If you can exclude all but one answer, it's probably correct, so mark it.

Try out these tips on the sample passages and questions in the "Practising with Sample Problems" section.

Questions about visual materials

The other type of question on the Science Test is the question based on visual materials. *Visual materials* are pictures that contain information you may need to answer the corresponding questions, and they can be in the form of tables, graphs, diagrams, or maps. Understanding information in visual materials takes more practice than doing so from textual passages, because many people aren't as familiar with getting information from pictures as they are with getting it from text. This section (and the practice tests in Chapters 15 and 17) helps you get the practice you need to do well on all the questions on the Science Test — including the ones based on pictures.

The following sections take a more detailed look at the different visual materials — tables, graphs, diagrams, and maps — that questions on the Science Test can refer to.

Tables

A *table* is a graphical way of organizing information (see Figure 14-1). This type of visual material lets you easily compare two or more sets of data. Some tables use symbols to represent information; others use words.

Science Subjects and Learning Time

Subject	Time to Prepare (Hours)	Average Grade
Earth science	10.8	A-
Biology	17.6	B+
Chemistry	17.5	B
Physics	25.2	B-

Figure 14-1: Table.

Most tables have titles that tell you what they're about. Always read the title first so you know right away what information the table includes. If a table gives you an explanation (or *key*) of the symbols, read the explanation carefully, too; doing so helps you know how to read the table itself.

Graphs

A *graph* is a picture that shows how different sets of numbers are related. On the Science Test, you can find the following three main types of graphs, each of which you can see in Figure 14-2:

✔ **Bar or column graphs:** Use bars (horizontal) or columns (vertical) to present and often compare information

✔ **Line graphs:** Use one or more lines to connect points drawn on a grid to show the relationships between data, including changes in data over time

✔ **Pie graphs (also called pie charts or circle graphs):** Use arcs of circles (pieces of a pie) to show how data relates to a whole

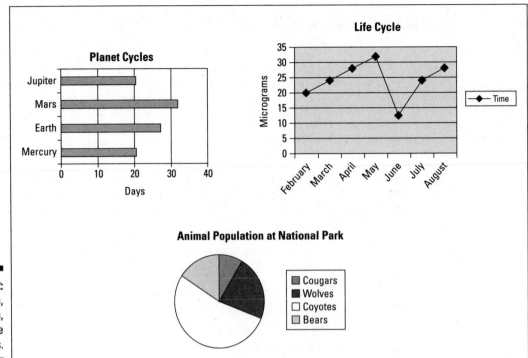

Figure 14-2:
Bar graphs,
line graphs,
and pie
graphs.

These types of graphs usually share the following characteristics:

- ✓ **Title:** The title tells you what the graph is about, so always read the title before reviewing the graph.

- ✓ **Horizontal axis and vertical axis:** Bar, column, and line graphs have a horizontal and a vertical axis. (Pie graphs don't.) Each axis is a vertical or horizontal reference line that's labelled to give you additional information.

- ✓ **Label:** The label on the axis of a graph usually contains units, such as feet or dollars. Read all axis labels carefully; they can either help you with the answer or lead you astray (depending on whether or not you read them correctly).

- ✓ **Legend:** Pie graphs usually have a *legend,* or printed material that tells you what each section of the graph is about. They may also contain labels on the individual pieces of the pie so that you know what each piece represents.

Graphs and tables are both often called *charts,* which can be rather confusing. To prepare for problems with graphs, look at plenty of graphs before the test. Remember that many graphs show relationships. If the numbers represented on the horizontal axis are in millions of dollars and you think they're in dollars, your interpretation of the graph will be incorrect.

Diagrams

A *diagram,* such as the one in Figure 14-3, is a drawing that helps you understand how something works.

Diagrams on the Science Test often have the following two components:

- ✓ **Title:** Tells you what the diagram is trying to show you
- ✓ **Labels:** Indicate the names of the parts of the diagram

Figure 14-3:
Diagram.

When you come to a question based on a diagram, read the title of the diagram first to know what the diagram is about. Then carefully read all the labels to find out the main components of the diagram. These two pieces of information can help you understand the diagram well enough to answer questions about it.

Maps

A *map* is a drawing of some section — large or small — of the earth or another planet, depending on how much space exploration has been done. Because the entire world is too large to show you on one small piece of paper, a section of it is drawn to scale and presented to you on the test.

Most maps give you the following information:

- **Title:** Tells you what area of the world the map focuses on
- **Legend:** Gives you general information about the colours, symbols, compass directions, or other graphics used on the map
- **Labels:** Indicate what the various points on the map represent
- **Scale:** Tells you what the distance on the map represents in real life (For example, a map with a scale of 1 cm = 100 km shows a distance of 500 km on the real earth as a distance of 5 cm on the map.)

Although maps are seldom used in science passages, they are used occasionally, so at least be familiar with them. The best way to get familiar with maps is to look at road maps and world atlases, which you can find in your local library or bookstore.

Examining Preparation Strategies That Work

To get better results from the time and effort you put into preparing for the Science Test, we suggest you try the following strategies:

- **Take practice tests.** Chapters 15 and 17 give you full-length practice Science Tests. Take them. If you need more, consider purchasing additional preparation manuals that offer sample tests. Take as many of these practice tests as you can. Be strict about time restrictions, and check your answers when you're finished. If you don't understand why some answers are correct, ask a tutor or a friend who understands science, take a preparation class, or look up the information in a book or on the Internet. Be sure you know why every one of your answers is right or wrong.

✔ **Create your own dictionary.** Get a notebook and keep track of all the new words (and their definitions) that you discover as you prepare for the Science Test. Make sure you understand all the science terminology you come across. Of course, you can't do this job in one night. Take some time and make sure this terminology becomes part of your brain.

✔ **Read as many passages as you can.** We may sound like a broken record, but reading is the most important way to prepare for the Science Test. After you read a paragraph from any source (textbook, newspaper, novel, magazine, and so on), ask yourself some questions about what you read. You can also have friends and family ask you questions about what you read.

Check out Chapter 3 for some general test-taking strategies to help you prepare to take the GED tests.

Managing Your Time for the Science Test

As we mention earlier in this chapter, the Science Test has 50 questions that you must complete in 80 minutes, which means you have about 90 seconds to read each textual or visual passage and answer each question that goes with it. If a passage has more than one question, you have slightly more time to answer those questions because you should read the passage only once.

To help you manage your time, we recommend you check out Chapters 2 and 3 for some general time-management strategies that you can use on all the tests. For the Science Test, specifically, we suggest you focus on these two time-saving strategies:

✔ **For questions about passages, read the questions first and then skim the material for the answers.** The passage always contains the answer, but your background knowledge in science and your familiarity with scientific terms can help you understand the material more easily and quickly. Reading the question first provides you with a guide to what is being asked and what the passage is about so that you know what to look for as you read it.

✔ **For questions about a visual material, such as a graph or table, read the questions first and then scan the visual material.** Look at the visual material to see the big picture; questions usually don't ask about minute details.

As a general tip, answer the easiest questions first. You can then go back and spend a little more time on the more difficult questions. Remember, though, to plan ahead and leave a few minutes at the end to review your answers.

Practising with Sample Problems

To increase your odds of doing well on the Science Test, become as familiar as possible with what you'll encounter on the actual test. The following questions are some sample problems for the Science Test. Read each question carefully, and find the best answer based on the passages.

Questions 1 and 2 refer to the following passage.

One of the great discoveries in earth science is rocks. Rocks have many useful purposes in science. You can use them as paperweights to keep academic papers from flying away in the wind. You can use rocks to prop laboratory doors open when the experiments go wrong and produce horrible smells. You can rub smooth rocks when pressure builds and you just need a mindless activity to get through the day.

1. According to the passage, one of the great discoveries in science is

   (1) atomic energy

   (2) static electricity

   (3) rocks

   (4) nectarines

   (5) DNA

   The correct answer is Choice (3). The important words in the question are "According to the passage." When you see this phrase, you know to look in the passage for the answer. Because none of the answers except rocks is even remotely mentioned, rocks must be the best answer.

2. How do rocks help scientists when experiments go horribly wrong and produce terrible odours?

   (1) They can be used to smash the windows.

   (2) They can prop open the doors.

   (3) They can be thrown in anger.

   (4) They can be rubbed.

   (5) Only scientists know the answer to this.

   The correct answer is Choice (2). According to the passage, the rocks can be used to hold open the door of the lab. Rocks can also be used to smash windows and can be thrown in anger, but the passage doesn't specifically mention these uses. The passage mentions rubbing rocks as a use, but it does so in another context.

   Questions 3 through 5 refer to the following passage.

   Dr. Y. Kritch was a world-famous botanist. He spent his life in search of an early blooming, colourful spring flower. He first developed the onelip flower, which bloomed so early that it immediately froze in the winter weather. After many years of research, he developed a new strain of flowers called the threelip, which bloomed in the late fall, just after the first frost. Frustrated, he decided to cross-pollinate the two blooms to develop a plant that would bloom in the spring. Using a special cross-averaging-pollination process, he managed to develop a plant that would bloom in the early spring and come in many colours. In honour of the averaging process, he called it a twolip, which was later changed to tulip.

3. Why did Dr. Kritch want to develop a new flower?

   (1) He was bored.

   (2) He wanted something named after him.

   (3) He wanted to sell the flowers to stores.

   (4) He needed a gift for his wife.

   (5) Not enough information is given.

The correct answer is Choice (5). The first four answers are all possible, but the passage doesn't mention any of them. The only correct answer is 5 because not much information is given about the doctor himself.

4. What was wrong with the onelip flower?

(1) It bloomed so late that everyone was tired of flowers.

(2) It never bloomed at all.

(3) It was an ugly colour.

(4) It bloomed too early.

(5) Not enough information is given.

The correct answer is Choice (4). The passage states that the onelip bloomed so early that it immediately froze in the winter weather.

5. Based on the information in the passage, what can you assume a botanist does?

(1) studies the averaging process

(2) studies plants

(3) freezes to death

(4) sells flowers

(5) not enough information given

The correct answer is Choice (2). The passage describes how Dr. Kritch studies and develops tulip plants. Although he uses the averaging process to develop the tulip, the passage doesn't mention that he studies that process. No mention is made of Dr. Kritch selling flowers or freezing to death.

Revealing Some Helpful Pointers

Here are a few pointers to remember as you take the Science Test. (See Chapter 1 for general rules that apply to all GED tests.)

✔ **Don't panic!** Your worst enemy on this or any other test is panic. Panicking takes time and energy, and you don't have a surplus of either. On the Science Test, you're expected to recognize and understand some scientific vocabulary, but, if you come across a word you don't understand, try to figure out its meaning from the rest of the sentence. If you can't do so quickly, leave the sentence till the end of the test when you know exactly how much time you have left to spend on it.

✔ **Remember that reading pictures is a science.** During this test, you have to answer questions based on visual materials, something you may not do every day. Remember that any visual object is like a short paragraph. It has a topic and makes comments or states facts about that topic. When you come across a question based on visual material, the first thing to do is to figure out what the visual material is about. Usually, visual objects have titles that help you figure out what they're about. After you figure out the main idea behind the visual object, ask yourself what information you're being given; rereading the question can be helpful. After you know these two pieces of information, you're well on your way to answering the question.

Chapter 15

Practice Test — Science Test

• •

*T*he Science Test consists of multiple-choice questions intended to measure general concepts in science. The questions are based on short readings that may include a graph, chart, or figure. Study the information given and then answer the question(s) following it. Refer to the information as often as necessary in answering the questions.

You have 80 minutes to answer the 50 questions in this booklet. Work carefully, but do not spend too much time on any one question. Be sure you answer every question.

Answer Sheet for Science Test

1 ① ② ③ ④ ⑤   26 ① ② ③ ④ ⑤

2 ① ② ③ ④ ⑤   27 ① ② ③ ④ ⑤

3 ① ② ③ ④ ⑤   28 ① ② ③ ④ ⑤

4 ① ② ③ ④ ⑤   29 ① ② ③ ④ ⑤

5 ① ② ③ ④ ⑤   30 ① ② ③ ④ ⑤

6 ① ② ③ ④ ⑤   31 ① ② ③ ④ ⑤

7 ① ② ③ ④ ⑤   32 ① ② ③ ④ ⑤

8 ① ② ③ ④ ⑤   33 ① ② ③ ④ ⑤

9 ① ② ③ ④ ⑤   34 ① ② ③ ④ ⑤

10 ① ② ③ ④ ⑤   35 ① ② ③ ④ ⑤

11 ① ② ③ ④ ⑤   36 ① ② ③ ④ ⑤

12 ① ② ③ ④ ⑤   37 ① ② ③ ④ ⑤

13 ① ② ③ ④ ⑤   38 ① ② ③ ④ ⑤

14 ① ② ③ ④ ⑤   39 ① ② ③ ④ ⑤

15 ① ② ③ ④ ⑤   40 ① ② ③ ④ ⑤

16 ① ② ③ ④ ⑤   41 ① ② ③ ④ ⑤

17 ① ② ③ ④ ⑤   42 ① ② ③ ④ ⑤

18 ① ② ③ ④ ⑤   43 ① ② ③ ④ ⑤

19 ① ② ③ ④ ⑤   44 ① ② ③ ④ ⑤

20 ① ② ③ ④ ⑤   45 ① ② ③ ④ ⑤

21 ① ② ③ ④ ⑤   46 ① ② ③ ④ ⑤

22 ① ② ③ ④ ⑤   47 ① ② ③ ④ ⑤

23 ① ② ③ ④ ⑤   48 ① ② ③ ④ ⑤

24 ① ② ③ ④ ⑤   49 ① ② ③ ④ ⑤

25 ① ② ③ ④ ⑤   50 ① ② ③ ④ ⑤

Science Test

Do not mark in this test booklet. Record your answers on the separate answer sheet provided. Be sure that all requested information is properly recorded on the answer sheet.

To record your answers, fill in the numbered circle on the answer sheet that corresponds to the answer you select for each question in the test booklet.

EXAMPLE:

Which of the following is the smallest unit in a living thing?

(1) tissue

(2) organ

(3) cell

(4) muscle

(5) capillary

(On Answer Sheet)

① ② ● ④ ⑤

The correct answer is "cell"; therefore, answer space 3 would be marked on the answer sheet.

Do not rest the point of your pencil on the answer sheet while you are considering your answer. Make no stray or unnecessary marks. If you change an answer, erase your first mark completely. Mark only one answer space for each question; multiple answers will be scored as incorrect. Do not fold or crease your answer sheet. All test materials must be returned to the test administrator.

Note: Refer to Chapter 16 for the answers for this practice test.

DO NOT BEGIN TAKING THIS TEST UNTIL TOLD TO DO SO

Directions: Choose the <u>one best answer</u> to each question.

Questions 1 and 2 refer to the following passage.

Insulation

During the winter, you need something to keep warmth in your home and cold air out. In the summer, you need something to keep heat outside and cooler air inside. What you need is insulation.

Insulation reduces or prevents the transfer of heat (called thermal transfer) from the inside out or the outside in. Fibreglass and plastic foam provide insulation because they contain trapped air. Normally, air is not a good insulator because the currents in air transfer the heat from one place to another. Trapping the air in small places, however, slows or prevents the transfer of heat. Think about these little packets of air the next time you sit in a warm home, safe from the frigid winter cold.

1. Why does a cinder block provide less thermal transfer than a window?

   (1) Cinder blocks are thicker.

   (2) Windows have little insulation value.

   (3) You can't see through cinder blocks.

   (4) There is no air in a cinder block.

   (5) Windows are necessary for safety.

2. Which would keep you warmest during the winter?

   (1) silk underwear

   (2) silk trousers

   (3) trousers padded with cotton

   (4) cotton underwear

   (5) fibreglass trousers

Questions 3 through 5 refer to the following passage.

Metabolism

The process of metabolism is an essential process in every living cell. Metabolism allows the cell to obtain and distribute energy, which is necessary for survival. Light from the sun is absorbed and converted into chemical energy by photosynthesis, and it is this chemical energy that is necessary for animals to survive.

One of the primary carbohydrates derived from plants is glucose. Through a process called glycolysis, energy is obtained from glucose. This reaction takes place in mitochondria, and the glucose molecule is broken down into pyruvic acids, which are further broken down into molecules, such as ethanol and lactic acid. This process is cyclical as the energy produced keeps the fermentation going.

Pyruvic acids are broken down to carbon dioxide and water by respiration, which releases far more energy. What started out as sunlight has become energy that keeps animals alive.

Go on to next page

3. How do animals depend on plants to stay alive?

   (1) Plants provide animals with protective cover.

   (2) Animals need the shade provided by plants.

   (3) Cures for some diseases originate in plants.

   (4) Plants provide a comfortable environment for animals.

   (5) Plants provide animals with chemical potential energy.

4. What would happen to a plant if you covered it with a cloth that does not allow light to pass through it?

   (1) The plant would stop growing.

   (2) The leaves would shrivel.

   (3) The flower would fall off.

   (4) The plant would starve to death.

   (5) The roots would die.

5. Which chemical is key to providing animals with energy?

   (1) pyruvic acid

   (2) carbon dioxide

   (3) chlorophyll

   (4) ethanol

   (5) lactic acid

Questions 6 and 7 refer to the following passage.

Velocity and Speed

Speed and velocity are different concepts, although sometimes you see the words used interchangeably. The velocity of a body is its rate of motion in a specific direction, such as a bicycle travelling 25 kilometres per hour due east. Because velocity has both magnitude (25 kilometres per hour) and direction (due east), it can be represented by a vector.

Speed has a magnitude only. If a bicycle travels at a speed of 28 kilometres per hour, you know its magnitude (kilometres per hour), but not its direction. Because speed has a magnitude but not a direction, it can be represented as a scalar.

6. If force is defined as that which is required to change the state or motion of an object in magnitude and direction, how should it be represented?

   (1) wavy lines

   (2) straight line

   (3) grams

   (4) scalar

   (5) vector

7. If a person travels seven blocks at 3 kilometres per hour but you do not know in which direction, what would represent the person's path?

   (1) kilometres

   (2) scalar

   (3) metres

   (4) vector

   (5) linear measure

Go on to next page

Questions 8 and 9 refer to the following diagram, which is excerpted from Physical Science: What the Technology Professional Needs to Know by C. Lon Enloe, Elizabeth Garnett, Jonathan Miles, and Stephen Swanson (Wiley).

Newcomen's Steam Engine

8. What properties of water and steam allow Newcomen's steam engine to operate?

    (1) Water is heavier than steam.

    (2) Steam condenses when cooled, occupying less space.

    (3) The boiler provides the energy to move the pump.

    (4) The pump rod is heavy enough to pull the arm down.

    (5) The cistern provides a positive pressure.

9. What effect does the condensation of steam in the cylinder with the piston have on the pump that fills the cistern?

    (1) controls the fire in the boiler

    (2) pumps water from the cistern to the boiler

    (3) causes the pump to fill the cistern with water

    (4) forces the piston down

    (5) sprays cold water into the main pump

Go on to next page ➡

Question 10 refers to the following figure.

The Food Chain

The Sun

Producers

Consumers

Decomposers

Green Plants

10. If the number of consumers in an ecosystem began to multiply without control, what would happen to the balance of the ecosystem?

(1) The green plants would increase.

(2) The herbivores would increase.

(3) Consumers would starve for lack of food.

(4) The decomposers would go out of business.

(5) The sun would stop shining.

Go on to next page

> *Questions 11 through 14 refer to the following passage.*

The Big Bang Theory

Imagining the universe as it is now is hard, and harder still is creating a theory about how it all began. In the 1940s, George Gamow began to develop such a theory. Georges Lemaitre, another scientist, had also been working on the problem, and Gamow used some of Lemaitre's ideas to develop his theory.

Gamow proposed the following theory: Somewhere between 10 and 21 billion years ago, a giant explosion in space occurred. Before the explosion, the universe was the size of an atomic nucleus, with a temperature of about 10 billion degrees. The explosion started the expansion of the universe. Quarks, or elemental particles, existed in huge numbers.

Within a millisecond, the universe had expanded to the size of a grapefruit. The temperature cooled to 1 billion degrees. The quarks began to clump into protons and neutrons. Minutes later, the universe was still too hot for electrons and protons to form into atoms: a super-hot, fog-like environment.

With passing time and cooling temperatures, nuclear reactions took place, and within 300,000 years, atoms of hydrogen and helium began to emerge. As the atoms formed, light began to shine. The universe was taking shape.

Gravity began to act on the atoms and transform them into galaxies. Within 1 billion years of that first great explosion, galaxies and stars began to form. Within 15 billion years, planets began to emerge from the heavy elements thrown off by the dying of stars. The universe started with a big bang and continues to grow and change according to this theory.

11. The temperature of the first tiny particles was thought to be

   (1) 1 billion degrees

   (2) 20 billion degrees

   (3) 10 billion degrees

   (4) 30 billion degrees

   (5) 15 billion degrees

12. Atoms were transformed into galaxies by

   (1) heat

   (2) pressure

   (3) centrifugal force

   (4) light

   (5) gravity

13. Quarks are

   (1) atoms

   (2) 1 billion degrees

   (3) elemental particles

   (4) hydrogen

   (5) helium

14. How is the formation of hydrogen and helium atoms related to the possible destruction from an atomic bomb?

   (1) Both use hydrogen.

   (2) No relation exists.

   (3) Both are scientific principles.

   (4) Both result from explosions.

   (5) Both are nuclear reactions.

Go on to next page ⇨

Questions 15 through 17 refer to the following passage.

The Jellyfish

One of the creatures living in all the world's oceans is the jellyfish. Although it lives in the ocean, it is not a fish. The jellyfish is an invertebrate; that is, an animal lacking a backbone. Not only does it lack a backbone, but the jellyfish has no heart, blood, brain, or gills and is over 95 percent water.

The jellyfish has a body and tentacles. These tentacles are the long tendrils around the bell-like structure that contain stinging cells, which are used to capture prey. The movement of the prey triggers the sensory hair in the stinging cell and the prey is then in trouble.

Unfortunately, people are also in trouble if they get too close to the tentacles of a jellyfish. The stings are not fatal to humans but can cause a great deal of discomfort.

15. Why is a jellyfish considered an invertebrate?

    (1) It has tentacles.

    (2) It has a small brain.

    (3) It has a primitive circulatory system.

    (4) It has no backbone.

    (5) It swims in the ocean.

16. Why do swimmers not like to be near jellyfish?

    (1) They look weird.

    (2) Swimmers can get caught in the tentacles.

    (3) Swimmers may accidentally swallow a jellyfish.

    (4) The stings are painful.

    (5) Swimmers don't like to be near ocean creatures.

17. Why do most small ocean creatures try to avoid jellyfish?

    (1) Jellyfish get in the way of the fish when they are feeding.

    (2) Jellyfish sting and eat small ocean creatures.

    (3) The fish are afraid of the strange-looking creatures.

    (4) Jellyfish and ocean creatures compete for the same food sources.

    (5) Fish cannot swim as fast as jellyfish.

Go on to next page

Questions 18 through 25 refer to the following passage.

Laws of Conservation

You are faced with laws every day. You cannot drive as fast as you want on the roads, and you cannot park wherever you choose.

Science has laws, as well. One such law is that energy cannot be created or destroyed. This law, called the Law of Conservation of Energy, makes sense because you cannot create something from nothing. And if you have an electrical charge, you cannot simply make it disappear.

A further law of conservation is the Law of Conservation of Matter, which says that matter cannot be created or destroyed. This means that when a chemical change occurs, the total mass of an object remains constant. When you melt an ice cube, the water that results is neither heavier nor lighter than the original ice cube.

18. When lightning strikes a tree, the tree gets damaged, but the lightning ceases to exist. What happens to the lightning?

    (1) It disappears.
    (2) The energy in the lightning is transformed into something else.
    (3) The tree absorbs the lightning.
    (4) Striking the tree creates new energy to damage the tree.
    (5) It is still there, but invisible.

19. Why does science have laws?

    (1) Science is an ordered discipline.
    (2) Laws keep scientists honest.
    (3) Science needs rules to operate carefully.
    (4) Laws make it easier to study science.
    (5) Lawyers like laws.

20. When a magician makes a rabbit appear out of a hat, it is an example of

    (1) physics
    (2) conservation of matter
    (3) entertainment
    (4) illusion
    (5) biology

21. When an iceberg melts, what is the result?

    (1) global warming
    (2) warmer ocean water
    (3) nothing
    (4) more food for fish
    (5) more water in the ocean

22. When you take a dead battery out of your flashlight, what has happened to its original charge?

    (1) It has been converted into light.
    (2) It has disappeared.
    (3) The battery has worn out.
    (4) The energy has been destroyed.
    (5) It went into the flashlight.

23. If you add 3 millitres of water to 1 gram of salt, what will be the effect on the final mass?

    (1) The salt will absorb the water.
    (2) You will get 1 gram of salty water.
    (3) The salt will disappear.
    (4) The total mass will remain the same.
    (5) The salt will dissolve.

Go on to next page

24. A ball rolling down a hill cannot stop by itself. What explains this?

    (1) There is a bump on the road.

    (2) The ball has no brakes.

    (3) The energy from rolling down the hill can't disappear.

    (4) The theory of the laws of conservation keeps the ball from stopping.

    (5) The ball always weighs the same.

25. Conservation of energy is an example of what?

    (1) something you have to memorize

    (2) a battery commercial

    (3) a statement by a famous scientist

    (4) a law of science

    (5) the title of a magazine article

Questions 26 through 28 refer to the following passage.

Why Do Birds Fly South for the Winter?

Every fall, birds fly south for the winter. Scientists have advanced theories about this phenomenon.

Some birds eat insects for food. In winter, many species of birds fly south, because that's where the food exists. In the southern United States, insects are available all year long, providing a banquet for the birds, whereas in most parts of Canada, insects (as well as other food sources, such as seeds and berries) are scarce or even non-existent during the winter because of the cold temperatures. The birds fly south for winter to follow the food. In the spring, when temperatures rise and insects become plentiful in Canada again, the birds still follow the food, this time to the north.

26. Why do migratory birds return to the north in the spring?

    (1) They miss their homes.

    (2) It gets too hot in the southern United States.

    (3) They are able to find food again.

    (4) They fly north out of habit.

    (5) Birds like to fly long distances.

27. Why are insects responsible for the migration of some birds?

    (1) Insects bite the birds.

    (2) The insects lead the birds south.

    (3) Some birds eat insects.

    (4) Birds have a habit of always eating the same insects.

    (5) Insects like to chase birds.

28. Why are scientists interested in the migration of birds?

    (1) It happens regularly and apparently without explanation.

    (2) Scientists like to go south.

    (3) Scientists like to listen to bird songs.

    (4) Scientists look for connections between travel and caterpillars.

    (5) Someone asked the scientists about it.

Go on to next page

Questions 29 and 30 refer to the following passage.

The Law of Unintended Consequences

Lake Victoria is the largest freshwater lake in Africa. It once had abundant fish, which provided protein for the local people who ate the fish. Unfortunately, a new species — the Nile Perch — was introduced into the lake by fishermen looking for a challenging fishing experience to attract tourists interested in exploring the area.

The Nile Perch is an aggressive predator and had no natural enemies in Lake Victoria. It quickly ate up large numbers of the smaller fish, which affected the diets of the local population. These smaller fish ate algae and parasite-bearing snails. Without the smaller fish eating them, the live algae spread over the surface of the lake. Dead algae sank to the bottom of the lake and decayed, a process that consumed oxygen necessary for the fish living deep in the lake.

Without natural predators, the snails and the parasites they carried multiplied, creating a serious health hazard to the population. Introducing fish to encourage tourism had a detrimental effect on the lake and the population that depended on it.

29. What destroyed the ecological balance in Lake Victoria?

    (1) local merchants

    (2) shrinking populations of snails

    (3) freshwater lake

    (4) growing populations of smaller fish

    (5) the Nile Perch

30. Why is it never a good idea to introduce a foreign species into a stable lake?

    (1) The foreign species has plenty of predators.

    (2) The foreign species is too attractive.

    (3) The other species in the lake would not have to compete for food.

    (4) The foreign species is bad for sport fishing.

    (5) The foreign species can upset the ecological balance.

Go on to next page

Questions 31 through 34 refer to the following table, which is adapted from Hands-On General Science Activities with Real-Life Applications by Pam Walker and Elaine Wood (Wiley).

Space Travel

Characteristic	Moon	Mars
Distance from earth	384,630 kilometres	78,214,000 kilometres
Gravity	⅙ earth's gravity	⅓ earth's gravity
Atmosphere	None	Thin carbon dioxide, 1% air pressure of earth
Trip time	3 days	1.88 earth years
Communication time	2.6 seconds, round trip	10 to 41 minutes, round trip

31. If you were an aeronautical engineer planning a journey to Mars, why would you prefer to go to a space station on the moon and then launch the rocket to Mars, rather than going directly from earth to Mars?

    (1) Lower gravity on the moon means you need less fuel for the launch.

    (2) You have more space to take off and land on the moon.

    (3) No atmosphere means an easier take off.

    (4) The moon is closer to earth than Mars.

    (5) Not enough information is given.

32. If you were a communications engineer trying to establish a safety network to warn a rocket ship of dangers, where would you place the transmitter for this rocket ship's journey to Mars?

    (1) on the moon

    (2) on earth

    (3) on Mars

    (4) at the space station

    (5) not enough information given

33. Why would a trip to the moon be a better first choice than a trip to Mars for space travellers?

    (1) You can see the moon from earth without a telescope.

    (2) The time of the trip is much shorter.

    (3) The moon has a better atmosphere.

    (4) There are already space vehicles on the moon.

    (5) You could phone home from the moon.

34. If you held a pole-vaulting contest on the moon and Mars, on which planet could the same contestant vault higher with the same expenditure of energy?

    (1) the moon

    (2) Mars

    (3) earth

    (4) no difference

    (5) not enough information given

Go on to next page

Questions 35 through 37 refer to the following passage.

Heredity, Then and Now

How often have you seen a young child and said, "She takes after her parents." Many traits in children do come from their parents. Physical characteristics such as hair colour and nose shape, as well as other characteristics, are transmitted from one generation to the next. These characteristics exist because of genetic code.

The first scientist to experiment with heredity was Gregor Mendel during the 19th century. Mendel experimented with pea plants and noted that characteristics appearing in "child" plants were similar to those in the "parent" plants. Mendel hypothesized that these characteristics were carried from generation to generation by "factors." It took many years of research to understand why children often look like their parents, but genetic code is now the basis of the study of heredity.

35. According to the passage, what is a primary determinant for characteristics of the next generation?

    (1) chance

    (2) hair colour

    (3) pea plants

    (4) heredity

    (5) nature

36. What are the factors that Mendel hypothesized carried traits from one generation to the next?

    (1) plants

    (2) peas

    (3) traits

    (4) protons

    (5) genetic code

37. If you want to grow monster-sized pumpkins, from what kind of pumpkins do you want to get seeds?

    (1) orange pumpkins

    (2) doesn't matter if you have special fertilizer

    (3) monster-sized pumpkins

    (4) larger-than-average pumpkins

    (5) healthy pumpkins

Go on to next page ⟶

Questions 38 and 39 refer to the following passage.

The Space Shuttle

NASA has designed and built six space shuttles: Atlantis, Challenger, Columbia, Discovery, Endeavor, and Enterprise. The space shuttles are made up of two distinct parts: the orbiter and the booster rocket. The booster rocket provides the additional thrust to get the space shuttle away from the gravitational pull of earth. The orbiter carries the people and payload as well as the workings of the shuttle. In a space flight, the booster is jettisoned after clearing earth's gravitational pull, and the orbiter continues on its way.

38. Why would the booster be jettisoned?

(1) to have more fuel for later in the trip

(2) because the shuttle needs to add weight

(3) to increase the size of the shuttle

(4) to make the shuttle less manoeuvrable for landing

(5) because it is no longer needed

39. Which part of a shuttle carries the payload?

(1) booster

(2) cockpit

(3) orbiter

(4) rocket

(5) Challenger

Questions 40 and 41 refer to the following figure, which is excerpted from Physical Science: What the Technology Professional Needs to Know *by C. Lon Enloe, Elizabeth Garnett, Jonathan Miles, and Stephen Swanson (Wiley).*

40. Work is defined as the product of force times displacement. Consider the diagram. If the force of gravity is greater than the forces being exerted by the muscles controlling the hand, what would happen?

(1) Nothing would happen.

(2) The hand would move downward.

(3) The hand would move to the right.

(4) The hand would move upward.

(5) The hand would move to the left.

41. If an athlete knows that building muscles requires doing work against a weight, what would the athlete want to change in this diagram?

(1) nothing

(2) moving the hand upward faster

(3) adding weight to the hand

(4) closing the fist as the arm is raised

(5) exhaling as the arm is raised

Go on to next page

Questions 42 and 43 refer to the following passage, which is adapted from The Sciences: An Integrated Approach, *6th Edition, by James Trefil and Robert M. Hazen (Wiley).*

Copying DNA Sequence

The polymerase chain reaction (PCR) copies a sequence of DNA. In order to do this, a strand of DNA is mixed with nucleotides (DNA precursors). Nucleotides target a specific piece of DNA, as well as polymerase, an enzyme that helps to assemble DNA. Heat is applied until the temperature reaches 94°C. The energy from the heating separates the DNA strands. The mixture is then cooled to 60°C. At this temperature, the primers attach themselves to the DNA strands. Raising the temperature to 71°C causes the nucleotides to begin to attach to the DNA strands. After all this, two copies of the DNA are created.

42. What process in the polymerase chain reaction separates the DNA strands?

    (1) heating
    (2) chemicals
    (3) pulling
    (4) gravity
    (5) chilling

43. To clone an organism, you require an identical DNA blueprint. Why would a scientist who is interested in cloning want to study the PCR?

    (1) It creates an identical copy of the DNA.
    (2) PCR clones animals.
    (3) Scientists should know everything.
    (4) A duplicate DNA structure cools clones.
    (5) The heat destroys clones.

Questions 44 and 45 refer to the following passage.

Dogs and Wolves — Relatives?

Current scientific theory is that the familiar family pet, the dog, descended from the wolf, but the dog has taken a very different path. The dog was the first animal to be domesticated, right around the end of the Ice Age.

Dogs are part of an extended family called Canidae, which contains 38 different species. Jackals, foxes, wolves, and dogs are all part of this family.

Although they are related, wolves and dogs are different. Wolves have smaller heads for the same body weight. Dogs have smaller teeth, a more curved lower jaw, and eyes that are more rounded and forward looking. At a distance, however, many of these differences are difficult to spot.

44. What feature makes the wolf better adapted to hunting in the wild?

    (1) heavier coat
    (2) larger body
    (3) larger teeth
    (4) larger paws
    (5) deeper growl

45. Of the members of the Canidae family that were mentioned, why is the dog the only household pet?

    (1) There are many types of dogs to choose from.
    (2) Dogs were domesticated.
    (3) Dogs are smaller than wolves.
    (4) Dogs protect people's houses.
    (5) Dogs can help the visually impaired.

Go on to next page ⟶

Questions 46 through 48 refer to the following passage.

Isotopes

Isotopes are chemical cousins. They are related to each other, but each isotope has slightly different — but related — atoms. Each of the related atoms has the same number of electrons or protons, but a different number of neutrons. Because the number of electrons or protons determines the atomic number, isotopes have the same atomic number.

The number of neutrons determines the mass number. Because the number of neutrons in each isotope is different, the mass number is also different. These cousins all have different mass numbers but the same atomic number. Their chemical properties are similar but not the same. Like most cousins, isotopes have family resemblances, but each has a unique personality.

46. What determines the atomic number?

    (1) number of isotopes

    (2) number of neutrons

    (3) number of electrons

    (4) number of atoms

    (5) number of chemicals

47. Isotopes of a chemical have the same

    (1) number of neutrons

    (2) number of atoms

    (3) mass number

    (4) size

    (5) atomic number

48. A scientist has found related atoms in two different substances. If both atoms have the same atomic number but different mass numbers, what preliminary conclusion can be reached about the atoms?

    (1) They are the same substance.

    (2) They are isotopes.

    (3) They are different substances.

    (4) One is a compound of the other.

    (5) It is too early to make any decisions.

Go on to next page ⟶

Questions 49 and 50 refer to the following passage.

How to Survive the Winter

When the temperature drops and the wind blows cold, you may think of animals that don't have homes to keep out the cold, and you may worry about their ability to survive the winter. Not much food is available, temperatures drop below zero, and shelter is limited. How do they survive the winter?

Many animals can hibernate for the winter. Hibernation is a sleep-like condition in which the animal's heartbeat, temperature, and metabolism slow down to adapt to the colder temperatures. This dormant condition prevents their starving or freezing during the harsh winters.

49. Bears survive the winter by

    (1) going south

    (2) living in warm caves

    (3) growing a heavy winter coat

    (4) absorbing the sun's rays to keep warm

    (5) finding a safe shelter and hibernating

50. Why should you not disturb a hibernating animal?

    (1) It gets grouchy when awakened suddenly.

    (2) It needs its sleep.

    (3) It could have trouble falling asleep again.

    (4) You should never bother a wild animal.

    (5) It would not be able to find enough food to survive.

END OF TEST

Chapter 16

Answers and Explanations for the Science Test

· ·

Answer Key

After taking the Science Test in Chapter 15, use this section to check your answers.

1. **2**	18. **2**	35. **4**
2. **3**	19. **1**	36. **5**
3. **5**	20. **4**	37. **3**
4. **4**	21. **5**	38. **5**
5. **1**	22. **1**	39. **3**
6. **5**	23. **4**	40. **2**
7. **2**	24. **3**	41. **3**
8. **2**	25. **4**	42. **1**
9. **3**	26. **3**	43. **1**
10. **3**	27. **3**	44. **3**
11. **3**	28. **1**	45. **2**
12. **5**	29. **5**	46. **3**
13. **3**	30. **5**	47. **5**
14. **5**	31. **1**	48. **2**
15. **4**	32. **5**	49. **5**
16. **4**	33. **2**	50. **5**
17. **2**	34. **1**	

Analysis of the Answers

If you aren't sure why an answer is incorrect, use this section to get quick explanations of the answers. If you correctly answered a question, you may still want to read the explanations to get a better understanding of the thought process that helped you choose the correct answer.

1. **2.** Glass contains no encapsulated air and, thus, provides neither insulation nor greater thermal flow. Choice (1), that cinder blocks are thicker, can be true, but it doesn't answer the question about heat transfer. Choice (2), that *windows have little insulation value*, is the best answer. Choice (3), that you can't see through cinder blocks, is true and may be interesting, but it's irrelevant to the question. Choice (4), that there is no air in a cinder block, is inaccurate. Choice (5), that windows are necessary for safety, is not only irrelevant, but also incorrect. To answer this question, you need to know that good insulators contain trapped air and that glass doesn't. This information is assumed to be general knowledge for someone at this educational level.

2. **3.** The passage says that insulation is necessary for reduced heat transfer, which keeps you warmer. All the answers except Choice (3) refer to clothing made of a single layer of material. The *cotton padding* acts as insulation for the trousers because the cotton contains trapped air.

3. **5.** The last paragraph of the passage states that animals must eat food with *chemical potential energy*, which is derived from plants. The other answers are irrelevant to the information in the passage.

This passage gives you a lot of interesting information, but because you have a time limit, you may want to read the question first and then look for the answer in the passage instead of reading the passage, reading the question, and then reading the passage again.

4. **4.** Plants produce food using energy from the sun. If you cut off the energy from the sun, you cut off the food supply, and *the plant starves*. The other answers may be symptoms of a plant's starving to death, but Choice (4) sums up the information in one answer.

5. **1.** According to the passage, *pyruvic acid* is key to energy production. This question is a good example of why a little bit of knowledge and familiarity with the words and names used in science is helpful on these tests. All the answer choices in this question are chemical names, and some familiarity with them would make answering the question easier. The answer is stated in the passage, and being comfortable with some scientific vocabulary makes the answer easier to find.

6. **5.** The passage states that velocity can be represented by a vector because it has both magnitude and direction. Force is defined as changing the state or motion of an object, either in magnitude or direction. Because a force has magnitude and direction, it's represented by a *vector*. The information needed to answer this question is in the last sentence of the first paragraph. You can ignore the first three answer choices completely because they have very little to do with the question. Choice (4) requires you to know the difference between a vector and a scalar. The last line of each paragraph in the passage contains the definitions you need.

7. **2.** If a person travels seven blocks from home to school, only the distance is defined. The person can go four blocks due east and three blocks due west. He or she can take a roundabout path involving all four points of the compass. You really don't know what the person is doing except somehow travelling seven blocks to school. This activity has only a magnitude and no direction, so it's represented by a *scalar*. After you understand the definition of a scalar, which you need to answer question 6, this question is easier to answer. You can ignore Choices (1) and (3) because they are measures of length and do not answer the question. Choice (4) is wrong because a vector has both magnitude and direction, and Choice (5) is irrelevant.

8. **2.** In the steam engine, water cools the steam, which then *condenses, occupying less space*. This action starts the entire cycle over again. You can eliminate the other answer choices when guessing is necessary. Choice (1) is incorrect because water and steam are both water, in different states. Their densities may be different, but their weights are the same. Only the volume differs when water turns to steam. Choice (3) is incorrect because the boiler doesn't provide the energy to move the pump, which you can see by looking at the diagram. Choice (4) isn't based on information given in the diagram; nowhere are you told the weight of the pump rod. Choice (5) isn't based on the diagram, on fact, or on general knowledge.

9. **3.** The *pump pushes water into the cistern*. The other choices don't answer the question based on the information provided in the diagram. Knowing how to answer questions based on diagrams is a useful skill to have for tests like this one.

10. **3.** The producers provide food for the consumers. If the producers stay the same but the consumers increase, the consumers won't have enough food, so *the consumers will starve*. The other answer choices are incorrect based on the information provided.

11. **3.** The passage states that the temperature of the first tiny particles was 10 billion degrees.

This question is a good one on which to practise your skimming skills to find the answer. When you skim the passage, the words "10 billion degrees" should jump out at you. By reading the whole sentence, you confirm that your answer is correct. The other answer choices are wrong, and skimming helps you figure that out. When an answer is as definite as this one, skimming the passage is usually helpful.

12. **5.** The last paragraph states that *gravity* transformed the atoms into galaxies. This question is another example of when a basic knowledge of science-related words can be helpful.

13. **3.** The passage states that quarks are *elemental particles*. This question asks for a definition. Skimming the passage guides you toward the last sentence in the second paragraph, which contains the definition you're looking for.

14. **5.** An atomic bomb uses a nuclear reaction to produce its massive damage. The passage states that hydrogen and helium atoms were formed by *nuclear reactions*. The other choices don't answer the question based on the passage. Choice (1) may be right, but it's irrelevant in this context. Choices (2) and (4) are incorrect; and Choice (3) may be interesting in another context, but it's wrong here.

15. **4.** According to the passage (third sentence in the first paragraph), *invertebrates have no backbones*. The other choices may be correct, but they don't answer the question. Here and in all questions on this test, you're looking for the best answer to the question posed. Don't get sidetracked by other choices that are correct based on your knowledge or even based on the passage. The answer to the question posed is always the best response on a multiple-choice test.

16. **4.** Jellyfish can sting swimmers, and the *stings are painful*. You find this information in the last sentence of the third paragraph. The other choices don't answer the question based on the passage. For example, Choice (3) may be the stuff nightmares are based on, but the information (or misinformation) isn't in the passage, so you can't consider it.

17. **2.** *Small ocean creatures* are always on the menu for jellyfish. Creatures, in general, avoid predators — that's general science knowledge.

Reading some science articles or books is good preparation for this test, but never base your answers on your prior reading. Rather, base all your answers on the material presented in the passages.

18. **2.** The passage states that energy can't be created or destroyed, so the energy from the lightning must be *transformed into another type of energy*. The other answer choices imply that the energy has somehow disappeared, which the passage says can't happen.

19. **1.** *Science is an ordered discipline* and, as such, needs laws to maintain its organization. The first sentence in the second paragraph spells out this idea. Choice (5) may be true, but it's irrelevant. Choice (2) is obviously incorrect. Choices (3) and (4) may be interesting for conversation, but they don't answer the question using the material in the passage.

20. **4.** Matter can't be created or destroyed. Thus, a rabbit can't appear except by *illusion*. The other answer choices seem scientific but have nothing to do with the question. Always read the question carefully to make sure you're answering it.

21. **5.** When ice melts, it turns into water. Although the amount of water in a melting iceberg is tiny compared to the amount of water in the ocean, it does *add some water to the ocean*. Choices (1) and (2) are incorrect answers because, although the melting of the iceberg and the warming of the water may be the results of global warming, these choices don't answer the question. Choices (3) and (4) are incorrect. This question is a good example of what can happen if you read a question too quickly and answer it from general knowledge. Use the information in the passage to find the best answer to the question.

22. **1.** Flashlights *provide light by using the energy in the battery*. The passage says that energy can't be created or destroyed, so the energy in the battery must have been converted or transformed into something else. In reality, even if you don't use a battery for an extended time, the battery grows weaker because of other reactions inside the cell. But this tidbit isn't mentioned in the passage and is just a reminder not to leave batteries in your flashlight forever.

23. **4.** If you add 3 millilitres of water to 1 gram of salt, you have 4 grams of combined ingredients. One millilitre of water weighs 1 gram. The combined mass is the same as the sum of the individual masses. The volume may be different, but the question doesn't ask you about the volume. Choices (1) and (5) may seem to be relevant if not correct, but they don't answer the question because they have nothing to do with mass. Choice (3) is also wrong because the salt doesn't disappear; it dissolves in the water.

24. **3.** The Law of Conservation of Energy states that energy can't be created or destroyed. Thus, the *energy developed by the ball rolling down the hill can't disappear*. In reality, friction exists between the ball and the ground that slows it down, and the hills don't go on forever — so the ball will eventually come to rest. You may have learned this information elsewhere, but it doesn't answer the question based on the passage. No information in the passage supports Choices (1) and (5). Choice (2) may be true, but it's irrelevant, and Choice (4) is cute but incorrect.

25. **4.** Conservation of energy is a *law of science*. You can immediately eliminate the other answers because they are obviously irrelevant. Choice (4) is the only choice that answers the question.

26. **3.** The passage states that the lack of food in the winter months makes most birds fly south *to find sources of food*. When the food returns to the north, so do the birds. The other choices don't answer the question based on the information in the passage.

27. **3.** *Some birds eat insects* for their food supply. If an area has no insects, the birds move to find a new source of food. General reading in science tells you that living creatures go where the food is. Even human beings, who can choose where to live, are unlikely to move somewhere that lacks food. Other creatures have a more basic instinct to move near a supply of food. Thus, the insects have a responsibility for the birds' migration — although their main contribution is being eaten.

28. **1.** Scientists are curious about anything that *happens regularly that can't be easily explained*. Migration is one such issue. Choice (5) may have happened, but the passage doesn't spell it out. The key word here is "every" at the beginning of the first sentence.

29. **5.** This question may have many answers, from sport fishermen to algae to snails. Of the potential answers given, however, *Nile Perch* is the best one because the introduction of this species caused all the subsequent problems.

30. **5.** This question asks you to make a general statement about foreign species of fish. Although this question doesn't ask you specifically to consider the Lake Victoria example, you're supposed to think about that example as you answer the question. Using the Lake Victoria example, you can safely say that a *foreign species upsets the local ecological balance*. You also know from the example that the other four choices are incorrect.

31. **1.** The less fuel you need to launch, the less you have to carry. The gravity on the moon is less than that on earth, so you need less force and *less fuel to break free of gravity*. Choices (2), (3), and (4) may seem to have a ring of truth, but they don't answer the question.

32. **5.** The only locations mentioned in the table are Mars and the moon, and you're supposed to answer the question based on the material given. Thus, you don't have enough information to answer the question.

33. **2.** According to the table, it takes just three days to get to the moon, which is a *much shorter* and better first choice than the 1.88 years needed to get to Mars. The other choices are irrelevant to the question and the given table.

34. **1.** Gravity on *the moon* is less than that on Mars. Because gravity is the force that attracts you to the moon (or to earth or to Mars), the less the gravity, the less attraction between you and the surface on which you stand, and, thus, the higher and farther you can jump — which, is the goal of a pole-vaulting contest.

35. **4.** The passage states that *heredity* determines the characteristics of the next generation. The only other answer choice mentioned in the passage is Choice (3), but this choice doesn't answer the question.

36. **5.** The passage states that "These characteristics, passed from one generation to the next, are called the genetic code." Thus, the best answer is Choice (5), *genetic code*.

37. **3.** If children inherit the traits of their parents, you want the desired traits of your child pumpkin to be a part of the traits of the parent pumpkins. *Monster-sized pumpkin seeds* have a better chance of producing extra large pumpkins than do the seeds from a regular-sized pumpkin. Although Choice (2) seems like a possibility, the passage doesn't mention the effects of fertilizer on monster-pumpkin production.

38. **5.** All the choices except Choice (5) — that the booster is *no longer needed* — are incorrect because they're in direct opposition to the passage. If you can quickly eliminate some or most of the answer choices, you can save time answering the question. In this case, you can eliminate four answers quickly and easily.

39. **3.** Because the booster is jettisoned after takeoff, the *orbiter* has to carry everything that continues on the trip. Choices (2), (4), and (5) are wrong, so you eliminate them quickly.

40. **2.** If the force pushing down is greater than the force pushing up, *the hand would move down*. Although this question is based on the diagram, which gives a general idea of what happens when a hand holds weight, the answer is in the first part of the question itself. If the force of gravity (the downward force) is greater than the force of the muscles moving upward, the resultant force would be downward.

41. **3.** A *heavier weight in the hand* would produce a greater force downward. Thus, the athlete would have to work harder against this extra weight (and, as a result, would build more muscle). Making the displacement of the hand larger would also increase the work done, but this isn't an answer choice.

42. **1.** The fourth sentence in the passage tells you that *heating* is the process that separates DNA strands. The other choices either don't answer the question or are wrong.

43. **1.** Cloning requires identical DNA. As you can see from the first sentence of the passage, *PCR provides identical copies of DNA*.

44. **3.** The *larger teeth* of the wolf are better for hunting. The third sentence of the third paragraph of the passage states that dogs have smaller teeth, which means wolves must have bigger teeth. Although this information isn't stated directly in the passage, it's implied. You're expected to be able to draw conclusions from the information given, so read carefully. The other answer choices are incorrect. True, some dogs have heavier coats, larger bodies, and so on, but this information isn't in the passage. You can answer the question using only information given or implied — not information from your general knowledge or prior reading.

45. **2.** The passage states that the dog was *domesticated* very long ago. A domesticated animal is preferable to a wild one for a household pet. The other answers may be factually correct, but they aren't part of the information included in the passage.

46. **3.** According to the first sentence of the passage, the *number of electrons* or protons determines the atomic number. Skimming the paragraph after reading the question for key words in the question makes choosing the correct answer faster and easier.

47. **5.** The last sentence of the first paragraph of the passage states that isotopes have the same *atomic number*.

In most cases, you don't have to memorize factual information for these tests; the passages give you the factual information you need to know. Remember that the answers are based on the factual information given.

48. **2.** The last sentence of the first paragraph of the passage states that *isotopes* have the same atomic number. The second sentence of the second paragraph tells you that isotopes have different mass numbers. This question requires using two bits of information from two different locations in the passage to decide on the right answer.

49. **5.** According to the first sentence of the second paragraph of the passage, bears survive the winter by *finding a safe shelter and hibernating*.

50. **5.** Animals hibernate in the winter when food is scarce (a fact implied from the last sentence in the second paragraph). If you wake up a hibernating animal, that animal awakes to a strange environment without its usual sources of food and *probably wouldn't be able to find enough food to survive*. The other answer choices may be right in some circumstances, but they don't relate to the passage. Choice (4) is good advice, but it isn't a good answer.

Chapter 17

Another Practice Test — Science Test

• •

*T*he Science Test consists of multiple-choice questions intended to measure general concepts in science. The questions are based on short readings that may include a graph, chart, or figure. Study the information given and then answer the question(s) following it. Refer to the information as often as necessary in answering the questions.

You have 80 minutes to answer the 50 questions in this test. Work carefully, but do not spend too much time on any one question. Be sure you answer every question.

Answer Sheet for Science Test

1 ① ② ③ ④ ⑤	26 ① ② ③ ④ ⑤
2 ① ② ③ ④ ⑤	27 ① ② ③ ④ ⑤
3 ① ② ③ ④ ⑤	28 ① ② ③ ④ ⑤
4 ① ② ③ ④ ⑤	29 ① ② ③ ④ ⑤
5 ① ② ③ ④ ⑤	30 ① ② ③ ④ ⑤
6 ① ② ③ ④ ⑤	31 ① ② ③ ④ ⑤
7 ① ② ③ ④ ⑤	32 ① ② ③ ④ ⑤
8 ① ② ③ ④ ⑤	33 ① ② ③ ④ ⑤
9 ① ② ③ ④ ⑤	34 ① ② ③ ④ ⑤
10 ① ② ③ ④ ⑤	35 ① ② ③ ④ ⑤
11 ① ② ③ ④ ⑤	36 ① ② ③ ④ ⑤
12 ① ② ③ ④ ⑤	37 ① ② ③ ④ ⑤
13 ① ② ③ ④ ⑤	38 ① ② ③ ④ ⑤
14 ① ② ③ ④ ⑤	39 ① ② ③ ④ ⑤
15 ① ② ③ ④ ⑤	40 ① ② ③ ④ ⑤
16 ① ② ③ ④ ⑤	41 ① ② ③ ④ ⑤
17 ① ② ③ ④ ⑤	42 ① ② ③ ④ ⑤
18 ① ② ③ ④ ⑤	43 ① ② ③ ④ ⑤
19 ① ② ③ ④ ⑤	44 ① ② ③ ④ ⑤
20 ① ② ③ ④ ⑤	45 ① ② ③ ④ ⑤
21 ① ② ③ ④ ⑤	46 ① ② ③ ④ ⑤
22 ① ② ③ ④ ⑤	47 ① ② ③ ④ ⑤
23 ① ② ③ ④ ⑤	48 ① ② ③ ④ ⑤
24 ① ② ③ ④ ⑤	49 ① ② ③ ④ ⑤
25 ① ② ③ ④ ⑤	50 ① ② ③ ④ ⑤

Science Test

Do not mark in this test booklet. Record your answers on the separate answer sheet provided. Be sure that all requested information is properly recorded on the answer sheet.

To record your answers, fill in the numbered circle on the answer sheet that corresponds to the answer you select for each question in the test booklet.

EXAMPLE:

Which of the following is the smallest unit in a living thing?

(1) tissue

(2) organ

(3) cell

(4) muscle

(5) capillary

(On Answer Sheet)
① ② ● ④ ⑤

The correct answer is "cell"; therefore, answer space 3 would be marked on the answer sheet.

Do not rest the point of your pencil on the answer sheet while you are considering your answer. Make no stray or unnecessary marks. If you change an answer, erase your first mark completely. Mark only one answer space for each question; multiple answers will be scored as incorrect. Do not fold or crease your answer sheet. All test materials must be returned to the test administrator.

Note: Refer to Chapter 18 for the answers for this practice test.

DO NOT BEGIN TAKING THIS TEST UNTIL TOLD TO DO SO

Directions: Choose the <u>one best answer</u> to each question.

Questions 1 through 3 refer to the following passage.

Hibernating Plants

Tulips are beautiful flowers that come up early every spring. They appear fragile but manage to survive the uncertain weather of spring, blooming for awhile, and then sleeping for the rest of the year. The next year, they are ready to peek out of the earth and brighten your spring again.

Tulips survive because they grow from bulbs. Each bulb stores moisture and food during good weather. When the weather turns, the plant hibernates: The roots and leaves dry out and fall off, but the bulb develops a tough outer skin to protect itself. The bulb becomes dormant until the following spring, when the whole cycle begins again.

1. Which part of the tulip allows it to survive a rough winter?

   (1) the leaves

   (2) the buds

   (3) the bulb

   (4) the roots

   (5) the stem

2. If you wanted an early blooming plant to give your garden colour in spring, which of the following would you plant?

   (1) roses

   (2) petunias

   (3) tulips

   (4) begonias

   (5) impatiens

3. When you are enjoying your garden in spring or summer, the flowers that look so pretty are composed of cells. These cells are the basic unit of all living things in the universe. Weeds, trees, and even you are also all composed of cells. Although garden plants are composed of cells, the cells are different from plant to plant. That is why some plants produce roses and others produce dandelions.

   Which of the following is not composed of cells?

   (1) dogs

   (2) flowers

   (3) gravity

   (4) Sir Isaac Newton

   (5) the forest

Go on to next page

Questions 4 and 5 refer to the following passage.

Gunpowder

As you watch a Western on television, have you ever wondered how the bullet is propelled out of the gun when the trigger is pulled?

Bullets are made of two parts, the jacket and the projectile. The jacket is filled with gunpowder and an ignition device, and when the ignition device is hit, the gunpowder explodes, hurling the projectile out of the barrel of the gun.

4. In the movies, guns with blank cartridges are used for effect. What part of the cartridge would be different from a cartridge used for target practice?

   (1) bullet

   (2) casing

   (3) barrel

   (4) gunpowder

   (5) projectile

5. If you wanted to reduce the force with which a projectile was hurled out of the barrel, what would you change?

   (1) Use a smaller jacket.

   (2) Use a smaller projectile.

   (3) Use a smaller gun.

   (4) Use less gunpowder in the jacket.

   (5) Use more gunpowder.

Questions 6 and 7 refer to the following passage.

Rocket Propulsion

Have you ever wondered how a rocket ship moves? Perhaps you have seen science-fiction movies in which a captain uses a blast of the rocket engines to save the ship and its crew from crashing into the surface of a distant planet.

Usually, a fuel, such as the gas in a car, needs an oxidizer, like air, to create combustion, which powers the engine. Space has no air and, thus, provides no oxidizer. The rocket ship, being a clever design, carries its own oxidizer. The fuel used may be a liquid or a solid, but the rocket ship always has fuel and an oxidizer to mix together. When the two are mixed and combustion takes place, a rapid expansion is directed out the back of the engine. The force pushing backward moves the rocket ship forward. In space, with no air, the rocket ship experiences no resistance to the movement. The rocket ship moves forward, avoids the crash, or does whatever the crew wants it to do.

6. Why is the rocket engine the perfect propulsion method for space travel?

   (1) It's very powerful.

   (2) It can operate without an external oxidizer.

   (3) It carries a lot of fuel.

   (4) You can't hear the noise it makes.

   (5) It accelerates quickly.

7. Fuel on a rocket ship may be

   (1) an oxidizer

   (2) a gas

   (3) an air

   (4) an expansion

   (5) a liquid

Go on to next page

Questions 8 through 16 refer to the following passage.

Where Does All the Garbage Go?

When we finish using something, we throw it away, but where is away? In our modern cities, away is usually a landfill site, piled high with all those things that we no longer want. A modern city generates solid waste or garbage at an alarming rate. Toronto shipped 696,327 tonnes of garbage to Michigan landfills in 2006. We each produce enough garbage every five years equal to over 40 times the volume of cement in the CN Tower. In spite of all the efforts to increase recycling, we continue producing garbage without thinking much about where it goes.

In any landfill, gone is not forgotten by nature. By compacting the garbage to reduce its volume, we slow the rate of decomposition, which makes garbage last longer. In a modern landfill, the process produces a garbage lasagna. A layer of compacted garbage is covered by a layer of dirt, covered by a layer of compacted garbage, and so on. By saving space for more garbage, we cut off the air and water needed to decompose the garbage and, thus, preserve it for future generations. If you could dig far enough, you might still be able to read 40-year-old newspapers. The paper may be preserved, but the news is history.

One of the answers to this problem is recycling. Any object that can be reused in one form or another is an object that shouldn't go to a landfill. Most of us gladly recycle our paper, which saves energy and resources. Recycled paper can be used again and even turned into other products. Recycled newspaper is not as valuable as hidden treasure, but when you consider the cost of landfills and the environmental impact of producing more and more newsprint, it can be a bargain. If plastic shopping bags can be recycled into a cloth-like substance that can be used to make reusable shopping bags, maybe Canadian ingenuity can find ways to reduce all that landfill garbage before the landfills overtake the space for cities.

8. Why are modern landfills as much a part of the problem as a part of the solution?

   (1) They look very ugly.

   (2) They take up a lot of valuable land.

   (3) The bacteria that aid decomposition do not thrive.

   (4) Newspapers are readable after 50 years.

   (5) Archaeologists have no place to dig.

9. Why is recycling paper important?

   (1) It looks neater.

   (2) It reduces the need for new landfill sites.

   (3) Newspaper is not biodegradable.

   (4) It saves money.

   (5) Newspapers do not fit into compost heaps.

10. Why is solid waste compacted in a modern landfill?

   (1) to reduce the odour

   (2) to help the bacteria decompose the waste

   (3) to make the landfill look better

   (4) to reduce the amount of space it occupies

   (5) to speed up the nitrogen cycle

11. What is the modern landfill compared to?

   (1) an efficient way of ridding cities of solid waste

   (2) a garbage lasagna

   (3) a place for bacteria to decompose solid waste

   (4) a site for archaeologists to explore

   (5) a huge compost bin

Go on to next page

12. Why is it important for cities to establish recycling programs?

    (1) Recycling makes people feel good about their garbage.

    (2) Recycling is cheaper.

    (3) Recycling lets someone else look after your problem.

    (4) You are running out of bacteria to decompose waste.

    (5) Recycling is cheaper than acquiring new landfill sites.

13. What can Canadians do to reduce the amount of waste that is going into landfills?

    (1) Eat less.

    (2) Reuse and recycle as much as possible.

    (3) Stop using paper.

    (4) Import more nitrogen.

    (5) Grow more bacteria.

14. Bacteria provide what helpful purpose in composting?

    (1) They help get rid of illness.

    (2) They make rodents sick.

    (3) They are part of the inorganic cycle.

    (4) They help decompose composting waste.

    (5) They make yogourt taste distinctive.

15. If municipalities lose money recycling paper, why do they continue?

    (1) The politicians don't know they are losing money.

    (2) Municipalities don't have to make money.

    (3) The public likes to recycle paper.

    (4) The cost is less than acquiring more landfill sites.

    (5) Recycling paper has become part of urban life.

16. How does recycling paper save money for the city?

    (1) Recycling trucks run on diesel fuel.

    (2) New landfill sites cost money to buy.

    (3) Municipalities don't have to burn the paper.

    (4) In a landfill site, the heavy machinery uses a lot of fuel.

    (5) Newspapers have to be delivered.

Go on to next page

Questions 17 and 18 refer to the following passage.

Airbags

Most new cars are equipped with airbags. In a crash, the airbags quickly deploy, protecting the driver and front-seat passenger by inflating to absorb the initial force of the crash. Airbags deploy so quickly and with such force that they can injure a short person sitting too close to the dashboard or a child in a car seat. This safety device has to be treated with respect. With the proper precautions, airbags save lives. In fact, a person in the front seat of a modern car equipped with airbags who also wears a seat belt stands a much better chance of surviving a crash than an unbelted person. The two safety devices work together to save lives but must be used properly.

17. In a front-end collision, what absorbs the force of the crash?

    (1) airbags

    (2) the car's frame

    (3) the seats

    (4) padded dashboards

    (5) the windshield

18. Where is the safest place for an infant in a car seat in a car equipped with air bags?

    (1) in the rear seat

    (2) in the front seat

    (3) on the right side of the car

    (4) on the left side of the car

    (5) where the infant can be tended by an adult

Go on to next page

Questions 19 through 22 refer to the following diagram, which is excerpted from The Sciences: An Integrated Approach *by James Trefil and Robert M. Hazen (Wiley).*

10^{-9} m

Molecule

10^{-10} m

Atom

$10^{-15} - 10^{-14}$ m

Nucleus

10^{-15} m

Neutron (or proton)

Less than 10^{-18} m

Quark

19. According to this diagram, what is the building block upon which the other particles are made?

   (1) atom

   (2) molecule

   (3) neutron

   (4) quark

   (5) proton

20. According to this diagram, how many times larger is a molecule than a quark?

   (1) 100

   (2) 1,000

   (3) 1,000,000

   (4) 1,000,000,000

   (5) 10,000,000,000

Go on to next page

21. Scientists thought that the atom was the smallest particle that existed, but they were wrong. Smaller particles than the atom exist, and the atom is not itself a solid. If people cannot see atoms, how can scientists know that smaller particles than atoms exist?

    (1) They guess.

    (2) They experiment.

    (3) They use powerful magnifying glasses.

    (4) They use logic.

    (5) Another scientist told them.

22. The seat you are sitting on seems solid, but it is composed of atoms. Each of the atoms is composed of a nucleus, which is composed of neutrons and protons, but much of the space occupied by an atom is just empty space. This means that the chair you are sitting on is mostly empty space. It follows that when you stand on the floor of a building, you are ultimately being supported by

    (1) wood

    (2) concrete

    (3) girders

    (4) atoms

    (5) chemical reactions

Questions 23 and 24 refer to the following passage.

The Surface of the Moon

The surface of the moon is a hostile, barren landscape. Astronauts have found boulders as large as houses in huge fields of dust and rock. They've had no maps to guide them but have survived, thanks to their training for the mission.

23. What is it about the lunar landscape that may make landing there dangerous?

    (1) Astronauts have to consider the possibility of hostile aliens.

    (2) The moon is full of large, uncharted spaces with very large boulders.

    (3) The moon has unlit landing fields with uncertain footings.

    (4) Not all maps of the moon are accurate.

    (5) Space crafts have poor brakes for this type of terrain.

24. What aspect of the moon makes the height of a boulder unimportant for the astronauts moving about?

    (1) Astronauts have training in flying.

    (2) Special tools exist for flying over boulders.

    (3) Astronauts can drive around an obstruction.

    (4) Low gravity makes climbing easier, if it's necessary.

    (5) The boulder is not that big.

Go on to next page

Questions 25 and 26 refer to the following passage.

Pushing Aside the Water

If you fill a glass right to the brim with water, you have to drink it at its present temperature. If you add ice, the water spills over the brim. The ice has displaced an amount of water equal to the volume of the ice.

When you lower yourself into a luxurious bubble bath in your tub, the water rises. If you could measure the volume of that rise, you could figure out the volume of your body. Because you would displace a volume of water in the tub equal to the volume of your body, the new combined volume of you plus the water, minus the original volume of the water, equals the volume of your body. Next time you sink slowly into that hot bathwater, make sure that you leave room for the water to rise or make sure that you are prepared to mop the floor.

25. When you sink into a tub of water, you displace

   (1) your weight in water
   (2) a lot of water
   (3) bubbles
   (4) a volume equal to the volume of your body
   (5) the soap

26. If you wanted to find the volume of an irregularly shaped object, how could you do it?

   (1) Put the object in a pre-measured volume of water and measure the increase.
   (2) Measure the object and calculate the volume.
   (3) Weigh the object and calculate the volume.
   (4) Put the object in an oven and heat it.
   (5) Look it up.

Go on to next page

Questions 27 through 29 refer to the following passage.

Newton's First Law of Motion

In 1687, Isaac Newton proposed three laws of motion. These laws are not the types of laws that we are familiar with; they are statements of a truth in the field of physics. Newton's First Law of Motion states that a body at rest prefers to remain at rest and a body in motion prefers to stay in motion unless acted upon by an external force. One example you may know is the game of billiards. Each of the balls will remain in its position unless hit by the cue ball. When the ball gets hit, it will continue to roll until the friction of the table's surface or an external force stops it.

Inertia is the tendency of any object to maintain a uniform motion or remain at rest. This law has been adopted in current language. When we say that businesses or people are being held back because of their inertia, we mean that they will either languish in their immobility or refuse to change direction in spite of all the input from employees and advisors. In 1687, when Newton was formulating his First Law of Motion, he was not aware of the profound effect it would have on the world of science and common language.

27. If your car becomes stuck in a snowbank, what must you do to free it?

   (1) Apply a force downward to increase the traction of the wheels.

   (2) Leave it at rest until it wants to move.

   (3) Apply a force in the direction you want it to move.

   (4) Sit on the hood to increase the weight on the front tires.

   (5) Blame Newton.

28. A company that refuses to change its ideas is said to suffer from

   (1) downturns

   (2) stability

   (3) manipulation

   (4) inertia

   (5) poor management

29. When you are driving at a steady speed on the highway, why does stopping suddenly take such great effort?

   (1) Cars should have the right of way.

   (2) It takes too much power to start driving again.

   (3) Pedestrians should stay in parks.

   (4) Your car tends to continue at the same rate.

   (5) Driving is difficult enough without distractions.

Go on to next page

Question 30 refers to the following passage.

Newton's Second Law of Motion

Newton's Second Law of Motion states that when a body changes its velocity because an external force is applied to it, that change in velocity is directly proportional to the force and inversely proportional to the mass of the body. That is, the faster you want to stop your car, the harder you must brake. The brakes apply an external force that reduces the velocity of the car. The faster you want to accelerate the car, the more force you must apply. Increasing the horsepower of an engine allows it to apply greater force in accelerating. That is why drag racer cars seem to be all engine.

30. If you want a car that accelerates quickly, which attributes give you the best acceleration?

    (1) lightweight and two doors

    (2) high horsepower and automatic transmission

    (3) automatic transmission

    (4) automatic transmission and two doors

    (5) lightweight and high horsepower

Question 31 refers to the following passage.

Newton's Third Law of Motion

Newton's Third Law of Motion states that for every action there is an equal and opposite reaction. If you stand on the floor, gravity pulls your body down with a certain force. The floor must exert an equal and opposite force upward on your feet, or you would fall through the floor.

31. A boxer is punching a punching bag. What is the punching bag doing to the boxer?

    (1) bouncing away from the boxer

    (2) reacting with a force equal and opposite to the force of his punch

    (3) swinging with a velocity equal to that of the punch

    (4) swinging back with a force greater than that of the punch

    (5) remaining still

Go on to next page

Questions 32 through 34 refer to the following passage.

Why Don't Polar Bears Freeze?

Watching a polar bear lumber through the frigid Arctic wilderness, you may wonder why it doesn't freeze. If you were there, you would likely freeze. In fact, you may feel cold just looking at photographs of polar bears.

Professor Stephan Steinlechner of Hanover Veterinary University in Germany set out to answer the question of why polar bears don't freeze. Polar bears have black skin. This means that polar bears have a huge solar heat collector covering their bodies. Covering this black skin are white hollow hairs. These hairs act as insulation, keeping the heat inside the fur covering. This is like an insulated house. The heat stays in for a long time.

This is an interesting theory and does answer the question, except you may still wonder how polar bears keep warm at night, when the sun isn't out!

32. The most important element in retaining the polar bear's body heat is its

    (1) paws
    (2) scalp
    (3) skin
    (4) blood
    (5) hair

33. What is the polar bear's solar heat collector?

    (1) caves
    (2) ice
    (3) its furry coat
    (4) the snow
    (5) its skin

34. If you had to live in the Arctic, what sort of clothing would be most appropriate?

    (1) insulated coats
    (2) silk underwear
    (3) black clothing with fur covering
    (4) white clothing with fur covering
    (5) heavy wool

Go on to next page

Questions 35 and 36 refer to the following diagram, which is excerpted from The Sciences: An Integrated Approach by James Trefil and Robert M. Hazen (Wiley).

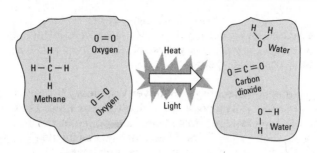

35. When methane burns, it produces light, heat, carbon dioxide, and water. Why would natural gas be a good choice for keeping your house warm in winter?

    (1) The chemical reaction produces carbon dioxide.

    (2) The chemical reaction produces light.

    (3) The chemical reaction produces water.

    (4) The chemical reaction uses oxygen.

    (5) The chemical reaction produces heat.

36. If firefighters were faced with a methane fire, what would they want to eliminate to put out the fire?

    (1) heat

    (2) light

    (3) water

    (4) carbon dioxide

    (5) oxygen

Questions 37 and 38 refer to the following passage.

Paternity Testing

DNA has become part of everyone's vocabulary, and several crime shows on television use it as a key plot element. DNA has put criminals in jail and freed others. It is used as proof in trials and is an important dramatic tool on many television dramas and talk shows.

Another use for DNA is not as dramatic. Because a child inherits the DNA of his or her parents, DNA testing can prove paternity. This is an example of a practical use for a scientific discovery.

37. Paternity testing compares the DNA of the child with the DNA of the

    (1) mother

    (2) father

    (3) father's aunt

    (4) father and grandfather

    (5) both sides of the family

38. Why is maternity testing not needed when a child is born?

    (1) A mother's DNA is always the same as her children's.

    (2) Fathers are liable for support.

    (3) Mothers give birth to their children.

    (4) It makes a better drama.

    (5) Fathers may have more than one child.

Go on to next page

> *Questions 39 through 44 refer to the following passage.*

Space Stuff

Each space flight carries items authorized by NASA, but the quirky little items carried in astronauts' pockets are what catch the interest of collectors. Auction sales have been brisk for material carried aboard space flights.

On the second manned Mercury flight, Gus Grissom carried two rolls of dimes. He was planning to give these to the children of his friends after he returned to earth. If you carried two rolls of dimes around the earth, they would be worth ten dollars. When Gus Grissom returned to earth, however, these dimes became space mementos, each worth many times their face value.

Although NASA does not permit the sale of items carried aboard space missions, many items have found their way to market. Eleven Apollo 16 stamps, autographed by the astronauts, sold for $27,000 at auction, but the corned beef sandwich that John Young offered to Gus Grissom never returned to earth.

39. What did Gus Grissom plan to do with his rolls of dimes?

   (1) Sell them at auction.

   (2) Use them in vending machines.

   (3) Give them to children.

   (4) Donate them to charity.

   (5) Keep them as souvenirs.

40. What happened to John Young's corned beef sandwich?

   (1) It is in storage.

   (2) It was sold.

   (3) It was left on the moon.

   (4) It was eaten.

   (5) Not enough information is given.

41. What is so special about items carried in an astronaut's pocket?

   (1) Weightlessness changes their composition.

   (2) They have been in space.

   (3) Lunar radiation affects them.

   (4) The pockets are made of a special material.

   (5) They are autographed.

42. What would NASA authorize astronauts to carry into space?

   (1) toys to bring home to their kids

   (2) a bulletproof vest

   (3) an extra cup of coffee for the flight

   (4) government documents

   (5) tools for experiments

43. Why would autographed stamps be worth so much money?

   (1) They are rare when personally autographed.

   (2) Stamps always become valuable.

   (3) People collect autographs.

   (4) Astronauts don't give autographs.

   (5) Auctions always get high prices.

44. Why would the contents of an astronaut's pocket become so valuable after a space flight?

   (1) NASA told them not to carry things in their pockets.

   (2) Auctions increase the value of articles.

   (3) Collectors value anything that exists in limited quantities.

   (4) Space travel makes articles magical.

   (5) The astronauts held out for the highest price.

Go on to next page ⟹

> *Questions 45 and 46 refer to the following passage.*

Work

When we think of work, we think of people sitting at desks using computers or building homes or making some other effort to earn money. When a physicist thinks of work, she probably thinks of a formula — force exerted over a distance. If you don't expend any energy — resulting in a force of zero — or if your force produces no movement, no work has been done. If you pick up your gigantic super-ordinary one-kilogram hamburger and lift it to your mouth to take a bite, you do work. If you want to resist temptation and just stare at your hamburger, you do no work. If your friend gets tired of you playing around and lifts your hamburger to feed you, you still do no work, but your friend does. In scientific terms, two elements are necessary for work to be done: a force must be exerted and the object to which the force has been exerted must move.

45. If the formula for work is Work = Force × Distance, how much more work would you do in lifting a 10-kilogram barbell 0.75 metres instead of 0.5 metres?

   (1) ½ as much

   (2) 3 times as much

   (3) ⅓ as much

   (4) 1½ times as much

   (5) 2⅓ times as much

46. While you may feel that you do work in climbing a flight of stairs, why do you also do work when you descend a flight of stairs?

   (1) Climbing down stairs is hard.

   (2) You have travelled a distance down the stairs.

   (3) You feel tired after descending stairs.

   (4) You have exerted a force over a distance.

   (5) If you do it at work, it's work.

Go on to next page

Questions 47 and 48 refer to the following figure and passages, which are excerpted from *Physical Science: What the Technology Professional Needs to Know* by C. Lon Enloe, Elizabeth Garnett, Jonathan Miles, and Stephen Swanson (Wiley).

Lead-Acid Storage Battery

Dry-Cell Battery

The Lead-Acid Storage Battery

One battery you rely on is the 12-volt lead-acid storage battery that cars and trucks use. This battery is composed of six separate cells, each developing about 2 volts. By connecting the six cells in series, the overall voltage becomes the sum, or 12 volts.

The Dry-Cell Battery

The traditional dry-cell or flashlight battery is a zinc-carbon battery. It derives its name from the fact that the liquid portion has been replaced by a moist paste of ammonium chloride, manganese dioxide, and carbon. These components are the anode portion of the cell, and the zinc container serves as the cathode.

Go on to next page

47. If you wanted a 48-volt lead-acid battery, how many cells would it need?

    (1) 24

    (2) 26

    (3) 28

    (4) 36

    (5) 48

48. What replaces the liquid acid portion of the lead-acid battery in a dry-cell battery?

    (1) a moist paste

    (2) a powder

    (3) dry acid

    (4) carbon and zinc

    (5) a stick of acid

Questions 49 and 50 refer to the following passage.

The Cell and Heredity

Each cell in a living organism consists of a membrane surrounding a cytoplasm. The cytoplasm is like jelly and has a nucleus in its centre. Chromosomes are part of the nucleus. They are important because they store DNA. DNA stores the genetic code that is the basis of heredity.

49. What determines what traits you inherit from your parents?

    (1) the cell

    (2) the atom

    (3) the nucleus

    (4) the neutron

    (5) DNA

50. What part of the chromosome carries the genetic code?

    (1) membrane

    (2) cytoplasm

    (3) nucleus

    (4) atom

    (5) DNA

END OF TEST

Chapter 18

Answers and Explanations for the Science Test

· ·

Answer Key

After taking the Science Test in Chapter 17, use this section to check your answers.

1. **3**	18. **1**	35. **5**
2. **3**	19. **4**	36. **5**
3. **3**	20. **4**	37. **2**
4. **5**	21. **2**	38. **3**
5. **4**	22. **4**	39. **3**
6. **2**	23. **2**	40. **5**
7. **5**	24. **4**	41. **2**
8. **3**	25. **4**	42. **5**
9. **2**	26. **1**	43. **1**
10. **4**	27. **3**	44. **3**
11. **2**	28. **4**	45. **4**
12. **5**	29. **4**	46. **4**
13. **2**	30. **5**	47. **1**
14. **4**	31. **2**	48. **1**
15. **4**	32. **5**	49. **5**
16. **2**	33. **5**	50. **5**
17. **1**	34. **3**	

Analysis of the Answers

If you aren't sure why an answer was incorrect, use this section to get quick explanations of the answers. If you correctly answered a question, you may still want to read the explanations to get a better understanding of the thought process that helped you choose the correct answer.

If you have trouble finishing the whole Science Test in Chapter 17 in the allotted time, turn to Chapter 16 and read over the answers to the first Science Test (which you can take in Chapter 15). Underline the sentence or sentences that tell you the correct answer to each question. Mark each passage in the test in Chapter 15 to indicate whether you can skim it or you need to read the entire passage to find the answer.

1. **3.** The passage describes how *the bulb* changes to allow the tulip to survive the winter. The complete explanation of how the bulb enables the tulip to survive is in the second paragraph.

2. **3.** The passage states that *tulips* bloom early and grow each year from the bulb.

3. **3.** All the answer choices except *gravity* are living substances that are made up of cells. Gravity is a force, not a living substance.

4. **5.** Because the *projectile* is the only part that leaves the gun, and because movie producers and directors don't want to hurt anyone, the guns are altered so that the projectile does no harm. In most cases, the gun has no projectile; it just makes a noise and a flash — nothing comes out of the barrel. The bullet still operates in a similar way with flash and noise, but the non-existent projectile is harmless.

5. **4.** The force that propels the projectile out of the barrel is the explosion of the gunpowder in the jacket. The force of the explosion is determined by the amount of powder in the jacket. If *less powder is in the jacket,* less force propels the projectile out of the barrel.

6. **2.** In space, no oxidizer exists to take part in the chemical reaction needed for combustion. A *rocket ship carries its own oxidizer* and, thus, can travel through airless space.

7. **5.** The passage states that "the fuel used may be a liquid or a solid." This question asks for only part of the information given in the passage.

8. **3.** The passage states that with the methodology used for burying solid waste in a modern landfill, *the bacteria needed for decomposition can't survive.* The reason for using landfills is that they require less space — not that they promote decomposition. Thus, the landfill and the processes used within it are as much a part of the problem as part of the solution.

9. **2.** Recycling *reduces the need for new landfill sites.* In large cities, land is expensive and few people want to live next to a landfill site. Even if you remove the garbage by shipping it elsewhere, as Toronto does, you have to dump it somewhere. This information, which the passage states, agrees with what you may have read in newspapers and seen on television. This passage is an example of a passage where previous knowledge blends in with the stated material.

Even though you may feel you know the answer, read the passage quickly to make sure because sometimes your prior knowledge conflicts with the passage.

10. **4.** Solid waste is compacted to *reduce the amount of space it occupies,* which also happens to make the landfill last longer. The waste is compacted in spite of the fact that doing so slows down decomposition and lengthens the life of the garbage.

11. **2.** A modern landfill is compared to *garbage lasagna* because it's made up of alternating layers of compacted garbage and dirt. This method prevents timely decomposition.

12. **5.** The passage states that recycling is *cheaper than continuing to acquire new landfill sites.* Choice (2) looks like a possible answer, but it isn't complete because it doesn't explain why recycling is cheaper. Be sure to read the answers carefully — you don't want to

choose an incomplete answer. The other answer choices don't address the question in light of the material presented in the passage.

13. **2.** As long as you dispose of waste by taking it to the curb or the dump, excess waste will go into landfills. Every piece of waste that you can *reuse or recycle* lives on to be useful again and, thus, eliminates some of the waste.

14. **4.** The passage states that *bacteria decompose waste*. Unfortunately, modern methods of waste disposal in landfills reduce the effectiveness of the bacteria.

15. **4.** Recycling *costs less than acquiring more landfill sites*. In most cities, people hope to find new uses for recycled materials, which could increase the value of garbage.

16. **2.** Recycling reduces the amount of space required in landfill sites. These sites are large and *expensive for any city to buy*. Needing fewer landfill sites (or smaller landfill sites) would save money.

You may notice a theme developing in these questions — something you may see as a pattern of answers. Be wary of looking for themes or patterns when answering questions on this test. If you think you've found one, be cautious because the theme or pattern may exist only in your head.

17. **1.** The purpose of the *airbag*, according to the passage, is to absorb some of the forces in a front-end crash. Choice (2) is incorrect because the passage doesn't mention anything about the car's frame as part of the energy-absorbing mechanism. Choices (3) and (5) would do little in the way of absorbing force in a crash. Padded dashboards provide minimal protection, but they're not as good as airbags.

One or more answer choices to a question may be correct according to your memory, but if the passage doesn't mention them, don't choose them. A correct answer in a multiple-choice question is either mentioned or suggested in the passage.

18. **1.** An infant is safest in the *rear seat* because, when deployed, the airbag is powerful enough to injure a small person (according to the third sentence of the first paragraph). The other four answer choices seem reasonable, but they're incorrect because the passage doesn't mention them.

19. **4.** The diagram (going from bottom to top) indicates the process of building up a molecule. The *quark* is the smallest particle, and the molecule is the largest. Sometimes you have to read a diagram in an unfamiliar way to answer the question.

20. **4.** According to the diagram, a quark is 10^{-18} m across and a molecule is 10^{-9} across. The molecule would be $10^{-9} \div 10^{-18} = 1 \div 10^{-9}$ or *1,000,000,000 times* the size of a quark.

A number with a negative exponent, like 10^{-9}, equals 1 ÷ 10 to the positive power of the negative exponent (for example, $10^{-9} = 1 \div 10^{9}$).

21. **2.** Scientists often *develop experiments* to test theories about items that are invisible to the naked eye. Curiosity drives scientists to try to find answers; experimentation proves that smaller particles than atoms exist. The other answers don't directly answer the question.

22. **4.** The passage states that everything is composed of *atoms*. As a result, the floor must be composed of atoms. Choices (1) and (2) are building materials and are themselves made of atoms. Choice (3) is a fabricated part of a building and is made of atoms, and Choice (5) doesn't even come close to answering the question.

23. **2.** Landing a space ship on *large boulders* is impossible, and the lack of charts makes accidentally meeting a boulder a possibility. A boulder as big as a house could do major damage to a space ship. The passage states that the surface of the moon has large boulders, and that few accurate charts exist of the surface.

24. **4.** Climbing requires lifting your weight against the force of gravity. The moon has less gravity than earth, so *climbing on the moon is easier*. With greatly reduced gravity, astronauts can jump fairly high. Whether or not they could jump over a house-sized boulder remains to be seen.

25. **4.** The passage tells you that you would displace a *volume equal to your own volume.* Choice (1) looks like it may be correct, but the passage is about volume, not weight.

26. **1.** The object would displace a volume of water equal to its volume. Thus, *putting an object in a pre-measured volume of water* is one way to measure the volume of an irregularly shaped object.

27. **3.** According to Newton, a force must be applied to move an object at rest. Newton, who never drove a car, said that you have to apply an external force on the object at rest (the car in this question) *in the direction you want it to move.* If you want your car to move deeper into the snow, you push it down. If you have a crane or a helicopter, which the passage doesn't mention, you apply a force upward to lift it out of the snow. Choice (3) is the best answer.

28. **4.** You find the answer (*inertia*) to this question in the second paragraph of the passage.

29. **4.** When driving at a uniform rate of speed, the car resists changes in speed. The car wants to *continue to travel at the same speed.* To change that speed suddenly, you must apply great effort to your brakes.

30. **5.** Newton's Second Law of Motion states that when a body changes its velocity because an external force is applied to it, that change in velocity is directly proportional to the force and inversely proportional to the mass of the body. If you *decrease the weight of the body* and *increase the size of the external force,* the acceleration increases.

31. **2.** Newton's Third Law of Motion states that for every action there's an equal and opposite reaction. If the boxer is exerting a force on the punching bag, *the bag is exerting an equal and opposite force* on the boxer's glove.

32. **5.** The passage states that the *hair* acts as insulation, retaining the polar bear's body heat.

33. **5.** The passage states that the polar bear's dark *skin* collects heat from the sun.

34. **3.** If you were in the Arctic, you'd want to duplicate the experience of the polar bear. *Black clothing with a fur covering* is the best answer.

35. **5.** In cold weather, you need a source of heat to warm your house, and methane *produces heat in the chemical reaction.* The other answers are incorrect.

36. **5.** Methane requires *oxygen* to produce light and heat. If there's no oxygen, the methane can't burn.

37. **2.** Paternity refers to the male half of a couple — the *father.* If mothers were tested, it would be called maternity testing.

38. **3.** No one ever has any doubt on the day of the birth about who the mother is, because the *mother gave birth to the child.* The mother is always obvious on that day. If the child were separated from the mother after birth, maternity could be an issue. But the question specifically asks about the day the baby is born.

39. **3.** According to the passage, Gus Grissom planned to *give the dimes to the children* of his friends.

40. **5.** The passage *doesn't tell you what happened to the sandwich,* other than that it didn't return to earth. Any of the other answer choices besides Choice (5) are speculation. On these tests, you need to stick to the information you're given.

41. **2.** Because *being in space* is a rare occurrence, anything that has been there takes on a certain importance. Collectors want objects that are rare and about to get rarer.

42. **5.** The purpose of space flights is scientific research, so you're looking for *items for carrying out experiments* or performing the daily routines of space travel. None of the other choices fills the bill.

43. **1.** Anything *autographed by a famous person is valuable*. When the object autographed is also available in limited quantities, it becomes more valuable still.

44. **3.** Collectors like to collect unique things. *Few items have flown in space*, which makes them rare.

45. **4.** Because the force remains constant, the work done is proportional to the distance travelled, which means you would do $3 \div 2$ or *1½ times as much* work.

46. **4.** Walking down the stairs, you have to *exert a force against the force of gravity for a distance* (the definition of work in physics). In real life, it seems easier to walk down a flight of stairs than walk up it, but, in both cases, you're doing work.

47. **1.** If you want a 48-volt lead-acid battery, and each cell produces 2 volts, you need *24 cells* $(48 \div 2 = 24)$.

48. **1.** The *moist paste* replaces the acid in the battery.

49. **5.** *DNA* stores the genetic code, which determines heredity, and you get your DNA from your parents.

50. **5.** *DNA* in the chromosome stores the genetic code, which determines heredity. Yes, this answer is the same answer as Question 49, but the question is different. Read the questions carefully, and don't spend your time looking for patterns or tricks.

Part V

Checking Your Comprehension: The Language Arts, Reading Test

The 5th Wave   By Rich Tennant

"C'mon Fogelman – talk! And I don't want to hear any of your non-parallel sentence structures, incomplete sentences, or dangling participles!"

In this part . . .

*H*ere you get to find out everything you ever wanted to know about the Language Arts, Reading Test. You discover what types of materials you're expected to read and answer questions about and how the test is formatted. You also find out some strategies that can help you do your best on this test, as well as a summary of what to read before the test to increase your chances for success. Finally, you get a chance to take two full-length practice tests.

The practice tests are serious business — as long as you choose to treat them that way. They give you a chance to see how you'd do on a real test and to check your answers. As a bonus, this part offers you detailed answer explanations you can read if you don't understand why answers are what they are.

Chapter 19

Reading between the Lines: The Language Arts, Reading Test

· ·

In This Chapter

▶ Identifying the skills the Language Arts, Reading Test covers

▶ Figuring out how the test is formatted

▶ Preparing for the different types of questions on this test

▶ Checking out a few helpful strategies and managing your time for this test

▶ Trying out some sample problems

· ·

*I*n a nutshell, the Language Arts, Reading Test determines how well you read and understand what you've read. Sounds simple enough, right? If you're looking for a few more details about the types of passages and questions that appear on this test, you've come to the right place. This chapter covers those topics and many more.

To do well on this test, you have to be in the practice of reading different types of material and comprehending what you read. If you're not a big fan of reading, start with something simple, like a daily newspaper or a weekly news magazine. Every day, switch off the TV for an hour and read something instead. Gradually advance to how-to books (like this one) and short stories from an *anthology* (a collection of short stories or poems). Eventually, begin reading novels, longer poems, and plays.

Looking at the Skills the Language Arts, Reading Test Covers

You may not understand why the GED wants to test your knowledge of literature comprehension. But comprehending, analyzing, and applying something you've read are important skills to have. The Language Arts, Reading Test has questions that focus on the following skills (which you're expected to be able to use as you read passages of prose, poetry, and plays):

✔ **Comprehension (20 percent):** Questions that test your *comprehension* skills test your ability to read a source of information, understand what you've read, and restate the information in your own words. If you understand the passage, you can rephrase what you read without losing its meaning. You can also create a summary of the main ideas presented in the passage and explain the ideas and implications of the passage.

✔ **Application (15 percent):** Questions that test your *application* skills test your ability to use the information you read in the passage in a new situation, such as answering questions. Application-focused questions are most like real life because they often ask you to apply what you read in the passage to a real-life situation. Reading a users' manual and then using the product it came with is a perfect example of using your application skills in real life.

✔ **Analysis (30 to 35 percent):** Questions that test your *analysis* skills test your ability to draw conclusions, understand consequences, and make inferences after reading the passage. To answer these questions successfully, you have to base your conclusions on the written text in the passage and not on your background knowledge or the book you read last week. Analysis questions try to find out if you appreciate the way a passage was written and if you see the cause-and-effect relationships within it. They also expect you to know when a conclusion is being stated and analyze what it means in the context of the passage.

✔ **Synthesis (30 to 35 percent):** Questions that test your *synthesis* skills test your ability to take information in one form and in one location and put it together in another context. You make connections between different parts of the passage and compare and contrast them. You may be asked to talk about a passage's tone, point of view, style, or purpose — and saying that the purpose of a passage is to confuse and confound test takers isn't the answer.

In some questions in this test, you may be asked to use information in the passage combined with information from the question to choose your answer. So make sure you read everything written in the test booklet — you never know where an answer may come from.

Understanding the Test Format

The Language Arts, Reading Test measures your ability to understand and interpret prose and poetry passages. It's plain and simple — no tricks. You don't have to do any math to figure out the answers to the questions. You just have to read, understand, and use the material presented to you to answer the corresponding questions. The passages in this test are similar to those works a high school student would come across in English class, and the questions that go with them check your knowledge in two specific areas: literary text and non-fiction text (we discuss both areas in the next section).

To help you feel more comfortable with taking the Language Arts, Reading Test, we give you a better idea of what this test looks like on paper. It consists of 40 multiple-choice questions and a number of textual passages to go with them. You have 65 minutes to complete the test, which means you have a little over a minute and a half to complete each question (and read the passage that goes with it).

Before each passage in the test is a question in bold — called a *purpose question*. You don't have to answer the purpose question; its sole job is to help you focus on what's important in the passage that follows it. The purpose question suggests the purpose for reading the passage and can give you hints about what the questions that follow will ask.

A passage of 200 to 400 words or a poem of 8 to 25 lines follows each purpose question. The passages in this test may come from workplace (on-the-job) materials or from academic reading materials. Thirty of the questions (or 75 percent of them) are based on literary texts (including plays, poetry, short stories, novels, and so on), and the other ten questions (or 25 percent) are based on non-fiction texts (including biographies, reviews, memos, directions, and so on). After each passage, you have to answer four to eight multiple-choice questions.

 Passages are passages. Although the next section describes what types of passages appear on the Language Arts, Reading Test to help you prepare, when taking the test, don't worry so much about what type of passage you're reading. Instead, spend your time understanding what information the passage presents to you.

Identifying the Types of Questions and Knowing How to Prepare for Them

To help you get comfortable with answering the questions on the Language Arts, Reading Test, we show you what these questions look like. This section focuses on the two main types of questions. We also give you some practical advice for preparing to take this test.

The simplest advice we can give you about this test is to read. Earlier in this chapter, we outline what's being tested and give you an idea of how much of the test focuses on each type of passage. Now comes your part — the reading. Read everything you can and decide what kind of reading you're doing as you do it. Ask yourself questions about everything you read — even if that means asking yourself questions about the sides of cereal boxes. Read instruction manuals for products you own — you may surprise yourself by learning something new about some of your more complicated electronic gadgets.

Literary passages

The Language Arts, Reading Test includes at least one passage from each of the following literary texts (and plenty of questions to go with them):

- ✔ **Drama:** *Drama* (that is, a play) tells a story using the words and actions of the characters. The description of the places and costumes are in the stage directions or in the head of the director. As you read passages from drama, try to imagine the dramatic scene and see the characters and their actions in your head. Doing so makes drama easier to understand.

  Stage directions are usually printed in italics, *like this.* Even though you're not an actor in the play, pay attention to the stage directions. They may provide you with valuable information you need to answer the questions that follow the passage.

- ✔ **Poetry:** *Poetry* is the concentrated juice of literature, meaning that the ideas and emotions are closely packed and aren't always obvious during your first reading. Read poetry slowly and carefully. If you take your time, poetry can make sense and be quite beautiful. As a matter of fact, popular music is often written as poetry. (Leonard Cohen is a wonderful example of a poet who can and does sing his poems.) We know you aren't taking this test as entertainment, but try to enjoy the poetry as much as you can.

  As you prepare for this test, read a lot of poetry — even if you hate it. Some poetry is beautiful and moving, and, if you read enough, you're sure to find at least one piece that you love. After you read a poem, decide what the poet is saying and how he or she is saying it. Why does the poet use certain words? What images are in the poem? Asking yourself these types of questions after reading poetry can really prepare you for the poetry portion of this test.

- ✔ **Prose fiction:** *Prose fiction* refers to novels and short stories. As you may already know, *fiction* is writing that comes straight from the mind of the author (in other words, it's made up; it's not about something that really happened). The only way to become familiar with prose fiction is to read as much fiction as you can. After you read a book, try to talk about it with other people who have read the book.

  This test includes prose fiction written during the following three time periods (look in the library for books written during these periods to get some ideas of what to read):

  - Before 1920

  - Between 1920 and 1960

  - After 1960

The difference between the time periods is usually evident in the words used and the situations described, but when the prose was written isn't the most important part of the passages. Spend your time reading and understanding the main ideas in the passages, and don't worry too much about when they were written. Just try to recognize that some passages are newer and some are older.

Non-fiction passages

As far as the non-fiction text on this test is concerned, you may have to read passages from any of the following sources (and answer questions about them, too, of course):

- ✔ **Critical reviews of visual and performing arts:** These prose passages are reviews written by people who have enough knowledge of the visual or performing arts to be critical of them. You can find examples of good critical reviews in the library, in some daily papers, and on the Internet. Enter *critical review* into a search engine, and you'll get more than you have time to read.

  To prepare for this part of the test, try to read critical reviews of books, movies, restaurants, and the like as often as you can. The next time you go to a movie, watch television, or go to a play, write your own critical review (what you thought of the piece of work). Put some factual material into your review, and make suggestions for improvement. Compare what the real critics have to say with your own feelings about the movie, television show, or play. Do you agree with their opinions?

- ✔ **Non-fiction prose:** *Non-fiction prose* is prose that covers a lot of ground — and all the ground is real. Non-fiction prose is material that the author doesn't create in his or her own mind — it's based on fact or reality. This book is classified as non-fiction prose, and so are the newspaper articles you read every day. The next time you read the newspaper or a magazine, tell yourself, "I'm reading non-fiction prose." Just don't say it out loud in a coffee shop or in your break room at work — you may get strange looks.

- ✔ **Workplace and community documents:** You run across these types of passages in the job- and community-related areas of life. Remember that time you bought an MP3 player and couldn't figure out how to transfer music to it or when your school had a student manual for behaviour? Well, the how-to manual that came with your MP3 player and the student manual are both examples of workplace documents. The following are some more examples:

  - **Mission statements:** Organizations and companies often write mission statements to tell the world what the company's role is in the community. You may have your own mission statement: "I live to party" or "I hate reading," for example. Of course, you may have to change it if you want to pass this test.

  - **Goal (or vision) statements:** Companies and organizations may also have goal statements, which tell the world what they intend to accomplish. The goal statement for your study group may be as follows: "We're all going to pass the GED tests on our first attempt."

  - **Rules for employee behaviour:** Every company, school, or organized group has rules for behaviour, which are sometimes referred to as a code of conduct. Some are written down, while others are unspoken but understood. Some of the passages on this test come from real or imaginary rules of behaviour. You probably already know how to read them.

  - **Legal documents:** Legal documents are drafted by lawyers and may include leases, purchase contracts, and bank statements. If you aren't familiar with legal documents, collect some examples from banks or libraries and review them. If you can explain these types of documents to a friend, you understand them.

- **Letters:** You certainly know what a letter is: a written communication between two people. It's not very often that you get to read other people's letters without getting into trouble — here's your chance.

✔ **Manuals:** Every time you invest in a major purchase, you get a users' manual that tells you how to use the item. Some manuals are short and straightforward; others are long and complicated.

Examining Preparation Strategies That Work

Now that you know what to read to prepare for this test, you need to focus on how to read. You can't easily skim the type of poetry and prose that appears on the test. You need to read each question and passage carefully to find the right answer.

Keep the following reading tactics in mind as you prepare for the test:

✔ **Read.** Read whatever you have available, but also look for the specific types of texts that we discuss in the preceding sections. Become a reading addict. Read labels, cereal boxes, novels, magazines, poems, plays, short stories, and newspapers. Read everything and anything. And don't stop with just reading — also digest and think about everything you read, just as this test asks you to do. When you read, read carefully. If you're unfamiliar with poetry and drama, read them even more carefully. The more carefully you read any material, the easier the test will be.

✔ **Ask questions.** Ask yourself questions about what you've read. Do you understand the main ideas well enough to explain them to a stranger? (Note that we don't advise going up to strangers to explain things to them in person. Pretend you're going to explain it to a stranger and do all the talking in your head. If you want to explain what you read to someone in person, ask your friends and family to lend you an ear — or two.)

Ask for help if you don't understand something you read. You may want to form a study group and work with other people. If you're taking a test-preparation course, ask the instructor for help when you need it. If you have family, friends, or co-workers who can help, ask them.

✔ **Use a dictionary.** Not many people understand every word they read, so use a dictionary whenever you need to. Looking up unfamiliar words increases your vocabulary, which, in turn, makes passages on the Language Arts, Reading Test easier to understand. If you have a thesaurus, use it, too. Often knowing a synonym for the word you don't know is helpful. Plus, it improves your Scrabble game.

✔ **Use new words.** A new word doesn't usually become part of your vocabulary until you put it to use in your everyday language. When you come across a new word, make sure you know its meaning and try to use it in a sentence. Then try to work it into conversation for a day or two. After a while, this challenge can make each day more exciting.

✔ **Practise.** Practise taking the Language Arts, Reading Tests in Chapters 20 and 22. Do the questions, and check your answers. Look at the explanations of the answers that we provide in Chapters 21 and 23. Don't move on to the next answer until you understand the preceding one. If you want more sample tests, look for additional test-prep books at your bookstore or local library. You can also find some abbreviated tests on the Internet. Enter *GED test questions* or *GED test questions + free* into your favourite search engine, and check out some of the results.

Take as many practice tests as you can. Stick to the time limits, and keep the testing situation as realistic as possible. When you go to the test centre for the official test, you will have done it before, which will hopefully make you feel more at ease.

This test doesn't test you on anything but reading. All the information you need to answer the questions is given in the passages or in the text of the questions that accompany the passages. You're not expected to recognize the passage and answer questions about what comes before it or what comes after it in context of the entire work. The passages are complete in themselves, so just focus on what appears on the test.

Many people get hung up on the poetry and drama passages. Don't stress. Keep in mind that these literary genres are just different ways of telling a story and conveying feelings. If you're not familiar with them, read poems and plays before taking this test. Discuss what you have read with others; you may even consider joining (or starting) a book club that discusses poems and/or plays.

Managing Your Time for the Language Arts, Reading Test

As we mention earlier in this chapter, the Language Arts, Reading Test consists of 40 questions that you have to answer in 65 minutes, which averages out to just over one and a half minutes per question. When you begin the test, the best way to manage your time is to answer the easiest questions first. Then move on to the more difficult questions that you may need to spend a little more time on.

Throughout the test, keep track of the time so it doesn't run out before you finish answering all the questions. Arrange to leave a little extra time for the sections you have the most difficulty with. If you have difficulty with poetry, leave a bit of extra time for poetry-based questions, and use less time for the prose sections. Keep in mind, however, that this is a timed test, so you can't spend too long on any one question. If you do, you won't have time to finish — and finishing is definitely important. Check out Chapter 2 for some general time-management tips.

Practising with Sample Problems

The following passage and sample problems give you some idea of what the Language Arts, Reading Test questions look like.

Choose the one best answer to each question. Questions 1 through 5 refer to the following passage.

Does Employment Need a New FACE?
Facilities for Access to Creative Enterprise (FACE)

Originally founded in 1982 to train unemployed youth in small "hand skill" craft workshops, this project provides occupational and entrepreneurial skills as an alternative to traditional manufacturing jobs. Beginning with glass engraving and sign writing, FACE now offers training in more than 200 hand skill occupations, including antique restoration, clothing manufacturing, graphic design, masonry, sail making, specialist joinery, weaving, and wood turning. Funded through the Youth Training Scheme, FACE provides 800 training places in the west and northeast of England under the premise that even if the young people can't secure employment, they at least will have the skills to create their own businesses.

Based on its experience, FACE has developed, with the Royal Society of Arts, a Certificate in Small Business and Enterprise Skills. The aim of the certificate is "to develop the basic skills of enterprise across a range of occupational sectors, within small business and in general employment and which are applicable in a wide range of personal and social contexts outside work." Competencies include self-evaluation, decision making, initiative taking, resource and time management, opportunism and self-motivation, problem solving, and learning-to-learn skills, as well as communication and number skills vital to personal effectiveness.

1. What is the overall purpose of the FACE project?

    (1) to provide manufacturing jobs

    (2) to engrave glass

    (3) to train unemployed youth

    (4) to write signs

    (5) to restore antiques

The correct answer is Choice (3). The overall purpose of the FACE project is to train unemployed youth. Glass engraving, sign writing, and antique restoring are just some of the skills the youth may develop through FACE. Manufacturing jobs are in short supply, resulting in the need for entrepreneurial skills.

2. What answer is not an example of a hand skill craft occupation?

    (1) weaving

    (2) wood turning

    (3) sail making

    (4) specialist joinery

    (5) robotic assembly

The correct answer is Choice (5). Robotic assembly is a high-tech computer-assisted approach to manufacturing that seeks to replace workers with robots. The other answers — weaving, wood turning, sail making, and joinery (carpentry) — are all examples of hand skill craft occupations according to the passage.

3. How can young people best secure employment in the northeast of England?

    (1) by engaging in traditional manufacturing

    (2) by creating new enterprises

    (3) by joining the Royal Society of Arts

    (4) by obtaining a Certificate in Small Business

    (5) by going to one of 800 training places

The correct answer is Choice (2). The best way for youth to secure employment is to "create new enterprises," as the passage states. Jobs are being lost in traditional manufacturing. The Royal Society, business certificate, and training places don't refer directly to securing employment.

4. Who helped FACE develop the Certificate in Small Business and Enterprise Skills?

    (1) Youth Training Scheme

    (2) west and northeast England

    (3) hand skill workshops

    (4) Royal Society of Arts

    (5) occupational sectors

The correct answer is Choice (4). The Royal Society of Arts assisted FACE in developing the Certificate in Small Business and Enterprise Skills. The Youth Training Scheme, while providing funding for FACE, wasn't directly involved with the certificate. Hand skill workshops and occupational sectors have no direct relation to the certificate. Choice (2) — west and northeast England — refers only to locations.

5. Which competency is not included in training for the Certificate?

   (1) self-evaluation

   (2) anger management

   (3) decision making

   (4) problem solving

   (5) number skills

The correct answer is Choice (2). Anger management isn't mentioned in the passage as one of the competencies; all the other skills are.

Revealing Some Helpful Pointers

This chapter includes several tips to help you achieve greatness on this test. This section hits on a few other general pointers that can help give you the edge you're looking for. As you work your way through the Language Arts, Reading Test, keep the following pointers in mind:

- ✔ **Look at the purpose question.** Before every passage is a purpose question (see the "Understanding the Test Format" section for details). Be sure to read it. You don't have to answer it, but it gives you a direction for reading the passage. Take any clues that you can get.

- ✔ **Ferret out the meaning of new words from the surrounding text.** Even the best readers sometimes come to a word they don't recognize or understand. Luckily, the sentences around a new word can give you clues to the meaning of the word. Ask yourself, "What word would make sense in place of the one I don't know?"

- ✔ **Recognize that everything's important.** In this test, you may find information in many places. It may be in explanatory notes set off in square brackets [like this]. It may be in stage directions, usually printed in italics, *like this*. It may be in the speaker's name before the dialogue. Read everything and skip nothing.

- ✔ **Develop your reading speed.** Reading is wonderful, but reading quickly is even better — it gets you through the test with time to spare. Check out *Speed Reading For Dummies* by Richard Sutz with Peter Weverka (Wiley), or check online to find plenty of material that can help you read faster. Whatever method you use, try to improve your reading rate without hurting your overall reading comprehension.

Chapter 20

Practice Test — Language Arts, Reading Test

· ·

*T*he Language Arts, Reading Test consists of excerpts from fiction and non-fiction. Each excerpt is followed by multiple-choice questions about the reading material.

Read each excerpt first and then answer the questions following it. Refer back to the reading material as often as necessary in answering the questions.

Each excerpt is preceded by a purpose question. The purpose question gives a reason for reading the material. Use these purpose questions to help focus your reading. You are not required to answer these purpose questions. They are given only to help you concentrate on the ideas presented in the reading material.

You have 65 minutes to answer the 40 questions in this booklet. Work carefully, but do not spend too much time on any one question. Be sure you answer every question.

Answer Sheet for Language Arts, Reading Test

1 ① ② ③ ④ ⑤   21 ① ② ③ ④ ⑤

2 ① ② ③ ④ ⑤   22 ① ② ③ ④ ⑤

3 ① ② ③ ④ ⑤   23 ① ② ③ ④ ⑤

4 ① ② ③ ④ ⑤   24 ① ② ③ ④ ⑤

5 ① ② ③ ④ ⑤   25 ① ② ③ ④ ⑤

6 ① ② ③ ④ ⑤   26 ① ② ③ ④ ⑤

7 ① ② ③ ④ ⑤   27 ① ② ③ ④ ⑤

8 ① ② ③ ④ ⑤   28 ① ② ③ ④ ⑤

9 ① ② ③ ④ ⑤   29 ① ② ③ ④ ⑤

10 ① ② ③ ④ ⑤   30 ① ② ③ ④ ⑤

11 ① ② ③ ④ ⑤   31 ① ② ③ ④ ⑤

12 ① ② ③ ④ ⑤   32 ① ② ③ ④ ⑤

13 ① ② ③ ④ ⑤   33 ① ② ③ ④ ⑤

14 ① ② ③ ④ ⑤   34 ① ② ③ ④ ⑤

15 ① ② ③ ④ ⑤   35 ① ② ③ ④ ⑤

16 ① ② ③ ④ ⑤   36 ① ② ③ ④ ⑤

17 ① ② ③ ④ ⑤   37 ① ② ③ ④ ⑤

18 ① ② ③ ④ ⑤   38 ① ② ③ ④ ⑤

19 ① ② ③ ④ ⑤   39 ① ② ③ ④ ⑤

20 ① ② ③ ④ ⑤   40 ① ② ③ ④ ⑤

Language Arts, Reading Test

Do not mark in this test booklet. Record your answers on the separate answer sheet provided. Be sure that all requested information is properly recorded on the answer sheet.

To record your answers, fill in the numbered circle on the answer sheet that corresponds to the answer you select for each question in the test booklet.

EXAMPLE:

It was Susan's dream machine. The metallic blue paint gleamed, and the sporty wheels were highly polished. Under the hood, the engine was no less carefully cleaned. Inside, flashy lights illuminated the instruments on the dashboard, and the seats were covered by rich leather upholstery.

The subject ("it") of this excerpt is most likely

(1) an airplane

(2) a stereo system

(3) an automobile

(4) a boat

(5) a motorcycle

(On Answer Sheet)
① ② ● ④ ⑤

The correct answer is "an automobile"; therefore, answer space 3 would be marked on the answer sheet.

Do not rest the point of your pencil on the answer sheet while you are considering your answer. Make no stray or unnecessary marks. If you change an answer, erase your first mark completely. Mark only one answer space for each question; multiple answers will be scored as incorrect. Do not fold or crease your answer sheet. All test materials must be returned to the test administrator.

Note: See Chapter 21 for the answers for this practice test.

DO NOT BEGIN TAKING THIS TEST UNTIL TOLD TO DO SO

Directions: Choose the <u>one best answer</u> to each question.

Questions 1 through 6 refer to the following poem, "In High Flight," by John Gillespie Magee Jr. (1941).

WHO CAN REACH TO THE HEAVENS?

_{Line} Oh, I have slipped the surly bonds of earth,
And danced the skies on laughter-silvered wings;
Sunward I've climbed and joined the tumbling mirth
Of sun-split clouds — and done a hundred things

(05) You have not dreamed of — wheeled and soared and swung
High in the sunlit silence. Hov'ring there,
I've chased the shouting wind along and flung
My eager craft through footless halls of air.

I've topped the wind-swept heights with easy grace,
(10) Where never lark, or even eagle, flew;
And, while with silent, lifting mind I've trod
The high untrespassed sanctity of space,
Put out my hand and touched the face of God.

1. What is the occupation of the poet?

   (1) aviator

   (2) mountain climber

   (3) sailor

   (4) clergyman

   (5) biologist

2. Which phrase best describes the weather in the poem?

   (1) laughter-silvered

   (2) footless halls

   (3) soared and swung

   (4) sun-split clouds

   (5) wind-swept heights

3. How does the poet describe the sky?

   (1) surly bonds

   (2) burning blue

   (3) easy grace

   (4) wind-swept

   (5) sunlit silence

4. What phrase tells us the poet is referring to the flight of an aircraft?

   (1) laughter-silvered wings

   (2) wheeled and soared

   (3) eager craft

   (4) hov'ring there

   (5) all of the above

5. What word best describes the poet's attitude as expressed in the poem?

   (1) free

   (2) fearful

   (3) delirious

   (4) silent

   (5) surly

6. How do you know the poet is a religious person?

   (1) He slipped the surly bonds.

   (2) He danced the skies.

   (3) He touched the face of God.

   (4) He topped the wind-swept heights.

   (5) He joined the tumbling clouds.

Go on to next page

Questions 7 through 12 refer to the following excerpt from Garrison Keillor's Prodigal Son (1989).

WHERE DOES EVIL COME FROM?

Line **DWIGHT:** *(sitting at table, reading newspaper)* Morning.

DAD: You see your brother this morning?

DWIGHT: In bed.

DAD: I promised Harry Shepherd I'd be over to his place by seven-thirty. He's got a lost
(05) sheep out on the mountain wild and steep.

DWIGHT: Says here that fatted calves are down one and three-quarter shekels on the
Damascus market, Dad. Makes me wonder if maybe lean calves wouldn't have a higher profit
margin, and then we could spend more time in the vineyard — Dad, are you listening to me?

DAD: I'm worried about your brother.

(10) **DWIGHT:** We can't afford to stand still, Dad. Look at the Stewarts — they're buying up land
left and right! You've got to move ahead or you lose ground . . . .

WALLY: *(thickly)* Morning, Dad. Morning, Dwight. *(He sits down, groans, puts his head in his
hands.)*

DAD: You look a little peaked, son.

(15) **WALLY:** I donno — it's some kind of morning sickness, Dad. I feel real good at night and
then I wake up and hurt all over.

DWIGHT: I noticed a couple empty wineskins behind the fig tree this morning.

WALLY: I dropped them, and they spilled! Honest!

DAD: Where were you taking them?

(20) **WALLY:** I was putting them outside! Wine's got to breathe, you know. And so do I, Dad. I've
got a real breathing problem here. I'm worried about my health, Dad. I read an article the
other day in Assyrian Digest that says bad feelings may be environmental. I donno. Maybe I
need to get away for a while, Dad. Get my head straight. Work out some things.

7. Why does Wally's father think Wally
doesn't feel well this morning?

(1) Wally feels bad that he spilled some
wine.

(2) Wally works on a tree farm in Judea.

(3) Wally drank too much wine.

(4) Wally needs a vacation.

(5) Wally wants to run the business.

8. What is the setting for the play?

(1) breakfast table

(2) fig tree

(3) market

(4) bed

(5) vineyard

Go on to next page

9. Why does Dwight feel it would be better to raise lean calves?

    (1) less profit

    (2) fat is bad for you

    (3) more profit

    (4) more expensive to produce

    (5) better than goats

10. Why isn't Dad paying attention to Dwight?

    (1) He wants to help find a lost sheep.

    (2) He wants to spend time in the vineyard.

    (3) He wants to buy more land.

    (4) He is reading the paper.

    (5) He is worried about Wally.

11. Why do you think Wally is late for breakfast?

    (1) He is sick.

    (2) He has a hangover.

    (3) He is doing the chores.

    (4) He is reading an article.

    (5) He is working in the fields.

12. What comparison does Wally make between himself and wine?

    (1) They both are sweet.

    (2) They both like to travel.

    (3) They both need to breathe.

    (4) They are both precious.

    (5) They both cause problems.

Go on to next page

Questions 13 through 18 refer to the following excerpt from Jack London's "In a Far Country" (1899).

HOW CAN I MAKE MY FORTUNE?

Line When the world rang with the tale of Arctic gold, and the lure of the North gripped the heartstrings of men, Carter Weatherbee threw up his snug clerkship, turned the half of his savings over to his wife, and with the remainder bought an outfit. There was no romance in his nature — the bondage of commerce had crushed all that; he was simply tired of the

(05) ceaseless grind, and wished to risk great hazards in view of corresponding returns . . . and there, unluckily for his soul's welfare, he allied himself with a party of men.

There was nothing unusual about this party, except its plans. Even its goal, like that of all the other parties, was the Klondike. But the route it had mapped out to attain that goal took away the breath of the hardiest native, born and bred to the vicissitudes of the Northwest. Even

(10) Jacques Baptiste, born of a Chippewa woman and a renegade voyageur (having raised his first whimpers in a deerskin lodge north of the sixty-fifth parallel, and had the same hushed by blissful sucks of raw tallow), was surprised. Though he sold his services to them and agreed to travel even to the never-opening ice, he shook his head ominously whenever his advice was asked.

Percy Cuthfert's evil star must have been in the ascendant, for he, too, joined this company

(15) of Argonauts. He was an ordinary man, with a bank account as deep as his culture, which is saying a good deal. He had no reason to embark on such a venture — no reason in the world, save that he suffered from an abnormal development of sentimentality. He mistook this for the true spirit of romance and adventure.

13. What caused Carter Weatherbee to leave his job?

   (1) Arctic gold

   (2) a woman

   (3) his snug clerkship

   (4) half of his savings

   (5) the heartstrings of men

14. What is meant by "bondage of commerce" in line 4?

   (1) the corresponding returns

   (2) the romance in his nature

   (3) the drudgery of life as a clerk

   (4) the risk of great hazards

   (5) half of his savings

15. What was the goal of the party?

   (1) to find the old trails

   (2) to reach the Klondike

   (3) to map out a route

   (4) to tell the tale of the Arctic

   (5) to buy outfits

16. How would you best describe the chosen route to the Klondike?

   (1) blissful

   (2) hardy

   (3) hushed

   (4) ominous

   (5) surprising

17. Why was Jacques Baptiste important to the party?

   (1) He was a native of the Northwest.

   (2) He was born of a Chippewa woman.

   (3) He was a renegade voyageur.

   (4) He was born in a deerskin lodge.

   (5) He sucked raw tallow.

18. Why do you think Percy Cuthfert joined the party?

   (1) to show that he is an ordinary man

   (2) to fill his bank account

   (3) to seek romance and adventure

   (4) to be able to say a good deal

   (5) because of his abnormal development

Go on to next page

> Questions 19 through 24 refer to the following excerpt from "My Financial Career" by Stephen Leacock (1923).

HOW DO YOU OPEN A BANK ACCOUNT?

Line When I go into a bank I get rattled. The clerks rattle me; the wickets rattle me; the sight of the money rattles me; everything rattles me.

The moment I cross the threshold of a bank and attempt to transact business there, I become an irresponsible idiot.

(05) I knew this beforehand, but my salary had been raised to fifty dollars a month, and I felt that the bank was the only place for it.

So I shambled in and looked timidly round at the clerks. I had an idea that a person about to open an account must needs consult the manager.

I went up to a wicket marked "Accountant." The accountant was a tall, cool devil. The very
(10) sight of him rattled me. My voice was sepulchral.

"Can I see the manager?" I said, and added solemnly, "alone." I don't know why I said "alone."

"Certainly," said the accountant, and fetched him.

The manager was a grave, calm man. I held my fifty-six dollars clutched in a crumpled ball
(15) in my pocket.

"Are you the manager?" I said. God knows I didn't doubt it.

"Yes," he said.

"Can I see you," I asked, "alone?" I didn't want to say "alone" again, but without it the thing seemed self-evident.

(20) The manager looked at me in some alarm. He felt that I had an awful secret to reveal.

"Come in here," he said, and led the way to a private room. He turned the key in the lock.

"We are safe from interruption here," he said; "sit down."

We both sat down and looked at each other. I found no voice to speak.

"You are one of Pinkerton's men, I presume," he said.

(25) He had gathered from my mysterious manner that I was a detective. I knew what he was thinking, and it made me worse.

"No, not from Pinkerton's," I said, seeming to imply that I came from a rival agency.

"To tell the truth," I went on, as if I had been prompted to lie about it, "I am not a detective at all. I have come to open an account. I intend to keep all my money in this bank."

Go on to next page ⟶

19. Why did the author go to the bank?

    (1) He felt rattled.

    (2) He got a raise in salary.

    (3) He worked for Pinkerton's.

    (4) He was an irresponsible idiot.

    (5) He felt timid.

20. Whom does the author think he needs to see to open an account?

    (1) the clerk

    (2) the accountant

    (3) the manager

    (4) Pinkerton's man

    (5) the president

21. How does the author describe the accountant?

    (1) irresponsible

    (2) timid

    (3) sepulchral

    (4) tall and cool

    (5) calm and grave

22. What gets the author rattled?

    (1) going into the bank

    (2) the clerks

    (3) the wickets

    (4) the sight of money

    (5) all of the above

23. Why does the manager take the author to a private room?

    (1) He wanted them to be safe from interruption.

    (2) He wanted them to be alone.

    (3) He thought the author was one of Pinkerton's men.

    (4) He thought the author was investigating the bank.

    (5) He suspected the author had an awful secret.

24. Why did the manager think the author was a detective?

    (1) He was rattled.

    (2) He looked timid.

    (3) He had a mysterious manner.

    (4) He was a grave, calm man.

    (5) He was a tall, cool devil.

Go on to next page

Questions 25 through 30 refer to the following excerpt from Anne of Green Gables by L. M. Montgomery (1908).

WHAT WAS RACHEL LYNDE WATCHING FOR?

Line Mrs. Rachel Lynde lived just where the Avonlea main road dipped down into a little hollow, fringed with alders and ladies' eardrops and traversed by a brook that had its source away back in the woods of the old Cuthbert place; it was reputed to be an intricate, headlong brook in its earlier course through those woods, with dark secrets of pool and cascade; but

(05) by the time it reached Lynde's Hollow it was a quiet, well-conducted little stream, for not even a brook could run past Mrs. Rachel Lynde's door without due regard for decency and decorum; it probably was conscious that Mrs. Rachel was sitting at her window, keeping a sharp eye on everything that passed, from brooks and children up, and that if she noticed anything odd or out of place she would never rest until she had ferreted out the whys and

(10) wherefores thereof.

There are plenty of people, in Avonlea and out of it, who can attend closely to their neighbours' business by dint of neglecting their own; but Mrs. Rachel Lynde was one of those capable creatures who can manage their own concerns and those of other folks into the bargain. She was a notable housewife; her work was always done and well done; she "ran"

(15) the Sewing Circle, helped run the Sunday-school, and was the strongest prop of the Church Aid Society and Foreign Missions Auxiliary. Yet with all this Mrs. Rachel found abundant time to sit for hours at her kitchen window, knitting "cotton warp" quilts — she had knitted sixteen of them, as Avonlea housekeepers were wont to tell in awed voices — and keeping a sharp eye on the main road that crossed the hollow and wound up the steep red hill

(20) beyond. Since Avonlea occupied a little triangular peninsula jutting out into the Gulf of St. Lawrence, with water on two sides of it, anybody who went out of it or into it had to pass over that hill road and so run the unseen gauntlet of Mrs. Rachel's all-seeing eye.

She was sitting there one afternoon in early June. The sun was coming in at the window warm and bright; the orchard on the slope below the house was in a bridal flush of pinky-

(25) white bloom, hummed over by a myriad of bees. Thomas Lynde — a meek little man whom Avonlea people called "Rachel Lynde's husband" — was sowing his late turnip seed on the hill field beyond the barn; and Matthew Cuthbert ought to have been sowing his on the big red brook field away over by Green Gables. Mrs. Rachel knew that he ought because she had heard him tell Peter Morrison the evening before in William J. Blair's store over at

(30) Carmody that he meant to sow his turnip seed the next afternoon. Peter had asked him, of course, for Matthew Cuthbert had never been known to volunteer information about anything in his whole life.

25. Where did Mrs. Rachel Lynde live?

(1) in a hollow on the main road to Avonlea

(2) back in the woods

(3) at the old Cuthbert place

(4) on the main road in Avonlea

(5) beside a pool and cascade

26. How would you best describe Mrs. Rachel?

(1) without decency or decorum

(2) a lazy housekeeper

(3) very observant

(4) quiet and well-conducted

(5) odd or out of place

Go on to next page

27. How do you know Mrs. Rachel was a leader?

    (1) She ran the Sewing Circle.

    (2) She helped run the Sunday-school.

    (3) She was the strongest prop of the Church Aid Society.

    (4) She was active in the Foreign Missions Auxiliary.

    (5) all of the above

28. According to the passage, where is Avonlea located?

    (1) up the steep red hill

    (2) on a peninsula

    (3) in the St. Lawrence

    (4) on the slope below

    (5) all of the above

29. How does the author describe Thomas Lynde?

    (1) a meek little man

    (2) Rachel Lynde's husband

    (3) an all-seeing eye

    (4) a turnip planter

    (5) a storekeeper

30. Where is Mrs. Rachel's favourite place?

    (1) on the hill beyond the barn

    (2) over by Green Gables

    (3) in William J. Blair's store

    (4) at the kitchen window

    (5) in the orchard on the slope

Questions 31 through 35 refer to the following excerpt, written by Dale Shuttleworth (originally printed in The Toronto Star, *January 2008).*

WHAT IS THE HISTORY OF THE SOCIAL ENTERPRISE MOVEMENT?

Line The Centre for Social Innovation, a renovated warehouse in the Spadina Ave. area of Toronto, houses 85 "social enterprises," including organizations concerned with the environment, the arts, social justice, education, health, technology and design. Tribute has been paid to the "social enterprise movement" in Quebec and Vancouver for providing the impe-
(05) tus for this very successful venture.

In fact, the cause of social enterprise has a rich history in the later part of the 20th century, including New Dawn Enterprises in Sydney, N.S. and the Mondragon Movement in the Basque Region of Spain. In each instance, these pioneers in "community economic development" had a built-in relationship with an educational and training facility to encourage co-
(10) operative enterprise and entrepreneurial skills.

Toronto, Ontario, also has provided leadership in the areas of community education and community economic development — essential components in the creation of social enterprises. In 1974, the Toronto Board of Education assisted in the establishment of the Learnxs Foundation Inc. as part of its Learning Exchange System.

(15) The foundation represented an additional source of support for the burgeoning "alternatives in education" movement. In 1973, the Ontario government had imposed ceilings on educational spending and together with reduced revenue due to declining enrolment the Toronto board had limited means to fund innovative and experimental programs. The Learnxs Foundation was an independent "arms-length" non-profit charitable enterprise,
(20) which could solicit funds from public and private sources and generate revenue through the sale of goods and services to support innovative programs within the Toronto system.

Go on to next page

What followed during the 1970s was a series of Learnxs — sponsored demonstration projects as a source of research and development in such areas as: School and community programs to improve inner-city education; a series of small enterprises to employ 14- to

(25) 15-year-old school leavers; Youth Ventures — a paper recycling enterprise employing at-risk youth; Artsjunction — discarded material from business and industry were recycled for use as craft materials for visual arts classes; Toronto Urban Studies Centre — a facility to encourage the use of the city as a learning environment; and Learnxs Press — a publishing house for the production and sale of innovative learning materials.

(30) The York Board of Education and its school and community organizations jointly incorporated the Learning Enrichment Foundation (LEF), modelled on Learnxs. Originally devoted to multicultural arts enrichment, LEF during the 1980s jointed with parental groups and the school board to establish 13 school-based childcare centres for infants, pre-school and school-age children.

(35) Training programs for youth, immigrants and refugees soon followed. Often with teachers in the workplace, provided by the board's Adult Day School, training programs included: renovation and construction, industrial maintenance, home helpers, healthcare aides, childcare assistants, food service and catering, courier/light delivery, bus drivers and clerical services.

In 1984, LEF was asked by Employment and Immigration Canada to convene a local commit-
(40) tee of adjustment in response to York's high rate of unemployment and plant closures. The York Community Economic Development Committee, besides LEF and the school board, included the City of York, the York Association of Industry, the United Steelworkers and the Ontario Ministry of Labour. Outcomes of the work of the Committee included:

York Business Opportunities Centre: In 1985, with support from the Ontario Ministry of
(45) Industry, Trade & Technology, LEF opened the first small business incubator operated by a non-profit charitable organization. Originally 28,000 square feet, the centre was later increased to 74,000 square feet providing small business incubator and training space for 40 enterprises creating 160 new jobs in the first three years. Business education students from the Adult Day School provided clerical and administrative services to tenants. An LEF child-
(50) care facility was also established at the front of the building.

Microtron Centre: This training facility was devoted to micro-computer skills, word and numerical processing, computer-assisted design, graphics and styling, and electronic assembly and repair. Located in three surplus classrooms at Vaughan Road Collegiate, it was jointly sponsored by the board of education, LEF, Commodore Business Machines,
(55) Comspec Systems, Corel Systems and the York Business Opportunities Centre. Microtron served York Board employees, small business and industry, government departments, voluntary organizations and the community at large.

Microtron Bus: This refurbished school bus incorporated eight workstations from the Microtron Centre. It visited small business, industry and service organizations on a scheduled
(60) basis to provide training in word and numerical processing for their employees and clients.

In 1996, the Training Renewal Foundation was incorporated as a non-profit charity to serve disadvantaged youth and other displaced workers seeking skills, qualifications and employment opportunities. Over the years TRF has partnered with governments, employers and community organizations to provide a variety of services including job-creation programs
(65) for: immigrants and refugees, GED high school equivalency, café equipment technicians, coffee and vending service workers, industrial warehousing and lift truck operators, fully expelled students, youth parenting, construction craft workers and garment manufacturing.

Go on to next page

These three community education and training organizations have been unique in the "social enterprise movement." They have combined the resources of the governmental, commercial (70) and voluntary sectors to address skill shortages in the labour market while providing entrepreneurial opportunities for some of the most disadvantaged segments of our society.

31. The Centre for Social Innovation is
    (1) a new restaurant
    (2) a centre housing social enterprises
    (3) the head office of a charity
    (4) part of LEF
    (5) a small enterprise to employ school leavers

32. The Learnxs Foundation supported
    (1) homeless people
    (2) scholarships for students specializing in computer studies
    (3) innovative programs
    (4) art programming
    (5) recycling projects

33. Artsjunction specialized in
    (1) making maps
    (2) assisting new artists in finding studios
    (3) helping artists learn about the city
    (4) publishing art booklets
    (5) distributing discarded materials to visual art classes

34. The Microtron bus helped to
    (1) provide transportation for computer science students to their labs
    (2) provide training in word and numerical processing to employees and clients
    (3) train auto mechanics in the digital controls in new cars
    (4) establish social enterprises
    (5) train young people as bus drivers

35. The Training Renewal Foundation serves
    (1) as a social innovator for youth
    (2) as a patron of the centre
    (3) dinner to the homeless
    (4) disadvantaged youth and displaced workers
    (5) as a business incubator

Go on to next page

> *Questions 36 through 40 refer to the following excerpt.*

HOW MUST EMPLOYEES BEHAVE?

Line It is expected that employees behave in a respectful, responsible, professional manner. Therefore, each employee must do the following:

- Wear appropriate clothing and use safety equipment where needed.

(05)
- Refrain from the use and possession of alcohol and/or illicit drugs and associated paraphernalia throughout the duration of the work day.

- Refrain from associating with those who pass, use, and are under the influence of illicit drugs and/or alcohol.

- Address all other employees and supervisors with courtesy and respect, using non-offensive language.

(10)
- Accept the authority of supervisors without argument. If you consider an action unfair, inform the Human Resources department.

- Respect the work environment of this company and conduct oneself in a manner conducive to the growth and the enhancement of our business.

(15)
- Refrain from inviting visitors to our place of work in order to keep the premises secure.

- Promote the dignity of all persons, regardless of gender, creed, or culture and conduct oneself with dignity.

If the employee chooses *not* to comply:

(20)
- On the first offense, the employee meets with his or her supervisor. A representative from Human Resources may choose to attend.

- On the second offense, the employee meets with the vice-president of Human Resources before returning to work.

- On the third offense, the employee is dismissed.

36. Which requirement relates to employee appearance?

(1) The employee must refrain from using alcohol.

(2) The employee must not use associated paraphernalia.

(3) The employee must wear appropriate clothing.

(4) The employee must use courtesy and respect.

(5) The employee must use non-offensive language.

37. Which requirement addresses relations with supervisors?

(1) Accept authority.

(2) Contribute to business growth and enhancement.

(3) Use non-offensive language.

(4) Do not use drugs and alcohol.

(5) Refrain from associating.

Go on to next page

38. Which requirement is concerned with the growth and enhancement of the business?

    (1) conducive to growth

    (2) enhancement of self

    (3) dressing unprofessionally

    (4) personal conduct

    (5) inviting visitors

39. How are safety and security protected?

    (1) by promoting dignity

    (2) by not inviting others in

    (3) by the types of interaction

    (4) through meetings with supervisors

    (5) by being respectful and responsible

40. What are the penalties for continued non-compliance?

    (1) You meet with the president of the company.

    (2) Your salary goes up.

    (3) You must avoid your supervisor.

    (4) You have to take behaviour classes.

    (5) You are fired.

END OF TEST

Chapter 21

Answers and Explanations for the Language Arts, Reading Test

Answer Key

After taking the Language Arts, Reading Test in Chapter 20, use this section to check your answers.

1. **1**	15. **2**	29. **1**
2. **4**	16. **4**	30. **4**
3. **2**	17. **1**	31. **2**
4. **5**	18. **3**	32. **3**
5. **1**	19. **2**	33. **5**
6. **3**	20. **3**	34. **2**
7. **3**	21. **4**	35. **4**
8. **1**	22. **5**	36. **3**
9. **3**	23. **1**	37. **1**
10. **5**	24. **3**	38. **4**
11. **2**	25. **1**	39. **2**
12. **3**	26. **3**	40. **5**
13. **1**	27. **5**	
14. **3**	28. **2**	

Analysis of the Answers

If you aren't sure why an answer was incorrect, use this section to get quick explanations of the answers. If you correctly answered a question, you may still want to read the explanations to get a better understanding of the thought process that helped you choose the correct answer.

1. **1.** The correct choice is *aviator*, which is a synonym for pilot. Although the poem speaks of wind-swept heights, the poet certainly isn't a mountain climber. Sailor, clergyman, and biologist are not relevant to the poem.

2. **4.** *Sun-split clouds* describe two important features concerning weather. Although wind-swept heights may also be part of a weather report, it is not the best answer. The other choices — laughter-silvered, footless halls, and soared and swung — are not related to weather.

3. **2.** The poet describes the sky as *burning blue*. Surly bonds refer to the earth, while wind-swept describes the heights. Sunlit silence does not refer directly to the sky.

4. **5.** All of the first four choices have some reference to an aircraft or its flight pattern: wings, soared, craft, and hovering.

5. **1.** The poet tells us that he is free of the earth. The other choices — fearful, delirious, silent, or surly — do not describe the poet's attitude.

6. **3.** The fact that the poet reached out his hand to touch the face of God would indicate that he has religious beliefs. The other choices are descriptions of his flight path as the aircraft climbed higher in the sky.

7. **3.** Wally isn't feeling well because he drank too much wine. You can draw this conclusion from Dwight's saying that he "noticed a couple empty wineskins behind the fig tree this morning."

8. **1.** *Breakfast table* is correct because the characters had just sat down for breakfast. The other locations — fig tree, market, bedroom, and vineyard — although mentioned in the excerpt, aren't the setting of the play.

9. **3.** Dwight felt it would be better to raise lean calves because they would represent *more profit*. Two of the answers — less profit and more expensive — are the opposite of what's stated in the passage. Fat may be bad for you, but that isn't mentioned in the passage. Goats aren't mentioned in the passage, either.

10. **5.** Dad isn't paying attention to Dwight because *he is worried about Wally*. Lost sheep, time in the vineyard, buying more land, and reading the paper aren't the best reasons for Dad's distraction.

11. **2.** Wally had been drinking wine the night before and is suffering from *a hangover*. The other reasons given — sickness, chores, reading, and working — aren't appropriate answers, based on the passage.

12. **3.** Both Wally and the wine *need to breathe*. Wally says, "Wine's got to breathe, you know. And so do I, Dad."

13. **1.** Carter left his job because he was lured by the promise of *Arctic gold*. Leaving his snug clerkship may be partially correct, but it isn't the best answer. The passage doesn't mention "a woman," except his wife, who stays behind. "Half of his savings" and "the heart-strings of men" don't answer the question.

14. **3.** He wanted to escape his everyday *drudgery of life as a clerk*. "Bondage of commerce" refers to his dislike of his daily routine in the business world. His need for wealth (returns), romance, risk taking, and savings are different factors that don't apply to the question.

15. **2.** The text says that "Even its [the party's] goal . . . was the Klondike."

16. **4.** It was *ominous* because there was a foreboding of ill-fortune. Throughout the passage, words such as "unluckily," "ominously," and "evil star . . . in the ascendant" give the passage an ominous feeling. The route certainly was not blissful or hushed. Surprising doesn't make sense, and hardiest refers to a native of the region.

17. **1.** The fact that Jacques was *a native of the Northwest* made him important to the party. The fact that he was a renegade voyageur, born of a Chippewa woman in a deerskin lodge where he sucked tallow, isn't as relevant as his knowledge of the area is to his importance to the party.

18. **3.** Percy was seeking some *romance and adventure* in his otherwise mundane life. The fact that he was an ordinary man with a bank account, who spoke a good deal and was abnormally sentimental, aren't the best answers.

19. **2.** The author had *his salary raised to fifty dollars per month* and needed to protect his savings. The other choices — feeling rattled, working for Pinkerton's, being an irresponsible idiot, or feeling timid — are not his reasons for opening an account.

20. **3.** The author thinks he needs to see *the manager* to open an account. He feels that seeing a clerk or an accountant would be inappropriate. Pinkerton's man or the president are not options for opening an account.

21. **4.** The author describes the accountant as "a tall, cool devil." He does not describe the accountant as irresponsible, timid, sepulchral, or calm and grave.

22. **5.** According to the passage, the author is rattled by all of the first four choices — *going into the bank, clerks, wickets,* and *money.*

23. **1.** The manager takes the author to a private room and says, "We are safe from interruption here." They also wanted to be alone, but that isn't the best answer. The fact that the manager thought the author might be one of Pinkerton's men or have an awful secret are other reasons for taking him to a place without interruption.

24. **3.** The manager most likely thought the author was a detective because he had a mysterious *manner*, rather than the fact that he was rattled. The other choices do not refer to the author.

25. **1.** Mrs. Rachel Lynde lived in *a hollow along the main road* to Avonlea. The other choices — the woods, the Cuthbert place, the main road in Avonlea, and beside a pool and cascade are incorrect answers.

26. **3.** Because Mrs. Rachel spent most of her time staring out the kitchen window, she was *very observant* of the comings and goings in Avonlea. The other choices do not describe Mrs. Rachel.

27. **5.** Mrs. Rachel demonstrated her leadership in the community through all of the first four choices.

28. **2.** The passage describes Avonlea as occupying "a little triangular peninsula" in the Gulf of St. Lawrence. The other answers do not adequately describe Avonlea's location.

29. **1.** The best description given in the passage for Thomas Lynde is "a meek little man." He also may have been Rachel Lynde's husband according to Avonlea people, but this is not the author's description. A turnip picker is also not a best description. Neither was he an all-seeing eye or a storekeeper.

30. **4.** According to the passage, Mrs. Rachel's favourite place is *at the kitchen window* so she could observe the comings and goings in Avonlea. The other choices are incorrect.

31. **2.** The column specifically states that the centre *houses 85 social enterprises*. Choice (1) is totally wrong and can be instantly eliminated on first reading. The other answers have a ring of correctness because the column is about social enterprises, charities, LEF, and school leavers, but they have nothing to do with the centre and, thus, are wrong.

32. **3.** The column states that the Learnxs Foundation supports *innovative programs*. All the other answers except for Choice (1) are mentioned or implied in the column; however, they aren't correct answers to the question. You have to read carefully and double-check the facts. Just because something is mentioned or is familiar doesn't mean it's the right answer to the question.

33. **5.** The passage clearly spells out that Artsjunction's function is to *distribute discarded materials to visual art classes*. The other answers may be worthy of effort on behalf of some charity or agency, but they aren't the mandate of Artsjunction.

34. **2.** The column is very specific about the purpose of the Microtron bus. It provided services to employees and clients of small businesses in *word and numerical processing*. The other answers sound like they could be right, but, after rereading the column, you can see that they aren't.

 When you're trying to answer these questions under time constraints, try to remember exactly what the passage said. If you only think you remember, go back as quickly as you can and skim the piece looking for key words to focus on. In this case the key word is *Microtron*.

35. **4.** The passage very precisely spells out the mandate of the Training Renewal Foundation as being to *serve disadvantaged youth and displaced workers*. The other answers may be worthy activities for any charity, but they aren't stated as part of the mandate and, thus, are wrong as answers. Choice (3) is just wrong and is a play on another meaning of *serves*. You can immediately exclude this answer and have only four others to consider.

36. **3.** Employees should *wear appropriate clothing* to project a professional appearance and maintain safety standards. The other requirements — such as refraining from alcohol use, not associating with paraphernalia, being respectful, and using non-offensive language — don't relate to appearance.

37. **1.** Employees must *accept the authority of supervisors*, as is stated clearly in the passage.

38. **4.** Employees must conduct themselves professionally so that *the business grows and improves*.

39. **2.** To ensure safety and security, *employees shouldn't invite other people in*. The promotion of dignity, interaction, supervisors, and respect don't directly relate to bringing outsiders into the workplace.

40. **5.** Repeated instances of non-compliance *lead to dismissal*. The passage doesn't back up the other answers.

Chapter 22

Another Practice Test — Language Arts, Reading Test

- -

*T*he Language Arts, Reading Test consists of excerpts from fiction and non-fiction. Each excerpt is followed by multiple-choice questions about the reading material.

Read each excerpt first and then answer the questions following it. Refer back to the reading material as often as necessary in answering the questions.

Each excerpt is preceded by a purpose question. The purpose question gives a reason for reading the material. Use these purpose questions to help focus your reading. You are not required to answer these purpose questions. They are given only to help you concentrate on the ideas presented in the reading material.

You have 65 minutes to answer the 40 questions in this test. Work carefully, but do not spend too much time on any one question. Be sure you answer every question.

Answer Sheet for Language Arts, Reading Test

1 ① ② ③ ④ ⑤   21 ① ② ③ ④ ⑤

2 ① ② ③ ④ ⑤   22 ① ② ③ ④ ⑤

3 ① ② ③ ④ ⑤   23 ① ② ③ ④ ⑤

4 ① ② ③ ④ ⑤   24 ① ② ③ ④ ⑤

5 ① ② ③ ④ ⑤   25 ① ② ③ ④ ⑤

6 ① ② ③ ④ ⑤   26 ① ② ③ ④ ⑤

7 ① ② ③ ④ ⑤   27 ① ② ③ ④ ⑤

8 ① ② ③ ④ ⑤   28 ① ② ③ ④ ⑤

9 ① ② ③ ④ ⑤   29 ① ② ③ ④ ⑤

10 ① ② ③ ④ ⑤   30 ① ② ③ ④ ⑤

11 ① ② ③ ④ ⑤   31 ① ② ③ ④ ⑤

12 ① ② ③ ④ ⑤   32 ① ② ③ ④ ⑤

13 ① ② ③ ④ ⑤   33 ① ② ③ ④ ⑤

14 ① ② ③ ④ ⑤   34 ① ② ③ ④ ⑤

15 ① ② ③ ④ ⑤   35 ① ② ③ ④ ⑤

16 ① ② ③ ④ ⑤   36 ① ② ③ ④ ⑤

17 ① ② ③ ④ ⑤   37 ① ② ③ ④ ⑤

18 ① ② ③ ④ ⑤   38 ① ② ③ ④ ⑤

19 ① ② ③ ④ ⑤   39 ① ② ③ ④ ⑤

20 ① ② ③ ④ ⑤   40 ① ② ③ ④ ⑤

Language Arts, Reading Test

Do not mark in this test booklet. Record your answers on the separate answer sheet provided. Be sure that all requested information is properly recorded on the answer sheet.

To record your answers, fill in the numbered circle on the answer sheet that corresponds to the answer you select for each question in the test booklet.

EXAMPLE:

It was Susan's dream machine. The metallic blue paint gleamed, and the sporty wheels were highly polished. Under the hood, the engine was no less carefully cleaned. Inside, flashy lights illuminated the instruments on the dashboard, and the seats were covered by rich leather upholstery.

The subject ("it") of this excerpt is most likely

(1) an airplane

(2) a stereo system

(3) an automobile

(4) a boat

(On Answer Sheet)
① ② ● ④ ⑤

(5) a motorcycle

The correct answer is "an automobile"; therefore, answer space 3 would be marked on the answer sheet.

Do not rest the point of your pencil on the answer sheet while you are considering your answer. Make no stray or unnecessary marks. If you change an answer, erase your first mark completely. Mark only one answer space for each question; multiple answers will be scored as incorrect. Do not fold or crease your answer sheet. All test materials must be returned to the test administrator.

Note: Refer to Chapter 23 for the answers for this practice test.

DO NOT BEGIN TAKING THIS TEST UNTIL TOLD TO DO SO

Directions: Choose the <u>one best answer</u> to each question.

Questions 1 through 6 refer to the following poem by Sheila Sarah Franschman (2010).

WHAT IS SPECIAL ABOUT MUIR WOODS?

Line Under the worn wooden sign ushering one and all
To wander along the broad plank path
And feast your eyes on the majestic redwoods
Some on earth longer than 1,000 years
(05) Their outer layers bathed in shades of brown and black
Towering above but below the clouds
Gazing now at the branches entwined in lovers knots
Nature providing the streams meandering through
Feeding the nourishments required to sustain
(10) Through the times
Fog settles on the highest branches
Elevating trees into the heavens above
Small animals dart about the ground cover
And birds choose between plant and branch
(15) The four seasons offer different hues
While spring follows a babbling stream,
Ending in catch basins
And summer opens to sunlight exposing their vulnerability
And their strength
(20) Fall foliage turns to red and yellow,
With a hint of orange
While winter envelopes the landscape
Wearing a coat of white
Vulnerable now
(25) Waiting again for seasons to renew themselves
For people and animals
To wander again along the broad plank path.

1. What is the overall setting for the poem?

   (1) a backyard

   (2) a barn

   (3) a city street

   (4) a forest

   (5) a playground

2. Some redwood trees live as long as

   (1) 400 years

   (2) 1,000 years

   (3) 200 years

   (4) 1,500 years

   (5) 80 years

3. When the author writes, "The four seasons offer different hues," she means that

   (1) Different birds and animals populate the setting each season.

   (2) Leaves change colour every season.

   (3) Falling leaves make the streams change colour.

   (4) Fog filters the light differently during the winter.

   (5) The colours of the setting change with the seasons.

Go on to next page →

4. In which season does the author describe the setting as "vulnerable"?

    (1) spring

    (2) summer

    (3) fall

    (4) winter

    (5) not enough information given

5. When someone looks at a redwood tree, what colour(s) does that person see?

    (1) green and red

    (2) red

    (3) brown and black

    (4) red and yellow

    (5) orange

6. What provides the nourishment for the giant trees to grow?

    (1) nature

    (2) gardeners

    (3) park workers

    (4) animals

    (5) birds

Go on to next page

> *Questions 7 through 12 refer to the following excerpt from George Bernard Shaw's*
> Major Barbara *(1905).*

WHY IS UNDERSHAFT INTERESTED IN THE SALVATION ARMY?

Line **UNDERSHAFT:** One moment, Mr. Lomax. I am rather interested in the Salvation Army. Its motto might be my own: Blood and Fire.

LOMAX: *(shocked)* But not your sort of blood and fire, you know.

UNDERSHAFT: My sort of blood cleanses: my sort of fire purifies.

(05) **BARBARA:** So does ours. Come down tomorrow to my shelter — the West Ham Shelter — and see what we are doing. We're going to march to a great meeting in the Assembly at Mile End. Come and see the shelter and then march with us: It will do you a lot of good. Can you play anything?

UNDERSHAFT: In my youth I earned pennies, and even shillings occasionally, in the streets
(10) and in public house parlors by my natural talent for stepdancing. Later on, I became a member of the Undershaft Orchestra Society, and performed passably on the tenor trombone.

LOMAX: *(scandalized, putting down the concertina)* Oh I say!

BARBARA: Many a sinner has played himself into heaven on the trombone, thanks to the Army.

(15) **LOMAX:** *(to BARBARA, still rather shocked)* Yes; but what about the cannon business, don't you know? *(to UNDERSHAFT)* Getting into heaven is not exactly in your line, is it?

LADY BRITOMART: Charles!!!

LOMAX: Well; but it stands to reason, don't it? The cannon business may be necessary and all that; we can't get along without cannons; but it isn't right, you know. On the other hand,
(20) there may be a certain amount of tosh about the Salvation Army — I belong to the Established Church myself — but still you can't deny that it's religion; and you can't go against religion, can you? At least unless you're downright immoral, don't you know.

7. Why did Barbara invite Undershaft to the shelter?

   (1) to march in the band

   (2) to attend a great meeting

   (3) to earn pennies

   (4) to stepdance

   (5) to be with them in the Assembly

8. What does stepdancing for pennies tell you about Undershaft?

   (1) He has natural talent.

   (2) He frequented public houses.

   (3) He had an impoverished youth.

   (4) He performed passably.

   (5) He was a skilled musician.

Go on to next page ⟶

9. What can Undershaft contribute to the march?

    (1) stepdancing

    (2) pennies

    (3) shillings

    (4) trombone playing

    (5) natural talent

10. How would you describe Lomax's treatment of Undershaft?

    (1) friendly

    (2) bitter

    (3) encouraging

    (4) philosophical

    (5) critical

11. Why might Undershaft's motto be "Blood and Fire"?

    (1) He makes cannons.

    (2) He plays the trombone.

    (3) He is a sinner.

    (4) He doesn't belong to the Established Church.

    (5) He marches for the Salvation Army.

12. How do you know Barbara is committed to doing good?

    (1) She is in the Salvation Army.

    (2) She operates a shelter.

    (3) She joins in marches.

    (4) She plays the concertina.

    (5) She recruits others to join.

Go on to next page

> *Questions 13 through 18 refer to the following excerpt from* Klee Wyck *by Emily Carr (1941).*

WHERE WAS THE MISSION HOUSE?

The lady Missionaries expected me. They sent an enormous Irishman in a tiny canoe to meet the steamer. We got to the Ucluelet wharf soon after dawn. Everything was big and cold and strange to me, a fifteen-year-old school girl. I was the only soul on the wharf. The Irishman did not have any trouble deciding which was I.

It was low tide, so there was a long, sickening ladder with slimy rungs to climb down to get to the canoe. The man's big laugh and the tipsiness of the canoe were even more frightening than the ladder. The paddle in his great arms rushed the canoe through the waves.

We came to Toxis, which was the Indian name for the Mission House. It stood just above high tide water. The sea was in front of it and the forest behind.

The house was of wood, unpainted. There were no blinds or curtains. It looked, as we paddled up to it, as if it were stuffed with black. When the canoe stuck in the mud, the big Irishman picked me up in his arms and set me down on the doorstep.

The Missionaries were at the door. Smells of cooking fish jumped out past them. People lived on fish at Ucluelet.

Both the Missionaries were dignified, but the Greater Missionary had the most dignity. They had long noses straddled by spectacles, thin lips, mild eyes, and wore straight, dart dresses buttoned to the chin.

There was only two of everything in the kitchen, so I had to sit on a box, drink from a bowl, and eat my food out of a tin pie-dish.

After breakfast came a long prayer. Outside the kitchen window, just a few feet away at the edge of the forest, stood a grand balsam pine tree. It was very tall and straight.

13. What is the name of the author's final destination in the passage?

    (1) Ucluelet
    (2) Mission House
    (3) the school
    (4) the Greater Missionary
    (5) the wharf

14. Which phrase best describes Mission House?

    (1) unpainted wood
    (2) no blinds or curtains
    (3) stuffed with black
    (4) smells of cooking fish
    (5) all of the above

Go on to next page

15. How did the author reach Ucluelet?

    (1) by airplane

    (2) by canoe

    (3) by steamer

    (4) by ladder

    (5) by car

16. Which of the following choices best describes the author's journey to Mission House?

    (1) sickening

    (2) big and cold

    (3) tipsiness

    (4) frightening

    (5) delightful

17. What is the Indian name for Mission House?

    (1) Toxis

    (2) Ucluelet

    (3) Klee Wyck

    (4) Esquimalt

    (5) Nanaimo

18. Which word best describes the Missionaries?

    (1) powerful

    (2) dignified

    (3) hungry

    (4) prayerful

    (5) straight

Go on to next page

Questions 19 through 24 refer to the following excerpt from Flowers for the Living by Nellie L. McClung (1931).

WHO WILL LOOK AFTER THE PILGRIMS NOW?

The old doctor, on his way home from Iron Springs, suddenly remembered the Pilgrims. He must run in and check them over, now that he happened to be in their neighbourhood. There was sure to be something he could do for them, for the Pilgrim family lived in an atmosphere of sin, sickness, and death. For ten years now, ever since the Pilgrim family had come to the vicinity of Mandonville, Dr. Laidlaw had ministered to them. He had ushered seven tiny Pilgrims into the world, and carried all but one of these through many infantile diseases; he had poulticed and lanced and dressed various portions of their anatomy, and set wrists and legs without number, for they were a brittle lot and fell downstairs, out of hay-mows, and into wells, and were stepped on and run over with alarming frequency.

When Mrs. Laidlaw accepted an invitation for herself and the doctor she often made their acceptance conditional on the good health of the Pilgrims. Even at church it was not an unusual sight to see an usher tiptoe up the aisle, guided by the doctor's bald head, and the congregation were pretty sure it betokened an upheaval of some kind at the home of John Pilgrim, though most of the alarms now came at night since they got their telephone.

And in all these ten years Dr. Laidlaw had not received a cent for his services, the elder Pilgrim believing that a doctor's services were included in his title of citizenship.

When the doctor, driving his chestnut mare, was about a mile from the house, he overtook Johnny Pilgrim, the eldest son, returning from school. Johnny was a pallid lad of eleven, who had recently come through an attack of tonsillitis followed by mumps.

Johnny was glad of the ride, but was surprised to see his old friend, Dr. Laidlaw.

"I guess you wondered why we haven't been sendin' for you," he began at once, "We're takin' off Dr. Slandt now. He's the new doctor in town, you know."

Yes, Dr. Laidlaw knew.

"He's an awful smart doctor, and drives a car, and can get here so quick. He came out in half an hour when the cow stepped on Ma's foot! Dad said it would have took you two hours, and when we want a doctor we want him in a hurry."

Johnny was evidently quoting.

"And Pa said we had patronized you for ten years, and now it was only fair to give the new man a chance."

"Fair enough," the old doctor agreed, with his whimsical smile.

Go on to next page

19. Which phrase best describes the way the Pilgrim family lived?

    (1) seven tiny Pilgrims

    (2) infantile diseases

    (3) sin, sickness, and death

    (4) many accidents

    (5) an attack of tonsillitis

20. When would Mrs. Laidlaw agree to visit the Pilgrims?

    (1) if they were healthy

    (2) to tend to their needs

    (3) to collect their fees

    (4) to help out during upheaval of some kind

    (5) to treat the mumps

21. How does Dr. Laidlaw travel to serve his patients?

    (1) by horseback

    (2) by car

    (3) by boat

    (4) by buggy

    (5) by foot

22. Why does Mr. Pilgrim believe that he never has to pay Dr. Laidlaw for services?

    (1) He goes to church.

    (2) He has a new doctor.

    (3) He doesn't drive.

    (4) He is a citizen.

    (5) He is too busy.

23. Why are the Pilgrims "takin' off Dr. Slandt now"?

    (1) He provides faster service.

    (2) He is awful smart.

    (3) He is a new man.

    (4) He charges less.

    (5) He has moved away.

24. How do you think Dr. Laidlaw felt about losing the Pilgrims as patients to the new doctor?

    (1) disappointed

    (2) relieved

    (3) angry

    (4) ashamed

    (5) hopeful

Go on to next page

> *Questions 25 through 30 refer to the following excerpt from* The Adventures of Sajo and her Beaver People *by Grey Owl (1935).*

WHY IS LIFE SO DIFFICULT FOR THESE PEOPLE?

Everybody in these villages has work to do; even the young people must do their share. Nearly all this work has to do with travelling, as Indians are constantly on the move. Some seasons, the animals on which the Indians depend for a living disappear out of a district, and the people must follow them or find new hunting-grounds, so that whole villages have to be pulled down, and everything (except the log cabins, of course) must be loaded in canoes or on toboggans, according to the time of year, and moved for many miles. On these Winter trips little boys and girls take their turn at breaking trail on snow-shoes, feeling very proud as they lead the long procession of dog-teams and toboggans and people, for a mile or two at a time. In Summer they paddle all day in the canoes with the older people, and each has his or her small load to carry on the portages. They really enjoy their work, and they are just as serious and business-like about their tasks as are their parents.

Those of the Indian children who spend their summers near a fur-post or on a reservation, have an opportunity to go to school, and often make good scholars; some, indeed become lawyers, others doctors, writers, or artists, and are very successful. But those of them who live the year round in the wild country have an education of another kind. The forest is their school, and in it they study the lessons so necessary to their way of life. Geography, history, or arithmetic or English would be of no use to them; their studies are plant and tree life, the ways and habits of animals and how to track them; how to catch fish at all times of the year and, most important of all, how to make fire in any kind of weather, such as rain, wind, or snow. They learn the calls of all the birds and beasts, and can imitate some of them very well. They are trained to observe the movements of water in the rivers and lakes, so as to become skillful in the handling of canoes, and they learn the proper use of snowshoes, guns, and axes, and how to drive a dog-team besides such everyday tasks as sewing moccasins, tanning hides, and finding firewood in places where there looks to be none at all; and they must be able to cook. Such a thing as a compass is unknown to them, and they can travel anywhere they wish in the forest by means of the sun, stars, moon, shapes of trees, formation of the hills, movements of animals, and many other signs far too numerous to mention here. Their knowledge of woodcraft is so great that they become very self-reliant, and are able to make long trips alone and face without fear many dangers, as did the Indian boy and girl in this story.

The Indian life is so hard and toilsome that no one in these villages can be lazy very long without quickly running short of food, clothing, or shelter; and while the people will help one another and divide up whatever they may have, a lazy person is very much looked down on. Yet in spite of all this hard work, the younger people find much time to play their simple and very active games. Sometimes, after the day is done and darkness falls, they will sit out beneath the glittering northern stars, around the blazing camp-fires, and listen to darkness falls, they will sit out beneath the glittering northern stars, around the blazing camp-fires, and listen to the tales of their elders. Some of these tales are about hunting trips, or far-off tribes of Indians or about great men of long ago; others are about strange adventures in the forest. But the strangest tales of all, to them, are told by those of the grown-ups who have visited that wonderful country so far away to the south, where the white people come from; where are great sleighs on wheels that run with the speed of wind over an iron trail, by which they mean the railroad, and where smoke-canoes, as they call steamboats, go nearly as fast on the water; where there are no Indians and not many trees, only rows of tall stone houses between which people walk in crowds, rushing, hurrying along, seeming to go nowhere and come from nowhere. A country, they are told, where if you have no money you cannot sleep or eat. And they find this last to be the very strangest thing of all, because in the woods travellers are always welcome to rest and eat in the camps of white trappers or in an Indian village, free of any charge.

Go on to next page

25. How would you best describe the lifestyle of the Indians?

    (1) difficult

    (2) proud

    (3) nomadic

    (4) serious and businesslike

    (5) focused on hunting and fishing

26. How do the children contribute in the winter?

    (1) loading toboggans

    (2) paddling canoes

    (3) harnessing the dogs

    (4) catching fish

    (5) breaking the trail

27. What place acts as a school for the children of the wild country?

    (1) the forest

    (2) the fur-post

    (3) the reservation

    (4) the village

    (5) the city

28. What do the children use to find their way in the forest?

    (1) a map

    (2) a compass

    (3) a GPS system

    (4) the sun, stars, and moon

    (5) woodcraft

29. What happens to lazy people in the village?

    (1) They play active games.

    (2) They run short of food.

    (3) They seek rewards.

    (4) They listen to tales.

    (5) They steal from the others.

30. What are smoke-canoes?

    (1) sleighs on wheels

    (2) iron trails

    (3) steamboats

    (4) railroads

    (5) white trappers

Go on to next page

> Questions 31 through 35 refer to the following excerpt from Russell Hart's *Photography For Dummies, 2nd Edition* (Wiley).

WHAT'S THE SECRET TO LOADING BATTERIES?

Line   If you've ever had to figure out where to stick batteries in your child's latest electronic
acquisition, then loading batteries in your point-and-shoot shouldn't be a challenge. Turn
off your camera when you install them; the camera may go crazy opening and closing its
lens. (Some cameras turn themselves off after you install new batteries, so you have to turn
(05)   them back on to shoot.)

With big point-and-shoot models, you typically open a latched cover on the bottom to
install batteries. More compact models have a battery compartment under a door or flap
that is incorporated into the side or grip of the camera. You may have to pry open such
doors with a coin.

(10)   More annoying are covers on the bottom that you open by loosening a screw. (You need a
coin for this type, too.) And most annoying are battery covers that aren't hinged and come
off completely when you unscrew them. If you have one of these, don't change batteries
while standing over a sewer grate, in a field of tall grass, or on a pier.

Whether loading four AAs or a single lithium, make sure that the batteries are correctly ori-
(15)   ented as you insert them. You'll find a diagram and/or plus and minus markings, usually
within the compartment or on the inside of the door.

If your camera doesn't turn on and the batteries are correctly installed, the batteries may
have lost their punch from sitting on a shelf too long. Which is where the battery icon
comes in.

(20)   If your camera has an LCD panel, an icon tells you when battery power is low.

31. Where will you be installing the batteries?
    (1) an electronic acquisition
    (2) a children's toy
    (3) a big point-and-shoot
    (4) a camera
    (5) a flashlight

32. What is the easiest model in which to replace the batteries?
    (1) compact models
    (2) big point-and-shoots
    (3) screw bottoms
    (4) covers not hinged
    (5) covers that come off completely

Go on to next page ⟶

33. Why should locations such as sewer grates and tall grass be avoided when changing batteries?

    (1) Water can get in the camera.

    (2) Your lens may get dirty.

    (3) The glare would ruin the picture.

    (4) Your film would get exposed.

    (5) The battery cover may be lost.

34. How do you ensure that the batteries are correctly oriented?

    (1) Use four AAs.

    (2) Use a single lithium.

    (3) Empty the compartment.

    (4) Find a diagram.

    (5) Check the inside of the film box.

35. What tells you whether the batteries are low?

    (1) the LCD panel

    (2) the battery icon

    (3) the battery compartment

    (4) a single lithium battery

    (5) markings on the diagram

Go on to next page

> *Questions 36 through 40 refer to the following excerpt written by Sheila Sarah Franschman (2010).*

WHAT'S THE MOST COMFORTABLE WAY TO SEE THE SIGHTS?

Line   San Francisco is a walking town and I trudged up and down the hills until my legs were
ready for a vacation. I walked through Chinatown; explored Union Square; looked up at Coit
Tower; down at the Golden Gate from the bridge; meandered in Fisherman's Wharf, and, of
course, shopped Macy's and Barney's. While looking at a pair of comfortable shoes in a
(05)   store window, I noticed, tucked away among the souvenir shops, an innocuous store front
selling tours. What an original idea — seeing San Francisco seated instead of walking.

Wading through various brochures extolling the virtues of many destinations, I noticed a
folder about the coastline from San Francisco to Carmel, California. The pictures were strik-
ing, but tourism pictures always are. The words jumped off the paper and into my brain
(10)   with tired feet providing the cheerleading. I was going to sit comfortably on a padded seat
and let someone else provide the motive power.

The next day a small white tour bus picked me up from my hotel at 8:15 a.m., a little earlier
than I would have preferred, but the anticipation of seeing beautiful California while seated
got me going. The bus was comfortable and not very crowded, and I found a window seat
(15)   with its view of the world or at least Mason Street.

We drove, or more precisely, the driver drove and I relaxed. City streets soon became highways, interrupted only by the calm voice of the driver announcing points of interest. This
was living — seeing the sights, seated. I was becoming a convert to guided tours.

Travelling the spectacular windswept coastline of northern California I anticipated the high-
(20)   light of the trip, called the seventeen-mile drive. I watched as the suburbs of San Francisco
faded into the distance and each mile took us closer to our destination. I looked at the pictures in the brochure and wondered if the reality was as glorious as the photographs.

Travelling on Highway 92, the Pacific Ocean rolled into focus and I sat glued to my seat,
staring at the sandy beaches and the rolling white-capped waves, anticipating the seventeen
(25)   miles of glorious ocean front that lay ahead.

The driver explained that this was a century-old route that was originally used by tourists in
covered wagons. Now, it was a gated community with luxury hotels and golf courses, which
are still the main attraction after all these years, but I was not there to see people swinging
clubs. I was there to see the power of the waves and the stillness of the deserted beaches. I
(30)   could tolerate golfers, oblivious to anything except their game, playing on the world famous
Pebble Beach Golf Links as long as I could commune with my beloved ocean.

Soon enough I saw it. The ocean pounded the beach, lapping up sand only to spit it out
again in a swirl of water. I was one with the ocean, and the rhythm of the waves washed
away all present-day concerns. This is what I had come to California to experience.

(35)   There are about twenty stops along the route and I watched in wonderment as we slowed to
enjoy each one. Stopping first at Point Joe, I disembarked with camera in tow, awe-struck by
the power of the waves and the beauty of the scenery. From this vista point, the terrain is
studded by rocks jutting above the turbulent waters that stream around them. Standing
against the backdrop of sky meeting water, people recorded memories to take back home.

(40)   People dressed in early winter attire stepped gingerly down steep terrain weathered by the
elements to get a closer look at the magnificent beach spread before them. All of us on the
bus had entered the seventeen-mile drive experience.

Go on to next page

The next stop is Bird Rock, housing countless shorebirds and sea lions, perched upon huge rocks vying for space. Their amazing sounds filled the air and definitely topped the experi-
(45) ence of shopping.

As the bus passed countless coves and scenic views, we encounter pure white sand while curious people move in a dream sequence aimlessly wandering about. I had entered the reality of Pebble Beach, the sand danced in the waves resembling an unfinished canvas which engulfed me and swirled my imagination.

(50) At the next stop, the Lone Cypress stands majestically perched on the rocky cliff watching over the Pacific Ocean, a symbol and landmark inspiring amateur photographers trying to capture the grandeur on a silicon chip. This tree, growing from a rock, is used as a trade-mark for the resort and typifies the pioneer spirit that must have been part of each early Californian as they struggled with nature for their existence. Now, sitting on a comfortable
(55) bus, I experienced the beauty of the area surrounded by native pine and cypress trees, twisted by nature becoming a foil for the Lone Cypress. I admire the independence and strength of this tree and the early pioneers as I continue my journey.

The Ghost tree, a Monterey Cyprus, bleached white from ocean spray, stands as a monu-ment to nature's fury and beauty. Along the cliffs are other blanched Cyprus trees, standing
(60) like a phalanx of apparitions haunting me. I have seen the raw beauty of California.

Leaving the ever-changing view, our next stop is Carmel. I wander the streets haunted by the majesty I have experienced, and the small town streets and shops fade into vistas of ocean waves, drifting sand, birds, animals, and rocks. Carrying memories to treasure, I return to the reality of San Francisco.

36. What means of getting around San Francisco did the author use at first?
(1) public transit
(2) bus
(3) walking
(4) automobile
(5) limousine

37. What was the highlight of the author's trip?
(1) the Golden Gate Bridge
(2) Chinatown
(3) Carmel
(4) the seventeen-mile drive
(5) Union Square

38. In reality, the seventeen-mile drive is a
(1) gated community
(2) deserted highway
(3) golf course
(4) luxury hotel
(5) beach resort

39. What impressed the author at Point Joe?
(1) the power of the waves and the beauty of the scenery
(2) the rhythm of the waves
(3) the manicured lawns
(4) the sea lions
(5) the covered wagons

40. The Lone Cyprus has become famous because it is
(1) very old
(2) used as a trademark for the resort
(3) growing out of a rock
(4) much taller than the other trees
(5) very well kept

END OF TEST

Chapter 23

Answers and Explanations for the Language Arts, Reading Test

Answer Key

After taking the Language Arts, Reading Test in Chapter 22, use this section to check your answers.

1. **4**	15. **3**	29. **2**
2. **2**	16. **4**	30. **3**
3. **5**	17. **1**	31. **4**
4. **4**	18. **2**	32. **2**
5. **3**	19. **3**	33. **5**
6. **1**	20. **1**	34. **4**
7. **1**	21. **4**	35. **2**
8. **3**	22. **4**	36. **3**
9. **4**	23. **1**	37. **4**
10. **5**	24. **2**	38. **1**
11. **1**	25. **3**	39. **1**
12. **2**	26. **5**	40. **2**
13. **2**	27. **1**	
14. **5**	28. **4**	

Analysis of the Answers

If you aren't sure why an answer was incorrect, use this section to get quick explanations of the answers. If you correctly answered a question, you may still want to read the explanations to get a better understanding of the thought process that helped you choose the correct answer.

1. **4.** From the description in the first part of the poem (trees, stream, birds, small animals, and so on), you can tell that the setting is a forest. None of the other answers fits the setting described in the poem.

2. **2.** The poem states that the redwood trees can live longer than 1,000 years (line 4). The other answers are factually incorrect. This question is a good example of when skimming can help you find an answer quickly because it's asking for a factual and numeric answer.

3. **5.** The author describes in detail the changes in colour of the setting each season. The other answers may look right, but the poem gives no evidence to support them.

4. **4.** The author writes, "While winter envelopes the landscape / Wearing a coat of white / Vulnerable now." The other seasons aren't described in this manner, so you know winter is the answer. Choice (5) is incorrect as more than enough information is given to answer the question. If you read the question and then skim the poem, you stand a very good chance of efficiently getting the right answer.

5. **3.** The author describes the trees as "bathed in shades of brown and black." If you have some knowledge of redwood trees, you know that the wood is red — not the bark. The other colours may be mentioned in the poem, but they aren't referring to the redwood trees.

6. **1.** The author says that nature provides the needed nourishment and that the streams carry it to the trees. Although the other answers are feasible, they're incorrect based on the poem. You must answer the questions based on only the information given in the passage. Don't let any prior knowledge sway you from this task. The correct answer is always in the passage.

7. **1.** Barbara was recruiting players for her marching band and saw Undershaft as a candidate. The other answer choices (attending a meeting, earning pennies, stepdancing, and being in the Assembly) don't express her interest in Undershaft.

8. **3.** You know Undershaft had an impoverished youth because he had to stepdance for pennies to survive. During this time, poor children danced as entertainment for people who might throw them pennies. This way of living was a bit above begging in that the children provided some entertainment for the money donated.

9. **4.** Undershaft is a trombone player who could contribute his musical talents to the marching band. Stepdancing, pennies, or shillings aren't contributions to the band. Natural musical talent could be a correct answer, but because a more specific answer exists, you need to rule out this one.

10. **5.** Lomax criticizes Undershaft's work as a cannon manufacturer, implying that Undershaft won't get to heaven because of his work with cannons. Lomax may be bitter and he may be philosophical, but those words don't describe his treatment of Undershaft. "Friendly" and "encouraging" certainly don't describe Lomax's demeanour, either.

11. **1.** Undershaft's motto could be "Blood and Fire" because he manufactures cannons used to kill people in war. Playing the trombone, being a sinner, belonging to the Church, and marching aren't related to blood and fire.

12. **2.** Barbara doesn't just preach about good works; she operates a shelter to help poor people. This reason is stronger than the other choices given, such as being in the Salvation Army, joining in marches, playing the concertina, or recruiting others.

13. **2.** The name of the author's final destination is Mission House. Although she had to travel to the wharf at Ucluelet to get there, that was not her final destination. The Greater Missionary refers to a person, and the school is not mentioned in the passage.

14. **5.** The best answer is Choice (5), because all of Choices (1) to (4) describe Mission House in the passage.

15. **3.** According to the passage the author reached Ucluelet by steamer. She later transferred to a canoe to continue her journey. The passage does not say that the author travelled by airplane, ladder, or car.

16. **4.** The author describes her trip to Mission House by canoe as "frightening," because of the tipsiness of the canoe and the big man's laughter. "Sickening" refers to the ladder while "big and cold" describes the environment. The journey certainly was not delightful.

17. **1.** Toxis is the Indian name for Mission House. Ucluelet is where the steamer landed and *Klee Wyck* is the title of the book from which the passage was taken. The passage does not mention Esquimalt or Nanaimo.

18. **2.** According to the passage, the best word to describe the Missionaries is dignified. They may have also been prayerful as missionaries, but that is not stated, nor is powerful or hungry. The word straight refers to the dresses.

19. **3.** The passage describes the Pilgrim family as living in an atmosphere of "sin, sickness, and death." The other options are relevant, but not one of them provides the best overall description.

20. **1.** To avoid any chance of contagion, Mrs. Laidlaw would only agree to accompany the doctor when he visited the Pilgrims if they were healthy.

21. **4.** According to the passage, Dr. Laidlaw was "driving his chestnut mare," which would indicate that he travels by buggy.

22. **4.** Mr. Pilgrim never pays the doctor for his services because Mr. Pilgrim thinks that as a citizen he is entitled to free care. The other options are not relevant to the question.

23. **1.** The reason Johnny Pilgrim gives for using the town's new doctor is that he provides faster service. That Dr. Slandt is smart or a new man are not the strongest reasons given for the decision. That the new doctor costs less or that he moved away are not relevant answers.

24. **2.** Dr. Laidlaw must have felt relieved that he no longer had to treat the Pilgrims and that they had found another source of medical attention. The other choices — disappointed, angry, ashamed, or hopeful — do not make sense.

25. **3.** Because the Indians depend on the availability of animals and must follow them or find new hunting grounds, they lead a *nomadic* lifestyle, which means they are always travelling. The other answers — difficult, proud, serious and businesslike, and focused on hunting and fishing — are not the best choices.

26. **5.** During the winter, the children's job is to break the trail on snow-shoes for the dog teams and toboggans. In summer, they paddle canoes or carry small loads. Loading toboggans, harnessing dogs, or catching fish are skills they learn later.

27. **1.** For the children who remain in the wild country, the forest acts as their school and provides them with their education. The other options do not relate to these children.

28. **4.** The children use the sun, stars, and moon to find their way in the forest. They do not have a map or compass, nor would woodcraft assist them. The GPS has not been invented yet.

29. **2.** Lazy people in the village run short of food. While they might also play active games, seek rewards, listen to tales, or steal from the others, these answers do not best describe their situation.

30. **3.** Smoke-canoes would seem to be vehicles that travel on water and emit some kind of vapour; therefore, steamboats is the best answer. Sleighs on wheels, iron trails, railroads, and white trappers all refer to land and are not relevant to the question.

31. **4.** The batteries are installed in a camera. Other answer choices, such as electronics, a children's toy, or a flashlight, have no meaning in this excerpt. Point-and-shoot, while another term for a camera, isn't the best answer.

32. **2.** The easiest model in which to replace batteries is the point-and-shoot camera. The other answer choices — compact models, screw bottoms, and different types of covers — don't relate directly to the question.

33. **5.** Avoid all the locations mentioned if you drop the battery cover. Sewer grates and tall grass are places where the cover could easily be lost. The rest of the answer choices refer to issues other than battery covers or getting lost.

34. **4.** To ensure that the batteries are correctly oriented, you must find the diagram and use it. Other choices, such as using four AAs or a single lithium, emptying the compartment, or checking inside the film box, don't answer the question.

35. **2.** You must check the battery icon to see whether the batteries are low. According to the passage, the LCD panel, compartment, lithium battery, and diagram markings aren't correct answers.

36. **3.** At first, the author walks around San Francisco. The author uses the bus for a trip outside the city after walking around the city itself, and the passage doesn't mention public transit, automobiles, or limousines. You can pick this answer easily by reading the questions first and then skimming the passage.

37. **4.** The author states quite emphatically that the seventeen-mile drive was the highlight of the trip. The author saw all the other places, but none elicited the response of the seventeen-mile drive.

38. **1.** In the passage, the bus driver explains to the passengers that the seventeen-mile drive is really a gated community. It also contains a golf course and a luxury hotel, but it is a gated community itself. You have to read the questions and passage carefully to make sure of the answer. Skimming may have provided you with three possible answers (3, 4, and 5) and one unlikely but still possible answer (2). More careful reading provides only one correct answer (1).

39. **1.** The first answer is a direct quote from the passage, so you know right away that it's right. The other answers are possible but not specifically mentioned as impressing the author. Two of the answers (3 and 4) aren't located at Point Joe, one answer (5) is from another century, and the last answer (2) isn't specifically associated with Point Joe. When you find a direct quote that answers the question, choosing the right answer is easy to do.

40. **2.** The Lone Cyprus is used as a trademark for the resort and, for this reason, has become famous. The other answers may or may not be right, but they aren't specifically mentioned by the author. You can use only items that are specifically mentioned or directly implied as your answer. Other answers may be possible, but the answer you want is the one that's in the passage.

Part VI
Counting All the Possible Solutions: The Mathematics Test

The 5th Wave   By Rich Tennant

"I hear you think you got all the angles figured. Well, maybe you do and maybe you don't. Maybe the ratios of the lengths of corresponding sides of an equiangular right-angled triangle are equal, then again, maybe they're not — let's see your equations."

In this part . . .

This part includes ways to use the mathematics you've learned over the years to pass the Mathematics Test. Here you discover why this test has different answer forms and how to use them. To help you build confidence for this part of the GED, we show you that you really do know a lot about math — and that you may have been too frightened of the subject before to think about everything you know. We do our best to show you that math can be fun — or at least not horrible — and we offer you strategies that can help you do your best on this test.

Like the other test parts, this part includes two complete practice tests. Take the allotted time to answer these problems, and then be sure to check your answers to see if you were right. If, by chance, you don't answer a question or two (or more) correctly, use the explanations we provide here to help you understand how to work out the problems.

Before you start preparing for the Mathematics Test, remember this: You can conquer math — and this part will help you do just that.

Chapter 24

Safety in Numbers: The Mathematics Test, Parts I and II

Welcome to the dreaded Mathematics Test. Although you may have done everything to avoid math in high school, you can't escape this test if you want to pass the GED. Some test takers may have nightmares about this test, but don't worry! This chapter helps you prepare not for having nightmares but for taking the test successfully.

Most of the questions in the other GED tests are about reading comprehension: You're given a passage and are expected to understand it well enough to correctly answer the questions that follow. Although you can prepare for the other tests by doing a lot of reading and taking sample tests, you don't have to come in with a lot of knowledge or great skills in the test areas themselves.

The Mathematics Test, however, tests your understanding of mathematical concepts and your ability to apply them to real-world situations, which means you have to spend time solving as many problems as you can and improving your math skills as much as possible before you take this test. This chapter gives you some tips and tricks for studying for the GED Mathematics Test.

Looking at the Skills the Math Test Covers

Math isn't scary, and it has yet to appear as the villain in any major Hollywood horror films (at least that we know about). In fact, math can be fun when you put your mind to it. In any case, the Mathematics Test tests you on math, so you have to be ready. This is the one GED subject that requires a special way of thinking and understanding — improving your ability to think mathematically will make passing this test easier.

To do well on the Mathematics Test, you need to have a general understanding of numbers, their relationships to one another, measurements, geometry, data analysis and statistics, probability, patterns, functions, and algebra. (If you don't know what we mean by these terms, check out the next section "Understanding the Test Format.") In essence, to be successful on this test, you need to have the mathematical knowledge base that most high school graduates have, and you need to know how to use it to solve real-life problems. If, after reading this chapter, you're still worried about solving different math problems, go through a few high school math books at your local library or sign up for a math prep class or a math study group.

Understanding the Test Format

The Mathematics Test consists of two parts, each with 25 questions. You have 90 minutes to complete both parts. Part I allows you to use a calculator; Part II bans the calculator in favour of your brain. (You're given scratch paper to use for rough calculations.) You have to pass both parts to pass this test.

A formula sheet is provided for you to use during the test. Keep in mind that you may not need all the formulas provided, and you may not need a formula for every question. Part of the fun of math is knowing which formula to use for which problems and figuring out when you don't need one at all.

The Mathematics Test is different from all the other tests in the GED because you have different ways to answer the questions on this test. This test assesses the following four areas. Each of the four areas gets approximately equal billing on the test. You can expect to find between 5 and 7 questions (or 20 to 30 percent of the total number of questions) on each area.

- **Number operations and number sense:** Surprise, surprise — these problems deal with numbers. Here's a breakdown of the two topics in this category:

    - *Number operations* are the familiar actions you take in math problems and equations, such as addition, subtraction, multiplication, and division. You probably mastered these operations in grade school; now all you have to do is practise them.

    - *Number sense* is the ability to understand numbers. You're expected to be able to recognize numbers (not a difficult task), know their relative values (that 5 is larger than 3, for example), and know how to use them (which takes us back to number operations). In addition, number sense includes the ability to *estimate* (or approximate) the result of number operations — which is always a handy skill on a timed test.

- **Measurement and geometry:** Here, you get a chance to play with mathematical shapes and manipulate them in your head. You get to use the Pythagorean Relationship (or Theorem) to do all sorts of interesting calculations, and you get to use measurements to do things like finding the volume of ice cream in a cone or the amount of paint you need to cover a wall. If you relax, you can have fun with these questions and then maybe even use a lot of the knowledge in real life. This category breaks down into two topics:

    - *Measurement* involves area, volume, time, and the distance from here to there. Measurement of time is a good thing to know when taking any test because you want to make sure you run out of questions before you run out of time!

    - *Geometry* is the part of mathematics that deals with measurement. It also deals with relationships and properties of points, lines, angles, and planes. This branch of math requires you to draw and use diagrams.

- **Data analysis, statistics, and probability:** If you pay attention and practise the concepts in this category, you'll be able to think more clearly about the next political poll that shows how every representative of the sponsoring party is good and all others are evil. This category breaks down into the following types:

    - *Data analysis* allows you to analyze data. You probably already practise this skill without realizing it. When you read about stock performance (or lack of performance), calculate or read about baseball statistics, or figure out how many litres per kilometre you car uses, you're doing data analysis.

- Statistics and probability are part of data analysis. *Statistics* is the interpretation of collections of random numbers and can be used to prove one thing or another; *probability* tells you how often an event happens.

✔ **Algebra, functions, and patterns:** You most likely use these concepts in everyday life, although you may not know it. Here's a breakdown of the three types in this category:

- *Algebra* is a form of mathematics used to solve problems by using letters to represent unknown numbers, creating equations from the information given, and solving for the unknown number — thus, turning it into a known number. If you ever said something like, "How much more does the $10 scarf cost than the $7.50 one?" you were really solving this equation: $7.50 + x = 10.00$.

- *Functions* are part of mathematics. They involve the concept that one number can be determined by its relationship with another. A dozen always consists of 12 units, for example. If you were buying two dozen eggs, you'd be buying $12 \times 2 = 24$ eggs.

- *Patterns* are the predictable repeat of a situation. For example, if someone told you the first four numbers in a pattern were 1, 2, 3, and 4 and asked you what the next number was, you'd say "5" pretty fast. This simple pattern involves adding one to each number to get the next one. Most patterns get more complicated than this one, but, if you keep your wits about you, you can figure out how to solve them.

Make sure you understand how to solve problems involving these four math concepts. (The "Practising with Some Sample Problems" section later in this chapter gives you examples on how to do so.) If you already have a firm grasp on these topics, go ahead and take the practice tests in Chapters 25 and 27. However, if you need to review most of this material, read the following sections for more info, and take the mini-practice test in this chapter. You can check your answers and read the explanations when you're done. If you need to review certain concepts even more, do so. Then you can take the full practice tests.

Identifying the Types of Questions and Knowing How to Tackle Them

The Mathematics Test breaks down into four main types of questions. With a basic understanding of these question types, you can avoid any surprises when you take the test. The following sections explain the four types of questions you encounter and offer advice on how to prepare for them so you can solve them with ease on test day.

Multiple-choice questions

Most of the questions in the GED tests are *multiple choice*. In these questions, you're given five possible answers, and you have to choose the one best answer. Most of the multiple-choice questions on the Mathematics Test give you some information or show you figures and ask you to solve the problem based on that info or those figures. But you may also see the following special types of questions:

✔ **Set-up questions:** These questions don't expect you to calculate specific answers but ask you what steps you'd take to solve them. Before you declare this type of question to be your favourite, keep in mind that you still have to choose the correct way to solve the problem. You just get to skip the final step of calculating the answer.

✔ **Not-enough-information questions:** These questions don't give you enough information to calculate specific answers. The only right answer is "not enough information given." Only 4 percent of the questions on the test are of this type, so if you answer more than two questions this way, you may not be looking at the questions carefully enough.

Some of the questions on this test may have extra information — just ignore it. Of course, you have to make sure that the information you decide is extra really is extra. You don't want to disregard anything essential to solving the problem.

Because you're assessed no penalty for guessing, if you don't know the answer to a question, guess. Although you can't get a point for a blank answer, you can get a point for eliminating all but the most possible answer and marking it (if you're correct, of course).

Alternate-format questions

Alternate-format questions ask you to calculate the answers without choosing from five possible answers. For these questions, you write down real numbers or fill in actual graphs. Because the Mathematics Test is machine graded, you can't just write down numbers on paper. Instead, you use an alternate-format grid, which comes in one of two formats (see the two following sections).

The test has about ten questions that require you to record your answers on an alternate-format grid. Don't panic: Just concentrate on reading the instructions and calculating your answers.

Standard grid

Questions that require you to use a standard grid (see Figure 24-1) to record your answers are very similar to multiple-choice questions except that they don't give you five answers to choose from. When you come up with your answer on a standard-grid question, record it on the standard grid by writing the numbers in the open spaces and filling in the corresponding circles below the numbers. (If you don't fill in the circles, you can't get a point for your answer.)

Figure 24-1: A standard grid.

Keep these tips in mind as you work your way through the standard-grid questions:

- ✔ **No answer entered on a standard grid can be a mixed number.** If your answer is a *mixed number* (a whole number and a fraction), convert your answer to a decimal before entering it on the grid. You convert to a decimal by dividing the top number of the fraction by the bottom number and adding that decimal to the whole number; for example, 1¾ becomes 1.75. If, on the other hand, your answer is an *improper fraction* (one in which the top number is larger than the bottom number), you have the choice of entering the number this way on the grid or converting it to a decimal and entering that number.

- ✔ **No answer entered on a standard grid can be negative.** If you come up with an answer that's a negative number, check your calculations, because it's wrong.

Coordinate-plane grid

Questions that require you to use a coordinate-plane grid to record your answers are mostly geometry problems. The *coordinate-plane grid* is a two-dimensional graph with circles placed at regular points. You indicate your answer by filling in a circle to indicate a point on the graph (as with all other questions on this test, make sure you fill in the circles completely). Take a look at the coordinate-plane grid in Figure 24-2 for the point (3, 2).

Figure 24-2: A coordinate-plane grid.

The best way to prepare for questions with coordinate-plane grids is to practise geometry questions. Borrow a high school geometry textbook to get your fill of sample questions. Just be sure you understand the answers to those questions, too. If you need more geometry problems, check out *Math Word Problems For Dummies* by Mary Jane Sterling (Wiley). With all the problems in this book and that book, you should have all the practice you need.

If you spend all your time doing problems to be 100 percent sure that you know everything possible, you may never get the chance to take the tests to prove what you know. So just do the best you can in the time you have before you take the GED tests.

Questions with a calculator

Part I of the Mathematics Test lets you use a calculator — not just any calculator, however. On test day, you'll receive a special calculator — the Casio FX-260 solar calculator — to use on this part of the Mathematics Test. This calculator may seem like a real bonus, but you have to return it along with your test booklet. If you're calculator-phobic or worried about using a scientific calculator, try to practise with one before the test. You can check out an interesting video on how to use the calculator at www.acenet.edu/programs/gedts/media/calc.wmv.

You're probably familiar with calculators that add, subtract, multiply, and divide. The Casio FX-260, however, is a *scientific calculator*, which means it does all those operations and a whole lot more. The Casio FX-260 calculates fractions, percents, exponents, problems involving parentheses, and so on. Note that you won't necessarily use all the keys on the calculator to take the test.

Using a calculator for Part I of the Mathematics Test has a downside, too. Because you can use a calculator, the questions in this part tend to be a bit harder with more steps than in the non-calculator part. However, in general, if you know how to set up the problems, the calculator makes them easier for you to solve.

Questions without a calculator

Part II of the Mathematics Test doesn't let you use a calculator — unless you count the calculator you were born with (that's right, your brain). You're given scratch paper on the test, but the more questions you practise in your head, the easier the non-calculator test questions will be. Here are some easy ways to practise solving problems in your head:

- ✔ When you go shopping, add up the cost of the items as you put them in the cart.
- ✔ Calculate discounts when you shop.
- ✔ Be the first at your table in a restaurant to figure out the tip.

For multiple-choice questions, sometimes estimating the answer to a question is easier and faster. For example, 4.2×8.9 is almost 4×9, which equals 36. If you see only one answer that's close to 36, that answer is probably correct. If you see five answers that are close to 36, however, you need to spend time calculating the exact answer.

Examining Preparation Strategies That Work

To get ready for the Mathematics Test, you first have to relax and realize that math is your friend — perhaps not a lifetime friend, but a friend at least until you finish this test. You also need to consider that you've been using math all your life (and probably didn't even know it). When you tell a friend that you'll be over in 20 minutes, for example, you use math. When you see a sale sign in the store and mentally figure out whether or not you can afford the sale-priced item, you use math. When you complain about your car's high fuel usage (and can prove it), you use math. Lucky for you, we're here to help you get more familiar with math (and how to use it) so that you're ready for everything the Mathematics Test throws at you. The following are some strategies you can implement to help you get better results:

- ✔ **Read and make sure you understand what you read.** What all the GED tests have in common is that they all test, in one way or another, reading comprehension; if you can't read and understand the questions, you can't answer them. As we mention time and time again in this book, just reading isn't always enough — you have to stop and ask yourself questions about what you read. A good way to practise this skill is to find an old math textbook. Don't worry about the grade level or even the content. If it's full of problems to solve, it'll work. Read through each problem and ask yourself these questions: What does this problem want me to find? What is the answer in general terms?

If you need more practice reading and understanding math problems, go to the "Practising with Some Sample Problems" section later in this chapter or check out one of the following (all published by Wiley):

- *Basic Math and Pre-Algebra For Dummies* by Mark Zegarelli
- *Basic Math and Pre-Algebra Workbook For Dummies* by Mark Zegarelli
- *Math Word Problems For Dummies* by Mary Jane Sterling

✔ **Solve the problem with the information on the page — not with the information in your head.** Some questions may not give you enough information to solve the problem. For example, a question may ask for a conclusion that you can't make from the information given on the page. Even if you know some information that would help you solve the problem, don't use it. The people who write the test questions include and exclude information for a purpose — extra information can make guessing more difficult and separate the test takers who are paying attention from those who aren't, and, sometimes, extra information is put in to make the question a bit more realistic. They don't depend on you to add information.

You bring with you to the test your knowledge of what the basic operations are and how to use them. You aren't expected to know the dimensions of some fictional character's room or how well Alice does on her reading scores. You're expected to know how to solve problems and to leave the specifics of the problems to the tester.

✔ **Realize that not every question is solvable.** Some questions don't include enough information to solve the problem, or they ask a question that can't be answered with the information in the question. If you come across a question you can't answer, don't panic! Reread the question to make sure it can't be answered.

One clue that a question may not be able to be answered is an answer choice that says, "Not enough information given." Don't assume this clue means you don't have enough information, because some questions that can be solved include this answer choice to make you think. Use this clue only when you've already determined that the question can't be solved.

✔ **Take the practice tests in this book, and check your answers.** Turn to Chapters 25 and 27 to take full-length practice tests. Hold yourself to the test's time constraints, and make sure you answer all the questions. Then, check your answers and read through all the answer explanations in Chapters 26 and 28. Going through the answers shows you what areas of the test you need extra help on.

Try not to be intimidated by the word *math* or the subject as a whole. A math teacher once said that mathematicians are lazy people — they always use the easiest way to find the right answer. We don't want to insult or irritate any mathematicians by calling them lazy, but finding the easiest way to solve a problem is usually the right way. If your way is too long and complicated, it's probably not right.

Managing Your Time for the Math Test

The Mathematics Test allows you 90 minutes to complete 50 questions (you get 45 minutes to answer the first 25 questions, followed by a short break, and then you get another 45 minutes for the last 25 questions). For the mathematically inclined, that equals one minute and 48 seconds for each question. If you want some time to review your answers, you have less than one and a half minutes for each question. To help you manage your time for the Mathematics Test, check out the following suggestions (refer to Chapter 1 for some general time-management tips):

✔ **Experiment.** You need a second person to complete this exercise. After finding a friend to help you, close your eyes and try to estimate how long one and a half minutes are. Indicate the beginning and end of the time by tapping the table with your finger or a pencil, and have your friend measure and report on your accuracy. Repeat this exercise many times until you can estimate one and a half minutes repeatedly and accurately. Next, pick a question from the "Practising with Some Sample Problems" section later in this chapter, and try to do it in one and a half minutes. Being able to manage your time is the most important indicator of success on any test like the GED.

If you can keep to your schedule of less than one and a half minutes per question, you'll have enough time to go over your answers and make any changes after you finish solving all the questions.

With such a tight schedule for taking the Mathematics Test, you have no time to panic. Aside from the fact that panicking distracts you from your overall goal, it also takes time — which you have very little of. So relax and do your best.

✔ **Time yourself.** If you don't see what's being asked by a question within a few seconds, reread the question and try again. If it still isn't clear, go on to the next question. Spending all your time to solve one problem at the expense of the others isn't a good idea. Watch your watch. Put it on the table in front of you. If it doesn't have a second hand or a second indicator, consider borrowing one that does.

Practise timing yourself as you work your way through the practice tests in Chapters 25 and 27. Getting familiar with how to keep track of your time before you get to the real test can help you make sure you run out of questions before you run out of time.

✔ **Speed-read.** The key to developing your speed-reading skills is making sure you don't sacrifice your understanding of the material you're reading along the way. Follow these steps to improve your speed-reading skills:

1. Find any book with short paragraphs and calculate the number of words in two typical paragraphs. The easiest way to do so is to count the number of words in three consecutive lines and divide by three. (Isn't it interesting how math creeps into everything?) Write down the average number of words per line so you don't forget it, and multiply it by the number of lines in a paragraph to figure out the number of words in the paragraph.

2. Now recruit your friend for help again. At a signal from your friend, start to read the paragraph and signal when you're finished. You can then calculate how long it took you to read a word by dividing the time you spent reading by the number of words.

3. Read other paragraphs in the same way, but try to read them faster. You may try leading your eyes with your fingers by moving your finger across the line of text and slowly speeding up the rate you read. Check out *Speed Reading For Dummies* by Richard Sutz (Wiley) for more tips and practice ideas. If you think increasing your reading speed would increase your test scores or reduce your anxiety about finishing all the questions in time, this book can help.

Practising with Some Sample Problems

The best way to get ready for the Math Test is to practise solving problems. You encounter problems on this test that evaluate your skills in a wide variety of areas, so check out the sample problems in this section to help you prepare for all of them. We provide several examples for each skill on the test. At the end of this section, we give you another minitest to help you practise even more. You can then check out Chapters 25 and 27 for additional practice.

Number operations and number sense

To do well on the questions that address number operations and number sense, you need to be able to use numbers in equivalent forms, such as integers, fractions, decimals, percents, exponents, and scientific notation, and recognize equivalences ($\frac{3}{30}$ = $\frac{1}{10}$ = 0.1 = 10%). You need to know how to use whole numbers, decimals, fractions, percents, ratios, proportions, exponents, roots, and scientific notation when appropriate and how to decide which operation to use to solve problems. For these types of problems, you also want to be able to relate basic arithmetic operations to one another (for example, knowing that addition and subtraction are opposite operations: 5 + 2 = 7 and 7 − 2 = 5). Finally, you must know how to perform calculations with pencil and paper, with a calculator, and in your head, as well as how to estimate the solution to a problem to ensure that your answer is reasonable.

Try out the following example problems for practice with number operations and number sense:

1. Vlad is shopping for a new shirt because all the stores are having end-of-season sales. Sam's Special Shirts offers Vlad 20% off all his purchases, while Hardworking Harry's Haberdashery has a special sale offering five shirts for the price of four. Which is the better deal?

   (1) neither

   (2) Sam's Special Shirts

   (3) both are the same

   (4) Hardworking Harry's Haberdashery

   (5) not enough information given

   In this case, the correct answer is Choice (3) because five shirts for the price of four represents a 20% discount. Consider buying four shirts for $10 each and getting one more free. Then your five shirts would cost you $40 or an average price of $8 each, which is 20% off the regular price ($10). Often prices that are the same are stated in different ways.

2. Lillian is drawing a scale diagram of her apartment to take with her while shopping for rugs. If she has taken all the measurements in her apartment, what operation would she use to draw the scale drawing?

   (1) decimals

   (2) exponents

   (3) addition

   (4) scientific notation

   (5) ratios

   The correct answer is Choice (5). A scale drawing involves representing one dimension with a smaller one while keeping the shape of the room the same. Lillian may have decided to represent one metre in real life by one centimetre on her drawing (a ratio of 1 metre to 1 centimetre), resulting in a 12-metre wall being represented by a 12-centimetre line. You can exclude all the answers that aren't operations.

3. Sylvia couldn't fall asleep one night and got to wondering how much water her bedroom would hold if she filled it to the ceiling. She measured all the walls and knew all the measurements, including length, width, and height. What operation should she use to calculate how many cubic metres of water would fill the room?

   (1) addition

   (2) subtraction

   (3) multiplication

   (4) division

   (5) roots

   The correct answer is Choice (3) because the formula to calculate the volume of a room is to multiply the length by the width by the height.

4. Hassan has developed a new trick to play on his classmates. He asks them to write down their ages and multiply by 4, divide by 2, then subtract 6, and, finally, add 8. When they tell him the resulting number, Hassan can always tell them their age. If one of his friends tells Hassan the resultant number is 52, how old is he?

   (1) 33

   (2) 25

   (3) 52

   (4) 24

   (5) 26

   The correct answer is Choice (2). Hassan knows that multiplication and division are opposite operations, which means that multiplying by 4 and dividing by 2 produces a number twice the original. Addition and subtraction are opposites, too, so subtracting 6 and adding 8 results in a number 2 larger than the original. If the number Hassan's friend tells him is 52, Hassan simply has to subtract 2 from the resultant number (52) and divide by 2, giving him an answer of 25.

5. Susie is shopping for a few groceries. She buys a loaf of bread for $1.29 and a litre of milk for $1.47. She sees her favourite cheese on sale for $2.07. If she has five dollars in her purse, can she buy the cheese?

   (1) unsure

   (2) yes

   (3) not enough money

   (4) too much information

   (5) not enough information

   The correct answer is Choice (2). The simplest way to solve this problem is to add the cost of the bread and milk to get $2.76. The cheese is $2.07, which added to the $2.76 gives you a total of $4.83, which is less than $5.00. You can also estimate the result by adding $1.30 (approximation of $1.29) and $1.50 (approximation of $1.47) to get $2.80. If you then add $2.10 (approximation of $2.07) for the cheese, the result is $4.90, which is less than $5.00. Using approximations can help you answer some questions quickly and give you an idea of whether or not an answer you calculated using a calculator makes sense.

Mathematics vocabulary refresher

In case you forget what some important words in math mean, check out these definitions:

- **Congruence:** Two or more triangles are *congruent* when they can be superimposed on one another exactly (same length of corresponding sides, same corresponding angles).

- **Parallelism:** Two or more lines are *parallel* to one another if they never meet.

- **Perpendicularity:** Two lines are *perpendicular* when the angle between them is 90 degrees or a right angle.

- **Similarity:** Two or more triangles are *similar* when they have equal angles and the corresponding sides are proportional to each other.

Measurement and geometry

To do well on the questions that address measurements and geometry, you need to be able to solve problems involving geometric figures using the ideas of perpendicularity, parallelism, congruence, and similarity. You need to know how to "see" geometric figures and their translations and rotations, as well as how to understand and use the Pythagorean Relationship (or Theorem) to solve problems. You also must be able to calculate and use the *slope* of a line (which is rise over run), the *y-intercept* of a line (the point at which the line crosses the *y*-axis), and the *intersection* of two lines (where two lines meet). And you need to know how to use coordinates to describe and draw geometrical figures on a graph.

You must be able to identify, estimate, and convert units of metric and customary measurement and solve problems involving uniform rates (kilometres per hour, for example). You need to be able to read and interpret scales, meters, and gauges. In addition, you need to know how to solve questions involving length, perimeter, area, volume, angle measurements, capacity weight, and mass. Finally, you need to be able to predict how a change in length and width affects the perimeter, area, and volume of an object.

The metric system is based on multiples of ten. Each unit uses the same prefixes, which makes it easy to convert. Table 24-1 presents the most common prefixes and their relative values (the unit without any prefix has a relative value of one);

Table 24-1	Metric Prefixes and Their Values
Prefix	**Factor**
Tera	10^{12}
Giga	10^9
Mega	10^6
Kilo	10^3
Hecto	10^2
Deca	10
Deci	10^{-1}
Centi	10^{-2}
Milli	10^{-3}

The most common base units in the metric system are as follows:

✔ Length: Metre

✔ Mass: Gram

Try out the following example problems for practice with measurement and geometry:

1. Alvin is drawing a diagram of his room. He has drawn the line representing the floor and is ready to draw the line representing the wall. How would that line be related to the line representing the floor?

   (1) congruent

   (2) parallel

   (3) similar

   (4) perpendicular

   (5) equal

   The correct answer is Choice (4), because walls are perpendicular to floors (if they weren't, the room would probably collapse).

2. Olga designed a logo consisting of an equilateral triangle in a circle for a new company. She designed it with one vertex of the triangle pointing north-northeast. The client said she liked the design but preferred that the vertex of the triangle point due south. What rotation would Olga have to perform to satisfy her client?

   (1) 90 degrees to the right

   (2) 45 degrees to the left

   (3) 110 degrees to the right

   (4) 135 degrees to the left

   (5) 135 degrees to the right

   The correct answer is Choice (5). If you visualize or draw the equilateral triangle within the circle with one vertex pointing north-northeast, you can see that the vertex is 45 degrees above the horizontal, which is due east. To go from due east to due south requires a rotation of 90 degrees to the right. The entire rotation would consist of 45 degrees + 90 degrees = 135 degrees to the right. If reading about this problem is confusing, draw it. Diagrams often make problems easier to visualize.

3. Georgio wants to climb a ladder perched beside his house to check the condition of the eaves, which are 7 metres above the ground. For safety, the ladder should be placed 3 metres from the house. What is the minimum length of ladder he would need to reach the eaves, rounded to the nearest metre?

   (1) 7

   (2) 8

   (3) 10

   (4) 64

   (5) 7.6

   The correct answer is Choice (2). You represent a ladder perched against a house by a right-angled triangle with the vertical height of 7 metres and a base of 3 metres. The ladder represents the hypotenuse of the triangle. To calculate the length of the ladder, you have to use the Pythagorean Relationship. If you represent the length of the ladder as x,

$x = \sqrt{7^2 + 3^2} = \sqrt{49 + 9} = \sqrt{58} = 7.62$. Because you want the ladder to be long enough to reach the wall, it has to be 8 metres long. Although Choice (5) is right according to your calculator, the question asks you to round to the nearest metre.

Pythagoras, a Greek mathematician, proved that the square of the hypotenuse of a right-angled triangle is equal to the sum of the squares of the other two sides. The *hypotenuse* is the side opposite the right angle. You find the Pythagorean Relationship on the formula sheet you get with your test, so don't forget to check it out for important information you may need as you work through the test.

4. Calvin and Kelvin, carpenters extraordinaire, are building a staircase for their clients, the Coalmans. The stairway is to bridge a space 3 metres high, and the distance from the front of the bottom step to the back of the top step is 4.25 metres. What is the slope of the stairway to 2 decimal places?

    (1) 1.68

    (2) 1.4

    (3) 1.50

    (4) 0.71

    (5) 0.72

The correct answer is Choice (4). To calculate the slope, you have to divide the rise by the run. That is $\frac{3}{4.25}$ = 0.7058823, or 0.71 to 2 decimal places. The answer on your calculator or scrap paper would be 0.7058823, and because the next figure is 5, you would round the number up to 0.71.

The *slope* of a line is rise over run. Thus, the slope of a stairway is equal to the distances above the floor of the last step over the distance from the front of the first step to the back of the top step.

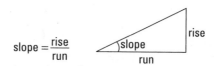

5. Describe where the point (–4, –4) would be on a graph by drawing it on the coordinate-plane grid.

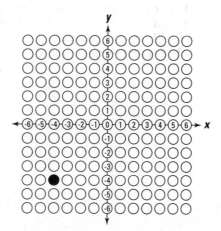

The point (–4, –4) would be 4 units to the left of the *y*-axis and 4 units below the *x*-axis.

6. Felix and Francis have just bought new cars. Felix, being American, has a car with a speedometer graduated in customary units. Francis, being Canadian, has a speedometer graduated in metric units. They know that 1 mile = 1.6 kilometres. When they're driving in Felix's car at a speed of 55 miles per hour, what would Francis's speedometer read in kilometres per hour rounded to the nearest kilometre?

   (1) 160

   (2) 88

   (3) 55

   (4) 77

   (5) 100

   The correct answer is Choice (2). Because one mile = 1.6 kilometres, 55 miles = 88 kilometres (55 × 1.6). The speeds are both in units per hour, so 55 mph = 88 kph.

7. Aaron wants to paint the floor of his apartment. His living room/dining room is 6 metres by 5 metres, his bedroom is 4 metres by 4 metres, and his hallway is 1.5 metres by 2.5 metres. Bowing to pressure from his friends, he has decided not to paint the floor of the kitchen or the bathroom. How many square metres of floor must he paint?

   (1) 94.75

   (2) 49.75

   (3) 47.95

   (4) 45.75

   (5) 57.50

   The correct answer is Choice (2). To find the area, you multiply the length by the width. The area of the living room/dining room is 6 × 5 = 30 square metres, the area of the bedroom is 4 × 4 = 16 square metres, and the area of the hallway is 2.5 × 1.5 = 3.75 square metres. The total area is the sum of the room areas or 30 + 16 + 3.75 = 49.75 square metres.

8. Read the following meter and enter the reading on the standard grid.

   The correct answer is 1,483. To show the answer of 1,483 on a standard grid, you simply darken the circles for the numbers 1, 4, 8, and 3, in that order.

	1	4	8	3
	⊘	⊘	⊘	
⊙	⊙	⊙	⊙	⊙
⓪	⓪	⓪	⓪	⓪
①	●	①	①	①
②	②	②	②	②
③	③	③	③	●
④	④	●	④	④
⑤	⑤	⑤	⑤	⑤
⑥	⑥	⑥	⑥	⑥
⑦	⑦	⑦	⑦	⑦
⑧	⑧	⑧	●	⑧
⑨	⑨	⑨	⑨	⑨

Questions 9 and 10 are based on the following information.

April is considering two apartments. They are of equal size except for the bedrooms. Bedroom A is 6 metres by 4.25 metres and bedroom B is 5.5 metres by 4.75 metres.

9. How many square metres larger is the larger bedroom?

    (1) 9.0

    (2) 25.5

    (3) 6.25

    (4) 0.625

    (5) 5.0

The correct answer is Choice (4). The area of bedroom A is $6 \times 4.25 = 25.5$ square metres. The area of bedroom B is $5.5 \times 4.75 = 26.125$ square metres. Bedroom B is larger by $26.125 - 25.5 = 0.625$ square metres.

10. April wants an area rug for the larger bedroom that would cover the floor leaving a space 30 centimetres from each wall. If the rug had a fringe all the way around it, how many metres of fringe would be needed?

    (1) 18.1

    (2) 0.6

    (3) 11.8

    (4) 1.8

    (5) 18.7

The correct answer is Choice (1). The measure of the fringe is the perimeter of the rug. Because the rug would cover the floor 30 centimetres in from each wall and 30 centimetres = 0.3 metres, the length of the rug would be $5.5 - 0.6 = 4.9$ metres, and the width would be $4.75 - 0.6 = 4.15$ metres. The reason you have to subtract 0.6 from each measurement is that the rug would be 0.3 metres from each wall, resulting in a rug that was 0.6 metres shorter than the room in each dimension. Perimeter = $2(l + w)$, where l is the length and w is the width, so the perimeter of the rug = $2(4.9 + 4.15) = 2(9.05) = 18.1$ metres.

Data analysis, statistics, and probabilities

To do well on the types of questions that address analyzing data, stats, and probabilities, you need to be able to construct, understand, and draw inferences from tables, charts, and graphs. You need to understand the difference between correlation and causation, and you need to be able to draw graphs based on the data presented and ensure that the graphs make sense. You also must know how to predict from data using an informal line of best fit.

For this portion of the GED, you must know how to calculate the mean, median, and mode of a group of data and evaluate what happens to these numbers when the data is changed. You also need to be able to recognize bias in statistical conclusions and make predictions from data produced by experiments or theoretical probabilities.

Try out the following example problems for practice with data analysis, stats, and probabilities:

Questions 1 and 2 refer to the following table.

Car Manufacturer	Sales — July 2009 (In Thousands)	Sales — July 2008 (In Thousands)	% Change
Commonwealth	90	105	−14
Frisky	175	147	+19
Goodenough	236	304	−22
Horsesgalore	99	64	+55
Silkyride	24	16	+50

1. From the table, which car manufacturer showed the greatest percentage increase in sales?

   (1) Commonwealth

   (2) Frisky

   (3) Goodenough

   (4) Horsesgalore

   (5) Silkyride

   The correct answer is Choice (4). The greatest percentage increase was Horsesgalore with a 55% increase in sales.

2. From the table, which of the following conclusions could be drawn from the data?

   (1) Car sales are increasing across the board.

   (2) Car sales are decreasing across the board.

   (3) Small manufacturers are selling more cars.

   (4) Large manufacturers are selling more cars.

   (5) No generalization is possible from this data.

   The correct answer is Choice (5). From the data given, no generalization is possible; some big manufacturers have rising sales, some have falling sales. This fact eliminates the first four statements.

Question 3 refers to the following table.

Week	Calories Consumed	Weight (Kilograms)	Height (Centimetres)
1	12,250	56.7	156.21
2	15,375	58.1	156.21
3	13,485	58.2	156.21
4	16,580	58.9	156.21
5	15,285	58.5	156.21

3. Alan kept track of his caloric intake, his weight, and his height for a period of 5 weeks. What conclusion can you draw from his observations?

    (1) Eating a lot makes you taller.

    (2) Some weeks Alan was hungrier than others.

    (3) Eating more calories will make you gain weight.

    (4) Eating more calories will make you taller.

    (5) There's no correlation between the data presented.

    The correct answer is Choice (3). The more Alan ate, the heavier he became (which represents a possible causal relationship). The table provides no basis for the other answers.

 If two values change in tune with each other, they have a *correlating* relationship. For example, a positive correlation exists between height and age during the teenage years. In other words, you get taller as you get older. If one event leads to another or causes another, the events form a *causal* relationship. For example, eating all the red jellybeans alters the percentage of orange jellybeans in a mixture of equal numbers of each colour, because eating a red jellybean removes it from the pool of jellybeans, which originally had the same number of each colour. As a result, the percentage of orange jellybeans increases.

4. Connect the following points to draw a geometric figure on the coordinate-plane grid: (3, 1), (–4, –3), (–5, 5).

    The correct answer should look like this:

TIP

Be prepared to draw graphs from data presented, but always remember that the only way to draw a graph for a question on this test is to use a coordinate-plane grid, which has size limitations. Always be sure that your graph makes sense. If the trend is declining, the graph should be headed downward toward the *x*-axis (horizontal axis). Negative values always appear on the left side of the *y*-axis (vertical axis) or below the *x*-axis.

Question 5 refers to the following table, which shows Sheila's marks in her final year of high school.

Subject	Grade (%)
Literature	94
Mathematics	88
Physical Education	86
Science	92
Spanish	90

5. On a standard grid, mark the mean grade that would result from a 6-point drop in Sheila's Spanish grade.

The mean mark with her grade in Spanish falling 6 points would be 94 + 88 + 86 + 92 + 84 ÷ 5 = 88.8. Here's what it would like on the standard grid:

Questions 6 and 7 refer to the following table, which shows the results Julio got from measuring and interviewing several of his classmates about their heights and birth months.

Month of Birth	Height (Centimetres)
March	162.6
June	167.6
March	155.0
January	172.7
August	165.1
January	162.6

6. What month would produce the shortest people according to this theory? Record the height in centimetres on the standard grid.

The grid should look like this:

1	5	5	.	0
	①	①	①	
⊙	⊙	⊙	●	⊙
⓪	⓪	⓪	⓪	●
●	①	①	①	①
②	②	②	②	②
③	③	③	③	③
④	④	④	④	④
⑤	●	●	⑤	⑤
⑥	⑥	⑥	⑥	⑥
⑦	⑦	⑦	⑦	⑦
⑧	⑧	⑧	⑧	⑧
⑨	⑨	⑨	⑨	⑨

7. From the table of Julio's results, what conclusion, if any, can be reached?

    (1) No conclusions can be reached.

    (2) People born in the darker months are taller.

    (3) People born in March are shorter.

    (4) People born in the warm months are similar in height.

    (5) Two of Julio's classmates were born in each of January and March.

The correct answer is Choice (5). The only conclusion that can be reached from such a small, biased sample is about the number of his classmates who were born in each month.

Question 8 refers to the following table.

Person Interviewed	Flavour Preference			
	Chocolate	Vanilla	Strawberry	Peanut
Donalda's mother	No	No	Yes	No
Donalda's father	No	No	Yes	No
Donalda's brother	No	No	No	Yes
Donalda's sister	No	No	Yes	No

8. Donalda collected the information in the table as part of her research on the most popular flavour of ice cream. After interviewing several subjects and entering her data into the table, she came up with the following results. Which is the most believable result?

    (1) Nobody likes chocolate ice cream.

    (2) Nobody likes vanilla ice cream.

    (3) Strawberry ice cream is the most popular flavour in the world.

    (4) No conclusion is possible from this data.

    (5) Peanut ice cream is the second most popular flavour in Canada.

The correct answer is Choice (4). The sample Donalda used is biased because the subjects are all related. A proper sample in an experiment is selected randomly. Because the data is from a biased sample, no conclusions can be drawn from the results.

Question 9 refers to the following table.

Age at Marriage for Those Who Divorce in Canada

Age	Women	Men
Under 20 years old	27.6%	11.7%
20 to 24 years old	36.6%	38.8%
25 to 29 years old	16.4%	22.3%
30 to 34 years old	8.5%	11.6%
35 to 39 years old	5.1%	6.5%

9. The information in this table indicates that to reduce the chance of divorce:

   (1) Younger women should marry older men.

   (2) Older men should marry younger women.

   (3) Nobody should get married.

   (4) Fewer men get divorced than women.

   (5) You can't draw conclusions from this table.

The correct answer is Choice (5). This table is a compilation of statistics and reflects the situation as of the date the statistics were gathered. You can't realistically draw conclusions from this type of data, except to state things such as, "5.1% of women who divorce got married between ages 35 and 39." Just because someone presents you with a table of data doesn't mean you can draw general conclusions from it.

Question 10 refers to the following table.

Make and Model	Price
Hopper Model A1	$249.99
Vacuous Vacuum Company Model ZZ3	$679.99
Clean-R-Up Special Series	$179.00
Electrified Home Upright	$749.99
Super Suction 101	$568.99

10. Pierre is looking for a vacuum cleaner for his apartment. He is on a limited budget and wants to spend the least he can for his purchase. Pierre's best friend told him that spending around the mean amount for a vacuum cleaner will get him an average unit. Pierre's father claims that spending about the median amount is the smartest way to get a good deal. Which vacuum cleaner comes the closest to satisfying both criteria?

    (1) Hopper Model A1

    (2) Vacuous Vacuum Company Model ZZ3

    (3) Clean-R-Up Special Series

    (4) Electrified Home Upright

    (5) Super Suction 101

The correct answer is Choice (5). You can calculate the mean price by adding all the prices and dividing the sum by the number of prices: (249.99 + 679.99 + 179.00 + 749.99 + 568.99) ÷ 5 = $485.39. To determine the median price, you put all the prices in order; the middle one is the median. In this case the median is $568.99, because it's in the middle of the prices: 749.99, 679.99, 568.99, 249.99, and 179.99. The machine that comes closest to satisfying both criteria is the Super Suction 101 because its price is the same as the median. The difference between the price of the Super Suction 101 and the mean price is $83.60. The difference between the price of the Hopper Model A1 and the mean price is $111.00, leaving the Super Suction 101 the clear mathematical winner.

One thing to keep in mind is that the mathematical problems on this test aren't always reflections of reality. The technique used for buying vacuum cleaners in question 10 isn't a reasonable way of buying anything, but it's a good test of your knowledge of the mean, median, and subtraction.

Algebra, functions, and patterns

To do well in the types of questions that address algebra, functions, and patterns, you need to be able to draw graphs or tables, create verbal descriptions and equations to represent presented data, and use the same data with different forms of representation. You need to understand that the same function may be used in different problems. You have to know how to solve problems using algebraic expressions and equations and how to evaluate formulas. You need to understand direct and indirect variation, use them to solve problems, and see patterns in tables and graphs. You also need to be able to explain how a change in one quantity in an equation results in changes in the other quantities in the equation. Finally, you must be able to understand, use, and solve problems involving linear, quadratic, and exponential functions.

Try out the following example problems for practice with algebra, functions, and patterns:

Question 1 refers to the following table.

Annual Production of the Wonderful World of Widgets	
Year	*Annual Production (In Million Units)*
2009	43
2008	29
2007	72
2006	70
2005	71

1. The general manager of the Wonderful World of Widgets wants to present these figures in a visual, easily understood way to the board of directors to help them understand the effect that the economic downturn is having on the production of widgets. What would be the best way to present the figures?

   (1) a graph

   (2) a series of tables

   (3) verbal descriptions

   (4) pictures of the plant exterior

   (5) a movie of how widgets are used in Canada

The best answer is Choice (1). A graph is a visual representation of data; it's easily understood and can be used to compare data visually. You could use some of the other choices to represent the data, but they would all be more complex than a graph.

2. Rachel and Ronda were planning for their first apartment, and they decided to split the required shopping tasks. Rachel was responsible for finding out how much it would cost to carpet their living room, and Ronda was responsible for finding out how much it would cost to paint the walls in the bedroom. What formula would they need to use to get an answer that would let them figure out the price for each job?

(1) $P = 2(l + w)$

(2) $A = l \times w$

(3) $V = l \times w \times d$

(4) $A = \pi r^2$

(5) $C = \pi d$

The correct answer is Choice (2). In each case, Rachel and Ronda have to calculate the area of the space they're dealing with to get a price for the carpet and the paint. The formula for area is $A = l \times w$.

3. Roger and Ekua went shopping together. Ekua spent twice as much for clothing as Roger did. If their total expenditure for clothing was $90.00, how much did Roger spend for clothing?

(1) $60.00

(2) $90.00

(3) $40.00

(4) $30.00

(5) $20.00

The correct answer is Choice (4). If you represent the amount of money Roger spent by x, the amount of money that Ekua spent is $2x$. You can represent their spending by the equation $90 = x + 2x$ or $3x = 90$, in which case $x = 30$. So Roger spent $30.00 for clothing.

4. Evaluate the following formula to 2 decimal places:

$N = \sqrt{a + c - 2ac}$, if $a = 25$ and $c = 9$

(1) 34.67

(2) 20.40

(3) 22.47

(4) no answer

(5) 27.99

The correct answer is Choice (4). You can't find the square root of a negative number, and $2ac$ will always be larger than $a + c$, which makes the difference of the two negative.

5. Solve the following equation for x:

$x = 2y + 6z - y^2$, if $y = 6$ and $z = 2$

(1) 12

(2) 11

(3) –12

(4) –11

(5) none of the above

The correct answer is Choice (3). You can solve this equation by substituting 6 for y and 2 for z, which produces this equation: $2(6) + 6(2) - 6^2 = -12$.

Question 6 refers to the following table.

Subject	Height (Metres)	Shoe Size (European)
1	1.6	37
2	1.75	41
3	1.68	37
4	1.85	43
5	1.7	38

6. Althea has a theory about the men in her class. She has decided that the taller men have larger shoe sizes than the shorter men. To prove her theory, she asked several of the men to measure their height in metres and tell her their shoe sizes. From her observations, she created this table.

   Using her observations, Althea decided to graph the results to see if her theory has any credibility. If she drew a graph to represent her findings with height as the x-axis and shoe size as the y-axis, the line would:

   (1) be level horizontally

   (2) be level vertically

   (3) slope upward to the right

   (4) slope downward to the right

   (5) not have a constant slope

   The correct answer is Choice (5). If you were to sketch the graph on your scrap paper, you would not have a straight line but could join the points with a line from point to point. This line would not have a constant slope.

7. The students in a math class are looking at the equation $A = l \times w$. The teacher asks what result doubling the length (l) would have on the area (A). What answer is correct?

   (1) none

   (2) makes it two times larger

   (3) makes it four times larger

   (4) makes it three times larger

   (5) can't determine the result without the value of w

   The correct answer is Choice (2). In this linear equation, any multiple of one term results in the same multiple of the answer. Multiplying l by 2 results in multiplying A by two.

As you prepare for the Mathematics Test, you definitely want to remember this rule about equations: Whatever you do to one side, you must do to the other.

Question 8 refers to the following table.

a	b	f
1	2	−16
2	1	−3
3	2	−18
2	3	−35
3	4	x

8. Herman developed the following function to amuse himself: $F = 2a + 3b^2 - 2ab$. He kept track of his results in this table.

Using Herman's function, what is the value of x?

(1) 53

(2) 82

(3) 88

(4) 66

(5) 42

The correct answer is Choice (4). Using Herman's function, $x = 2(3) - 3(4)(4) - 2(3)(4) = 6 - 48 - 24 = 66$.

A little pre-test to help you prepare for the Mathematics Test

For some extra practice for the Mathematics Test, take this short pre-test. After you finish each question in this pre-test, check your answer and read the explanation provided. The more you know and the more you practise, the better you'll do on test day.

1. A wall is 6 metres long and 2.5 metres high. If all of it is to be painted with two coats of blue paint, how many square metres of wall have to be covered?

(1) 17

(2) 15

(3) 23

(4) 30

(5) 40

The correct answer is Choice (4). The area of the wall is $6 \times 2.5 = 15$ square metres. Each coat requires that you paint 15 square metres, but because you have to paint two coats, the answer is $2 \times 15 = 30$. If your first choice for the answer was Choice (2), you forgot about the second coat of paint. If you picked Choice (1), you confused perimeter with area. Remember that *perimeter* is the distance all the way around an object — in this case $2(6 + 2.5) = 17$. Choices (5) and (3) are just plain wrong; you can eliminate these answers immediately.

2. Barry earns $1,730 per month after taxes. Each month, he spends $900 for rent and $600 for living expenses like food and utilities. How much does he have left over to buy luxuries and spend on entertainment?

   (1) $170

   (2) $230

   (3) $390

   (4) $320

   (5) $180

   The correct answer is Choice (2). Barry spends $900 + $600 = $1500 for rent and living expenses. He has $1730 – $1500 = $230 left over. The other answer choices are simply wrong. Some of them may look correct if you don't know how to do the question.

3. On Monday, Mary walked 12 blocks. On Tuesday, she walked 10 blocks, and, on Wednesday, she walked 14 blocks. If she wants to beat her average trip for those three days on Thursday, at least how many blocks must she walk?

   (1) 10

   (2) 11

   (3) 9

   (4) 13

   (5) 12

   The correct answer is Choice (4). Her average trip for those three days was (12 + 10 + 14) ÷ 3 = 36 ÷ 3 = 12 blocks. To beat her average, she has to walk 13 blocks on Thursday. If she walks 12 blocks, she will equal (not beat) her average trip. All the other answers are less than her average.

4. Solve the following equation for x: $3x + 12 = 24$

   (1) 12

   (2) 24

   (3) 3

   (4) 4

   (5) 36

   The correct answer is Choice (4). If $3x + 12 = 24$, you can subtract 12 from both sides so that $3x = 24 - 12$, or $3x = 12$, or $x = 4$. Again, remember the cardinal rule of equations: Whatever you do to one side; you must do to the other.

5. Where are all the points with an x-coordinate of –4 located on a graph?

   (1) 4 units above the x-axis

   (2) 4 units to the left of the x-axis

   (3) 4 units from the y-axis

   (4) 4 units above the y-axis

   (5) 4 units to the left of the y-axis

   The correct answer is Choice (5). All points with x-coordinates that are negative are located to the left of the y-axis (the vertical axis). Therefore, if a point has an x-coordinate of –4, it's located on a line 4 units to the left of the y-axis.

Revealing Some Helpful Pointers

As you prepare for the Mathematics Test, do the following:

- **Master arithmetic fundamentals.** About half the test depends on basic arithmetic (addition, subtraction, multiplication, division, decimals, and fractions). The better you know the fundamentals, the better you can do on this test.

- **Understand how to solve problems.** To get a handle on how to solve basic mathematical problems, do a lot of practice problems before the test. The more problems you solve, the more natural solving problems will become. Borrow or buy as many math books as you can, and use the sample questions in them to develop your problem-solving skills. (Be sure to get books that have answers in the back so you can check your work.) Check every answer immediately after you work the question. If you answered it wrong, figure out why. If you can't answer it, ask someone to explain the solution to you.

- **Understand the rules of math.** Textbooks are full of rules, theorems, hypotheses, and so on. Read over as many of these rules as you can, and try to explain the main ones to a friend. If you can explain a particular rule (the Pythagorean Theorem, for example) to a friend and he or she understands it, you've mastered the relationship. If you can't explain it, ask someone to help you better understand the rule.

- **Take practice tests.** See Chapters 25 and 27 for two full-length practice tests. If two aren't enough, buy or borrow additional test-prep books that include sample Mathematics Tests. Be strict about time constraints. After checking your answers, figure out the correct answers for any mistakes you made.

The only part of the test you can't duplicate is the feeling of sitting in the examination room just before you start the test. But the more practice tests you take, the more comfortable you'll be when test day finally arrives.

Chapter 25

Practice Test — Mathematics Test: Parts I and II

· ·

*T*he Mathematics Test consists of multiple-choice questions intended to measure general mathematics skills or problem-solving ability. The questions are based on short readings that often include a graph, chart, or figure.

The Mathematics Test is made up of two parts. Part I allows you to use a calculator to help you answer the questions; Part II doesn't. Each part consists of 25 questions.

You will have 45 minutes to complete each part. Work carefully, but do not spend too much time on any one question. Be sure to answer every question.

Formulas you may need are given on the page before the first test question in each part. Only some of the questions will require you to use a formula. You will not need all the formulas given.

Some questions contain more information than you will need to solve the problem; other questions do not give enough information. If the question does not give enough information to solve the problem, the correct answer choice is "not enough information given."

Answer Sheet for Mathematics Test: Part 1

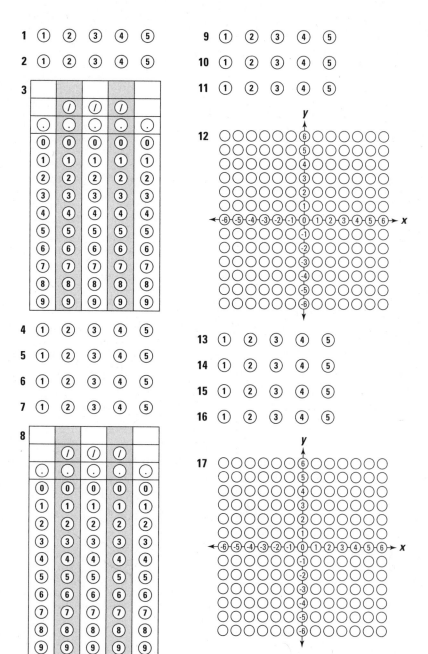

Answer Sheet for Mathematics Test: Part II

Mathematics Test: Part 1

The use of calculators is allowed in Part I only.

Do not write in this test booklet. The test administrator will give you a blank paper for your calculations. Record your answers on the separate answer sheet provided. Be sure all information is properly recorded on the answer sheet.

To record your answers, fill in the numbered circle on the answer sheet that corresponds to the answer you select for each question in the test booklet.

EXAMPLE:

If a grocery bill totaling $15.75 is paid with a $20.00 bill, how much change should be returned?

(1) $5.25

(2) $4.75

(3) $4.25

(4) $3.75

(5) $3.25

(On Answer Sheet)

① ② ● ④ ⑤

The correct answer is "$4.25"; therefore, answer space 3 would be marked on the answer sheet.

Do not rest the point of your pencil on the answer sheet while you are considering your answer. Make no stray or unnecessary marks. If you change an answer, erase your first mark completely. Mark only one answer space for each question; multiple answers will be scored as incorrect. Do not fold or crease your answer sheet. All test materials must be returned to the test administrator.

Note: Refer to Chapter 26 for the answers for Parts I and II of this practice test.

Calculator Directions

To prepare the calculator for use the ***first*** time, press the [ON] (upper-rightmost) key. "DEG" will appear at the top-centre of the screen and "0" at the right. This indicates the calculator is in the proper format for all your calculations.

To prepare the calculator for ***another*** question, press the [ON] or the red [AC] key. This clears any entries made previously.

To do any arithmetic, enter the expression as it is written. Press [=] (equals sign) when finished.

EXAMPLE A: 8 – 3 + 9

First press [ON] or [AC]

Enter the following: [8] , [–] , [3] , [+] , [9] , [=]

The correct answer is 14.

If the expression in parentheses is to be multiplied by a number, press [×] (multiplication sign) between the number and the parenthesis sign.

EXAMPLE B: 6(8 + 5)

First press [ON] or [AC]

Enter the following: [6] , [×] , [( ] , [8] , [+] , [5] , [ )] , [=]

The correct answer is 78.

To find the square root of a number

- ✔ Enter the number.
- ✔ Press the [SHIFT] (upper-leftmost) key ("SHIFT" appears at the top-left of the screen).
- ✔ Press [x^2] (third from the left on top row) to access its second function: square root.

DO NOT press [SHIFT] and [x^2] at the same time.

EXAMPLE C: $\sqrt{64}$

First press [ON] or [AC]

Enter the following: [6] [4] , [SHIFT] , [x^2] , [=]

The correct answer is 8.

To enter a negative number, such as –8:

- ✔ Enter the number without the negative sign (enter 8).
- ✔ Press the "change sign" ([+/–]) key, which is directly above the [7] key.

All arithmetic can be done with positive and/or negative numbers.

EXAMPLE D: –8 – (–5)

First press [ON] or [AC]

Enter the following: [8] , [+/–] , [–] , [5] , [+/–] , [=]

The correct answer is –3.

The Standard Grid

Mixed numbers, such as 3½, cannot be entered in the standard grid. Instead, represent them as decimal numbers (in this case, 3.5) or fractions (in this case, ⁷⁄₂). In addition, no answer on a standard grid can be a negative number, such as –8.

To record your answer for a standard-grid question:

> ✔ Begin in any column that will allow your answer to be entered.

> ✔ Write your answer in the boxes on the top row.

> ✔ In the column beneath a fraction bar or decimal point (if any) and each number in your answer, fill in the circle representing that character.

> ✔ Leave blank any unused column.

Points to remember:

> ✔ The answer sheet will be machine scored. **The circles must be filled in correctly.**

> ✔ Mark no more than one circle in any column.

> ✔ Grid only one answer even if more than one answer is correct.

> ✔ Mixed numbers, such as 3½, must be gridded as 3.5 or ½.

> ✔ No answer on a standard grid can be a negative number.

The Coordinate-Plane Grid

To record an answer on the coordinate-plane grid, you must have an *x*-value and a *y*-value. No answer for a coordinate-plane question will have a value that is a fraction or decimal.

Mark only the <u>one</u> circle that represents your answer.

EXAMPLE:

The coordinates of point A, shown on the graph below, are (2,–4).

The coordinates of point B, not shown on the graph, are (–3,1). What is the location of point B?

DO NOT MARK YOUR ANSWER ON THE GRAPH ABOVE.

Mark your answer on the coordinate-plane grid on the answer sheet (at right).

CORRECT RESPONSE:

Formulas

AREA of a:

square	Area = side^2
rectangle	Area = length × width
parallelogram	Area = base × height
triangle	Area = ½ × base × height
trapezoid	Area = ½ × (base$_1$ + base$_2$) × height
circle	Area = π × radius^2; π is approximately equal to 3.14

PERIMETER of a:

square	Perimeter = 4 × side
rectangle	Perimeter = (2 × length) + (2 × width)
triangle	Perimeter = side$_1$ + side$_2$ + side$_3$

CIRCUMFERENCE of a circle   Circumference = π × diameter; π is approximately equal to 3.14

VOLUME of a:

cube	Volume = side^3
rectangular solid	Volume = length × width × height
square pyramid	Volume = ⅓ × (base edge)^2 × height
cylinder	Volume = π × radius^2 × height; π is approximately equal to 3.14
cone	Volume = ⅓ × π × radius^2 × height; π is approximately equal to 3.14

COORDINATE GEOMETRY

distance between points = $\sqrt{(x_2 - x_1)^2 + (y_2 - y_1)^2}$; (x_1, y_1) and (x_2, y_2) are two points in a plane

slope of a line = $\dfrac{y_2 - y_1}{x_2 - x_1}$; (x_1, y_1) and (x_2, y_2) are two points on the line

PYTHAGOREAN RELATIONSHIP

$a^2 + b^2 = c^2$; a and b are sides, and c is the hypotenuse of a right triangle

MEASURES OF CENTRAL TENDENCY

mean = $\dfrac{x_1 + x_2 + ... + x_n}{n}$; where the x's are the values for which a mean is desired and n is the total number of values for x

median = the middle value of an odd number of *ordered* scores, and halfway between the two middle values of an even number of *ordered* scores

SIMPLE INTEREST   interest = principal × rate × time

DISTANCE   distance = rate × time

TOTAL COST   total cost = (number of units) × (price per unit)

DO NOT BEGIN TAKING THIS TEST UNTIL TOLD TO DO SO

Directions: Choose the <u>one best answer</u> to each question.

1. Dharma is making sale signs for the Super Summer Sale at the Super Saver Swim Shop. Sales tax in Dharma's province is 5%. She makes a series of signs:

   Sign A: ½ off all merchandise

   Sign B: Buy one item, get the second item of equal value free

   Sign C: 50% off all merchandise

   Sign D: Nine times your sales tax back

   What would a shrewd consumer notice about the signs?

   (1) Sign A offers a better buy.

   (2) Sign C offers the worst deal.

   (3) Sign D offers the worst deal.

   (4) Sign B offers a better deal.

   (5) All signs offer the same deal.

2. Daryl is framing a picture. He draws the following diagram to help him make it:

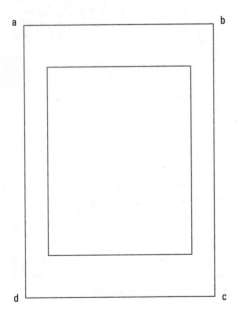

   Which of the following is true about the above diagram?

   (1) *ab* must be perpendicular to *ad*

   (2) *ab* must be parallel to *bc*

   (3) *ad* must be parallel to *ab*

   (4) *ab* and *dc* must be perpendicular

   (5) *ab* and *ad* must be parallel

3. The Hammerhill family is building a deck behind their house. The deck is to be 4.88 metres long and 6.40 metres wide, and the decking material was priced at $45.00 a square metre. What would be the cost, in dollars, of the decking material? Mark the answer on the standard grid on the answer sheet.

4. Margaret Millsford, the chief financial officer of Aggravated Manufacturing Corporation, has to report to the board of directors. She has been instructed to analyze the sales of each of the company's product lines and recommend dropping the least profitable line. She found that although the per-unit profit of each of their lines was the same, the volume produced differed. She prepared the following graph to back up her recommendation:

   What should be her recommendation of the least profitable line to drop?

   (1) widgets

   (2) grommets

   (3) gadgets

   (4) grommets and widgets

   (5) gadgets and widgets

Go on to next page ⟹

5. Quan wants to build steps down from the 1.8-metre-high porch behind his house. The bottom step should be 2.1 metres away from the house to allow for a gentle slope. How long, in metres, will the steps be (answer to two decimal places)?

    (1) 8.22

    (2) 7.65

    (3) 2.92

    (4) 3.22

    (5) 2.77

6. Alice was trying to explain how the length of time she could run each morning had improved each month since she started, except for the month she twisted her ankle. She drew the following graph to show her friends Mary and Kevin the average length of time she ran each day each month:

    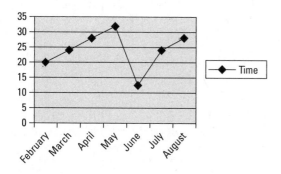

    In which month did Alice twist her ankle?

    (1) June

    (2) February

    (3) August

    (4) September

    (5) May

7. Dominic and Paula were comparing their report cards, as follows:

    Dominic's Report Card

Subject	Grade (%)
Mathematics	63
Social Studies	76
Science	65
Language Arts	84
Physical Education	72

    Paula's Report Card

Subject	Grade (%)
Mathematics	80
Social Studies	64
Science	76
Language Arts	72
Physical Education	88

    The teacher told them that the ratio of their total marks was very close. What is the ratio of Paula's marks to Dominic's marks on these report cards?

    (1) 9:10

    (2) 18:19

    (3) 10:9

    (4) 19:18

    (5) 2:1

8. In the series, 4, 6, 10, 18, . . . , which is the first term that is a multiple of 11? Mark the answer on the standard grid on the answer sheet.

Go on to next page

9. Simone follows the stock market very carefully. She has been carefully following Cowardly Corporation the last few months, keeping track of her research in the following table:

Date	Closing Price (in Canadian Dollars)
August 7	15.03
August 17	16.12
September 1	14.83
September 9	15.01
September 16	14.94
September 20	15.06
September 23	15.17
September 24	15.19

Simone bought shares of the stock on September 24 and wants to make money before selling it. She paid 3% commission to her broker for buying and will pay the same again for selling. What is the lowest price (in Canadian dollars) for which Simone can sell each of her shares in order to break even?

(1) 16.48

(2) 16.13

(3) 15.66

(4) 20.00

(5) 15.99

10. If $22.4 = \dfrac{56a}{5a+10}$, what is the value of a?

(1) 0

(2) –56

(3) 4

(4) –4

(5) 56

Questions 11 and 12 refer to the following graph.

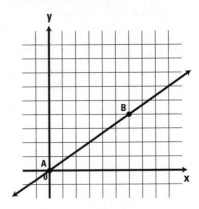

11. Calculate the slope of the line *AB*.

(1) ⅔

(2) ½

(3) ⅓

(4) ¼

(5) –½

12. If the slope of *AB* remains the same, but it intercepts the *y*-axis at C(0,4), where does it intersect the *x*-axis? Use the coordinate-plane grid on the answer sheet to draw the point where *AB* intersects the *x*-axis.

13. If a fire is built in the centre of a square barbecue pit, where is the safest place to stand to avoid the intense heat of the fire?

(1) at a corner

(2) along the left side

(3) along the right side

(4) 1.83 metres from the middle

(5) not enough information given

Go on to next page

14. Lydia and Wayne are shopping for carpets for their home and are looking for the best carpet at the best price. Carnie's Carpets offers them a wool carpet for $26.00 per square metre. Flora's Flooring says they will match that same carpet for only $0.003 per square centimetre, while Dora's Deep Discount offers them a 2.44-by-3.66 metre rug of the same carpet material for $210.24. What is the lowest price per square metre offered to Lydia and Wayne?

    (1) $24.50
    (2) $2.35
    (3) $21.90
    (4) $23.54
    (5) $2.19

15. Miscellaneous Appliances Limited is concerned about its output at Plant A. For its annual report, company officials prepared the following graphs to show the output for each quarter of the last two years:

    Output at Plant A – 2007

    - ▦ 1st Qtr
    - ■ 2nd Qtr
    - ☐ 3rd Qtr
    - ▦ 4th Qtr

    Output at Plant A – 2008

    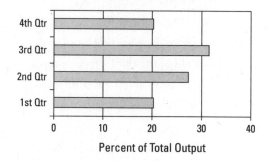

    Which quarter showed a dramatic decrease in production in 2008?

    (1) 3rd quarter
    (2) 1st quarter
    (3) 4th quarter
    (4) 2nd quarter
    (5) no significant change

16. The Ng's are looking to expand their two-storey house and have calculated that they need at least another 100 square metres to live comfortably. They want to use the basement level for storage and the rest for living. A contractor quotes them $146.00 per square metre for the renovation without redecoration. A real estate agent tells them that they can increase the value of their home by about $18,000 by building the addition. If they want to add as much additional space as possible for the $18,000 they will recover, how much additional space, in square metres, should they add on?

    (1) 630
    (2) 126
    (3) 162
    (4) 124
    (5) 132

17. In an experiment involving throws of a 20-sided die, the following results were obtained:

Throw	Left-Handed	Right-Handed
1	2	4
2	4	12
3	5	2
4	9	6
5	11	13
6	10	15
7	4	17
8	6	3
9	7	5

    Using the coordinate-plane grid on the answer sheet, plot the point representing the combined medians of the throws using the median of the left-handed results as the *x*-value and the median of the right-handed results as the *y*-value.

Go on to next page ⇨

18. LeeAnne is shopping for a new vehicle. She drives about 18,000 kilometres per year. She is most concerned about the cost of gasoline and other operating costs, like insurance and maintenance. She expects gasoline to average $.93 a litre during the five years she will own the car and is basing her decision on that price. As she shops, she makes the following chart:

Type of Vehicle	Litres per 100 Kilometres	Operating Costs per Kilometre
SUV	5.44	$0.78
Sedan	8.33	$0.48
Two-door	8.29	$0.54
All-wheel drive	7.31	$0.62
Sports car	7.91	$0.66

Based on her criteria, which car should LeeAnne buy?

(1) SUV

(2) sedan

(3) two-door

(4) all-wheel drive

(5) sports car

19. Tom is worried about getting to the GED testing centre on time. He knows that he averages 64 kilometres per hour on the route to the tests. If the test site is 75 kilometres from Tom's house, and he wants to arrive 20 minutes early, how much time does he have to leave for travel and waiting?

Choose the answer that indicates which operations need to be performed and the order in which they need to be performed to answer this question.

(1) add then divide

(2) multiply then add

(3) divide then add

(4) add then multiply

(5) divide then multiply

20. Leonora has just received her mid-term report card. Her grades are as follows:

Leonora's Report Card	
Subject	Grade (%)
English	84
Geography	78
Mathematics	68
Physical Education	77
Physics	82

Her average grade is 77.8%. In order to get into the university of her choice, she needs an average of 80%. English is her best subject. By how many percentage points will her English score have to go up, assuming all her other subjects stay the same, to get into university?

(1) 7

(2) 8

(3) 9

(4) 10

(5) 11

21. Sonia has an amazing recipe for rice. For each 1 cup of rice, she adds 2 cups of vegetable soup and a quarter cup of lentils. This weekend, she is having a large dinner party and figures she needs to cook 3½ cups of rice for her guests. How much of the other two ingredients should she use?

(1) 7 cups of soup and ⅞ cup of lentils

(2) 3½ cups of soup and ½ cup of lentils

(3) 7 cups of soup and 1 cup of lentils

(4) 1 cup of soup and 7 cups of lentils

(5) 6 cups of soup and ⅞ cup of lentils

Go on to next page ⟹

22. In drawing cards from a deck, any single card has an equal chance of being drawn. After six cards have been drawn and removed, what is the probability of drawing an ace of hearts if it has not yet been drawn?

    (1) 1:52

    (2) 1:50

    (3) 1:48

    (4) 1:46

    (5) 1:44

23. The Symons are redecorating a room in their house. They have some interesting ideas. They want to put a rug on the floor surrounded by a border of tiles. They are considering teak panelling halfway up each wall. In addition, they may cut away part of the ceiling to put in a skylight. This is a diagram of their room:

    The rug costs $67.50 a square metre, and tile costs $54.00 a square metre. One rug they like is 4.88 metres by 3.05 metres, leaving just a little area around the rug for tiles. At the store, however, they see another rug that is only 3.66 metres by 2.44 metres, but it's just the right pattern and colors for their room. Which floor treatment is less expensive?

    (1) both are the same cost

    (2) the larger rug

    (3) the smaller rug without the panelling

    (4) the smaller rug

    (5) not enough information given

Go on to next page

24. Brad is a secret shopper for the Friendly Furniture store. His job is to go to competitive stores and price a series of items to make sure his employer can advertise that he has the best prices. His boss wants to start a new advertising campaign: "Friendly Furniture — always lower than the average price of our competitors." Brad's job is to shop several stores to make sure the claim is accurate. Brad's results are recorded in the following table:

Item	Store A	Store B	Store C	Store D	Friendly Furniture
Couch	$1,729	$1,749	$1,729	$1,699	$1,719
Dining room set	$4,999	$4,899	$5,019	$4,829	$4,899
Loveseat	$1,259	$1,199	$1,279	$1,149	$1,229
Coffee table	$459	$449	$479	$429	$449
Reclining chair	$759	$799	$739	$699	$739

Which item cannot be advertised as "lower than the average price"?

(1) couch

(2) dining room set

(3) loveseat

(4) coffee table

(5) reclining chair

25. In a pistachio-eating contest, Sarah eats 48 pistachios in 18 minutes. If she could maintain her rate of eating pistachios, how many could she eat in 2 hours? Record your answer on the standard grid on the answer sheet.

END OF PART I

Mathematics Test: Part II

The use of calculators is <u>not</u> allowed in Part II.

Do not write in this test booklet. The test administrator will give you a blank paper for your calculations. Record your answers on the separate answer sheet provided. Be sure all information is properly recorded on the answer sheet.

To record your answers, fill in the numbered circle on the answer sheet that corresponds to the answer you select for each question in the test booklet.

EXAMPLE:

If a grocery bill totaling $15.75 is paid with a $20.00 bill, how much change should be returned?

(1) $5.25

(2) $4.75

(3) $4.25

(4) $3.75

(5) $3.25

> (On Answer Sheet)
>
> ① ② ● ④ ⑤

The correct answer is "$4.25"; therefore, answer space 3 would be marked on the answer sheet.

Do not rest the point of your pencil on the answer sheet while you are considering your answer. Make no stray or unnecessary marks. If you change an answer, erase your first mark completely. Mark only one answer space for each question; multiple answers will be scored as incorrect. Do not fold or crease your answer sheet. All test materials must be returned to the test administrator.

Note: Refer to Chapter 26 for the answers for Parts I and II of this practice test.

The Standard Grid

Mixed numbers, such as 3½, cannot be entered in the standard grid. Instead, represent them as decimal numbers (in this case, 3.5) or fractions (in this case, ½). No answer on a standard grid can be a negative number, such as –8.

To record your answer for a standard-grid question:

  ✔ Begin in any column that will allow your answer to be entered.

  ✔ Write your answer in the boxes on the top row.

  ✔ In the column beneath a fraction bar or decimal point (if any) and each number in your answer, fill in the circle representing that character.

  ✔ Leave blank any unused column.

Points to remember:

  ✔ The answer sheet will be machine scored. **The circles must be filled in correctly.**

  ✔ Mark no more than one circle in any column.

  ✔ Grid only one answer even if more than one answer is correct.

  ✔ Mixed numbers, such as 3½, must be gridded as 3.5 or ½.

  ✔ No answer on a standard grid can be a negative number.

The Coordinate-Plane Grid

To record an answer on the coordinate-plane grid, you must have an *x*-value and a *y*-value. No answer for a coordinate-plane question will have a value that is a fraction or decimal.

Mark only the <u>one</u> circle that represents your answer.

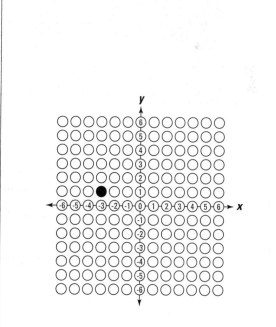

EXAMPLE:

The coordinates of point A, shown on the graph below, are (2,–4).

The coordinates of point B, not shown on the graph, are (–3,1). What is the location of point B?

DO NOT MARK YOUR ANSWER ON THE GRAPH ABOVE.

Mark your answer on the coordinate-plane grid on the answer sheet (at right).

CORRECT RESPONSE:

Formulas

AREA of a:

square	Area = side^2
rectangle	Area = length × width
parallelogram	Area = base × height
triangle	Area = ½ × base × height
trapezoid	Area = ½ × (base$_1$ + base$_2$) × height
circle	Area = π × radius^2; π is approximately equal to 3.14

PERIMETER of a:

square	Perimeter = 4 × side
rectangle	Perimeter = (2 × length) + (2 × width)
triangle	Perimeter = side$_1$ + side$_2$ + side$_3$

CIRCUMFERENCE of a circle — Circumference = π × diameter; π is approximately equal to 3.14

VOLUME of a:

cube	Volume = side^3
rectangular solid	Volume = length × width × height
square pyramid	Volume = ⅓ × (base edge)^2 × height
cylinder	Volume = π × radius^2 × height; π is approximately equal to 3.14
cone	Volume = ⅓ × π × radius^2 × height; π is approximately equal to 3.14

COORDINATE GEOMETRY

distance between points = $\sqrt{(x_2 - x_1)^2 + (y_2 - y_1)^2}$; (x_1, y_1) and (x_2, y_2) are two points in a plane

slope of a line = $\dfrac{y_2 - y_1}{x_2 - x_1}$; (x_1, y_1) and (x_2, y_2) are two points on the line

PYTHAGOREAN RELATIONSHIP

$a^2 + b^2 = c^2$; a and b are sides, and c is the hypotenuse of a right triangle

MEASURES OF CENTRAL TENDENCY

mean = $\dfrac{x_1 + x_2 + ... + x_n}{n}$; where the x's are the values for which a mean is desired, and n is the total number of values for x

median = the middle value of an odd number of *ordered* scores, and halfway between the two middle values of an even number of *ordered* scores

SIMPLE INTEREST — interest = principal × rate × time

DISTANCE — distance = rate × time

TOTAL COST — total cost = (number of units) × (price per unit)

DO NOT BEGIN TAKING THIS TEST UNTIL TOLD TO DO SO

Directions: Choose the <u>one best answer</u> to each question.

1. Kevin wants to paint his room, which is 2.82 metres long, 2.51 metres wide, and 2.49 metres high. The label on the paint can cautions that air must be exchanged in the room every 12 minutes. When Kevin looks for exhaust fans to keep the air moving, he finds that they are calibrated in cubic metres per hour. What operation does Kevin have to perform first to figure out which size fan he needs?

   (1) multiplication

   (2) division

   (3) addition

   (4) subtraction

   (5) square root

2. Which of these shapes has the same relationship to the horizontal after a 90-degree rotation about a point on the perimeter?

   (1) square

   (2) isosceles triangle

   (3) circle

   (4) pentagon

   (5) not enough information given

3. In a large company, the top four positions are organized as follows:

   Each department has the following budget:

Department	Budget ($ Millions)
Operations	14.7
Human Resources	2.1
Marketing	5.6

   What is the ratio of the largest budget to the smallest budget?

   (1) 7:1

   (2) 14:1

   (3) 5:2

   (4) 7:5

   (5) 14:5

Go on to next page

4. A company has doubled its sales from the 1st to the 3rd quarters. Which graph indicates this pattern?

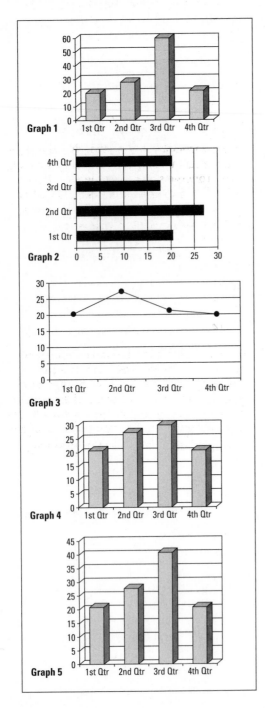

(1) Graph 1

(2) Graph 2

(3) Graph 3

(4) Graph 4

(5) Graph 5

5. A 1.8-metre tall forester standing some 5 metres from a tree uses his digital range-finder to calculate the distance between his eye and the top of the tree to be 8 metres. How tall is the tree?

(1) $\sqrt{41}$

(2) $\sqrt{881}$

(3) $\sqrt{256}$

(4) $\sqrt{97}$

(5) not enough information given

6. Lawrie is trying to save money and keeps her money in both chequing and savings accounts. Each week, she puts $24.00 from her paycheque into her savings account. However, the fourth week she overdraws her chequing account by $7.50, and the bank transfers the money from her savings account. For providing this service, the bank charges Lawrie $10.00. What is her savings account balance after the fourth week?

(1) $88.50

(2) $96.00

(3) $86.00

(4) $78.50

(5) $24.00

7. Sarah is negotiating the price of a chair for her room. The original price was $96.00. Store A offers her ⅓ off. Store B offers her a discount of 30%. How much will she save by taking the lower price? Use the standard grid on the answer sheet to record your answer in dollars.

Go on to next page

Questions 8 through 10 are based on the following information and figure.

While a rock band is setting up for a concert, the audio engineer is calibrating the amplifiers used for the concert. He has an instrument that develops and displays a graph for each setting on the amplifier controls. The graph appears like this:

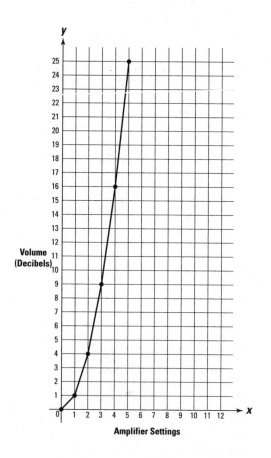

8. From the graph, calculate the volume in decibels for a setting of 10 on the amplifier.

(1) 20

(2) 30

(3) 50

(4) 100

(5) 10

9. The equation that produced this graph is $V = S^2$, where V is the volume in decibels and S is the volume setting. If the volume is 144, what is the volume setting on the amplifier?

(1) 8

(2) 9

(3) 10

(4) 11

(5) 12

10. In this particular auditorium, the volume of sound decreases by half for every 3 metres away from the stage a person sits. If the volume at the stage is 144 decibels, what will be the volume in decibels for a person sitting 6 metres from the stage?

(1) 24

(2) 36

(3) 48

(4) 60

(5) 72

11. Gary and Georgina George bought a new car and are trying to estimate the gas usage. The new car travels 400 kilometres at a cost of $54.00. The price of gasoline is $1.10 per litre. Show the gasoline usage per 100 kilometres on the standard grid on the answer sheet, rounded to one decimal point.

Go on to next page

Question 12 is based on the following figures, which are reprinted from Physical Science: What the Technology Professional Needs to Know *by C. Lon Enloe, Elizabeth Garnett, Jonathan Miles, and Stephen Swanson (Wiley).*

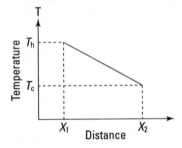

12. If the person pictured wants to remain at a constant temperature, what geometrical shape should he follow as a path?

    (1) hexagon

    (2) ellipse

    (3) line

    (4) square

    (5) circle

13. Igor is in charge of the diving pool at the local recreation centre. The pool is 36.5 metres long and 7.25 metres wide and holds 1,365 cubic metres of water. What is the average depth of the pool in metres? Record your answer on the standard grid on the answer sheet, rounded to two decimal points.

Questions 14 through 16 refer to the following table.

Average Fuel Consumption and Annual Fuel Cost of Selected Vehicles

Vehicle	Fuel Consumption (Litres per 100 Kilometres)		Annual Cost ($)*
	City	Highway	
A	10.2	8.4	840
B	11.2	8.1	875
C	12.4	9.4	1,000
D	13.0	9.8	1,050
E	13.8	10.8	1,105
F	14.7	10.7	1,167
G	15.7	11.2	1,235
H	16.8	12.4	1,314
I	18.0	13.0	1,400
J	20.0	14.7	1,823

*Annual cost includes 15,000 kilometres driven annually; 55% of kilometres are in the city and 45% on the highway; standard price of fuel and maintenance according to manufacturer's schedule.

14. If you were in the market for a car, how much could you save, in dollars, over a three-year period, by buying the most economical car over the least economical car?

    (1) $840

    (2) $983

    (3) $2,520

    (4) $5,469

    (5) $2,949

15. What is the difference in fuel consumed in litres between the mean city fuel usage and the median of the city fuel usage for these vehicles?

    (1) 1⅔

    (2) ⅓

    (3) 17

    (4) 2½

    (5) 2

Go on to next page

16. Graph the results for Vehicle E on the coordinate-plane grid, with the difference between city and highway fuel usage as the appropriate point on the *y*-axis.

17. To solve a problem in her mathematics class, Jan had to solve the following set of equations:

    $2x + 3y = 10$

    $5x + 6y = 13$

    What is the correct value of *y*?

    (1) +4

    (2) –8

    (3) –6

    (4) +6

    (5) +8

18. An international survey found the following information about participation in adult education:

Percent of Population Over Age 21 Participating in Adult Education in 2003

Country	Total Participation Rate (%)
Denmark	62.3
Hungary	17.9
Norway	43.1
Portugal	15.5
United States	66.4

Compare the participation rates of the countries with the highest and lowest participation rates by calculating approximately how many more adults participate in adult education in the country with the highest participation rate than in the country with the lowest participation rate.

(1) 2 times as many

(2) 4 times as many

(3) 6 times as many

(4) 8 times as many

(5) not enough information given

19. Gordon has the following six bills to pay this month:

Bill Payable To	Amount
Bedding by Vidalia	$23.00
Chargealot Credit Corp.	$31.00
Dink's Department Store	$48.00
Furniture Fit for a Princess Shoppe	$13.00
Highest Fidelity Sound Shop	$114.00
Overpriced Gas Corporation	$39.00

Each month, he allocates $250.00 to pay his bills. This month, his bills are over this budget. How much extra money must he find from other parts of his budget to pay all of his bills?

(1) $8.00

(2) $268.00

(3) $28.00

(4) $18.00

(5) $38.00

20. If a flight of stairs is 4.6 metres long, and the second floor is 2.75 metres above the floor below, how much floor space in length will the staircase occupy? Use the standard grid on the answer sheet to record your answer, rounded to one decimal point.

21. Andrew just bought a small circular swimming pool for his children to play in. The diameter of the pool is 4 metres, and Andrew can fill it safely to a depth of 22 centimetres. If a cubic metre of water weighs 1,000 kilograms, how many kilograms does the water in Andrew's pool weigh?

(1) approximately 2,700

(2) approximately 22,700

(3) approximately 26,000

(4) approximately 1,300

(5) approximately 2,790

Go on to next page →

22. If Giorgio borrows $100 for one year and three months and repays $108 dollars including simple interest, what rate of interest was he charged?

    (1) 6.4%

    (2) 8.0%

    (3) 4.0%

    (4) 4.6%

    (5) 8.4%

23. Chico went shopping for some groceries for his family. His shopping list was as follows:

    • 2 kilograms of apples

    • 5 bananas

    • 1 container of milk

    • 1 loaf of bread

    If apples were $.79 a kilogram, bananas $.23 each, milk $1.27 a carton, and bread $.98 a loaf, what is the approximate total cost of the groceries?

    (1) $3.90

    (2) $4.10

    (3) $4.90

    (4) $5.50

    (5) $6.00

24. What is the next number in the series: 4, 7, 12, 19, . . . ?

    (1) 28

    (2) 26

    (3) 24

    (4) 32

    (5) 30

25. A rectangle 5 units long and 4 units high is represented on a graph. If three of the corners are placed at (3, 2), (3,–2), and (–2, 2), where should the fourth corner be placed?

    (1) (–2, 2)

    (2) (2,–2)

    (3) (–2,–2)

    (4) (2, 2)

    (5) (5, 4)

END OF TEST

Chapter 26

Answers and Explanations for the Mathematics Test

Answer Key for Part 1

After taking the Mathematics Test, Part I, in Chapter 25, use this section to check your answers.

1. **3**

2. **1**

3. **1405** (on standard grid)

4. **2**

5. **5**

6. **1**

7. **4**

8. **66** (on standard grid)

9. **3**

10. **4**

11. **1**

12.

13. **5**

14. **4**

15. **1**

16. **4**

17.

18. **2**

19. **3**

20. **5**

21. **1**

22. **4**

23. **2**

24. **3**

25. **320** (on standard grid)

Analysis of the Answers for Part 1

If you aren't sure why an answer was incorrect, use this section to get quick explanations of the answers. If you correctly answered a question, you may still want to read the explanations to get a better understanding of the thought process that helped you choose the correct answer.

Note: In all the following explanations, the answers given are the ones that would be read from the display on the calculator if the correct numbers were entered. Calculators always calculate to the maximum number of digits possible on their display. It is up to the person operating the calculator to either set the number of decimal places, if possible, or to make sense of the answer.

1. **3.** This problem tests your understanding of numbers and their equivalents (integers, fractions, decimals, and percents) in a real-world situation. Signs A, B, and C give customers 50% off. Sign D gives them 45% (9 × 5% sales tax). *Sign D offers the least discount.*

2. **1.** This problem involves measurement and geometry and tests your understanding of perpendicular and parallel lines in a geometrical figure. Frames are rectangles. *Each pair of opposite sides must be parallel* for this to be a rectangle and adjacent sides must be perpendicular.

3. **1405 on standard grid.** This problem tests your knowledge and mastery of number operations and number sense.

   Area of the deck is 4.88 × 6.40 = 31.232 square metres

   1 square metre of decking costs $45.00

   31.232 square metres of decking costs $1,405.44 or $1,405 rounded to the nearest dollar. (Because the next number is 4, you round down.)

4. **2.** This problem tests your data-analysis skills. You're asked to interpret and draw inferences from the bar graph. Because the profit per unit is the same for all products, the product selling the least units provides the lowest profit. In each quarter, according to the bar graph, grommets sold the fewest numbers. *Grommets were the least profitable* product and, therefore, are recommended as the one to drop.

5. **5.** This problem tests your skills in measurement and geometry. You're asked to use the Pythagorean Relationship to calculate a distance. This is a good question on which to use the calculator because it involves squaring, adding, and calculating the square root.

The *Pythagorean Relationship* says that the square of the hypotenuse of a right-angled triangle is equal to the sum of the squares of the other two sides. (You may remember this term being called the *Pythagorean Theorem*.) The hypotenuse is the side opposite the right angle.

To help you figure out this problem, draw a sketch that looks something like this:

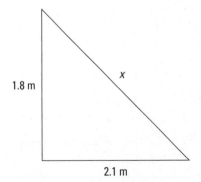

x represents the length of the hypotenuse. Thanks to the Pythagorean Relationship, which you're given on the formula sheet of the Mathematics Test, you know that the square of x is equal to the square of 1.8 plus the square of 2.1, or

$$1.8^2 + 2.1^2 = x^2$$

$$3.24 + 4.41 = 7.65$$

Then $x^2 = 7.65$

$x = 2.77$

The length of the stairs is *2.77 metres*, rounded to two decimal places.

6. **1.** Alice has converted her story into a graph, and you're being asked to interpret the line graph in conjunction with her story. Because her average daily time had been increasing until May, dropped in June, and recovered in July and August, you can assume that the twisted ankle slowed her down. It likely happened in June.

7. **4.** Number operations are involved in solving this problem. You're asked to average a set of grades for each person and compare them using a ratio. You can simplify this question using the calculator.

The total of Paula's marks is $80 + 64 + 76 + 72 + 88 = 380$.

The total of Dominic's marks is $63 + 76 + 65 + 84 + 72 = 360$.

Because you divide each total by 5 to get the averages for Paula and Dominic, you can simply use the ratio of the totals to get the answer because it will equal the ratio of the averages. (Note that if one of the students had six grades and the other had five, for example, you'd have to use the ratio of the averages, not of the totals.)

The ratio of Paula's marks to Dominic's marks is 380:360, which you can simplify by dividing top and bottom by 20 to get *19:18*. Note that Choice (2) is the ratio of Dominic's marks to Paula's marks, but that's not what the question asked for.

8. **66 on standard grid.** This problem involves algebra, functions, and patterns. The numbers 4, 6, 10, 18, . . . form a pattern (also called a *series*). After looking carefully at the series, you see that the second term is formed by subtracting 1 from the first term and multiplying by 2. Try this on the third number: $(6 - 1) \times 2 = 10$. You've found your pattern. Continuing the series: 4, 6, 10, 18, 34, 66, . . . , the first term you come to that is a multiple of 11 is 66.

9. **2.** This problem involves data analysis and manipulation of numbers and is best done using the calculator. Most of the information given is irrelevant, except to decide that Simone may have bought at a high point. The important price to consider is $15.19. In addition to this price per share, Simone has to pay her broker 3% commission.

Therefore, her final price per share on September 24 is $15.19 + 0.03(15.19) = $15.6457. Because you're dealing with money, you have to round the number to two decimal places, making her final price per share $15.65. This amount of money came out of her bank account for each share she bought.

If she decides to sell the shares at this price, $15.65, she has to pay her broker another 3% commission, or 0.03(15.65) = $0.4695. Rounded to two decimals, she has to pay a commission of $0.47 per share. She then receives the value of the shares, $15.65, minus the commission of $0.47, for a total of $15.18 per share. That is, for each share she sells, the broker deposits $15.18 into her account. Notice that this amount is less than the amount she paid for each share.

In order to break even, Simone has to receive $15.65 per share — after the commission.

Set the equation up this way:

$1x - x(0.03) = 15.65$, where x is the selling price

$1x - 0.03x = 15.65$, where x is the selling price

$0.97x = 15.65$

Now divide both sides by 0.97 and $x = 16.13$.

10. **4.** This question involves algebra. You have to solve a linear equation, as follows:

$$22.4 = \frac{56a}{5a + 10}$$

Cross-multiply and write this equation as $22.4(5a + 10) = 56a$

Getting rid of the parentheses, the equation looks like this: $112a + 224 = 56a$

Bringing all the a's to the left and the numbers to the right, you have: $112a - 56a = -224$

Combining the a's, you have: $56a = -224$

Divide both sides by 56 to get one a on the left: $a = -4$

11. **1.** This question tests your skills in measurement and geometry. You're asked to find the slope of a line drawn for you.

The *x-axis* runs horizontally across the paper. The *y-axis* runs vertically, up and down the paper. The *origin* is where the two axes (that's the plural of axis) intersect. Points to the left of the *y*-axis have negative *x*-values. Points below the *x*-axis have negative *y*-values. The *x-intercept* of a line is the point where the line cuts the *x*-axis. The *y-intercept* of a line is the point where the line cuts the *y*-axis. All lines parallel to the *x*-axis have slopes of 0.

The *slope* of a line is the rise over the run. The rise is 4 and the run is 6. This means that the slope is ⅘ or ⅔ (divide top and bottom by 2 to simplify).

12. **(–6,0) on coordinate-plane grid.** This question tests your skills in measurement and geometry. You're asked to identify the *x*-intercept and the *y*-intercept and to draw a line with a slope of ⅔ on the coordinate-plane grid.

If you draw a line through the point on the *y*-axis having the same slope, it crosses the *x*-axis at (–6,0). Simply count over 3 points to the left (the run), down 2 (the rise), and you're at (–3,2). But you're asked for the *x*-intercept, so repeat this process. Go over 3 more points to the left and down 2 more, and you're at (–6,0).

13. **5.** This question *doesn't provide enough information* for you to give an accurate answer. If the fire were rectangular in shape, the answer would be different from a circular fire, or an irregularly shaped fire. The question provides information only about the shape of the barbeque.

14. **4.** Consider the price per square metre at each store:

Carnie's Carpets: $26.00 per square metre

Flora's Flooring: $0.003 per square centimetre = $30.00 per square metre

Dora's Deep Discount: The area of an 2.44-by-3.66 metre rug is $2.44 \times 3.66 = 8.9304$ square metres. The cost for 8.9304 square metres is $210.24 or $210.24 \div 8.9304 = $23.54 per square metre*.

15. **1.** In this question, you're asked to analyze graphs to identify patterns in a workplace situation.

In the first graph for 2007, the 3rd quarter produces about half the output for the year. In the 2nd graph, the 3rd quarter of 2008 produces only a little over 30% of the output. The best answer for this question is the *3rd quarter.*

16. **4.** This problem involves measurement, specifically, area and money. Assuming that the estimate for renovation is accurate, the number of square metres of renovation that the Ng's can afford for $18,000 is $18,000 \div 146 = 123.28767$ square metres. Round this number to *124 square metres* because you usually don't add part of a square metre.

17. **(6,6) on coordinate-plane grid.** This problem involves data analysis, statistics, and probability. You're being asked to graph a point representing the medians of two sets of data. First, find the median (the middle number, when put in order) of the first set of numbers. The median is 6. Then find the median of the second set of numbers. Again, it is 6.

Neatness doesn't count in your rough work. Don't spend time making beautiful tables on your scratch paper. Just sketch out the answer.

18. **2.** This problem is based on measurement using uniform rates, and it asks you to make a decision based on factual information. To figure the cost of gasoline over the five years, set up the problem this way:

$$\frac{18,000}{100} \times 1 \times 0.93 \times 5 = \text{total gas costs, where l = litres/100 km}$$

To figure the operating costs over five years, set up the problem this way:

$18,000 \text{ km} \times O \times 5 = \text{operating costs over 5 years, where O = operating costs/km}$

To help you decide which car LeeAnne should buy, create a chart like the following:

Vehicle Type	Litres/100 Kilometres	Total Gas Costs	Operating Costs/ Kilometre	Total Operating Cost	Total Cost
SUV	5.44	$4,553.28	$0.78	$14,040.00	$18,593.28
Sedan	8.33	$6,972.21	$0.48	$8,640.00	$15,612.21
Two-door	8.29	$6,938.73	$0.54	$9.720.00	$16,658.73
All-wheel drive	7.31	$6,118.47	$0.62	$11,160.00	$17,278.47
Sports car	7.91	$6,620.67	$0.66	$11,880.00	$18,500.67

From these figures, you can see that *the sedan is the best buy*.

19. **3.** This problem involves number operations. Instead of asking you for the answer, which is pretty simple, you're asked to provide the operations that are required to solve the problem. First, you *divide* (kilometres to site ÷ kilometres per hour), and then you *add* (the amount of time Tom wants to arrive early).

20. **5.** This question involves data analysis. You're asked to apply measures of central tendency (the mean) and analyze the effect of changes in data on this measure. If Leonora's present average is 77.8% and she wants to get an average of 80%, she needs enough marks to get an additional 2.2% (80 – 77.8).

Because she is taking five subjects, she requires 5 extra points for each percent increase. Thus, she requires $2.2 \times 5 = 11$ *additional points*. The problem says that English is her best subject, so she would need the 11 extra points in English.

21. **1.** This question tests your ability to figure out how a change in the amount of rice used results in changes to the amount of soup and lentils needed.

Because each cup of rice requires 2 cups of soup, 3½ cups of rice require $2 \times 3½ = 7$ cups of soup

Because each cup of rice requires ¼ cup of lentils, 3½ cups of rice require $3½ \times ¼ = ½ \times ¼ = ⅞$ *cup of lentils*.

22. **4.** This question is a test in probability. You're asked to figure out the probability of an event occurring. If you had an entire deck of 52 cards, the probability of drawing an ace of hearts would be 1:52. If you remove six cards and none of them is the ace of hearts, you may as well have a 46-card deck (52 – 6). The probability of drawing an ace of hearts from a 46-card deck is *1:46*.

23. **2.** This problem tests your measurement skills and logic. You're asked to predict the impact of changes in the linear dimensions of the rug on its area and cost. Choice (3) seems logical, but the question never mentions the cost of the panelling, so you can't consider it as an answer.

The larger rug is the least expensive floor treatment. The smaller the rug, the more tile that has to be used to cover the floor and tile is more expensive than carpet.

Because tile costs more per square foot than carpeting, you know without doing any figuring that having more tile will result in higher costs. You have to read each question carefully to ensure that you answer the question without doing a lot of extra work.

24. **3.** This question is an exercise in data analysis. You're asked to compare sets of data based on the mean (average) prices of four other stores. You can summarize the average prices on a sketch table like this one:

Item	Store A	Store B	Store C	Store D	Average Price	Friendly Furniture
Couch	$1,729.00	$1,749.00	$1,729.00	$1,699.00	$1,726.50	$1,719.00
Dining room set	$4,999.00	$4,899.00	$5,019.00	$4,829.00	$4,936.50	$4,899.00
Loveseat	$1,259.00	$1, 199.00	$1,279.00	$1,149.00	$1,221.50	$1,229.00
Coffee table	$459.00	$449.00	$479.00	$429.00	$454.00	$449.00
Reclining chair	$759.00	$799.00	$739.00	$699.00	$749.00	$739.00

You can see that the only item Friendly Furniture sells for over the average price is the *loveseat*, which is the answer to the question.

25. **320 on standard grid.** This question tests your knowledge of number operations by asking you to solve a problem involving calculations. Sarah ate $48 \div 18$ pistachios per minute. In 2 hours, or 120 minutes, she could eat $120 \times \dfrac{48}{18} = 320$.

Answer Key for Part II

After taking the Mathematics Test, Part II, in Chapter 25, use this section to check your answers.

1. **1**

2. **5**

3. **1**

4. **5**

5. **5**

6. **4**

7. **3.20** (on standard grid)

8. **4**

9. **5**

10. **2**

11. **12.3** (on standard grid)

12. **5**

13. **5.16** (on standard grid)

14. **5**

15. **1**

16.

17. **5**	22. **1**
18. **2**	23. **3**
19. **4**	24. **1**
20. **3.7** (on standard grid)	25. **3**
21. **5**	

Analysis of the Answers for Part II

If you aren't sure why an answer was incorrect, use this section to get quick explanations of the answers.

1. **1.** This question is about number operations; it asks you to select the appropriate operation to solve a problem. Because the first operation performed is to find the volume of the room, and the formula for volume is length × width × height, the first operation you use to solve the problem is *multiplication*.

2. **5.** This question tests your knowledge of measurement and geometry. You're asked to visualize and describe geometrical figures under a 90-degree rotation. Each of the figures is changed by the rotation. Try drawing each of these shapes, picking a point on the perimeter, and rotating it 90 degrees. Because this is a timed test, try drawing one or two, noticing that they change quite a bit. Use your imagination to check the rest. After discovering that none of the four shapes has the same relationship to the horizontal after a 90-degree rotation about a point on its perimeter, you have your answer — *not enough information given*.

3. **1.** This question tests your data-analysis skills by asking you to interpret a chart and answer a question involving calculation.

   The largest budget is the Operations budget, while the smallest budget is Human Resources. The ratio between these two budgets is 14.7 to 2.1 or *7:1* (dividing both sides by 2).

   If you wanted to do this in your head, notice that 14:2 is double 7:1.

4. **5.** This question tests your knowledge of patterns by asking you to compare different graphs to extract information. *Graph 5* has the first and third quarters in the required ratio.

5. **5.** This problem involves measurement and geometry, and it asks you to use the Pythagorean Relationship to solve a problem.

   You can't actually solve this problem, however. Because the rangefinder is measuring the distance from the forester's eye and you don't know how high his eye is above the ground, you can't calculate the height of the tree. You can calculate the distance from the forester's eye to the top of the tree by using the Pythagorean Relationship, but the question asks for the height of the tree (which is the distance from the ground — not the forester's eye — to the top of the tree). Thus, *you don't have enough information*.

6. **4.** This question tests your knowledge of number operations by asking you to perform several operations to calculate an answer. After the fourth week, Lawrie would've deposited 4 × $24.00 = $96.00. There would've been two withdrawals totaling $7.50 + $10.00 = $17.50. Her balance after the fourth week would be $96.00 – $17.50 = *$78.50*.

7. **3.20 on standard grid.** This question tests your skills in using percentages and discounts. Store A offers Sarah ⅓ off or 96 ÷ 3 = $32.00 off the original price. Store B offers her 30% off. Because 30% is 0.30, she'll get 96 × 0.30 = $28.80 off the original price. By buying at store A, she'd get the chair for $32.00 – $28.80 = $3.20 less. Thus, she'd save $3.20.

8. **4.** This question tests your skills by asking you to use information from a graph to solve a problem. From the graph, you can figure out that the volume in decibels is the square of the volume setting. For a volume setting of 4, the volume is 16 decibels. Therefore, for a setting of 10, the volume is *100 decibels* (10^2).

9. **5.** This question tests your skills in algebra by asking you to solve equations. The equation given is $V = S^2$. If $S^2 = 144$, the square root of 144 is 12. Thus, the answer is 12.

10. **2.** If the volume decreases by half for every three metres away from the stage you get and the volume at the stage is 144 decibels, a person sitting 3 metres from the stage would hear at a volume of *72 decibels* ($144 \div 2$), and a person sitting 6 metres from the stage would hear at a volume of 36 decibels ($72 \div 2$). This explanation is given in two parts to show that mental calculations are easy if you break them down into parts.

11. **12.3 on standard grid.** This question involves number operations. You're asked to calculate the average gas usage for a vehicle. Rather than provide you with the number of litres used, you're given the cost of gasoline and the cost of the 400-kilometre trip. To calculate the amount of fuel used, you divide $54.00 by $1.10 to get 49.090909 or 49.1 (rounded to one decimal point which is reasonable) litres. Next, you would divide each number by 4, since gas usage is defined as litres per 100 kilometres. This would give you 49.1 divided by 4 = 12.275 or 12.3 rounded to one decimal point.

12. **5.** This question tests your skills in measurement and geometry. To remain at a constant temperature, you have to remain at a constant distance from the fire.

    The path of a point that travels a constant distance from a point is a *circle*.

13. **5.16 on standard grid.** This problem tests your ability to do calculations and use a formula. The area of the pool surface is length × width or $36.5 \times 7.25 = 264.625$ square metres. Volume = length × width × depth. Thus, 1,365 cubic metres = 264.625 × average depth. The average depth is $1,365 \div 264.625 = 5.16$ *metres* (the answer is rounded to two decimal points).

14. **5.** This question tests your ability to make a decision based on data presented in a table and then to use that information to answer a question. The least economical car costs $1,823 to drive for a year, while the most economical car costs $840 for the same time under the same conditions. The difference in cost for one year is $1,823 – $840 = $983. The cost for three years is $983 × 3 = *$2,949*.

15. **1.** This question tests your ability to analyze data using the mean and median to answer a question about the data given. The mean of the city fuel consumptions is the sum of the entries divided by 10 (the number of entries), which equals 16.8. The median of fuel usages is the one midway between the two in the middle, or 16.5. The difference between the two numbers (16.8 – 16.5) is 0.3.

16. **(0,3) on coordinate-plane grid.** This question tests your ability to analyze data by representing data graphically.

    For Vehicle E, the difference between the city and highway fuel consumption is 3 litres per 100 kilometres (13.8 – 10.8). The point you want on the *y*-axis is (0,3), which you need to mark on the coordinate-plane grid.

17. **5.** This question tests your skill in algebra by asking you to solve a system of linear equations:

    $2x + 3y = 10$

    $5x + 6y = 13$

    Remember that a *linear equation* is one in which the powers of the variables are all equal to 1. To solve this system, you have to eliminate x by multiplying each equation by a number that allows you to subtract one from the other and end up with just y's. Multiply the first equation by 5 and the second equation by 2:

    $5(2x + 3y = 10) = 10x + 15y = 50$

    $2(5x + 6y = 13) = 10x + 12y = 26$

Subtract the second equation from the first, and you get $3y = 24$; $y = 8$. (Note that you can also multiply the second equation by –2 and add the two equations together. Either way gets you the same answer.) Next, substitute 8 for y in either equation to get $2x + 3(8) = 10$ or $2x = 10 – 24 = -14$.

18. **2.** This question asks you to analyze a situation presented in a table. The table tells you that the country with the highest participation rate is the United States, with a participation rate of 66.4. The country with the lowest participation rate is Portugal, with a participation rate of 15.5. Because you're asked for an approximation, you can say that the participation rate in the United States is 60 and in Portugal is 15, which means that *4 times as many adults* participate in adult education in the United States than in Portugal.

19. **4.** This problem involves number operations. The total amount of Gordon's bills is $23.00 + $31.00 + $48.00 + $13.00 + $114.00 + $39.00 = $268.00. If Gordon allocates only $250.00 to pay these bills, he ends up $268.00 – $250.00 = *$18.00 short*. Be wary of Choice (2), which is a special trap for people who don't read the question carefully.

20. **3.7 on standard grid.** This question tests your ability to use the Pythagorean Relationship to solve a problem.

If the hypotenuse is 4.6 metres and the vertical height is 2.75 metres, the square of the third side is equal to $4.6^2 – 2.75^2$, which equals $21.16 – 7.56$, which equals 13.6. The square root of 13.6 is 3.6878177 or 3.7 rounded to one decimal point.

21. **5.** This problem tests your knowledge of measurement and geometry by asking you to solve a problem involving volume and weight.

The formula for volume of a cylinder (the cylinder is the circular inside of the pool to a height of 22 centimetres) is $\pi \times r^2 \times h$, where π = approximately 3.14, r = radius, and h = height. If the diameter is 4 metres, the radius is 2 metres. If the height is 22 centimetres, or .22 metres, it's $\pi r^2 h$, which can be simplified to $3.14 \times 2 \times 2 \times 0.22$ cubic metres. If you wanted to simplify this, you would use 22/7 for π and multiply $22 \times 2 \times 2 \times 22/7 \times 100$ (remembering that 0.22 is 22/100) = 1,936/700 = 2.77 cubic metres which would weigh 2,770 kilograms. If you used 3.14 for π, you would get 2.79 cubic metres or *2,790 kilograms*. The only answer close to this is 5.

In solving a problem, the easiest way is the best. In the above problem, we remembered that π could be expressed by either 3.14 or 22/7 and in this case, 22/7 was a little easier to work with and the answers were very close. If you can make your life easier on the test and still get the right answer, go for it.

22. **1.** This question tests your ability to evaluate an answer using a formula. This formula, $I = p \times r \times t$ isn't in the format you want it because you want to calculate the rate, which means solving for r. You can change the equation to $r = \dfrac{I}{p \times t}$, which allows you to calculate the rate from the information given. Substituting into this equation, you get $r = \dfrac{8}{100 \times 1.25}$. (Remember that 1 year and 3 months is 1¼ or 1.25 of a year.)

Then $r = \dfrac{8}{125} = 0.064 = 6.4\%$.

23. **3.** This question involves number operations. You're asked to calculate — in your head — the answer to a problem. Most problems that ask for approximate answers can be calculated in your head. If you are unsure of the calculator living between your ears, use the scrap paper.

To use mental math to solve this problem, round off everything. Consider the apples at $.80 a pound, bananas at $.20 each, milk at $1.30, and a loaf of bread at $1.00. The total for this approximation is $(2 \times \$.80) + (5 \times \$.20) + \$1.30 + \$1.00 = 4.90. Looking at the answer choices, Choice (3) is the same as this approximation. When you are doing approximations, you will not always get the exact answer but you should get a close answer.

24. **1.** This question tests your knowledge of patterns by asking you to figure out the next number in a series. By looking at the series, it looks like each number is the square of the placement of the number in the list, plus 3. That is, the first number is 1^2 plus 3, or 4. The second number is 2^2 plus 3, or 7. The third term is 3^2 (or 9) plus 3, or 12. The fifth term would be 5^2 (or 25) plus 3, which is *28*.

25. **3.** This question tests your skills in geometry by asking you to visualize a graph of an object. Because the object is a rectangle, the opposite sides are equal in length and are parallel, the fourth corner will be 2 units to the left of the *y*-axis, giving it an *x*-coordinate of –2, and 2 units below the *x*-axis, giving it a *y*-coordinate of –2. Therefore, the point would be *(–2,–2)*.

The *x-coordinate* is the distance from the *y*-axis, and the *y-coordinate* is the distance from the *x*-axis.

Chapter 27

Another Practice Test — Mathematics Test: Parts I and II

· ·

The Mathematics Test consists of multiple-choice questions intended to measure general mathematics skills or problem-solving ability. The questions are based on short readings that often include a graph, chart, or figure.

The Mathematics Test is made up of two parts. Part I allows you to use a calculator to help you answer the questions; Part II doesn't. Each part consists of 25 questions.

You will have 45 minutes to complete each part. Work carefully, but do not spend too much time on any one question. Be sure to answer every question.

Formulas you may need are given on the page before the first test question in each part. Only some of the questions will require you to use a formula. You will not need all the formulas given.

Some questions contain more information than you will need to solve the problem; other questions do not give enough information. If the question does not give enough information to solve the problem, the correct answer choice is "not enough information given."

Answer Sheet for Mathematics Test: Part 1

1 ① ② ③ ④ ⑤

2 (grid-in: . / 0 1 2 3 4 5 6 7 8 9)

3 ① ② ③ ④ ⑤

4 ① ② ③ ④ ⑤

5 ① ② ③ ④ ⑤

6 (grid-in: . / 0 1 2 3 4 5 6 7 8 9)

7 ① ② ③ ④ ⑤

8 ① ② ③ ④ ⑤

9 ① ② ③ ④ ⑤

10 (grid-in: . / 0 1 2 3 4 5 6 7 8 9)

11 ① ② ③ ④ ⑤

12 ① ② ③ ④ ⑤

13 (grid-in: . / 0 1 2 3 4 5 6 7 8 9)

14 ① ② ③ ④ ⑤

15 ① ② ③ ④ ⑤

16 ① ② ③ ④ ⑤

17 ① ② ③ ④ ⑤

18 (grid-in: . / 0 1 2 3 4 5 6 7 8 9)

19 ① ② ③ ④ ⑤

20 ① ② ③ ④ ⑤

21 ① ② ③ ④ ⑤

22 ① ② ③ ④ ⑤

23 ① ② ③ ④ ⑤

24 ① ② ③ ④ ⑤

25 ① ② ③ ④ ⑤

Answer Sheet for Mathematics Test: Part II

1 ① ② ③ ④ ⑤
2 ① ② ③ ④ ⑤
3 ① ② ③ ④ ⑤
4 ① ② ③ ④ ⑤
5 ① ② ③ ④ ⑤
6 ① ② ③ ④ ⑤
7 ① ② ③ ④ ⑤
8 ① ② ③ ④ ⑤
9 ① ② ③ ④ ⑤
10 ① ② ③ ④ ⑤
11 ① ② ③ ④ ⑤
12 ① ② ③ ④ ⑤
13 ① ② ③ ④ ⑤
14 ① ② ③ ④ ⑤

15

16 ① ② ③ ④ ⑤
17 ① ② ③ ④ ⑤
18 ① ② ③ ④ ⑤
19 ① ② ③ ④ ⑤

20

21 ① ② ③ ④ ⑤
22 ① ② ③ ④ ⑤

23

24 ① ② ③ ④ ⑤
25 ① ② ③ ④ ⑤

Mathematics Test: Part 1

The use of calculators is allowed in Part I only.

Do not write in this test booklet. The test administrator will give you a blank paper for your calculations. Record your answers on the separate answer sheet provided. Be sure all information is properly recorded on the answer sheet.

To record your answers, fill in the numbered circle on the answer sheet that corresponds to the answer you select for each question in the test booklet.

EXAMPLE:

If a grocery bill totaling $15.75 is paid with a $20.00 bill, how much change should be returned?

(1) $5.25

(2) $4.75

(3) $4.25

(4) $3.75

(5) $3.25

(On Answer Sheet)

① ② ● ④ ⑤

The correct answer is "$4.25"; therefore, answer space 3 would be marked on the answer sheet.

Do not rest the point of your pencil on the answer sheet while you are considering your answer. Make no stray or unnecessary marks. If you change an answer, erase your first mark completely. Mark only one answer space for each question; multiple answers will be scored as incorrect. Do not fold or crease your answer sheet. All test materials must be returned to the test administrator.

Note: Refer to Chapter 28 for the answers for Parts I and II of this practice test.

Calculator Directions

To prepare the calculator for use the *first* time, press the | ON | (upper-rightmost) key. "DEG" will appear at the top-centre of the screen and "0" at the right. This indicates the calculator is in the proper format for all your calculations.

To prepare the calculator for *another* question, press the | ON | or the red | AC | key. This clears any entries made previously.

To do any arithmetic, enter the expression as it is written. Press | = | (equals sign) when finished.

EXAMPLE A: $8 - 3 + 9$

First press | ON | or | AC |

Enter the following: | 8 |, | – |, | 3 |, | + |, | 9 |, | = |

The correct answer is 14.

If the expression in parentheses is to be multiplied by a number, press | × | (multiplication sign) between the number and the parenthesis sign.

EXAMPLE B: $6(8 + 5)$

First press | ON | or | AC |

Enter the following: | 6 |, | × |, | (|, | 8 |, | + |, | 5 |, |) |, | = |

The correct answer is 78.

To find the square root of a number

- ✔ Enter the number.
- ✔ Press the | SHIFT | (upper-leftmost) key ("SHIFT" appears at the top-left of the screen).
- ✔ Press | x^2 | (third from the left on top row) to access its second function: square root.

DO NOT press | SHIFT | and | x^2 | at the same time.

EXAMPLE C: $\sqrt{64}$

First press | ON | or | AC |

Enter the following: | 6 |, | 4 |, | SHIFT |, | x^2 |, | = |

The correct answer is 8.

To enter a negative number, such as –8:

- ✔ Enter the number without the negative sign (enter 8).
- ✔ Press the "change sign" (| +/– |) key, which is directly above the | 7 | key.

All arithmetic can be done with positive and/or negative numbers.

EXAMPLE D: $-8 - (-5)$

First press | ON | or | AC |

Enter the following: | 8 |, | +/– |, | – |, | 5 |, | +/– |, | = |

The correct answer is –3.

The Standard Grid

Mixed numbers, such as 3½, cannot be entered in the standard grid. Instead, represent them as decimal numbers (in this case, 3.5) or fractions (in this case, ⁷⁄₂). In addition, no answer on a standard grid can be a negative number, such as –8.

To record your answer for a standard-grid question:

✔ Begin in any column that will allow your answer to be entered.

✔ Write your answer in the boxes on the top row.

✔ In the column beneath a fraction bar or decimal point (if any) and each number in your answer, fill in the circle representing that character.

✔ Leave blank any unused column.

Points to remember:

✔ The answer sheet will be machine scored. **The circles must be filled in correctly.**

✔ Mark no more than one circle in any column.

✔ Grid only one answer even if more than one answer is correct.

✔ Mixed numbers, such as 3½, must be gridded as 3.5 or ½.

✔ No answer on a standard grid can be a negative number.

The Coordinate-Plane Grid

To record an answer on the coordinate-plane grid, you must have an *x*-value and a *y*-value. No answer for a coordinate-plane question will have a value that is a fraction or decimal.

Mark only the <u>one</u> circle that represents your answer.

EXAMPLE:

The coordinates of point A, shown on the graph below, are (2,–4).

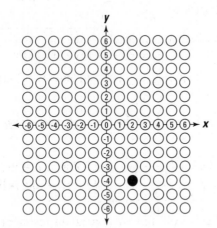

The coordinates of point B, not shown on the graph, are (–3,1). What is the location of point B?

DO NOT MARK YOUR ANSWER ON THE GRAPH ABOVE.

Mark your answer on the coordinate-plane grid on the answer sheet (at right).

CORRECT RESPONSE:

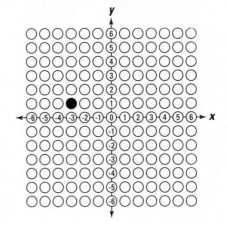

Formulas

AREA of a:

square	Area = side^2
rectangle	Area = length $\times$ width
parallelogram	Area = base $\times$ height
triangle	Area = ½ $\times$ base $\times$ height
trapezoid	Area = ½ $\times$ (base$_1$ + base$_2$) $\times$ height
circle	Area = $\pi \times$ radius^2; π is approximately equal to 3.14

PERIMETER of a:

square	Perimeter = 4 $\times$ side
rectangle	Perimeter = (2 $\times$ length) + (2 $\times$ width)
triangle	Perimeter = side$_1$ + side$_2$ + side$_3$

CIRCUMFERENCE of a circle — Circumference = $\pi \times$ diameter; π is approximately equal to 3.14

VOLUME of a:

cube	Volume = side^3
rectangular solid	Volume = length $\times$ width $\times$ height
square pyramid	Volume = ⅓ $\times$ (base edge)^2 $\times$ height
cylinder	Volume = $\pi \times$ radius^2 $\times$ height; π is approximately equal to 3.14
cone	Volume = ⅓ $\times \pi \times$ radius^2 $\times$ height; π is approximately equal to 3.14

COORDINATE GEOMETRY — distance between points = $\sqrt{\left(x_2 - x_1\right)^2 + \left(y_2 - y_1\right)^2}$; (x_1, y_1) and (x_2, y_2) are two points in a plane

slope of a line = $\dfrac{y_2 - y_1}{x_2 - x_1}$; (x_1, y_1) and (x_2, y_2) are two points on the line

PYTHAGOREAN RELATIONSHIP — $a^2 + b^2 = c^2$; a and b are sides, and c is the hypotenuse of a right triangle

MEASURES OF CENTRAL TENDENCY — **mean** = $\dfrac{x_1 + x_2 + \ldots + x_n}{n}$; where the x's are the values for which a mean is desired, and n is the total number of values for x

median = the middle value of an odd number of *ordered* scores, and halfway between the two middle values of an even number of *ordered* scores

SIMPLE INTEREST — interest = principal $\times$ rate $\times$ time

DISTANCE — distance = rate $\times$ time

TOTAL COST — total cost = (number of units) $\times$ (price per unit)

DO NOT BEGIN TAKING THIS TEST UNTIL TOLD TO DO SO

> **Directions:** Choose the <u>one best answer</u> to each question.

> *Question 1 refers to the following table.*

Room Level Dimensions (in metres)

Dining Room	2.95 x 2.44
Living Room	5.94 x 3.05
Kitchen	4.20 x 2.20
Solarium	5.79 x 2.44
Master Bedroom	4.20 x 3.78
Second Bedroom	3.48 x 2.62

1. Singh has bought a new apartment and wants to carpet the living room, dining room, and master bedroom. If he budgets $29.25 per square metre for carpeting and installation, how much should he budget for these rooms?

    (1) $1,674.08

    (2) $1,457.08

    (3) $1,204.84

    (4) $1,500.08

    (5) $1,745.08

2. After asking for directions to a restaurant, Sarah was told it was 1,140 metres ahead, but her car's odometer reads distances in kilometres and hectometres. How many kilometres should she drive to find the restaurant to the nearest tenth of a kilometre? Write your answer on the standard grid on the answer sheet.

3. Arthur is making a circular carpet made up of small pieces of cloth glued to a backing. If he wants a carpet that is 2.35 metres across, including a 5-centimetre fringe all around the carpet, how many square metres of backing does he need to cover, rounded to one decimal place?

    (1) 15.9

    (2) 3.97

    (3) 4.7

    (4) 4.3

    (5) 4.0

4. The vertices of a triangle are A(–6,4), B(–8,–6), and C(8,7). Which side is the longest?

    (1) AB

    (2) BC

    (3) CA

    (4) AC

    (5) not enough information given

> *Question 5 refers to the following graph.*

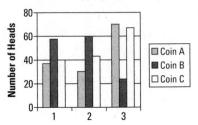

Results of Flipping Unbalanced Coins

5. As an experiment, a class flips three coins 100 times each and charts the results. The coins are not accurately balanced. From the graph, which coin during which series of tosses is closest to being balanced?

    (1) coin B, third set

    (2) coin C, third set

    (3) coin A, second set

    (4) coin B, first set

    (5) coin C, first set

6. Sam and Arnold were eating ice cream cones. Arnold wondered what volume of ice cream his cone would hold. Sam measured the cone and found it to be 6.36 centimetres across the top and 13.9 centimetres high. How many cubic centimetres of ice cream would the cone hold, rounded to one decimal place, if it were filled to the top of the cone? Record your answer on the standard grid on the answer sheet.

Go on to next page ⟩

7. Donna was very involved with speed walking. In order to keep from getting too bored, she started counting how many breaths she takes for each of her steps. She figured that she takes 3 breaths for every 68.5-centimetre step. How many breaths does she take in a 1-kilometre walk?

   (1) 5,332

   (2) 4,280

   (3) 2,126

   (4) 4,767

   (5) 4,380

8. Yvonne is studying a map. She is 75 kilometres due south of where she wants to go, but the road goes 27 kilometres due west to an intersection that then goes northeast to her destination. Approximately how much farther must she travel in kilometres because of the way the road goes?

   (1) 3

   (2) 15

   (3) 16

   (4) 50

   (5) 45

Questions 9 and 10 are based on the following information.

Carlos wants to buy a used car. He has been told that a car loses 4.3 cents from its book value for every kilometre over 100,000 that it has travelled. He sees just the car he wants, but it has 137,046 kilometres on the odometer. If the book value of the car is $13,500, what is the car actually worth?

9. Estimate the realistic value of the car to the nearest $10.

   (1) $10,907

   (2) $13,750

   (3) $87,046

   (4) $12,020

   (5) $12,000

10. Calculate the realistic value of the car to the nearest dollar. Record your answer on the standard grid on the answer sheet.

11. Elena wants to draw a mural on the wall of her house. The wall is 2.75 metres high and 5.20 metres long. In order to plan the mural, she draws a scale drawing that is 25 centimetres long of the area for the mural on a piece of paper 28 centimetres long and 22 centimetres high. How high, in centimetres, should the drawing be to maintain scale?

   (1) 10.2

   (2) 14.8

   (3) 8.5

   (4) 12.4

   (5) 15.0

12. If the slope of a line is 0.75, and $y_2 = 36$, $y_1 = 24$, and $x_1 = 12$, what is the value of x_2?

   (1) 14

   (2) −28

   (3) 28

   (4) −14

   (5) 22

Questions 13 and 14 are based on the following table.

Literacy Rates in Selected Countries

Country	Population	Literacy Rate (%)
China	1,315,844,000	90.9
Canada	31,612,897	99.0
Cuba	11,269,000	99.8
Ethiopia	77,431,000	35.9
Haiti	8,895,000	54.8
India	1,103,371,000	61.0
Israel	6,725,000	97.1
Russia	143,202,000	99.4
South Africa	47,432,000	82.4
United States	298,213,000	99.0

13. If the literacy rates of China, Canada, and Russia were compared, how many times larger would the greatest literacy rate be than the least? Record your answer, rounded to one decimal point, on the standard grid on the answer sheet.

Go on to next page

14. How many more people (in billions) are literate in India than Israel?

    (1) 1.0000009
    (2) 0.0000667
    (3) 0.0000009
    (4) 1.0
    (5) 1.0000003

15. The probability of an event taking place, *P*, is equal to the number of ways a particular event can occur, divided by the total number of ways, *M*, or $P = N \div M$. To test this theory, a student removes all the face cards from a deck. What is the probability that a card less than the number 6 will be drawn? (Aces are low in this case.)

    (1) 1 in 3
    (2) 1 in 5
    (3) 1 in 2
    (4) 1 in 4
    (5) 1 in 6

> *Questions 16 and 17 are based on the following information.*

Peter's grades in his final year of high school classes are 81, 76, 92, 87, 79, and 83.

16. In order to get a scholarship, Peter's median grade must be above the median grade for the school, which was 82. By how many points is he above or below that standard?

    (1) 4
    (2) 2
    (3) 1
    (4) 0
    (5) 3

17. If Peter's goal is to graduate with a mean grade of 90%, by how many total points is he failing to achieve his goal?

    (1) 42
    (2) 43
    (3) 44
    (4) 45
    (5) 46

18. Olga has a propane-powered car. She was told it was safe to fill her cylindrical propane tank at a rate of 0.433 cubic metres per minute. If the propane tank measures 1.46 metres long and 0.64 metres in diameter and is empty, how long in minutes will it take to fill it? Record your answer, rounded to one decimal, on the standard grid on the answer sheet.

19. The formula for compound interest on a loan is $M = P(1 + i)^n$, where *M* is the final amount including the principal, *P* is the principal amount, *i* is the rate of interest per year, and *n* is the number of years invested.

    If Amy invested the $1,574 she got as gifts for graduating from elementary school in a Guaranteed Investment Certificate paying 3.75% compound interest calculated annually for the 7 years until she graduates from college, how much money would she have?

    (1) $341.18
    (2) $1,978.18
    (3) $462.67
    (4) $2,036.67
    (5) $1,878.18

20. Consider the equation $E = mc^2$. If the value of *m* triples and the value of *c* remains constant, what is the effect on *E*?

    (1) 36 times larger
    (2) 9 times larger
    (3) 27 times larger
    (4) 3 times larger
    (5) no effect

21. An accident investigator calculates a car's speed during a skid by multiplying the following: the square root of the radius of the curve that the centre of mass, *r*, follows × a constant, *k*, × the drag factor of the road, *m*. If the speed calculated was 75 kilometres per hour and the drag factor was 0.65, what was the radius of the curve that the car's centre of mass followed?

    (1) 11.6
    (2) 8.5
    (3) 5.8
    (4) 4.9
    (5) not enough information given

Go on to next page ⟹

22. Vladimir is designing gas tanks for trucks. The length of the tanks is fixed, but the diameter can vary from 1 to 1.5 metres. How many more cubic metres of gas does the largest tank hold?

    (1) 8.50

    (2) 3.00

    (3) 2.75

    (4) 4.75

    (5) not enough information given

Questions 23 through 25 are based on the following table.

Summary of Winning Numbers in Seven Consecutive Lottery Draws

Draw Number	Winning Numbers
1	8, 10, 12, 23, 25, 39
2	1, 29, 31, 34, 40, 44
3	1, 14, 26, 38, 40, 45
4	1, 6, 14, 39, 45, 46
5	10, 12, 22, 25, 37, 44
6	13, 16, 20, 35, 39, 45
7	10, 16, 17, 19, 37, 42

23. Based only on the results in the table and assuming that 49 possible numbers exist in the set to be drawn, what are your chances of drawing a 1 in your first draw?

    (1) 1 in 343

    (2) 3 in 343

    (3) 3 in 7

    (4) 1 in 49

    (5) not enough information given

24. If you had to pick one number in this lottery, what would be the odds based on these results that a number greater than 25 would appear in the winning numbers?

    (1) 26 in 49

    (2) almost certain

    (3) 20 in 49

    (4) 17 in 49

    (5) 21 in 26

25. Louise had a theory that the median of the winning numbers in each draw in this lottery would be very close. Considering the winning numbers presented, is Louise's hypothesis accurate?

    (1) not at all

    (2) almost always

    (3) about half the time

    (4) occasionally

    (5) about a quarter of the time

END OF PART I

Mathematics Test: Part II

The use of calculators is <u>not</u> allowed in Part II.

Do not write in this test booklet. The test administrator will give you a blank paper for your calculations. Record your answers on the separate answer sheet provided. Be sure all information is properly recorded on the answer sheet.

To record your answers, fill in the numbered circle on the answer sheet that corresponds to the answer you select for each question in the test booklet.

EXAMPLE:

If a grocery bill totaling $15.75 is paid with a $20.00 bill, how much change should be returned?

(1) $5.25

(2) $4.75

(3) $4.25

(4) $3.75

(5) $3.25

(On Answer Sheet)

① ② ● ④ ⑤

The correct answer is "$4.25"; therefore, answer space 3 would be marked on the answer sheet.

Do not rest the point of your pencil on the answer sheet while you are considering your answer. Make no stray or unnecessary marks. If you change an answer, erase your first mark completely. Mark only one answer space for each question; multiple answers will be scored as incorrect. Do not fold or crease your answer sheet. All test materials must be returned to the test administrator.

Note: See Chapter 28 for the answers for Parts I and II of this practice test.

The Standard Grid

Mixed numbers, such as 3½, cannot be entered in the standard grid. Instead, represent them as decimal numbers (in this case, 3.5) or fractions (in this case, ½). No answer on a standard grid can be a negative number, such as –8.

To record your answer for a standard-grid question:

- Begin in any column that will allow your answer to be entered.
- Write your answer in the boxes on the top row.
- In the column beneath a fraction bar or decimal point (if any) and each number in your answer, fill in the circle representing that character.
- Leave blank any unused column.

Points to remember:

- The answer sheet will be machine scored. **The circles must be filled in correctly.**
- Mark no more than one circle in any column.
- Grid only one answer even if more than one answer is correct.
- Mixed numbers, such as 3½, must be gridded as 3.5 or ½.
- No answer on a standard grid can be a negative number.

The Coordinate-Plane Grid

To record an answer on the coordinate-plane grid, you must have an *x*-value and a *y*-value. No answer for a coordinate-plane question will have a value that is a fraction or decimal.

Mark only the <u>one</u> circle that represents your answer.

EXAMPLE:

The coordinates of point A, shown on the graph below, are (2,–4).

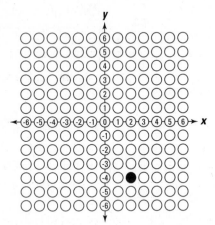

The coordinates of point B, not shown on the graph, are (–3,1). What is the location of point B?

DO NOT MARK YOUR ANSWER ON THE GRAPH ABOVE.

Mark your answer on the coordinate-plane grid on the answer sheet (at right).

CORRECT RESPONSE:

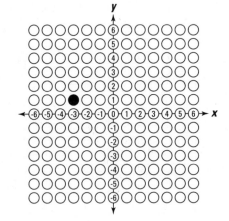

Formulas

AREA of a:

square	Area = side^2
rectangle	Area = length × width
parallelogram	Area = base × height
triangle	Area = ½ × base × height
trapezoid	Area = ½ × (base$_1$ + base$_2$) × height
circle	Area = π × radius^2; π is approximately equal to 3.14

PERIMETER of a:

square	Perimeter = 4 × side
rectangle	Perimeter = (2 × length) + (2 × width)
triangle	Perimeter = side$_1$ + side$_2$ + side$_3$

CIRCUMFERENCE of a circle   Circumference = π × diameter; π is approximately equal to 3.14

VOLUME of a:

cube	Volume = side^3
rectangular solid	Volume = length × width × height
square pyramid	Volume = ⅓ × (base edge)^2 × height
cylinder	Volume = π × radius^2 × height; π is approximately equal to 3.14
cone	Volume = ⅓ × π × radius^2 × height; π is approximately equal to 3.14

COORDINATE GEOMETRY

distance between points = $\sqrt{(x_2 - x_1)^2 + (y_2 - y_1)^2}$; (x_1, y_1) and (x_2, y_2) are two points in a plane

slope of a line = $\dfrac{y_2 - y_1}{x_2 - x_1}$; (x_1, y_1) and (x_2, y_2) are two points on the line

PYTHAGOREAN RELATIONSHIP

$a^2 + b^2 = c^2$; a and b are sides, and c is the hypotenuse of a right triangle

MEASURES OF CENTRAL TENDENCY

mean = $\dfrac{x_1 + x_2 + ... + x_n}{n}$; where the x's are the values for which a mean is desired, and n is the total number of values for x

median = the middle value of an odd number of *ordered* scores, and halfway between the two middle values of an even number of *ordered* scores

SIMPLE INTEREST   interest = principal × rate × time

DISTANCE   distance = rate × time

TOTAL COST   total cost = (number of units) × (price per unit)

DO NOT BEGIN TAKING THIS TEST UNTIL TOLD TO DO SO

Directions: Choose the <u>one best answer</u> to each question.

1. Jerry has started a business selling computers. He can buy a good used computer for $299, and sell it for $449. The only question he has is will he make money. If his overhead (rent, light, heating, and cooling) amounts to $48 per unit and his taxes amount to $3 per unit, how many computers will he have to sell to make $700 per-week profit?

   (1) 6
   (2) 9
   (3) 7
   (4) 8
   (5) 10

2. To be awarded a scholarship at Constant College, a student must score above the median of all the students in his or her year and have a mean of at least 90%. Georgio was hoping for a scholarship. Here are his marks:

   Mathematics: 94

   Applied Science: 92

   English: 87

   Spanish: 96

   Physics: 90

   The median mark for the graduating students was 86.5. How many percentage points above the required minimum mean score did Georgio score?

   (1) 3.2
   (2) 1.8
   (3) 86.5
   (4) 91.8
   (5) 93.2

Question 3 refers to the following table.

Geothermal-Electric Capacity in Selected Countries 2004

Country	Installed Capacity (Megawatts)
China	6
Italy	502
New Zealand	248
Russia	26
United States	1,850

3. What is the approximate ratio of Installed Capacity of the largest to the smallest?

   (1) 1850:26
   (2) 274:2
   (3) 308:1
   (4) 5:4
   (5) 803:1

Go on to next page

4. Elayne wants to buy a new fuel-efficient car. She notices that a new hybrid car is advertised as getting 2.3 litres per 100 kilometres in city driving and 3.4 litres per 100 kilometres on the highway. After a week of record keeping, she produces the following table for her old car.

Day	City Driving (Kilometres)	Highway Driving (Kilometres)
Monday	48	8
Tuesday	56	40
Wednesday	40	16
Thursday	48	32
Friday	32	8
Saturday	8	112
Sunday	8	120

If her old car consumes 13.1 litres per 100 kilometres in the city and 19.6 litres per 100 kilometres on the highway and gas costs $0.95 per litre, how much would she save in a week by buying this new fuel-efficient hybrid car?

(1) $74.71

(2) $22.50

(3) $71.74

(4) $47.25

(5) $69.75

Question 5 refers to the following table.

Interest Rates Offered by Different Car Dealerships

Dealer	Interest Rate Offered
A	Prime + 2%
B	7.5%
C	½ of prime + 5%
D	Prime + 20% of prime for administrative costs

5. Donald is confused. He is looking for a new car, but each dealership offers him a different interest rate. If the prime lending rate is 6%, which dealer is offering Donald the best terms to finance his car?

(1) Dealer D

(2) Dealer C

(3) Dealer B

(4) Dealer A

(5) not enough information given

6. The formula for average deviation in statistics is as follows:

Average deviation = $\dfrac{|x|}{n}$, where x is the deviation, $|x|$ is the absolute value of x, and n is the number of values.

If the values for the deviation are –7, +6, +2, –13, –9, and +17, what is the average deviation?

(1) 5

(2) 6

(3) 7

(4) 8

(5) 9

7. Henry wanted to find out how many people watched *Four's a Mob,* the newest sitcom. He did a survey of 12 of his favourite friends and found that 10 of them had seen the last episode. Knowing that the population of Canada is more than 34,074,000, Henry calculated that 28,000,000 people watched his new favourite sitcom. What is wrong with Henry's conclusion?

(1) There are more people than that in Canada.

(2) His sample is too small.

(3) Some people may have gone out that evening.

(4) His calculation is wrong.

(5) Nothing is wrong.

Go on to next page ⟹

Questions 8 and 9 are based on the following information.

In September, Ken and Ben wanted to lose some weight by the following July. They figured that by supporting each other, eating a balanced diet with reduced calories, and exercising, they could lose 0.25 kilograms per week.

8. What mathematical operation(s) would you use to calculate the amount of weight they could lose between the beginning of September and the end of June?

    (1) division

    (2) counting and adding

    (3) division and counting

    (4) counting and multiplication

    (5) subtraction

9. If they stuck to their plans, approximately how much could they each lose in kilograms between the beginning of September and the end of June?

    (1) 10

    (2) 25

    (3) 30

    (4) 18

    (5) 24

10. Mary and Samantha are planning a 1,450-kilometre trip. Mary says that she can drive at an average speed of 80 kilometres per hour. Samantha says that she will fly, but it takes her 45 minutes to get to the airport and 1 hour and 15 minutes to get from the airport to her destination after she lands. If she has to be at the airport 3 hours before take-off and the airplane travels an average of 480 kilometres per hour, how many hours will Samantha have to wait for Mary?

    (1) 2

    (2) 11.6

    (3) 9

    (4) 10.1

    (5) 16

Question 11 refers to the following information and graph.

The Queenly Hat Company of Lansing, Michigan, produces designer hats for women who feel that a hat completes an outfit. Their sales vary from quarter to quarter and factory to factory. The chart below reflects their sales for one year.

Hat Sales in Regional Offices

11. Of the three factories, which factories and in which quarters are sales figures approximately in the ratio of 2:1?

    (1) east and west in 2nd quarter

    (2) west and north in 3rd quarter

    (3) east and north in 3rd quarter

    (4) west and east in 1st quarter

    (5) east and west in 1st quarter

Questions 12 and 13 are based on the following table.

Life Expectancy for Urban Dwellers

Age (in Years)	Males	Females
10	61.4	67.3
20	50.3	55.1
30	40.4	45.1
40	32.8	36.5
50	22.1	26.4
60	15.2	17.8
70	9.9	10.7

Go on to next page

12. From the data presented in the table, what interpretation could be reached?

    (1) Women age better than men.

    (2) Men live longer than women in all age categories.

    (3) The number of years yet to live decreases with increasing age.

    (4) Urban dwellers live longer than rural dwellers in all age categories.

    (5) Not enough information is given.

13. From the data presented, hypothesize why women live longer than men in an urban environment?

    (1) Women take better care of their health.

    (2) A greater percentage of men work in an urban setting.

    (3) Men are involved in more auto accidents in an urban setting.

    (4) Rural populations live longer.

    (5) Not enough information is given.

14. The cost of a finished item is equal to 2 times the production cost, plus 120% of the overhead costs at the retail level, plus profit. If three stores, A, B, and C, each sell the product, and store B has a 50% raise in rent, how will this affect the selling price for the item?

    (1) The selling price would go down.

    (2) The selling price would remain the same.

    (3) The selling price would go up.

    (4) Everybody would raise their prices.

    (5) Everybody would lower their prices.

15. Sol wanted to write the population of Canada in scientific notation for a project he was working on. If the population of Canada is 34,074,000, what is the value for x, if he wrote the population out as 3.4×10^x? Mark your answer on the standard grid on the answer sheet.

16. Harry and Kerry are preparing for the big race. They have been keeping track of their times in the following table:

Comparative Times	
Harry's Times (in Seconds)	Kerry's Times (in Seconds)
15.6	15.9
14.9	16.1
16.0	15.8
15.8	16.2
16.1	14.8

    What conclusion can you reach from comparing their mean times?

    (1) Kerry is slightly faster.

    (2) Harry is slightly slower.

    (3) They are about even.

    (4) Kerry has a higher mean time.

    (5) Harry has a higher mean time.

17. Maria bought an apartment. The total floor area is 130 square metres. If the ceilings are 3 metres high, and her air system withdraws and replaces 1.8 cubic metres of air each minute, how long, in minutes, does it take to withdraw and replace all the air in her apartment?

    (1) 180.9

    (2) 216.7

    (3) 220.3

    (4) 240.0

    (5) 260.7

18. Peter is emptying his swimming pool. He can pump 0.25 cubic metres of water per minute. If his pool measures 14 metres by 3.6 metres with an average depth of 1.2 metres, when will his pool be empty if he starts pumping at noon on Tuesday?

    (1) 9:00 a.m. on Wednesday

    (2) 4:00 a.m. on Wednesday

    (3) 6:00 p.m. on Tuesday

    (4) 2:00 p.m. on Tuesday

    (5) 4:00 p.m. on Tuesday

Go on to next page

19. Mohammed works in sales. He compares his average paycheques for the last 4 weeks and finds that he has earned an average of $420.00 per week for the 4-week month. If he earned $480.00 the first week, $400.00 the third week, and $550.00 the final week, how much did he earn the second week of the month?

    (1) $250.00

    (2) $280.00

    (3) $340.00

    (4) $190.00

    (5) $300.00

20. Georgia started shopping with $500.00 in her purse. When she returned home after shopping, she had $126.00 in her purse and $83 in credit card receipts. How much did she spend shopping? Record your answer in dollars on the standard grid on the answer sheet.

21. If you open a can flat along the seam and cut almost all the way around each end, what shape would you end up with?

    (1) a circle

    (2) a rectangle with a circle on each end

    (3) a rectangle

    (4) a circle with two rectangles on each end

    (5) a cone

22. Sonya's car uses gasoline in direct proportion to her speed. If she increases her average speed by 10 kilometres per hour to save time, what is the economic consequence?

    (1) She would save time.

    (2) She would save money.

    (3) She would arrive at about the same time.

    (4) She would spend more money on fuel.

    (5) She would spend the same amount as before.

23. A circle is drawn with its centre at the origin and a diameter of 8 units. Where will the circumference intersect the negative y-axis? Mark this point on the coordinate-plane grid on the answer sheet.

24. An accurate fuel gauge reads ⅛ full. If the fuel tank holds 90 litres, how many decilitres of fuel will fill it?

    (1) 718.6

    (2) 819

    (3) 209

    (4) 787.5

    (5) 227.4

25. As part of a mathematics test, Ying was given the following equations to solve:

    $4x + 2y = 20$

    $2x + 6y = 35$

    What is the value of y?

    (1) 4

    (2) 5

    (3) 6

    (4) 7

    (5) 8

END OF TEST

Chapter 28

Answers and Explanations for the Mathematics Test

· ·

Answer Key for Part 1

After taking the Mathematics Test, Part I, in Chapter 27, use this section to check your answers.

1. **3**

2. **1.1** (on standard grid)

3. **5**

4. **2**

5. **4**

6. **147.1** (on standard grid)

7. **5**

8. **2**

9. **4**

10. **11907** (on standard grid)

11. **2**

12. **3**

13. **1.1** (on standard grid)

14. **2**

15. **3**

16. **4**

17. **1**

18. **3.4** (on standard grid)

19. **4**

20. **4**

21. **5**

22. **5**

23. **4**

24. **3**

25. **4**

Analysis of the Answers for Part 1

If you aren't sure why an answer was incorrect, use this section to get explanations of the answers. If you correctly answered a question, you may still want to read the explanations to get a better understanding of the thought process that helped you choose the correct answer.

Note: In all the following explanations, the answers given are the ones that would be read from the display on the calculator if the correct numbers were entered. Calculators always calculate to the maximum number of digits possible on their display. It is up to the person operating the calculator to either set the number of decimal places, if possible, or to make sense of the answer.

---

1. **3.** In this question, you're given more information than you need. You're given the dimensions of every room in the apartment, but Singh doesn't want to carpet all of them. Because you can use the calculator in this part of the test, you can calculate an accurate answer. The first thing to do is calculate the area of each of the rooms Singh wants to carpet.

   Area = length × width, and the length and width must be in the same units.

   Here are the areas you come up with:

   Living room: 5.94 × 3.05 = 18.117

   Dining room: 2.95 × 2.44 = 7.198

   Master bedroom: 4.20 × 3.78 = 15.876

   Next, you have to total the areas: 18.117 + 7.198 + 15.876 = 41.191.

   Because the lengths and widths are in metres, the answer is in square metres.

   You don't need all these decimal places, but because they're already entered into the calculator, you can keep them.

   The carpet budget was for $29.25 a square metre, so you have to multiply the total area Singh wants to carpet by the cost per square metre: 41.191 × 29.25 = 1,204.8367.

   You need an answer in dollars and cents, so you have to round to two decimal points. (The third decimal integer is 6, so you need to round up.) Therefore, the budget for the carpet is *$1,204.84* — Choice (3).

   This isn't a good question for guessing, because you can't logically eliminate any of the answers without doing the calculations.

2. **1.1 (on standard grid).** To convert metres into kilometres, divide by 1,000 (because one kilometre equals 1,000 metres). Odometers usually read to one decimal point, so Sarah should drive about 1.140 or *1.1 kilometres*, which would make her destination slightly before the restaurant, but the distance is approximately right.

3. **5.** The circular carpet has a diameter of 2.35 metres, and it has a 5-centimetre fringe all the way around it. To calculate the diameter that will be covered by the backing, you have to subtract twice the width of the fringe (which you get by multiplying 5 centimetres by 2 because the fringe adds 5 centimetres to each side of the circle):

   2.35 metres – 10 centimetres (0.1 metre) = 2.25 metres

   The diameter is twice the radius, thus the radius of the covered area = 2.25/2 = 1.125 metres.

   Now you can use the formula for the area of a circle given on the formula page, $A = \pi \times r^2$, where π is approximately 3.14. Thus, the area is 3.14 × 1.125 × 1.125 = 3.9740625 square metres, which rounds up to *4.0 square metres*.

   Choice (4) is what you would've calculated if you forgot to subtract the fringe, and Choice (1) is the result of using the diameter in the formula rather than the radius. Choice (2) is the result of not reading the question carefully; it's close, but it has two decimal places.

4. **2.** This question tests your skill in geometry by asking you to calculate the lengths of sides of a triangle when given the *vertices* (corners of a triangle).

   The length of the line joining the points (x_1, y_1) and (x_2, y_2) is $\sqrt{(x_2 - x_1)^2 + (y_2 - y_1)^2}$. Thus, when you substitute the three points of the triangle into this equation, you get the following lengths of *AB, BC,* and *CA* (or *AC*):

   $$AB = \sqrt{(-8 - [-6])^2 + (-6 - 4)^2} = 10.198039 = 10.20$$

   $$BC = \sqrt{(-8 - [-8])^2 + (7 - [-6])^2} = 20.615528 = 20.62$$

   $$CA = \sqrt{(-8 - [-6])^2 + (-7 - 4)^2} = 11.180339 = 11.18$$

From these lengths, you can see that the longest side of the triangle is *BC*.

If you sketch out a graph and locate the points of this triangle, *BC* is obviously the longest side. Sketching could save you a lot of time calculating when the answer is this obvious, so try sketching first.

5. **4.** This question asks you to draw an inference from a graph. Looking carefully at the graph, *coin B in the first set* comes closest to 50%, which is the theoretical chance of a head or tail landing when the coin is balanced.

6. **147.1 (on standard grid).** The shape of an ice cream cone is a cone, and the volume of a cone = ⅓ × π × radius² × height, where π is approximately equal to 3.14 (this equation appears on the formula sheet given to you on the test).

Now you have to insert the values from the question into the equation (remember that you find the radius by dividing the diameter by 2):

Volume = 0.3333333 × 3.14 × (6.36 ÷ 2)² × 13.9 = 147.1219, or *147.1 cubic centimetres*, rounded to one decimal place.

7. **5.** This problem asks you to solve a problem using basic operations. If Donna takes 3 breaths for every 68.5-centimetre step, and she walks 1 kilometre, she takes 100,000 ÷ 68.5 = 1,459.854 or 1,460 steps rounded to the nearest step. If she takes 3 breaths per step, she takes 3 × 1,460 = 4,380 breaths during her 1 kilometre walk.

8. **2.** This problem is a test of your knowledge in how to use the Pythagorean Relationship. Sketch out a map for this problem: Due south and due west are at right angles. So Yvonne's journey is a triangle, with the last part of Yvonne's journey as the hypotenuse. Pythagoras (the guy who, as you may expect, came up with the Pythagorean Relationship) said that the square of the hypotenuse of a right triangle is equal to the sum of the squares of the other two sides. Thus, the square of the last leg of Yvonne's journey equals $25^2 + 27^2 = 1,354$. The square root of which is 36.79673899. Because none of the numbers in this problem has any numbers beyond the decimal point, you can round the answer to 37. However, the question asks how much farther she travelled: She ended up travelling 27 + 25 = 52 kilometres. Therefore, she travelled 52 – 37 = *15 kilometres farther*.

9. **4.** If you want to use approximate values in this problem, you could say that the car depreciates about 4 cents a kilometre over 100,000 kilometres. This car is about 37,000 kilometres over that milestone, which means it has depreciated about 4 × 37,000 cents. You want to solve this in terms of dollars, though. To change cents into dollars, you divide by 100 (because each dollar has 100 cents): 4 × 370 = 1,480.

You can then subtract this approximate value from the original price: $13,500 – $1,480 = *$12,020*.

10. **11,907 (on standard grid).** Using the same calculation that you use in problem 9, but using exact values, you get 13,500 – (4.3 × 37,046) ÷ 100 = 11,907.02 or $11,907, when rounded to the nearest dollar.

11. **2.** This problem tests your skills in geometry by asking you to solve a problem involving similarity of geometrical figures. In order to draw a scale drawing, the lengths and widths must be reduced in the same ratio. If the wall is 5.20 metres (or 5.20 × 100 = 520 centimetres) long, and the paper is 28 centimetres long, the ratio of paper length to real length is 28:520. The width of the drawing must stay in the same ratio. If the height of the drawing is *H*, then 28:520 = *H*(275). In other words, $\frac{28}{520} = \frac{H}{275}$. By cross multiplying, you get *H* = (28 × 275) ÷ 520 = *14.8 centimetres*.

12. **3.** This question tests your skills in algebra by asking you to evaluate a term in an equation. The equation for the slope of a line is $\frac{y_2 - y_1}{x_2 - x_1}$.

Substituting into the equation, you get $0.75 = \frac{36 - 24}{x_2 - 12}$

Then, because 0.75 is the same thing as ¾, you can say the following: $\frac{3}{4} = \frac{12}{x_2 - 12}$

Cross multiplying, you get $3(x_2 - 12) = 4 \times 12$

$$3x_2 - 36 = 48$$

$$3x_2 = 48 + 36$$

$$3x_2 = 84$$

$$x_2 = \frac{84}{3} = 28$$

13. **1.1 (on standard grid).** From the table, you can see that the highest literacy rate is Russia at 99.4% and the lowest is China at 90.9%. Looking at Russia and Canada, you can see that their literacy rates are so close that, for all intents and purposes, they're equal, and, thus, you don't need to calculate the comparison.

If we consider the literacy rate for Russia divided by that for China, we get 99.4 ÷ 90.9 = 1.093509351 or *1.1*, rounded to one decimal place.

The literacy rate of Russia is 1.1 times the literacy rate of China.

14. **2.** The population of India is 1,103,371,000 of which 61.0% are literate. To calculate the number of literate people in India, calculate 61.0% of 1,103,371,000: 1,103,371,000 × 0.61 = 673,056,310.

Note that you have to change 61.0% to a decimal, 0.61, before you can do the calculation.

The population of Israel is 6,725,000 of which 97.1% are literate. To calculate the number of literate people in Israel, calculate 97.1% of 6,725,000: 6,725,000 × 0.971 = 6,529,975.

To calculate how many more illiterate people there are in India, you have to subtract the number of illiterate people in Israel from the number in India: 673,056,310 – 6,529,975 = 666,526,335. Thus, there are 666,526,335 or 0.0000667 billion more illiterate people in India than in Israel, which really doesn't tell you anything except that the population of India is substantially larger than that of Israel.

Choice (1) is the number of illiterate people in India, which the question didn't ask for directly. The other answers are just wrong.

In problems involving calculating big numbers, be really careful reading the digits from the calculator and copying them to the page.

15. **3.** This question tests your ability to calculate a probability. Use the formula given ($P = N \div M$) to calculate the results. To draw a card less than 6, the possible cards to be drawn are 5 (less than 6) × 4 (the number of suits) = 20. The total possible number of cards is 52 (total cards in a deck) – the face cards (4 jacks, 4 queens, and 4 kings), which is 52 – 12 = 40. Now, using the equation, the probability is 20 ÷ 40 = ½. This is another way of writing *1 in 2*.

16. **4.** This question tests your skill in statistics by asking you to solve a problem involving the median of a group of numbers. *Peter's median grade was 82*, which you find by putting his marks in ascending order — 76, 79, 81, 83, 87, 92 — and taking the grade that's right in the middle. If you had an odd number of grades, choosing the grade that's in the middle would be easy. Because you have an even number of grades, the median is the mean (or average) of the two middle numbers, or $\frac{81+83}{2} = 82$.

17. **1.** This question is a test of your skills in data analysis. Peter's average grade was (81 + 76 + 92 + 87 + 79 + 83) ÷ 6 = 83. He failed to meet his goal by 7%. Each percent is equivalent to one point per subject, or 7 × 6 = 42 points.

18. **3.4 (on standard grid).** This question tests you on your skills in measurement involving uniform rates, such as kilometres per hour, litres per minute, or, in this case, cubic metres per minute. The tank fills at a uniform rate, which means you can do the question without getting involved in a series of calculations. The volume of a cylinder = π × radius² × height. Substitute the numbers from the question into this equation:

Volume of cylinder = 3.14 × (0.64 ÷ 2)² × 1.46 = 1.47405

The safe fill rate is 0.433 cubic metres per minute. It would take 1.47405 ÷ 0.433 = *3.4 minutes* (rounded to the nearest tenth) to fill the tank.

19. **4.** Using the formula given, you can calculate the total amount Amy would have at the end.

Using the formula, we can calculate the principal at the end of the 7 years.

When a Guaranteed Investment Certificate or any investment is paid back to you, you get the interest earned plus the principal, so Amy would be paid: $1,574 + $462.67 = *$2,036.673* which is Choice (4).

If you picked Choice (3), you forgot to add back the principal and were paying poor Amy only the interest on her investment. The other answers are mixed-up digits.

20. **4.** This question tests your knowledge of equations by asking you to analyze how a change in one quantity in an exponential equation, $E = mc^2$, results in a change in another quantity. The variation between E and m in this function is linear and direct, which means that whatever happens to m also happens to E. If m is *3 times larger*, so is E.

21. **5.** This question tests your ability to figure out when you don't have enough information to complete a problem. Without the value of the constant, the answer can be anything.

22. **5.** Without the length of the tank, you don't have enough information to answer the question.

23. **4.** This question tests your skill in probability. If there are 49 possible numbers in a set, the probability of drawing any one number is *1 in 49*.

24. **3.** This problem tests your skills in data analysis by asking you to make inferences from data. If there are 49 numbers drawn in each draw, the odds of drawing a number greater than 25 is *20 in 49*. If you count the numbers greater than 25 in the table, you find 20 of them.

Although the table contains a lot of data, lottery draws are discrete events (they aren't dependent on one another), and the results of one don't affect the results of another. Thus, you can consider only one draw for this question.

25. **4.** This question tests your knowledge of statistics and measures of central tendency (in this case, the median). Consider the following adaptation of the given table. (The median is always the middle number when numbers are lined up from smallest to largest; when you have an even number of numbers, as you do here, take the two middle numbers, add them, and divide by 2 to get the median.)

Summary of Winning Numbers in Seven Consecutive Lottery Draws

Draw Number	Winning Numbers	Median
1	8, 10, 12, 23, 25, 39	17.5
2	1, 29, 31, 34, 40, 44	32.5
3	1, 14, 26, 38, 40, 45	32.0
4	1, 6, 14, 39, 45, 46	26.5
5	10, 12, 22, 25, 37, 44	23.5
6	13, 16, 20, 35, 39, 45	27.5
7	10, 16, 17, 19, 37, 42	18.0

Louise's theory is a curious one in that she seems to have no basis for it. When considering the numbers presented, two of the medians are close, so the best answer is *occasionally*.

Answer Key for Part II

After taking the Mathematics Test, Part II, in Chapter 27, use this section to check your answers.

1. **4**
2. **2**
3. **3**
4. **3**
5. **1**
6. **5**
7. **2**
8. **4**
9. **1**
10. **4**
11. **3**
12. **3**
13. **5**
14. **3**
15. **7** (on standard grid)
16. **4**
17. **2**

18. **5**
19. **1**
20. **457** (on standard grid)
21. **2**
22. **4**
23. **(0,-4)** (on coordinate-plane grid)

24. **4**
25. **2**

Analysis of the Answers for Part II

If you aren't sure why an answer was incorrect, use this section to get quick explanations of the answers.

1. **4.** To calculate the basic cost of the computer, you have to add the net cost plus the overhead (299 + 48 + 3 = 350). Because each computer costs Jerry $350 and he sells it for $449, he has a net profit of $99 (449 − 350 = 99).

   To calculate the number of computers he'd have to sell to make $700 a week, divide the amount of profit he wants to make by the gross cost of each computer:

   700 ÷ 99 = 7.070707071

   Because you can't sell less than one of a computer, *the correct answer is 8.*

2. **2.** Georgio's mean mark was (94 + 92 + 87 + 96 + 90) ÷ 5, or 459 ÷ 5, or 91.8. Because the minimum requirement was 90%, Georgio was 91.8 – 90 = *1.8%* above the minimum, which is Choice (2). If you answered Choice (4), you forgot to subtract the minimum mark.

3. **3.** The largest installed capacity is the United States with 1,850 megawatts, and the smallest is China with 6 megawatts. To calculate the ratio, you have to divide the largest by the smallest or divide 1,850 by 6, which gives you 308.3333333, which is approximately 308. *The ratio is 308:1.*

4. **3.** The simplest way to figure out this problem is to create a chart by figuring out the costs of the old car per day and the costs of the new car per day by multiplying the fuel consumption per 100 kilometres by the kilometres driven divided by 100 and multiplying by the cost per litre. For example, on Monday, Elayne spends this much for her old car in the city: 13.1 × (48 kilometres ÷ 100) × 0.95 = $5.97.

   After you find out how much Elayne spends on her old car and would spend on her new car per day, you have to add the costs for the 7 days of the week together to get the costs per week for each car.

Day	City Driving	Cost in Old Car $	Cost in New Car $	Highway Driving	Cost in Old Car $	Cost in New Car $
Mon	48	3.66	1.05	8	1.50	0.26
Tues	56	6.97	1.22	40	7.45	1.29
Wed	40	4.98	0.87	16	2.98	0.52
Thurs	48	3.66	1.05	32	5.96	1.03
Fri	32	3.98	.0.70	8	1.50	0.26
Sat	8	1.00	0.17	112	20.85	3.62
Sun	8	1.00	0.17	120	22.34	3.88
TOTAL	240	25.25	5.23	336	62.58	10.86

   The savings are the difference between the old car's costs and the new car's costs: ($25.25 + $62.58) – ($5.23 + $10.86) = *$71.74.*

5. **1.** This question tests your ability to use number operations. If you adapt the table, it looks like this:

Interest Rates Offered by Different Car Dealerships		
Dealer	**Interest Rate Offered**	**Equivalent Rate**
A	Prime + 2%	8% (6% + 2%)
B	7.5%	7.5%
C	½ of prime + 5%	8% (½ of 6% + 5% = 3% + 5%)
D	Prime + 20% of prime for administration	7.2% (6% + [20% of 6%] = 6% + 1.2%)

   Dealer D is offering the best terms for financing the car.

6. **5.** This question tests your skills in algebra because it asks you to use an equation to solve a problem.

   Using the formula given in the question, you can figure out that the average deviation is (7+6+2+13+9+17) ÷ 6 = 54 ÷ 6 = *9*. Because the absolute values are used, the numbers without the signs are used. You divide by 6 because you have 6 values to consider.

   The *absolute value* (what's inside the two vertical lines) of a number is its value without regard to its sign. So, the absolute value of a negative number is always a positive number.

7. **2.** In statistics, for results to be valid, samples must be large and random. In this question, the sample is too small to tell anyone anything of statistical significance, and the entire sample consists of friends, not randomly selected people. The best answer is that *the sample is too small*.

8. **4.** This question tests your skills in number operations by asking you to select the appropriate operations to solve this problem. To solve it, you count the number of weeks between September and the end of June and multiply by 0.25 (that is, 0.25 kilograms) to get the answer, so you use *counting and multiplication*.

9. **1.** This question tests your skills in using estimation to solve a problem involving number operations. There are ten months between the beginning of September and the end of June. If you estimate that each month has 4 weeks (each month actually has about 4.3 weeks), you have 40 weeks in this period of time. Each of them could lose about 10 kilograms (40×0.25).

10. **4.** This question tests your skills in measurement to solve a problem involving uniform rates. If Mary can drive at an average speed of 80 kilometres per hour, it will take her 1,450 ÷ 80 = 18.125, or 18.1 rounded to one decimal point, hours to drive the 1,450 kilometres. Samantha, on the other hand, will travel at 480 kilometres per hour on a plane for a time of 1,450 ÷ 480 = 3.02, or 3 hours rounded to one decimal point, hours, but she will add 45 + 75 (1 hour and 15 minutes is 75 minutes) + 180 (that's 3 hours in minutes) = 300 minutes, and 300 minutes is 5 hours (300 ÷ 60). Her total trip would be 3 hours + 5 hours = 8 hours in duration, or *10.1 hours* shorter than Mary's trip.

11. **3.** Looking at the graph, in the 3rd quarter, the east plant seems to have produced twice (ratio of 2:1) as many hats as the north plant.

    This answer is considered an approximation because the graphs aren't perfectly accurate.

12. **3.** This question tests your ability to interpret data presented in a table. The data presented is the number of years left to live at different age levels. The only valid interpretation you can reach from this data is that *the number of years yet to live decreases with increasing age*, which is Choice (3).

    Read the answers as carefully as you read the questions. Women may have a greater life expectancy, but that doesn't necessarily mean they age better or worse than men. That's a topic for another question.

13. **5.** This question tests your skills in data analysis by asking you to evaluate arguments. You also have to discover whether you have enough information to decide on a reason for why women live longer than men. In this case, *you don't have enough information* in the table to develop any hypothesis, which means Choice (5) is correct. In question 12, you have enough information to make a broad, sweeping generalization, but that isn't the case in this question. Always read questions carefully to make sure the question is answerable before choosing an answer.

14. **3.** This question tests your skills in analysis by asking you to explain how a change in one quantity affects another quantity. The price of the article is set by a linear function involving the overhead (the costs of doing business that don't change with how many products you sell — things like rent, utility bills, salaries, and so on), the cost of acquiring the item, and the profit. If any of these numbers goes up, *the selling price goes up*, too, which is why the correct answer is Choice (3). In this equation, each of the terms affects the answer in a linear manner. If the rent goes up, either the selling price goes up or the profit goes down, but, in either situation, the raise in rent will have an effect on the basic cost of an item and, thus, the selling price, as well.

15. **7 (on standard grid).** This question tests your skills in number operations by asking you to write a large number in scientific notation. To write 34,074,000 in scientific notation, you start with an approximation — 34,000,000 is close enough. The number of zeros defines the

power of *x*. The population could be written as 34×10^6. Because Sol wants to write it more properly as $3.4 \times$ a power of ten, the power would have to be one higher than 6, or *7*.

16. **4.** This question tests your skills in statistics by asking you to compare measurements of central tendency (the means or averages). Harry's mean time is $(15.6 + 14.9 + 16.0 + 15.8 + 16.1) \div 5 = 15.68$. Kerry's mean time is $(15.9 + 16.1 + 15.8 + 16.2 + 14.8) \div 5 = 15.76$. *Kerry has a higher mean time* (which means that Harry is slightly faster).

17. **2.** This question tests your skills in measurement by asking you to solve a problem involving volume. If the total floor area is 130 square metres and the ceilings are 3 metres high, the volume of the apartment is $130 \times 3 = 390$ cubic metres. If the air system can replace 1.8 cubic metres per minute, it requires $390 \div 1.8 = $ *216.7 minutes* to withdraw and replace all the air, which is Choice (2). The other answer choices are wrong, but Choices (1) and (3) are close enough that if you tried to do the question using approximations you might become confused.

When some of the answers are close in value, doing the calculations instead of estimating is worth the extra effort.

18. **5.** This question tests your skills in measurement and geometry. You have to solve a problem involving uniform rates. Peter's swimming pool holds $14 \times 3.6 \times 1.2 = 60.48$ cubic metres of water. He can pump 0.25 cubic metres per minute. It would take him $60.48 \div 0.25 = 241.9$ minutes. To get from hours to minutes, divide by 60 (because every hour has 60 minutes). So it would take Peter $241.9 \div 60 = 4$ hours to empty his pool. If he started pumping at noon on Tuesday, Peter would finish four hours later, which is at *4:00 p.m. on Tuesday*.

An easy way to simplify this problem is to divide one number by 9 first: $45 \div 9 = 5$. Then you can multiply: $5 \times 12 \times 4 = 240$. This calculation is easier to do in your head than the other way.

19. **1.** This question tests your skills in algebra by asking you to analyze data used to calculate the mean of a set of numbers. If Mohammed earned an average of $420.00 for 4 weeks, he earned a total of $420 \times 4 = \$1,680.00$. The other 3 weeks he earned $480.00 + $400.00 + $550.00 = \$1,430.00$. The remaining week he earned $1,680.00 - $1,430.00 = *\$250.00*.

20. **457 (on standard grid).** This question tests your skills in number operations. Georgia spent $500.00 - $126.00 = \$374.00$ plus $83.00 in credit card purchases. Calculate $374.00 + $83.00 = \$457.00$, *or 457 in dollars*, on the standard grid.

21. **2.** This question tests your skills in geometry and spatial visualization. If you opened a can flat along the seam, you'd have *a rectangle and two circles, one on each end*. Questions of this type require the use of imagination. Imagine a can and cut it along the seam in your head, and then cut around the bottom and top to make it lay flat. The result would be a rectangle from the can itself and a circle on each end from the top and bottom.

22. **4.** This question tests your skills by asking you to read carefully to answer a question. If Sonya's car uses gasoline in direct proportion to her speed, the faster she goes, the more gas she uses. The more gas she uses, the more it costs her to drive, so the economic consequence is that *she spends more money on fuel* — so Choice (4) is correct. Choice (1) isn't an economic consequence, although it is true in fact.

Read the answers carefully. A right answer that doesn't answer the question is wrong.

23. **(0,–4) (on coordinate-plane grid).** If the centre is at the origin and the diameter (which is twice the radius) is 8 units, the circle will intersect each of the axes (that's the plural of axis) at a distance of 4 units from it. Therefore, it intersects the negative *y*-axis at (0,–4).

24. **4.** If the gauge reads ⅛ full, it has $90 \div 8 = 11.25$ litres of fuel left in it. Because it holds 90 litres, it needs $90 - 11.25 = 78.75$ litres to fill it. Because 1 litre = 10 decilitres, it would take 787.5 decilitres.

25. **2.** To solve these equations, you need to subtract one from the other and end up with just y's. To get rid of one of the variables using this method, you need to have the same coefficient in front of the variable you're planning to eliminate. You can multiply each term of an equation by a number and still maintain the equation. Here's how:

Multiply the second equation by 2 and leave the first equation as it is (or multiply by 1, which is the same thing).

$1(4x + 2y = 20) = 4x + 2y = 20$

$2(2x + 6y = 35) = 4x + 12y = 70$

Subtract, and you get $10y = 50$; $y = 5$.

Note that you can also multiply the second equation by –2 and add the two equations together. Either way gets you the same answer.

Part VII
The Part of Tens

The 5th Wave
By Rich Tennant

In this part . . .

This part — which appears in all *For Dummies* books — includes lists of tens that amaze, astonish, astound, amuse, clarify, edify, educate, elucidate, expound, and explain. (Note that we use ten verbs here.)

This part gives you tips for succeeding on the GED tests, maximizing your test scores, and using that wonderful diploma after you pass all the tests.

If you use the material in this book seriously and have some fun with what we provide you, you'll be prepared for the tests. Only you can make a difference in your life. Start with this part and make up your own list of how a GED diploma will change your life for the better.

Chapter 29

Ten (Plus One) Surefire Ways to Maximize Your GED Test Scores

---

In This Chapter

▶ Finding ways to improve your skills for each test

▶ Giving yourself time to study and sleep

▶ Preparing yourself for the big day

Of course you want to do well on the GED — otherwise, you wouldn't be reading this book. But we also know that your time is limited, so this chapter gives you ten (er, eleven — we got a little carried away!) ideas and tips for doing well on your tests.

Studying Subject-Matter Books

If you've taken all the practice tests in this book (see Chapters 5, 7, 10, 12, 15, 17, 20, 22, 25, and 27), you may have identified key areas in which you're lacking skills. Although those practice tests can't predict your score, they do give you practice and a general idea of your strengths and weaknesses. If you didn't get 80 percent correct on any of the sample tests, you need to improve your skills in that area.

We recommend that you visit your local bookstore or library for the many *For Dummies, CliffsNotes,* and *CliffsQuickReview* books (Wiley) that are meant just for students. For example, consider the following fun, interesting, and easy-to-read *For Dummies* books that can either improve your skills or simply make you more familiar with (and, therefore, more comfortable with) certain subjects:

A word of warning: many of these books are American in content, so they all use American spellings and non-metric measure. They are worth looking at for the content, but don't learn American spellings or Imperial measure. Just read them for the content and vocabulary.

- ✔ *Algebra For Dummies* by Mary Jane Sterling (mathematics)
- ✔ *Algebra II For Dummies* by Mary Jane Sterling (mathematics)
- ✔ *Algebra Workbook For Dummies* by Mary Jane Sterling (mathematics)
- ✔ *Anatomy and Physiology For Dummies* by Donna Rae Siegfried (science)
- ✔ *Biology For Dummies* by Donna Rae Siegfried (science)
- ✔ *Astronomy For Dummies,* 2nd Edition, by Stephen P. Maran (science)
- ✔ *English Grammar For Dummies,* 2nd Edition, by Geraldine Woods (language arts)

- *Everyday Math For Dummies* by Charles Seiter (mathematics)
- *Geography For Dummies* by Charles Heatwole (social studies, science)
- *Geometry For Dummies,* 2nd Edition, by Mark Ryan (mathematics)
- *Poetry For Dummies* by The Poetry Center, John Timpane, and Maureen Watts (language arts)
- *Politics For Dummies,* 2nd Edition, by Ann DeLaney (social studies)
- *Shakespeare For Dummies* by John Doyle and Ray Lischner (language arts)
- *The Civil War For Dummies* by Keith D. Dickson (social studies)
- *Canadian History For Dummies,* 2nd Edition, by Will Ferguson (social studies)
- *Vocabulary For Dummies* by Laurie E. Rozakis (language arts)
- *World History For Dummies,* 2nd Edition, by Peter Haugen (social studies)
- *Physics Essentials For Dummies* by Steven Holzner (science)
- *Chemistry Essentials For Dummies* by John T. Moore (science)
- *World War II For Dummies,* by Keith D. Dickson (social studies)

To find out what other helpful *For Dummies* books have been published since this book was written, check out www.dummies.com.

In addition, consider browsing through the *For Dummies* travel books to help with social studies. You may also want to review some of the *For Dummies* workplace books on managing people and running a business to get acquainted with workplace reading material, which often appears on the Language Arts, Reading Test.

Some GED preparation books also include tutoring in test-content areas. (Those books are usually from 800 to 1,000 pages long, which is far more pages than this book had room for.) Visit your bookstore or local library and look for an up-to-date test-preparation book that gives you at least two additional sets of practice tests, is understandable, and includes some skill-building material in the areas in which you need help. You may also want to try taking an Official GED Practice Test. This test is available at testing centres and preparation classes. The official practice test can help you predict your score, which helps you focus your study.

You may also want to check out *The SAT I For Dummies,* 6th Edition, by Geraldine Woods and *The ACT For Dummies,* 4th Edition, by Michelle Rose Gilman, Veronica Saydak, and Suzee Vlk (Wiley). Although they're aimed at American students who are taking college entrance exams, if you can master the review material and sample questions, you prepare yourself not only for the GED but also for university entrance exams after you receive your GED certificate or diploma.

Enrolling in a GED Preparation Class

If you like to interact with people and prefer a teacher to guide you through your preparation, consider taking a *GED preparation class:* A class designed to prepare you to take and pass the GED tests. Some classes cost money, some may be free.

To find a class near you, ask around: Try people you know who have taken the GED, your local high school or college, or your local GED testing centre. You may also be able to take distance-learning courses (which means you do your assignments on your own and contact your instructor through e-mail, online message boards, or chat rooms), which may be a good choice for you. Do your research and check out everything about a class before enrolling.

New Brunswick has developed an online GED preparation program, which is available to people across Canada, although the high cost of the licence makes it more feasible if an agency or school sponsors the program. You can find out more about it at www.nald.ca/info/whatnew/headline/2001/connecnb.htm.

After deciding on a few potential classes, visit the class or instructor, if possible. Make sure that the teaching style matches your learning style. The preparation class is a big investment of your time, so shop around wisely.

After choosing a preparation class, form a _study group_ — a small group of other GED test takers who help each other with study questions to prepare for the tests. Then you can help each other study and ask each other questions. Not to mention, you can still go out with your friends and have a good time without boring everyone by talking only about the GED.

Be wary before committing to a group, though: If the other group members' idea of studying is to party for three hours and study for five minutes, and you want to study for three hours, you won't be happy. Talk to the other members of the study group and listen to what their goals are. If you can find a suitable group, commit to it.

Scheduling Time to Prepare

Whether you study on your own, with a group, or with an instructor, set aside time each day to prepare. Stick to your schedule as if your grade depends on it (and, by the way, it does!). Prepare regularly by doing the following:

1. **Take practice tests to find out which subject area(s) you struggle with.**

   Check each answer on the practice tests, and read all the answer explanations. Make sure you understand your mistakes.

2. **Focus your studies on the subject area(s) in which you're weak.**

3. **Take more practice tests.**

Preparing for the Test in Your Mind

To ease your anxiety about the GED tests, visualize yourself at the tests. In your mind, see yourself enter the room, sit down at the desk, listen to the instructions, and pick up your pen or pencil. Go through this routine in your mind until it feels familiar. Then see yourself opening the question booklet and skimming the questions (questions that are likely familiar to you because you've taken many practice tests). See yourself noting the easy questions and beginning to answer them. By repeating this visual sequence over and over again in your mind, it becomes familiar — and less stressful.

Getting Good Rest the Week before

As part of your plan for preparation, include some social time, some down time, and plenty of rest time because everyone performs better when well rested. In fact, your memory and ability to solve problems improve remarkably when you're properly rested.

Whatever you do, don't panic about your upcoming tests and stay up all night (or every night for a week) right before your tests. Instead, plan your last week before the test so that you get plenty of sleep and are mentally and physically prepared for the test.

Wearing Comfortable Clothes

Consider the following situation. You're about to sit for up to seven and a half hours on what is probably an uncomfortable chair. The room may be too warm or too cold.

So, choosing from the following answers, what's the appropriate dress for the GED tests?

(1) formal dress because this is an important occasion

(2) a parka over a bathing suit because one can never predict the weather

(3) something very comfortable so that you can concentrate on the tests

(4) your best clothes because you need to impress others

(5) whatever is handiest in your closet

If you answered Choice (3), you have the idea. Dress comfortably and in layers. All of your concentration should be on the tests, not your clothes, not on the people around you, and not on the conditions in the room.

Making Sure You Have the Proper Identification

To take the GED tests, you need acceptable picture identification. Because what's *acceptable* may vary from region to region, check with your local GED office or your local testing centre (or check the information they send to you after you sign up) before the test.

You probably already have the proper picture ID for the tests, such as a driver's licence or passport. Just check in advance for what's required, and make sure you bring it with you to the tests.

Practising Your Route to the Test Site

On certain days, you just don't want to get lost. These days include your wedding day, an important interview, and the day you're taking the GED tests. Make sure you plan a route from your home to the testing site. Map it out and practise getting there.

Leave extra time for surprises. You never know when your street could be declared an elephant crossing and a pack of pachyderms decides to meander across your road. The crowd and elephants could make you late for the tests unless you allow yourself some extra time.

Arriving Early

Consider the following two scenarios:

✔ Test Taker One arrives 15 seconds before the beginning of the tests and feels nothing but panic. Test Taker One barely arrives at the desk in time to lift a pencil and begin the test. Test Taker One is so distracted that he takes 15 minutes to calm down, and by then, the first test is well underway.

✔ Test Taker Two arrives 40 minutes early. Test Taker Two has time to drink some coffee and compose herself before the test. Sitting calmly at the desk, Test Taker Two listens to the instructions and begins to take the first test in a relaxed manner.

Which test taker would you rather be? Leave early for the test! Let other people stress and panic. Be the relaxed, prepared test taker.

A couple of weeks before the tests, confirm the time your test is supposed to begin. You may receive a letter of confirmation before your testing date. If not, call the testing centre to follow up.

Starting with Easy Questions

As you open each test, start with the easy questions — the ones you know you can do. As soon as you get the test, skim the questions, identify the easy ones, and do those problems first. Only after doing so are you ready to tackle the other questions in a relaxed, confident mood.

Whatever you do, don't mark in the test book as you move through the questions! Doing so could get you tossed out of the test.

Using Relaxation Techniques

Feeling a bit of stress before taking the GED tests is normal. A little bit of stress can actually help you function better, but you don't want to become so stressed that you can't think.

You need to find some ways to relax. The following techniques may work for you:

✔ **Think positively.** Instead of listing all the negative things that may happen, list the positive things. You can pass the GED tests. You can go on to college or university. You can get a great job. You can win the lottery — well, maybe that's going too far. Don't be greedy. Just be positive!

✔ **Breathe deeply.** The first thing to remember during a stressful situation is to breathe. The second thing is to breathe deeply. You can do so by following these steps:

   1. **Find your diaphragm.**

      Not a diagram, although you could use a diagram to find your diaphragm. Your diaphragm is that flat muscle under your ribcage that fills your lungs with air. It's above your navel.

   2. **Breathe in and make your diaphragm rise as much as you can.**

   3. **Exhale slowly.**

   4. **Repeat, making your diaphragm rise higher each time.**

   After you see how this process relaxes you, try it before each test.

✔ **Count backward from ten (in your head).** You can do this before any test, not just the math one. Start to count backward from ten with no thoughts in your mind. If a thought, even a teeny one, enters your mind, you have to start counting over. See how many times it takes to count from ten to one without a single thought entering your mind.

   Don't do this *during* the tests, only *before*. This exercise could eat up precious time if you try it during one of the tests.

✔ **Clench and unclench your fists.** This simple relaxation technique involves your hands and reminds your mind to relax:

1. **Sit with your hands in front of you.**

2. **Inhale deeply as you slowly clench your fists.**

3. **After they're clenched, slowly exhale as you unclench them.**

You may have to repeat this process several times, but within a couple of repetitions, you'll begin to feel relaxed.

✔ **Stare out a window.** Stare out the window, far into the distance. Try to see a point beyond the horizon. As you do, feel your eyes relax. Let your eyes relax until the feeling spreads to every part of your body. Enjoy the feeling long enough to let go of all the stress that has built up. When you're calm and full of energy, return to the test. This should only take a few seconds. If you spend too much time staring out the window to relax, you may relax your way through the test and not have enough time to answer questions.

If your testing room doesn't have a window, stare at a blank wall and envision your favourite relaxing scene. Don't be tempted, however, to close your eyes. If you're the least bit tired or stressed, you may fall asleep and not wake up until the test is over.

Chapter 30

Ten Ways to Succeed on the GED Tests

You want to succeed on the GED tests. If you didn't, you wouldn't have this book in your hands and spend all your spare time preparing for the tests, right? For your benefit, this chapter presents ten quick and easy ways to help you achieve your goal.

Selecting the Best Possible Test Date

Why plan to take your GED tests when you have a million other things to do? Sure, you probably live a busy life all the time, but do your best to find a period in that busy life when you can concentrate on preparing for and passing the tests. Choose the test date wisely. If you have enough time to prepare, you'll do well. It's just that simple. Select a date that gives you enough time to prepare, but not one that's so far off that you'll retire before you take the tests. Check out Chapter 1 for information on scheduling the test.

Preparing, Preparing, and Preparing Some More

If you're thinking of just signing up for the test, waiting until the test day comes, and walking in to take it — without ever preparing or studying — you'll likely be disappointed in your results. You wouldn't start to build a house by arriving at the construction site with nothing but your good looks and a smile, right? Accomplishing any goal requires careful and complete planning. Check out Chapter 3 to read about some general tips for preparing for the tests. Also spend some time reviewing Chapters 4, 9, 14, 19, and 24, which give you specific tips and hints for preparing for each individual test.

Being confident is great. Being overconfident can do you in. If you think you may be overestimating your knowledge, take as many practice tests as you can, and take them under the same time conditions as the actual tests. If your confidence exceeds the results you get on the practice tests, don't knock the practice tests — they show you what areas you need to work on. Then start seriously preparing for what may turn out to be a life-changing situation. Preparation is never wasted, and time wasted is never preparation.

Remaining Realistic

When you take the test, you need to keep a level head. Preparing (see the previous section) is the best way to do so. Optimism alone won't assure success. But an optimistic attitude combined with realistic preparation will get you far in this world. Your mental attitude can steer you in that direction. Look at the bright side, but be realistic.

Another part of keeping a level head is not allowing yourself to become preoccupied with worries. While you might have many things on your mind, from world events to personal or financial issues, remember that, realistically, most of what we worry about never happens, and worrying about such things will only distract you from the one and only thing that should be on your mind: passing the GED tests. Try thinking about the positive changes that could come about in your life after you pass. Then your thoughts won't be clouded by fear and you can look forward to the future — not the gloom.

Being on Time for When the Tests Start

If you're late to the test site, you probably won't be allowed to enter and you'll have to take the tests on another day. And you'll probably have to pay again to take the tests. Who needs all this grief? All you have to do to prevent this tragedy is to be early for the tests, which, contrary to popular belief, isn't as difficult as it may seem. You can prepare for your route and arrival the way you prepare for the tests. Check out some route maps on the Internet. Look into the schedules for public transit. Do your research, leave extra time for unforeseen situations, and arrive on time and ready for the tests.

Keeping Your Comments to Yourself

A little bit of stress is normal when you walk into a test. The last thing you want, though, is to increase your stress levels. Although it may seem anti-social, keep your serious conversations to a minimum just before the tests. If you want to exchange pleasantries about the weather, go ahead. If you want to arrange to go for coffee after the tests, plan away. If you want to get into a serious conversation about how everything you've done to this point will only guarantee failure, run away as fast as you can and don't talk to anyone! People hanging around the test centre or walking into the tests that have a hundred hints to tell everybody are guaranteed to increase your stress level. If you've prepared, you're ready. Listen to the voice in your head that says you're ready. Don't listen to the sidewalk experts who are going into the tests with you.

Staying Focused on the Task at Hand

An archer who wants to hit the bull's eye keeps all his mental faculties focused on the goal. Nobody ever hit the centre of the target daydreaming about a friend's birthday party. For this reason, put your mind on a leash; don't let it wander during the test. Letting your mind wander back to the greatest vacation you ever had can be very relaxing, but letting it wander during a test can be a disaster. You want your mind sharp, keen, and focused before and during the tests, so concentrate on doing your best and passing the GED.

Be sure to get plenty of sleep in the nights and weeks before the test. If you're well rested, you'll have an easier time focusing on each question and answering it correctly.

Looking at Only Your Test

If a Biggest Mistake Award for test takers existed, it would be awarded to someone who looks at his or her neighbour's paper during the test. This action is called cheating and is a very serious matter. Not only will you be asked to leave the testing centre, but you may have to wait several months to a year before you're allowed to schedule another test. Look at only your test. For the duration of the tests, your test and answer booklets are the most beautiful, fascinating items in the world — you can't help but spend all your time looking only at them.

Don't even give the slightest hint that you may, possibly, be looking at someone else's paper. The test proctor probably won't care about what you were actually doing; what he saw was you looking in the general direction of another person's paper, which, as you know, is considered cheating.

Writing Clearly and Carefully

The GED has only one test that allows you to write out an answer (as opposed to filling in circles). For the essay in Part II of the Language Arts, Writing Test (see Part II of this book), make sure you write clearly and carefully. Two test graders have to read it, and if they mis-read it because the writing is impossible to read, you'll lose marks. If your writing is naturally sloppy, spend some time improving it or figure out how to speed print. Be kind to your test graders — write clearly. Check out Chapter 4 for more advice.

Thinking Positive

Young children often proclaim, "I'm the boss of me!" Although this idea may not be true for a four-year-old child, it's certainly true for an adult. You're in charge of your thoughts. You can think positive thoughts, or you can think negative thoughts. All we can say is that positive thoughts will make you happier, more productive, and more confident, all of which can help you do your best on the GED tests.

Doing Your Best, No Matter What

Not everyone passes the GED tests the first time. If you've taken the tests before, don't see your not passing them as a failure — see it as a learning experience. Use your last test as motivation to discover your academic weaknesses. Sometimes you can gain more from not succeeding than from succeeding. Whether you're taking the tests for the first time or not, focus on doing your best.

Life is full of ups and downs. Although you may do your best on the test, unfortunately, fate may scheme against you. You may be a bit under the weather, or your children may have gotten on your last nerve right before you left the house. Regardless, don't worry. You can always retake the tests. Keep in mind that doing your best can build your confidence to achieve more at the next opportunity.

You can retake the tests, if needed. Failing once isn't a permanent condition, but not doing your best can become one.

Chapter 31

Ten Ways to Use Your GED After You Pass the Tests

In This Chapter
▶ Getting the most out of your diploma in your work life
▶ Reaping a few more personal benefits from your diploma

*P*assing the GED tests makes life more rewarding, because it opens doors that you may not have even known were closed before you passed the tests. You've probably already figured out why you want your GED; if not, this chapter shares ten great advantages the GED certificate or diploma can give you.

Getting a Job

Many employers want to see a high school diploma or its equivalent before they even think about giving you an interview. In fact, a high school diploma or its equivalent is often used as a pre-interview screening tool. A GED allows you to jump this hurdle. It shows potential employers that you've mastered skills equal to most high school graduates. This accomplishment can help you get an interview, and, when the interviewer sees how brilliant you are, it can help you get a job.

Being Promoted

If you're already working, you want to show your supervisor that you're ready for a promotion. The GED says, "I worked hard for this diploma and achieved something special!" Passing the GED helps you show your employer that you're ready to do the same — that is, work hard — on the job. It also shows that you've taken responsibility for your life and are ready to take on additional responsibility at work. Earning a GED gives you a document that shows you've mastered skills and are ready to master some more. You've solved problems and read charts and diagrams, and you're ready to do the same at work.

Showing Others What You Can Achieve

When you earn your GED, you show the world that you accomplished — on your own — what most other high school students needed a building, teachers, counsellors, principals, and at least four years to accomplish. Now's the time to visit old teachers and go to reunions to show your past acquaintances what you've accomplished on your own.

Sometimes we even think you should get to wear a badge that says, "GED — I Did It!" After all, being able to show others that you've accomplished something major thanks to your own hard work is important — in both your personal and professional lives.

Including Your GED in Your Portfolio

You need a portfolio to highlight your skills and accomplishments when applying for a job or further education. This portfolio is a binder that lists all your skills and experiences in an organized manner. Many employers and colleges have a particular format they want you to use; if yours doesn't, career counsellors can suggest generic formats. You can also make up a format yourself. The important thing is to have a place where you list all your skills and experiences that you can take with you to college and job interviews.

Your GED is the centrepiece of your portfolio. The diploma is a stamp of approval on all your prior learning. It shows that you officially know what high school graduates know.

Proving You're Ready for Further Education

After you master the skills equal to most high school graduates, you're ready to go on to the next step: college or university. Many colleges and universities accept the GED as proof of the equivalency to high school graduation. If your goal is further education, remind the registrars at the schools you want to attend that you're a mature student, who has worked hard to get where you are. Emphasize the real-world skills you've mastered by working and explain how those skills make you a great candidate for their institution.

Setting an Example for Your Kids

If you're like most people, you want your kids (or grandchildren) to be better educated and better off than you are. As soon as you pass the GED tests, you set the bar a little higher for them. Your accomplishment also reminds your kids that education is important — for you and them.

Enhancing Your Wall Décor

You may already have interesting mementos of your life hanging on your wall, but what could be more interesting than a GED with your name on it? A diploma looks great on your wall because it represents all the hard work you put in to passing the tests — not to mention your accomplishment in doing so.

If you plan to frame your GED diploma, make a couple of copies for prospective employers and colleges before you do so. Make copies of the transcript of your test results, as well. That way, you're ready to include these copies with your job and post-secondary applications.

Making You Feel like Part of a Select Group

Earning the GED means that you've outperformed 40 percent of high school seniors, which in itself is impressive. It also places you among great company. Comedian Bill Cosby and Dave Thomas, the late founder of Wendy's, are GED graduates. Although no one can promise that passing the GED tests will make you a show-business star or help you start a fast-food chain, it will make you feel very special. Who knows when you'll become famous enough to be listed in this section of a future edition of this book?

Motivating Yourself

One thing about challenging tests is that you have to face them on your own. You can use the fact that you overcame those challenges thanks to your hard work and determination to motivate yourself in your future endeavours. If you successfully passed the GED tests through rigid preparation and planning, nothing can stop you. After all, you've accomplished something not everyone can do. Enjoy the feeling you get from passing the GED, and use it in the future as you go on to bigger and better pursuits.

Improving Your Self-Esteem

When you pass the GED tests, you're essentially a high school graduate and can prove it (thanks to the handy diploma and transcript you receive upon passing the test). But the piece of paper is only concrete proof of your accomplishment. The real results are in your brain and in your own feelings about yourself. You need to remember that you passed the tests by yourself, with a little help from preparation texts, perhaps — but the real work was yours. Enjoy the feeling of accomplishment you deserve after passing the tests, and use it to feel better about yourself.

Index

BUSINESS & PERSONAL FINANCE

978-0-470-83878-5   978-0-470-73684-5

Also available:
- 76 Tips For Investing in an Uncertain Economy For Canadians For Dummies 978-0-470-16099-2
- Bookkeeping For Canadians For Dummies 978-0-470-73762-0
- Business Plans For Canadians For Dummies 978-0-470-15420-5

- Canadian Small Business Kit For Dummies 978-0-470-83818-1
- Investing For Canadians For Dummies 978-0-470-16029-9
- Trading For Canadians For Dummies 978-0-470-67744-5
- Wills & Estate Planning For Canadians For Dummies 978-0-470-67657-8

EDUCATION, HISTORY & REFERENCE

978-0-7645-2498-1   978-0-470-46244-7

Also available:
- Algebra For Dummies 978-0-7645-5325-7
- Art History For Dummies 978-0-470-09910-0
- Canadian History For Dummies 978-0-470-83656-9
- Chemistry For Dummies 978-0-7645-5430-8
- English Grammar For Dummies 978-0-470-54664-2

- French For Dummies 978-0-7645-5193-2
- Math Word Problems For Dummies 978-0-470-14660-6
- Speed Reading For Dummies 978-0-470-45744-3
- Statistics For Dummies 978-0-7645-5423-0
- World History For Dummies 978-0-470-44654-6

FOOD, HOME, & MUSIC

978-0-7645-9904-0   978-0-470-43111-5

Also available:
- 30-Minute Meals For Dummies 978-0-7645-2589-6
- Bartending For Dummies 978-0-470-05056-9
- Brain Games For Dummies 978-0-470-37378-1
- Gluten-Free Cooking For Dummies 978-0-470-17810-2

- Home Improvement All-in-One Desk Reference For Dummies 978-0-7645-5680-7
- Violin For Dummies 978-0-470-83838-9
- Wine For Dummies 978-0-470-04579-4

GARDENING

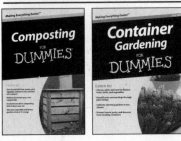

978-0-470-58161-2   978-0-470-57705-9

Also available:
- Gardening Basics For Canadians For Dummies 978-0-470-15491-5
- Organic Gardening For Dummies 978-0-7645-5320-2
- Sustainable Landscaping For Dummies 978-0-470-41149-0
- Vegetable Gardening For Dummies 978-0-470-49870-5

GREEN/SUSTAINABLE

978-0-470-84098-6   978-0-470-17569-9

Also available:
- Alternative Energy For Dummies 978-0-470-43062-0
- Energy Efficient Homes For Dummies 978-0-470-37602-7
- Green Building & Remodeling For Dummies 978-0-470-17559-0
- Green Cleaning For Dummies 978-0-470-39106-8
- Green Your Home All-in-One For Dummies 978-0-470-40778-3

HEALTH & SELF-HELP

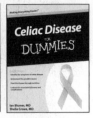

978-0-471-77383-2   978-0-470-16036-7

Also available:
- Borderline Personality Disorder For Dummies 978-0-470-46653-7
- Breast Cancer For Dummies 978-0-7645-2482-0
- Cognitive Behavioural Therapy For Dummies 978-0-470-01838-5
- Depression For Dummies 978-0-7645-3900-8
- Emotional Intelligence For Dummies 978-0-470-15732-9
- Diabetes For Dummies 978-0-7645-6820-6
- Healthy Aging For Dummies 978-0-470-14975-1
- Improving Your Memory For Dummies 978-0-7645-5435-3
- Neuro-linguistic Programming For Dummies 978-0-7645-7028-5
- Superfoods For Dummies 978-0-470-445-39-6
- Understanding Autism For Dummies 978-0-7645-2547-6

HOBBIES & CRAFTS

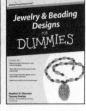

978-0-470-28747-7   978-0-470-29112-2

Also available:
- Crochet Patterns For Dummies 97-0-470-04555-8
- Digital Scrapbooking For Dummies 978-0-7645-8419-0
- Home Decorating For Dummies 978-0-7645-4156-8
- Knitting Patterns For Dummies 978-0-470-04556-5
- Oil Painting For Dummies 978-0-470-18230-7
- Quilting For Dummies 978-0-7645-9799-2
- Sewing For Dummies 978-0-7645-6847-3
- Word Searches For Dummies 978-0-470-45366-7

HOME & BUSINESS COMPUTER BASICS

 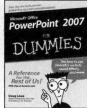

978-0-470-49743-2   978-0-470-04059-1

Also available:
- Excel 2007 For Dummies
  978-0-470-03737-9
- Office 2007 All-in-One Desk
  Reference For Dummies
  978-0-471-78279-7
- Pay Per Click Search Engine
  Marketing For Dummies
  978-0-471-75494-7

- PCs For Dummies
  978-0-7645-8958-4
- Search Engine Marketing For
  Dummies 978-0-471-97998-2
- Web Analytics For Dummies
  9780-470-09824-0

INTERNET & DIGITAL MEDIA

978-0-470-44417-7   978-0-470-39062-7

Also available:
- Blogging For Dummies
  978-0-471-77084-8
- MySpace For Dummies
  978-0-470-09529-4
- The Internet For Dummies
  978-0-470-12174-0

- Twitter For Dummies
  978-0-470-47991-9
- YouTube For Dummies
  978-0-470-14925-6

MACINTOSH

978-0-470-27817-8   978-0-470-43541-0

Also available:
- iMac For Dummies
  978-0-470-13386-6
- iPod Touch For Dummies
  978-0-470-50530-4
- iPod & iTunes For Dummies
  978-0-470-39062-7

- MacBook For Dummies
  978-0-470-27816-1
- Macs For Seniors For Dummies
  978-0-470-43779-7
- Switching to a Mac For Dummies
  978-0-470-46661-2

NETWORKING & SECURITY

978-0-470-53405-2   978-0-470-53791-6

Also available:
- Active Directory For Dummies
  978-0-470-28720-0
- Firewalls For Dummies
  978-0-7645-4048-6
- Identity Theft For Dummies
  978-0-470-56521-6

- TCP/IP For Dummies
  978-0-470-45060-4
- Wireless All-in-One For Dummies
  978-0-470-49013-6

PETS

978-0-764-58418-3   978-0-470-06805-2

Also available:
- Birds For Dummies
  978-0-7645-5139-0
- Boxers For Dummies
  978-0-7645-5285-4
- Cockatiels For Dummies
  978-0-7645-5311-0

- Ferrets For Dummies
  978-0-470-12723-0
- Golden Retrievers For Dummies
  978-0-7645-5267-0
- Horses For Dummies
  978-0-7645-9797-8
- Puppies For Dummies
  978-0-470-03717-1

SPORTS & FITNESS

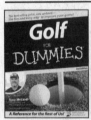

978-0-471-76871-5   978-0-470-73855-9

Also available:
- Exercise Balls For Dummies
  978-0-7645-5623-4
- Coaching Hockey For Dummies
  978-0-470-83685-9
- Coaching Volleyball For Dummies
  978-0-470-46469-4
- Curling For Dummies
  978-0-470-83828-0
- Fitness For Dummies
  978-0-7645-7851-9

- Mixed Martial Arts For Dummies
  978-0-470-39071-9
- Rugby For Dummies
  978-0-470-15327-7
- Ten Minute Tone-Ups For
  Dummies 978-0-7645-7207-4
- Wilderness Survival For Dummies
  978-0-470-45306-3
- Yoga with Weights For Dummies
  978-0-471-74937-0

WEB DEVELOPMENT

978-0-470-38541-8   978-0-470-38535-7

Also available:
- Adobe Creative Suite 4 Web
  Premium All-in-One For Dummies
  978-0-470-41407-1
- CSS Web Design For Dummies
  978-0-7645-8425-1
- HTML, XHTML & CSS For Dummies
  978-0-470-23847-9

- Joomla! For Dummies
  978-0-470-43287-7
- Web Design For Dummies
  978-0-471-78117-2
- Wikis For Dummies
  978-0-470-04399-8